MEASURED LANGUAGE

The Georgetown University Round Table on Languages and Linguistics Series
Selected Titles

Discourse 2.0: Language and New Media
DEBORAH TANNEN AND ANNA MARIE TRESTER, EDITORS

Educating for Advanced Foreign Language Capacities: Constructs, Curriculum, Instruction, Assessment
HEIDI BYRNES, HEATHER D. WEGER-GUNTHARP, AND KATHERINE A. SPRANG, EDITORS

Implicit and Explicit Language Learning: Conditions, Processes, and Knowledge in SLA and Bilingualism
CRISTINA SANZ AND RONALD P. LEOW, EDITORS

Language in Use: Cognitive and Discourse Perspectives on Language and Language Learning
ANDREA E. TYLER, MARI TAKADA, YIYOUNG KIM, AND DIANA MARINOVA, EDITORS

Linguistics, Language, and the Professions: Education, Journalism, Law, Medicine, and Technology
JAMES E. ALATIS, HEIDI E. HAMILTON, AND AI-HUI TAN, EDITORS

Telling Stories: Language, Narrative, and Social Life
DEBORAH SCHIFFRIN, ANNA DE FINA, AND ANASTASIA NYLUND, EDITORS

MEASURED LANGUAGE
Quantitative Approaches to Acquisition, Assessment, and Variation

Jeffrey Connor-Linton and Luke Wander Amoroso, Editors

GEORGETOWN UNIVERSITY PRESS
Washington, DC

Georgetown University Press, Washington, D.C. www.press.georgetown.edu

© 2014 by Georgetown University Press. All rights reserved. No part of this book may be reproduced or utilized in any form or by any means, electronic or mechanical, including photocopying and recording, or by any information storage and retrieval system, without permission in writing from the publisher.

Library of Congress Cataloging-in-Publication Data
   Measured language : quantitative studies of acquisition, assessment, and variation / Jeffrey Connor-Linton and Luke Wander Amoroso, Editors.
      pages cm. — (Georgetown University Round Table On Languages And Linguistics Series)
  Includes bibliographical references and index.
  ISBN 978-1-62616-037-8 (pbk. : alk. paper)
  1. Linguistics—Methodology. 2. Linguistics—Statistical methods. 3. Language and languages—Versification. 4. Computational linguistics. I. Connor-Linton, Jeff, editor. II. Amoroso, Luke Wander, editor.
  P126.M39 2014
  410.72'7—dc23
                      2013024841

∞ This book is printed on acid-free paper meeting the requirements of the American National Standard for Permanence in Paper for Printed Library Materials.

15 14   9 8 7 6 5 4 3 2
First printing

Printed in the United States of America

Contents

Acknowledgments — xi

Introduction — xiii
Jeff Connor-Linton and Luke Wander Amoroso, Georgetown University

1. The Ubiquitous Oral versus Literate Dimension: A Survey of Multidimensional Studies — 1
Douglas Biber, Northern Arizona University

2. When Ethnicity Isn't Just about Ethnicity — 21
Penelope Eckert, Stanford University

3. Does Language Zipf Right Along? Investigating Robustness in the Latent Structures of Usage and Acquisition — 33
Nick C. Ellis, University of Michigan; Matthew Brook O'Donnell, University of Michigan; Ute Römer, Georgia State University

4. Subjectivity and Efficiency in Language Assessment: Explorations of a Compensatory Rating Approach — 51
Steven J. Ross, University of Maryland

5. Subgrouping in Nusa Tenggara: The Case of Bima-Sumba — 63
Emily Gasser, Yale University

6. Young Learners' Storytelling in Their First and Foreign Languages — 79
Yuko Goto Butler and Wei Zeng, University of Pennsylvania

7. Measuring Quechua to Spanish Cross-Linguistic Influence — 95
Marilyn S. Manley, Rowan University

8. Speedup versus Automatization: What Role Does Learner Proficiency Play? — 111
Jessica G. Cox and Anne M. Calderón, Georgetown University

9. Frequency Effects, Learning Conditions, and the Development of Implicit and Explicit Lexical Knowledge — 125
Phillip Hamrick, Georgetown University; Patrick Rebuschat, Lancaster University

10. The Differential Role of Language Analytic Ability in Two Distinct Learning Conditions   141
Nadia Mifka Profozic, University of Zadar, Croatia

11. U-Shaped Development: Definition, Exploration, and Falsifiable Hypotheses   155
Hiroyuki Oshita, Ohio University

12. Using Simulated Speech to Assess Japanese Learner Oral Proficiency   171
Hitokazu Matsushita and Deryle Lonsdale, Brigham Young University

13. Keys to College: Tracking English Language Proficiency and IELTS Test Scores in an International Undergraduate Conditional Admission Program in the United States   183
Reese M. Heitner, Barbara J. Hoekje, and Patrick L. Braciszewski, Drexel University

14. How Does Foreign Language Proficiency Change over Time? Results of Data Mining Official Test Records   199
Amber Bloomfield, Steven Ross, Megan Masters, Kassandra Gynther, and Stephen O'Connell, University of Maryland

15. The Development of Complexity in a Learner Corpus of German   213
Colleen Neary-Sundquist, Purdue University

Index   229

Illustrations

Figures

1.1	Mean Scores of Registers along Dimension 1: Involved vs. Informational Production	8
1.2	Mean Scores for Registers along Dimension 2: Narrative vs. Nonnarrative Discourse	10
2.1	Negative Concord at Belten High (p=.000)	22
2.2	Negative Concord by Gender and Social Category	22
2.3	Negative Concord by Subgroups of Jocks and Burnouts	23
2.4	The Coastal California Shift	25
2.5	The Fields Pattern: Rachel's TRAP	29
2.6	The Steps Pattern: Selena's TRAP	29
2.7	Linda's TRAP in Sixth and Seventh Grades	30
3.1	BNC Verb Type Distribution for 'V *across* n' and for 'V n n'	42
3.2	A Semantic Network for 'V *across* n' from the BNC Using WordNet as a Base	44
4.1	OPI Task Difficulties	53
4.2	Probability of Rating Difference by Rater Severity	55
4.3	Risk of Not Improving over Time Attributable to Severity Differences	58
4.4	Martingale Residuals for Rater Severity Differences	59
4.5	Rater Co-Calibration Scheme	60
4.6	Risk of Not Improving over Time after Rating Co-Calibration	61
5.1	Five Subgrouping Hypotheses	64
5.2	Language Map	67
5.3	Unrooted Distance-Based Network	72
5.4	Stochastic Dollo Maximum Clade Credibility Tree	74
6.1	Structural Coherence in L1 and L2 and FL Fourth Graders ($N = 32$)	86
6.2	Structural Coherence in L1 and FL Sixth Graders ($N = 32$)	86
6.3	Structural Coherence in L1 and FL Eightn Graders ($N = 32$)	87
6.4	Structural Coherence in FL and PPVT in FL	89
6.5	Number of Idea Units Fourth Grade ($N = 16$)	90
6.6	Number of Idea Units Sixth Grade ($N = 16$)	90

6.7	Number of Idea Units Eighth Grade (*N* = 16)	91
7.1	Number of Participants Using the Thirty-One Features	101
7.2	Cross-Linguistic Feature Implicational Scale	102
9.1	Simple Screenshot Sequence from the Exposure Phase	131
9.2	Accuracy at Test by Input Frequency When Using Implict and Explicit Knowledge	135
11.1	Group Differences in Judgment of Active and Passive Sentences	163
12.1	Generated SS Scores for Students by Level across SOPI Tasks	179
12.2	Means of Generated SS Scores by Student Level across SOPI Tasks	179
12.3	Differences in Generated SS Scores across Class Level	180
12.4	Distribution of Generated SS Scores across All Items	181
13.1	Demographic Data of Gateway Participants	187
13.2	Average IELTS Scores of Matriculated Students Grouped by Test Date	188
13.3	Average L/R/W/S IELTS Scores of Matriculated Students by Test Date	189
13.4	Average and Range of IELTS Scores of Full Cohort Grouped by ELC Levels 2-6	189
13.5	Average and Range of Gateway CoAS GPAs for Matriculated Students	190
14.1	Latent Growth Model Fit to the 1–4 Listening Test Administrations in the Dataset	204
14.2	Latent Growth Model Fit to the 1–4 DLPT Reading Test Administrations	205
14.3	The Latent Growth Model Fit to the 2–4 Speaking Test Administrations	206
14.4	Retention of Listening Skills between First and Most Recent Test	208
14.5	Retention of Reading Skills between the First and Most Recent Test	209
14.6	Retention of Speaking Skills between Second and Most Recent Test	209
14.7	Retention of Speaking Skills between Second and Most Recent Speaking Test by Initial Proficiency Level	210
15.1	Subordination Rate for Speaking vs. Writing	224
15.2	Coordination Rate for Speaking vs. Writing	224
15.3	Mean Length Clause for Speaking vs. Writing	225

Tables

1.1.	MD studies of English discourse domains	12
1.2.	MD studies of discourse domains of other languages	14
5.1.	Languages analyzed	68
5.2.	Sample data (cognate judgments)	70
5.3.	Sample data for "old", with coding converted to binary	71

6.1.	Descriptive statistics (means and standard deviations) of structural coherence scores in L1 and FL	85
6.2.	Regression analyses predicting the story grammar scores in FL from those in L1	85
6.3.	Correlations among variables	88
7.1.	Participant characteristics	97
7.2.	Classification of thirty-one cross-linguistic features	98
8.1.	Participant characteristics by proficiency level	118
8.2.	Mean RT (ms), SDRT, CVRT, and error rate for L1 and L2 (standard deviations in parentheses)	121
9.1.	Ambiguous and unambiguous target items and their referents	130
9.2.	Accuracy and proportions (%) across source attributions	135
10.1	Descriptive statistics for language analysis test	146
10.2	Descriptive statistics for test scores in oral production	147
10.3	Descriptive statistics for test scores in written production	148
10.4	Between group differences on each posttest: RE and CR group	148
10.5	Correlations between gains and LAT scores	149
12.1	Simulated speech test items selected for administration and analysis	174
12.2	Features used for ASR-based fluency analysis	176
12.3	Classification accuracy for k-NN learning of SS test items	177
12.4	Prediction accuracy rate (%) for machine learning of SS test items using decision trees	178
12.5	Factors and their calculation for SS score generation	178
13.1	AY 2010-2011 Gateway Curriculum	186
13.2	Matriculated Gateway GPA compared to direct admission GPA	191
13.3	Average 1-term, 2-term, 3-term, and 4-term interval IELTS score gains of matriculated students (one term = 11 weeks)	193
15.1	Grammatical complexity in writing	220
15.2	Effect sizes and statistical significance for complexity measures in writing	220
15.3	Grammatical complexity in speaking	222
15.4	Effect sizes and statistical significance for complexity measures in speaking	223

Acknowledgments

THIS VOLUME OFFERS A selection of the many excellent papers presented at the 2012 Georgetown University Round Table on Languages and Linguistics (GURT), titled *Measured Language: Quantitative Approaches to Acquisition, Assessment, and Variation*. This volume would not have been possible without the help of all who gave their time and expertise to make the conference a success.

We are most deeply indebted to Mari Sakai, who was involved in every aspect of the conception, planning, and execution of GURT 2012. Mari was the designer, promoter, and organizer extraordinaire responsible for the realization of this intellectually stimulating and fun conference. Thank you, Mari.

We would also like to thank the Center for Applied Linguistics, Georgetown's Faculty of Languages and Linguistics, the Linguistics Department, and the Communication, Culture, and Technology program for their generous support.

Special thanks go to Manela Diez, who helped us avoid and resolve the many issues that inevitably arose while organizing an event of this kind. Her knowledge, patience, and kindness were indispensible. We are also grateful to the many student volunteers who helped with registration, book displays, technology, receptions, and every other aspect of the conference that made it a hospitable and stimulating venue for sharing research.

Finally, we would like to thank our colleagues for reviewing abstracts and helping us choose the best papers and posters for inclusion in the conference: Mark Arehart, Dwight Atkinson, Helene Blondeau, Melissa Bowles, Diana Boxer, Donna Christian, Eniko Csomay, Catherine Davies, Dan Douglas, Nydia Flores, Carolin Fuchs, John Hedgcock, Scott Jarvis, Antony Kunnan, Meg Malone, Lourdes Ortega, Hiroyuki Oshita, Lucy Pickering, Charlene Polio, Deborah Poole, Vaidehi Ramanathan, Leila Ranta, Peter Robinson, Carsten Roever, Yas Shirai, Susan Strauss, Elvis Wagner, Sara Weigle, Jessica Williams, George Wilson, Paula Winke, and Alla Zareva.

Introduction

JEFF CONNOR-LINTON AND LUKE WANDER AMOROSO
Georgetown University

THE GEORGETOWN UNIVERSITY ROUND Tables on Languages and Linguistics (GURT) and their attendant published volumes of selected papers have historically offered seminal contributions to the field of linguistics; papers from GURT volumes are frequently referenced in journal articles and are often required reading for graduate linguistics courses. The continued relevance of GURT publications stems from their coverage over the years of the many different areas of inquiry that constitute linguistics. With topics ranging from language teaching and education to discourse analysis, technology, and language-specific research, GURT conferences draw linguists from around the world.

The 2012 Round Table focused on the ways in which various aspects of language can be quantified, and how measurement informs and advances our understanding of language. The metaphors and operationalizations of quantification serve as an important lingua franca for much linguistic research, allowing methods and constructs to be translated from one area of linguistic investigation to another. A primary goal of the conference and this volume was to provide a forum for exploring relations among constructs developed from seemingly disparate theoretical and methodological perspectives.

While many previous GURT volumes have focused on a single method of linguistic analysis or considered a particular theoretical problem from many different perspectives, we took a different approach. We called for studies that employed quantitative methods of measuring language acquisition, assessment, and variation in the belief that quantification for one particular purpose would prove useful to researchers investigating other linguistic questions.

We believe that researchers in these areas of linguistics have much to learn from each other, both conceptually and methodologically, so conference contributors were asked to share the relevance of their perspectives and findings to other areas of linguistic inquiry.

For this volume we have selected papers that illustrate forms of measurement and quantitative analysis that are current in diverse areas of linguistic research, from language assessment to language change, from generative linguistics to psycholinguistic experimentalism, and from longitudinal studies to classroom research. The range and clarity of the research collected here ensures that even linguists who would not traditionally use quantitative methods will find this volume useful.

Quantification is central to many of the core principles of the modern scientific method—from falsifiability of hypotheses to arguments for the reality of underlying constructs, reliable measurement of those constructs, and the use of inferential statistics to estimate the risks of generalizing results of a study. As the philosopher of science Karl Popper pointed out, we cannot conclusively affirm a hypothesis—we can only conclusively negate it. Therefore, the validity of a claim (knowledge) is related to the probability that that claim can be falsified. Measurement and quantification help us to operationalize constructs and relations that comprise hypotheses. The more specifically and concretely a hypothesis is stated, the greater the possibility that it can be negated, and the more clearly its validity can be tested in the "trial by fire" of replicated research. The importance of replicable research—and therefore replicable measurement—to linguistics cannot be overstated; it is what separates a coherent field of study from a loose collection of individual case studies. Quantification also enhances the scientific process dialectically through the rigor of explicitly operationalizing a construct, developing a reliable way to measure it, and validating that measurement.

One of the more obvious values of quantification is that it facilitates classification and comparison of phenomena. In his plenary paper, "The Ubiquitous Oral versus Literate Dimension: A Survey of Multidimensional Studies," Douglas Biber first reviews his original multidimensional analysis of register variation in English speech and writing, in which he compared the frequencies of use of a variety of linguistic features across genres. His analysis of functionally motivated co-occurrence relations among linguistic features transmuted the qualitative folk notion of genres into measurable function-motivated text-types. The foundation of co-occurrence as an indicator of a shared function then allows him to compare how languages and their cultures build and organize their distinctive repertoires of text-types.

Where Biber uses factor analysis to identify underlying co-occurrence patterns, Emily Gasser uses Bayesian modeling in her paper titled "Subgrouping in Nusa Tenggara: The Case of Bima-Sumba" to expose underlying lexical similarities and differences—and therefore historical relations—between languages in the Central Malayo-Polynesian family. Gasser provides an example of an approach which, in addition to historical applications, has been useful in modeling morphology, child language acquisition, and sentence processing.

In a study of children's narratives, "Young Learners' Storytelling in Their First and Foreign Languages," Yuko Butler and Wei Zeng operationalize an abstract construct into measurable elements by identifying and counting idea units. This allows them to measure and compare the coherence of young foreign language learners' stories in L1 (Chinese) and L2 (English), and also to identify differences in both content and focus.

The rigor of operationalizing and measuring a construct can help expose assumptions underlying qualitative conceptualizations of a construct. Of course, measurement of a construct also entails its own assumptions and, as Penelope Eckert points out in her plenary paper, "When Ethnicity Isn't Just about Ethnicity," quantitative patterns must still be *interpreted*. Eckert shows that identifying patterns of speech attributed to large demographic categories, such as gender, is only part of the challenge. We have to understand the social functions of those patterns—their indirect indexicality—or we misconstrue their meaning.

Quantification allows us to see how different levels of a scale or components of a complex whole are related. Eckert's analysis shows how seemingly monolithic constructs like ethnicity are made up of smaller and smaller groups of language users; she also explores how linguistic change in a community is constructed by the practices of individual speakers within that community. Her paper demonstrates how a quantitative study can help define even such inherently qualitative constructs as community and ethnicity.

In her study of Quechua-Spanish communities in Cuzco, Peru, "Measuring Quechua to Spanish Cross-Linguistic Influence," Marilyn Manley problematizes the notion of cross-linguistic influence (specifically of Quechua into Spanish), which is both an index of individual speaker identity and of language change in speech communities. Her analysis demonstrates the value of comparing and assessing alternative measures of an underlying construct. Convergence of the measures can indicate the validity of the construct; divergence provides useful clues for reconceptualizing the construct.

In "Speedup versus Automatization: What Role Does Learner Proficiency Play?" Jessica Cox and Anne Calderòn provide a fine-grained psycholinguistic example of how a quantitative difference can index a qualitative difference. They parse a gross measure of processing reaction time into component parts in order to identify a distinction between two closely related concepts in language learning: increasing speed of language processing and automaticity of processing.

In their plenary paper "Does Language Zipf Right Along? Investigating Robustness in the Latent Structures of Usage and Acquisition," Nick Ellis, Matthew O'Donnell, and Ute Römer discuss evidence that word frequency influences how easily a word is acquired. They identify a quantitative fact—that word frequencies in corpora follow a scale-free Zipfian distribution. This distribution can then be used to test hypotheses of statistical learning. Ellis, O'Donnell, and Römer's paper exemplifies another benefit of quantification: the ability to measure phenomena, such as language form, meaning, and usage, on different scales—and to then relate those scales through statistical learning.

In "Frequency Effects, Learning Conditions, and the Development of Implicit and Explicit Lexical Knowledge," Phillip Hamrick and Patrick Rebuschat, working within a statistical learning paradigm, provide evidence that frequency of input influences word learning under both incidental and intentional learning conditions. This study supports Ellis, O'Donnell, and Römer's idea that the input from which learners acquire language is robust and useful. Their study shows how quantification of subjective phenomena (e.g., learners' ratings of how confident they are about their learning) may be useful in studies relating observable linguistic phenomena, like input frequency, to phenomena that are not directly observable, like awareness and language learning.

In her paper "The Differential Role of Language Analytic Ability in Two Distinct Learning Conditions," Nadia Mifka Profozic offers another study comparing learning conditions—whether a language instructor responds to learners' errors with recasts of the problematic form or clarification requests—and their relation to learners' analytic ability. Her study highlights an important standard for quantitative research: the need to explicitly assess reliability when classifying and coding discourse.

Another benefit of quantification is the ability to measure some behavior or perception at different developmental points. In "U-Shaped Development: Definition, Exploration, and Falsifiable Hypotheses," Hiroyuki Oshita investigates the acquisition of two kinds of intransitive verbs—unergatives and unaccusatives—by measuring learners' grammatical judgments at different stages of development using a cross-sectional design. By identifying and measuring two aspects of learners' grammaticality judgments—uneasiness versus overpassivization—he refines the notion of U-shaped development as "relative U-shaped development"—the relation of one aspect of interlanguage to another over time. Oshita's paper also shows how quantification can help the researcher assess a series of hypotheses that are closely related in order to render those hypotheses not just testable, but falsifiable.

In his plenary paper "Subjectivity and Efficiency in Language Assessment: Explorations of a Compensatory Rating Approach," Steven Ross traces the shift in language assessment from hermeneutics to quantification and points out that the development of quantitative methods has made the assessment of validity arguments possible in language testing. His paper discusses ways to quantify and then compensate for subjectivity in oral proficiency ratings. His description of compensatory adjustment of holistic oral proficiency exemplifies the confluence of the academic and the professional; that is, how language is represented in useful ways in the real world.

Hitokazu Matsushita and Deryle Lonsdale take a more analytic approach to measuring oral proficiency in "Using Simulated Speech to Assess Japanese Learner Oral Proficiency." To evaluate students' progress in a language program, they begin with a constrained sample of oral production, simulated speech, and use automatic speech recognition technology to assess a variety of measurable features. They then use supervised machine learning to identify which features best predict students' level of instruction within the language program. They show that the combination of simple measures—like number of tokens, types, pauses, fillers, and bursts—can reliably represent a much more complex underlying construct.

In "Keys to College: Tracking English Language Proficiency and IELTS Test Scores in an International Undergraduate Conditional Admission Program in the United States," Reese Heitner, Barbara Hoekje, and Patrick Braciszewski address a difficult but increasingly important question in education—the efficacy of instruction. They use scores on the IELTS exam to measure the developing proficiency of students in an Intensive English Program and to assess the amount of instruction students need to matriculate to an American university. Their study offers a useful metric for program evaluation and highlights the importance of carefully measured program data to make academic and policy decisions.

Concluding the volume are two papers that measure development of different aspects of language. In "How Does Foreign Language Proficiency Change over Time? Results of Data Mining Official Test Records," Amber Bloomfield, Steven Ross, Megan Masters, Kassandra Gynther, and Stephen O'Connell offer a glimpse into the usefulness of "big data." They analyze language proficiency scores of more than 800 government employees over many years. The size of their sample allows them to perform a latent growth analysis to identify the trajectory of language skills over time. Understanding the rate at which people lose language skills is important to policies informing language training and assessment, as well as to theories of second language acquisition.

In the final paper, "The Development of Complexity in a Learner Corpus of German," Colleen Neary-Sundquist compares three measures of complexity (subordination, coordination, and clause length) across the speech and writing of German learners at four levels of instruction. Previous studies have measured complexity in several different ways. Neary-Sundquist responds to the challenge made by Norris and Ortega in 2001 and demonstrates the importance of examining effect sizes, not just categorical statistical significance, to relate different measures of complexity.

Together, the papers collected here represent the quality and range of research presented at the 2012 Georgetown University Round Table on Languages and Linguistics, and they exemplify the virtues of quantitative analysis for many linguistic questions.

REFERENCES

Norris, John M., and Lourdes Ortega. 2009. "Towards an organic approach to investigating CAF in instructed SLA: The case of complexity." *Applied Linguistics* 30 (4): 555–78.

Popper, Karl R. 1959. *Logic of Scientific Discovery*. London: Hutchinson.

———. 1974. Replies to my critics. In *The Philosophy of Karl Popper*, 963–1197, edited by P. A. Schilpp. La Salle: Open Court.

1

The Ubiquitous Oral versus Literate Dimension: A Survey of Multidimensional Studies

DOUGLAS BIBER
Northern Arizona University

THE METHODOLOGICAL INNOVATIONS OF corpus-based linguistics have enabled researchers to ask fundamentally different kinds of research questions from previous research, sometimes resulting in radically different perspectives on language variation and use. Corpus linguistic research offers strong support for the view that language variation is systematic and can be described using empirical, quantitative methods. Variation often involves complex patterns consisting of the interaction among several different linguistic parameters, but in the end, it is systematic. Beyond this, the major contribution of corpus linguistics is to document the existence of linguistic constructs that are not recognized by current linguistic theories.

Research of this type—referred to as a corpus-driven approach—identifies strong tendencies for words and grammatical constructions to pattern together in particular ways, while other theoretically possible combinations rarely occur. That is, in a corpus-driven analysis, the "descriptions aim to be comprehensive with respect to corpus evidence" (Tognini-Bonelli 2001, 84), so that even the linguistic categories are derived "systematically from the recurrent patterns and the frequency distributions that emerge from language in context" (Tognini-Bonelli 2001, 87). Corpus-driven research has shown that these tendencies are much stronger and more pervasive than previously suspected, and that they usually have semantic or functional associations.

Much corpus research has focused on particular linguistic features and their variants, showing how these features vary in their distribution and patterns of use across registers. This relationship can also be approached from the opposite perspective, with a focus on describing the registers rather than describing the use of particular linguistic features.

However, the distribution of individual linguistic features cannot reliably distinguish among registers, as there are simply too many different linguistic characteristics to consider and individual features often have idiosyncratic distributions. Instead, sociolinguistic research has argued that register descriptions must be based on linguistic co-occurrence patterns (see, e.g., Ervin-Tripp 1972; Hymes 1974; Brown and Fraser 1979, 38–39; Halliday 1988, 162).

Multidimensional (MD) analysis is a corpus-driven methodological approach that identifies the frequent linguistic co-occurrence patterns in a language—the dimensions of variation (see, e.g., Biber 1988, 1995). Frequency plays a central role in the analysis, since each dimension represents a constellation of linguistic features that frequently co-occur in texts. MD analysis is corpus-driven because the linguistic constructs—the dimensions—emerge from quantitative analysis of linguistic co-occurrence patterns in the corpus, rather than being posited on theoretical grounds.

MD analyses have been carried out to study register variation in many different discourse domains of English and across many different languages. One of the most surprising findings across these studies is the existence of a basic oral/literate dimension. In most cases, this is the first dimension identified in the statistical analysis. Therefore, it is the most important dimension because it accounts for more linguistic variation than any of the other dimensions. In almost all of these analyses, this first oral/literate dimension is composed of a similar set of linguistic features that are distributed in a similar way across oral and literate registers, as demonstrated below.

This finding is surprising because it is reasonable to expect that diverse languages and discourse domains within languages would be governed by different dimensions of linguistic variation. MD research shows that this is indeed the case: the analysis of each language and discourse domain has identified dimensions that are peculiar to that language/domain. At the same time, though, these analyses have identified dimensions that might be considered universal, and the oral/literate dimension is the strongest of these.

This finding is also surprising because it contrasts with earlier researchers who argued that there are essentially no meaningful linguistic differences between speech and writing. Many of these researchers took an ethnographic perspective, studying literacy practices in communities where writing is used for specific, local functions. Having noticed that those functions do not necessarily include the stereotypical purposes of informational exposition, these researchers have made general claims minimizing the importance of literacy as a technology. For example:

> Literacy can be used (or not used) in so many different ways that the technology it offers, taken on its own, probably has no implications at all. (Bloch 1993, 87)

> It seems quite evident that speech may have all the characteristics Olson ascribes to text and written prose may have none of them. . . . Thus, the characteristics of linguistic performance at issue here have no intrinsic relation to whether performance is spoken or written. (Halverson 1991, 625)

> In sum, orality and literacy share many common features and the features that have been identified with one or the other have more to do with the context in which language is used than with oral versus literate use. (Hornberger 1994, 114)

The findings from MD analyses, as well as other corpus-based investigations (see, e.g., Biber 2006, 2009; Biber and Gray 2010; Biber, Gray, and Poonpon 2011), show that these generalizations about speech and writing are not accurate. However, it is not the case that MD studies have uncovered a dichotomous distinction between speech and writing. Rather, four general patterns and conclusions about spoken and written language have emerged from multidimensional studies:

1. Some dimensions are strongly associated with spoken and written differences, but other dimensions have little or no relation to speech and writing.
2. There are few, if any, absolute linguistic differences between spoken and written registers.
3. There are strong and systematic linguistic differences between stereotypical speech and stereotypical writing—that is, between conversation and written informational prose.
4. The spoken and written modes differ in their linguistic potential; they are not equally adept at accommodating a wide range of linguistic variation. In particular, there is an extremely wide range of linguistic variation among written registers because writers can choose to employ linguistic features associated with stereotypical speech. In contrast, there is a restricted range of linguistic variation among nonscripted spoken registers, which is associated with the real time production circumstances of the spoken mode.

Thus, the oral/literate dimensions that have emerged from MD studies do not identify absolute differences between spoken and written registers. They are, however, consistently associated with orality versus literacy. In the following sections I first introduce the methodology for MD analysis, followed by a survey of the studies that have replicated this finding across discourse domains and across languages.

Overview of Methods

The MD analytical approach was originally developed to investigate the linguistic patterns of variation among spoken and written registers (see, e.g., Biber 1988, 1995; Conrad and Biber 2001; Biber and Conrad 2009). Studies in this research tradition have used large corpora of naturally occurring texts to represent the range of spoken and written registers in a language. These registers are compared with respect to dimensions of variation (identified through a statistical factor analysis), comprising constellations of linguistic features that typically co-occur in texts. Each dimension is distinctive in three respects; they are defined by a distinct set of co-occurring linguistic features, associated with particular communicative functions, and related to different patterns of register variation.

MD analysis is based on the assumption that all registers have their own linguistic patterns of use that are associated with their defining situational characteristics. Thus, MD studies of speech and writing set out to describe the linguistic similarities and differences among a range of spoken and written registers and to then compare speech and writing within the context of a comprehensive linguistic analysis of register variation.

The MD approach uses statistical factor analysis to reduce a large number of linguistic variables to a few basic parameters of linguistic variation. In MD analyses, the distribution of individual linguistic features is analyzed in a corpus of texts.

Factor analysis is used to identify the systematic co-occurrence patterns among those linguistic features—the dimensions—and then texts and registers are compared along each dimension. Each dimension comprises a group of linguistic features that usually co-occur in texts (e.g., nouns, attributive adjectives, prepositional phrases), and these co-occurrence patterns are identified statistically using factor analysis. The co-occurrence patterns are then interpreted to assess their underlying situational, social, and cognitive functions.

The original MD analyses investigated the relations among general spoken and written registers in English, based on analysis of the LOB Corpus (fifteen written registers) and the London-Lund Corpus (six spoken registers). Sixty-seven different linguistic features were analyzed computationally in each text of the corpus. Then, the co-occurrence patterns among those linguistic features were analyzed using factor analysis, identifying the underlying parameters of variation: the factors or dimensions. In the 1988 MD analysis, the sixty-seven linguistic features were reduced to seven underlying dimensions (see, e.g., Biber 1988, chapters 4–5; Biber 1995, chapter 5).

The dimensions are interpreted functionally, based on the assumption that linguistic co-occurrence reflects underlying communicative functions. That is, linguistic features occur together in texts because they serve related communicative functions. Table 1.1 summarizes the factor analysis from the first major MD analysis of English spoken and written registers (Biber 1988), including a list of the most important linguistic features comprising each dimension, as well as the functional label assigned to each one. Below is a summary of the major linguistic features co-occurring on dimensions 1–6 from the 1988 MD analysis of register variation:

Dimension 1: Involved versus Informational Production
Positive features:

> mental (private) verbs, *that* complementizer deletion, contractions, present tense verbs, *wh*-questions, first- and second-person pronouns, pronoun *it*, indefinite pronouns, *do* as pro-verb, demonstrative pronouns, emphatics, hedges, amplifiers, discourse particles, causative subordination, sentence relatives, *wh*-clauses

Negative features:

> nouns, long words, prepositions, type/token ratio, attributive adjectives

Dimension 2: Narrative versus Nonnarrative Discourse
Positive features:

> past-tense verbs, third-person pronouns, perfect aspect verbs, communication verbs

Negative features:

> present-tense verbs, attributive adjectives

Dimension 3: Situation-Dependent versus Elaborated Reference
Positive features:

   time adverbials, place adverbials, other adverbs

Negative features:

   wh-relative clauses (including subject gaps, object gaps), phrasal coordination, nominalizations

Dimension 4: Overt Expression of Argumentation
Positive features:

   prediction modals, necessity modals, possibility modals, suasive verbs, conditional subordination, split auxiliaries

Dimension 5: Abstract/Impersonal Style
Positive features:

   conjuncts, agentless passives, BY-passives, past participial adverbial clauses, past participial postnominal clauses, other adverbial subordinators

Dimension 6: Real Time Informational Elaboration
Positive features:

   that clauses as verb complements, *that* clauses as adjective complements, *that* relative clauses, demonstratives

Each dimension can have positive and negative features. Rather than reflecting importance, positive and negative signs identify two groupings of features that occur in a complementary pattern as part of the same dimension. That is, when the positive features occur together frequently in a text, the negative features are markedly less frequent in that text, and vice versa.

On dimension 1, the interpretation of the negative features is relatively straightforward. Nouns, word length, prepositional phrases, type/token ratio, and attributive adjectives all reflect an informational focus, a careful integration of information in a text, and precise lexical choice. Text sample 1 illustrates these co-occurring linguistic characteristics in an academic article:

Text sample 1: Technical academic prose

   Apart from these very general group-related aspects, there are also individual aspects that need to be considered. Empirical data show that similar processes can be guided quite differently by users with different views on the purpose of the communication.

This text sample is typical of written expository prose in its dense integration of information: frequent nouns and long words, with most nouns being modified by attributive adjectives or prepositional phrases (e.g., general-group related aspects, individual aspects, empirical data, similar processes, users with different views on the purpose of the communication).

The set of positive features on dimension 1 is more complex, although all of these features have been associated with interpersonal interaction, a focus on personal stance, and real time production circumstances. For example, first- and second-person pronouns, *wh*-questions, emphatics, amplifiers, and sentence relatives can all be interpreted as reflecting interpersonal interaction and the involved expression of personal stance (feelings and attitudes). Other positive features are associated with the constraints of real-time production, resulting in a reduced surface form, a generalized or uncertain presentation of information, and a generally fragmented production of text; these include *that* deletions, contractions, pro-verb DO, the pronominal forms, and final (stranded) prepositions. Text sample 2 illustrates the use of positive dimension 1 features in a workplace conversation:

Text sample 2: Conversation at a reception at work

SABRINA: I'm dying of thirst.
SUZANNA: Mm, hmm. Do you need some M&Ms?
SABRINA: Desperately. <laugh> Ooh, thank you. Ooh, you're so generous.
SUZANNA: Hey, I try.
SABRINA: Let me have my Snapple first. Is that cold—cold?
SUZANNA: I don't know but there should be ice on uh, <unclear>.
SABRINA: I don't want to seem like I don't want to work and I don't want to seem like a stuffed shirt or whatever, but I think this is really boring.
SUZANNA: I know.
SABRINA: I would like to leave here as early as possible today, go to our rooms, and pick up this thing at eight o'clock in the morning.
SUZANNA: Mm, hmm.

Overall, factor 1 represents a dimension marking interactional, stance-focused, and generalized content (the positive features on table 1.1) versus high informational density and precise word choice (the negative features). Two separate communicative parameters seem to be represented here: the primary purpose of the writer/speaker (involved versus informational), and the production circumstances (those restricted by real-time constraints versus those enabling careful editing possibilities). Reflecting both of these parameters, the interpretive label "involved versus informational production" was proposed for the dimension underlying this factor.

The second major step in interpreting a dimension is to consider the similarities and differences among registers with respect to the set of co-occurring linguistic features. To achieve this, dimension scores are computed for each text by summing the individual scores of the features that co-occur on a dimension (see Biber 1988, 93–97). For example, the dimension 1 score for each text was computed by adding together the frequencies of private verbs, *that* deletions, contractions, present-tense verbs, etc.—the features with positive loadings—and then subtracting the frequencies of nouns, word length, prepositions, etc.—the features with negative loadings.

Once a dimension score is computed for each text, the mean dimension score for each register can be computed. Plots of these mean dimension scores allow linguistic characterization of any given register, comparison of the relations between any two registers, and a fuller functional interpretation of the underlying dimension.

For example, figure 1.1 plots the mean dimension scores of registers along dimension 1 from the 1988 MD analysis. The registers with large positive values, such as face-to-face and telephone conversations, have high frequencies of present-tense verbs, private verbs, first- and second-person pronouns, contractions, etc.—the features with salient positive weights on dimension 1. At the same time, registers with large positive values have markedly low frequencies of nouns, prepositional phrases, long words, etc.—the features with salient negative weights on dimension 1. Registers with large negative values, such as academic prose, press reportage, and official documents, have the opposite linguistic characteristics: very high frequencies of nouns, prepositional phrases, etc., as well as low frequencies of private verbs, contractions, etc.

The relations among the registers shown in figure 1.1 confirm the interpretation of dimension 1 as distinguishing among texts along an oral-literate continuum reflecting communicative purpose (involved versus informational) and different production circumstances (real time versus planned/edited). At the positive extreme, conversations are highly interactive and involved regarding the language produced under real-time circumstances. Registers such as public conversations, like interviews and panel discussions, are intermediate: they have a relatively informational purpose, but participants interact with one another and are still constrained by real-time production. Finally, at the negative extreme, registers such as academic prose are noninteractive but highly informational in purpose, produced under circumstances that permit extensive revision and editing.

Figure 1.1 shows that there is a range of variation among spoken registers with respect to the linguistic features that comprise dimension 1 (involved versus informational production). Conversation has extremely large positive dimension 1 scores, spontaneous speeches and interviews have moderately large positive scores, and prepared speeches and broadcasts have scores around zero, reflecting a balance of positive and negative linguistic features on this dimension. The written registers show a more extensive range of variation along dimension 1. Expository informational registers, like official documents and academic prose, have very large negative scores, the fiction registers have scores around zero, and personal letters have a relatively large positive score.

This distribution shows that no single register can be taken as representative of the spoken or written mode. At the extremes, written informational prose is dramatically different from spoken conversation with respect to dimension 1 scores. However, written personal letters are relatively similar to spoken conversation, while spoken prepared speeches share some dimension 1 characteristics with written fictional registers. Overall, the oral versus literate extremes of each mode (i.e.,

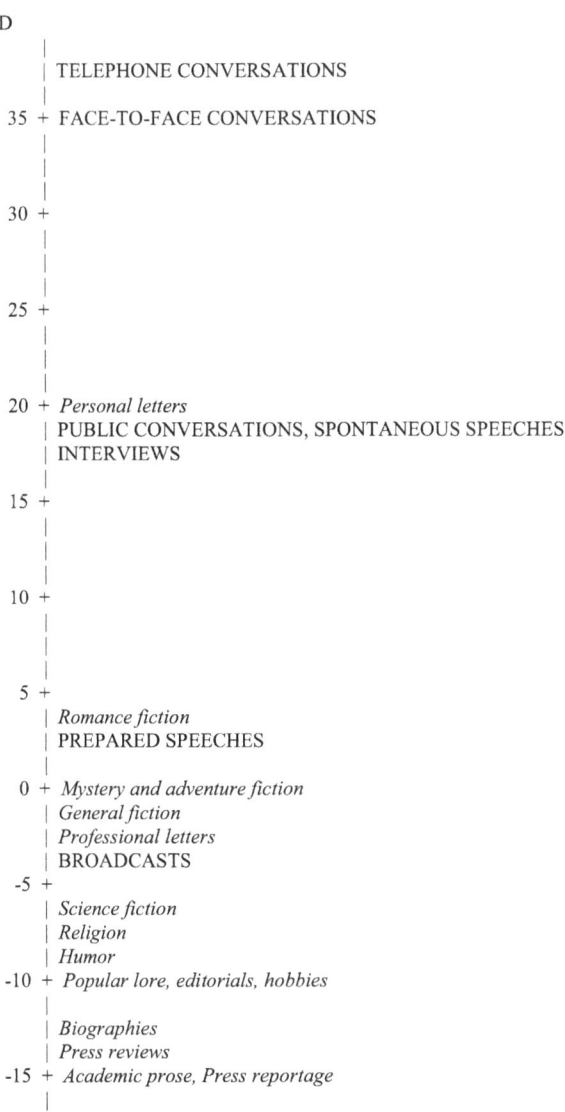

Notes: Written registers are in *italics*; spoken registers are in CAPS. (F = 111.9, p < .0001, r^2 = 84.3%). Adapted from figure 1.7 in Biber 1988.

Figure 1.1 Mean Scores of Registers along Dimension 1: Involved vs. Informational Production

conversation versus informational prose) are sharply distinguished from one another with respect to dimension 1. At the same time, there is extensive overlap between the spoken and written modes in these linguistic characteristics. However, that overlap is largely unidirectional; writing can be oral or literate, but speech is restricted primarily to the oral end of this dimension.

The overall comparison of speech and writing resulting from the 1988 MD analysis requires consideration of all six dimensions of variation, which each define a different set of relations among spoken and written registers (see table 1.1). For example, dimension 2 is interpreted as "narrative versus nonnarrative concerns." The positive features—past-tense verbs, third-person pronouns, perfect-aspect verbs, communication verbs, and present participial clauses—are associated with past-time narration. In contrast, the negative features—present-tense verbs and attributive adjectives—have nonnarrative communicative functions.

The distribution of registers along dimension 2, shown in figure 1.2, supports the interpretation as narrative versus nonnarrative concerns. All types of fiction have markedly high positive scores, reflecting their emphasis on narrating events. In contrast, registers that are typically more concerned with events currently in progress (e.g., broadcasts) or with building arguments rather than narrating (e.g., academic prose) have negative scores on this dimension. Finally, some registers have scores around zero, reflecting a mix of narrative and other features. For example, face-to-face conversation will often switch back and forth between narration of past events and discussion of current interactions.

Each of the dimensions in the analysis can be interpreted in a similar way. Overall, the 1988 MD analysis showed that English registers vary along several underlying dimensions associated with different functional considerations, including interactiveness, involvement and personal stance, production circumstances, informational density, informational elaboration, narrative purposes, situated reference, persuasiveness or argumentation, and impersonal presentation of information.

The Oral/Literate Dimension in MD Studies of English
Discourse Domains

Numerous other studies have undertaken MD analyses of other discourse domains in English (e.g., Biber 2001, 2006, 2008; Biber and Jones 2005; Biber, Connor, and Upton 2007; Biber and Gray 2013; Friginal 2008, 2009; Kanoksilapatham 2007; Crossley and Louwerse 2007; Reppen 2001; White 1994). Given that each of these studies is based on a different corpus of texts representing a different discourse domain, it is reasonable to expect that they would each identify a unique set of dimensions. This expectation is reinforced by the fact that the more recent studies have included additional linguistic features not used in earlier MD studies (e.g., semantic classes of nouns and verbs). However, despite these differences in design and research focus, there are certain striking similarities in the set of dimensions identified by these studies.

Most important, in nearly all of these studies, the first dimension identified by the factor analysis is associated with an oral/literate opposition, representing a personal/involved focus (personal stance, interactivity, and/or real-time production features)

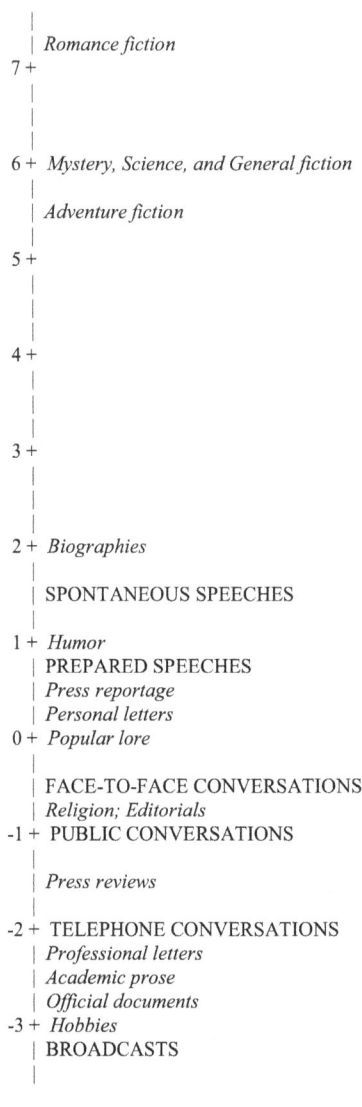

```
        NARRATIVE

         |
         | Romance fiction
       7 +
         |
         |
         |
       6 + Mystery, Science, and General fiction
         |
         | Adventure fiction
         |
       5 +
         |
         |
         |
       4 +
         |
         |
         |
       3 +
         |
         |
         |
       2 + Biographies
         |
         | SPONTANEOUS SPEECHES
         |
       1 + Humor
         | PREPARED SPEECHES
         | Press reportage
         | Personal letters
       0 + Popular lore
         |
         | FACE-TO-FACE CONVERSATIONS
         | Religion; Editorials
      -1 + PUBLIC CONVERSATIONS
         |
         | Press reviews
         |
      -2 + TELEPHONE CONVERSATIONS
         | Professional letters
         | Academic prose
         | Official documents
      -3 + Hobbies
         | BROADCASTS
         |

         NON NARRATIVE
```

Notes: Written registers are in *italics*; spoken registers are in CAPS. (F = 32.3, p < .0001, r^2 = 60.8%). Adapted from figure 7.2 in Biber 1988.

Figure 1.2 Mean Scores for Registers along Dimension 2: Narrative vs. Nonnarrative Discourse

versus an informational focus. Linguistically, this opposition is realized as two fundamentally different ways of constructing discourse: clausal versus phrasal. That is, across studies, the oral pole of this dimension consists of verb classes (e.g., mental verbs, communication verbs), grammatical characteristics of verb phrases (e.g., present tense, progressive aspect), and modifiers of verbs and clauses (e.g., adverbs and stance adverbials). Interestingly, in most studies these oral features also include various kinds of dependent clauses that function as clausal constituents, including adverbial clauses and finite complement clauses. In contrast, the literate pole usually consists of phrasal devices that mostly function as elements of noun phrases, especially nouns, nominalizations, attributive adjectives, and prepositional phrases.

In many studies, this first dimension is clearly oral versus literate because it distinguishes between spoken registers and written-informational registers. However, other studies have focused exclusively on only spoken registers or only written registers, considering variation within a restricted discourse domain. The most surprising finding to emerge from those studies is the existence of a similar oral/literate dimension, even though the corpus for analysis does not include both spoken and written texts. Thus, consider:

Perhaps, it is not surprising that dimension 1 in the original 1988 MD analysis was strongly associated with an informational versus (inter)personal focus, given that the corpus in that study ranged from spoken conversational texts to written expository texts. For the same reason, it is somewhat predictable that a similar dimension would have emerged from the study of eighteenth-century general written and speech-based registers. However, it is surprising that more restricted comparisons of spoken and written registers would uncover a first dimension with a similar set of co-occurring linguistic features that are associated with a similar opposition between oral and information-literate registers. To date, such studies include analyses of spoken and written university registers, elementary school registers, and spoken and written English as a second language (ESL) exam responses.

The most surprising finding here, however, is the existence of a similar first dimension in MD studies of register variation within a highly restricted discourse domain from a single mode. Those studies include studies focused exclusively on spoken registers (call center interactions, job interviews, and conversations), as well as those focused exclusively on written registers (fictional novels and research articles). In all of these cases, the linguistic composition of dimension 1 is surprisingly similar, generally opposing verbs, dependent clauses, and interpersonal devices to nouns and phrasal devices for elaborating information in noun phrases. Of course, the patterns of register variation differ here, distinguishing between more or less oral versus literate registers within a single mode. But the linguistic differences are strikingly similar, suggesting that this is a fundamental parameter of linguistic variation among registers in any discourse domain.

Table 1.1.
MD studies of English discourse domains

Discourse domain	Linguistic features defining Dimension 1	Register pattern along Dimension 1
University spoken and written registers Biber (2006)	contractions, pronouns, mental / activity / communication verbs, present tense, progressive aspect, time / place / stance adverbials, WH-questions, *that*-clauses, *WH*-clauses, adverbial clauses	service encounters, office hours, study groups, classroom teaching
	VERSUS nouns, nominalizations, attributive adjectives, prepositional phrases, long words, passives, *WH* relative clauses	VERSUS textbooks, course packs, institutional writing
Elementary school spoken and written registers Reppen (2001)	initial *and*, time adverbials, 3rd person pronouns	student conversations, oral narratives
	VERSUS nouns, long words, nominalizations, passives, attributive adjectives, prepositional phrases	VERSUS science and social science textbooks
ESL spoken and written exam responses Biber and Gray (2013)	mental verbs, present tense, modals, 3rd person pronouns, *that*-clauses, adverbial clauses	spoken, independent tasks (low-scoring)
	VERSUS nouns, attributive adjectives, prepositional phrases, long words, passives	VERSUS written, integrated tasks (high-scoring)
18th c. speech-based and written registers Biber (2001)	1st and 2nd person pronouns, present tense, possibility and prediction modals, *that*-deletion, mental verbs, emphatics	drama, letters
	VERSUS prepositions, passives, nouns, long words, past tense verbs	VERSUS academic prose, legal prose, newspaper prose
Call center discourse Friginal (2009)	1st person pronouns, past tense, perfect aspect, *that*-deletion, mental verbs, *WH*-clauses, *I mean/You know*	callers
	VERSUS 2nd person pronouns, long words, nouns, nominalizations, possibility modals, *please/thanks*	VERSUS agents

Table 1.1. (continued)

Discourse domain	Linguistic features defining Dimension 1	Register pattern along Dimension 1
Job interviews White (1994)	1st person pronouns, contractions, adverbs, discourse particles, emphatics	interviewees
	VERSUS nouns, nominalizations, prepositional phrases, long words, *WH* questions, 2nd person pronouns	VERSUS interviewers
Conversational text types Biber (2008)	contractions, 1st and 2nd person pronouns, activity verbs	casual conversations
	VERSUS long words, abstract nouns, nominalizations, attributive adjectives, prepositional phrases, relative clauses	VERSUS work-place conversations
19th c. fictional novels Egbert (2012)	mental verbs, existence verbs, perfect aspect, verb + *that*-clause; desire verb + *to*-clause; *WH*-clauses; adverbs, stance adverbials, indefinite pronouns	Henry James, Louisa May Alcott, Mark Twain
	VERSUS nouns, attributive adjectives, prepositions	VERSUS Herman Melville, Rudyard Kipling
Moves in biochemistry research articles Kanoksilapatham (2007) (cf. Biber and Jones 2005)	---	methodological moves describing procedures and materials
	VERSUS long words, nouns, attributive adjectives, numerals, technical jargon	VERSUS moves introducing the topic and study

The Oral/Literate Dimension in MD Studies of Other Languages

These same general patterns have emerged from MD studies of languages other than English, including Spanish (Biber et al. 2006; Biber and Tracy-Ventura 2007; Parodi 2007), Brazilian Portuguese (Berber-Sardinha 2012), Nukulaelae Tuvaluan (Besnier 1988), Korean (Kim and Biber 1994), Somali (Biber and Hared 1992, 1994), Taiwanese (Jang 1998), Czech (Kodytek 2007), and Dagbani (Purvis 2008). Taken together, these studies provide the first comprehensive investigations of register variation in European and non-Western languages.

Biber (1995) synthesizes several of the earlier studies to investigate the extent to which the underlying dimensions of variation and the relations among registers are configured in similar ways across languages. These languages show striking similarities in their basic patterns of register variation, as reflected by:

- the co-occurring linguistic features that define the dimensions of variation in each language;
- the functional considerations represented by those dimensions; and
- the linguistic/functional relations among analogous registers.

The most important of these similarities is the existence of a major dimension that reflects a basic oral-literate opposition. In almost all studies, this is the first dimension identified by the factor analysis. And despite large differences in the linguistic inventories available in different languages, this first dimension is strikingly similar in opposing verbs, pronouns, clausal modifiers, and dependent clauses versus nouns and phrasal modifiers.

Table 1.2.
MD studies of discourse domains of other languages

Language	Linguistic features defining Dimension 1	Register pattern along Dimension 1
Spanish Biber et al. (2006)	mental / desire / communication / simple occurrence verbs, indicative mood, present tense, progressive aspect, pronouns (1st, 2nd, 3rd person), 1st person pro-drop, time / place / manner adverbs, existential *haber*, yes-no questions, causal subordinate clauses, *que* verb complement clauses (indicative), tag questions, *el que* clauses, *que* relative clauses (indic.), *CU* verb complement clauses, conditional subordinate clauses	conversations (casual, business), political debates, drama
	VERSUS singular / plural nouns, derived nouns, postmodifying adjectives, definite articles, prepositions, type token ratio, postnominal past participles, premodifying attributive adjectives, long words, *se* passives	VERSUS newspaper reportage, academic prose, encyclopedias
Korean Kim and Biber (1994) (cf. Biber 1995)	questions, contractions, short negation, informal postpositions, demonstratives, discourse markers	conversations, TV drama
	VERSUS postposition-noun ratio, relative clauses, attributive adjectives, nonfinite clauses, 3rd person pronouns, noun complementation	VERSUS scripted speeches, textbooks, literary criticism

THE UBIQUITOUS ORAL VERSUS LITERATE DIMENSION

Table 1.2. (continued)

Language	Linguistic features defining Dimension 1	Register pattern along Dimension 1
Taiwanese Jang (1998)	discourse particles, contractions, demonstrative pronouns, questions, 1st and 2nd person pronouns, perfect aspect, existential aspect, progressive aspect, communication verbs	conversation, drama, spoken folktales
	VERSUS nouns, modifier markers, attributive adjectives, type/token ratio, additive conjunctions, prepositions	VERSUS academic essays, editorials, scripted broadcast news
Czech Kodytek (2007)	2sg reference, 1sg present tense, 3rd person pronouns, demonstrative pronouns, questions, time reference causative adverbial clauses likelihood adverbs	conversation, letters
	VERSUS attributive adjectives, verbal nouns, abstract nouns, prepositions, relative clauses	VERSUS newspaper prose, academic prose
Nukulaelae Tuvaluan Besnier (1988) [Dimension 2]	1st and 2nd person pronouns, 1st and 2nd person deictics, coordinators, subordinators	personal letters, conversations
	VERSUS possessive / definite noun phrases, nominalizations, prepositions, nominal focus markers	VERSUS political meetings, written sermons
Dagbani Purvis (2008)	3rd pers. animate pronouns, purpose particles, temporal subordination, nonphrasal coordination, new event particle, time depth particle, verb in SVC, public verbs, fronting, ideophones	Fables, novels, histories, court testimony, (conversation)
	VERSUS -*bu* nouns (gerunds), SVC as abstract complement, NP coordination, subject relatives, word length, possessive noun phrases, copula *ny*, Hausa loan words (nouns), -*im* / -*gu* abstract nouns, suasive verbs, compound nouns, postpositional (NP) phrases	VERSUS legal documents, scripted television news, grammar/educational materials

Table 1.2. (continued) MD studies of discourse domains of other languages

Language	Linguistic features defining Dimension 1	Register pattern along Dimension 1
Somali Biber and Hared (1992), Biber (1995)	simple responses, questions, contrast-clause coordination (*eh*), 1st and 2nd person pronouns, stance adjectives, contractions, independent verbs, time deictics, focus markers (*waa, baa*), main clauses, downtoners, imperatives, conditional clauses	conversations, family meetings, spoken narratives
	VERSUS relative clauses, *waxaa* clefts reduced (*ah*) relative clauses, clause / phrase coordination, word length, common nouns, derived adjectives, *-eed* genitives, verb complement clauses, case particle sequences	VERSUS newspaper reportage, editorials, political pamphlets

Conclusion

There are additional similarities in the patterns of linguistic variation found across languages and discourse domains. For example, a second parameter found in most MD analyses corresponds to narrative versus nonnarrative discourse, reflected by the co-occurrence of features like past tense, third-person pronouns, perfect aspect, and communication verbs (see, e.g., the Biber 2006 study of university registers; Biber 2001 on eighteenth-century registers; and the Biber 2008 study of conversation text types). In some studies, a similar narrative dimension emerged with additional special characteristics. For example, in Reppen's (2001) study of elementary school registers, narrative features like past tense, perfect aspect, and communication verbs co-occurred with once-occurring words and a high type/token ratio; in this corpus, history textbooks rely on a specialized and diverse vocabulary to narrate past events. In the job interview corpus (White 1994), the narrative dimension reflected a fundamental opposition between personal/specific past events and experiences (past tense verbs co-occurring with first-person singular pronouns) versus general practice and expectations (present tense verbs co-occurring with first-person plural pronouns). In Biber and Kurjian's (2007) study of web text types, narrative features co-occurred with features of stance and personal involvement on the first dimension, distinguishing personal narrative web pages, such as personal blogs, from the various kinds of more informational web pages.

At the same time, most MD studies have identified some dimensions that are unique to the particular discourse domain. For example, the factor analysis in Reppen (2001) identified a dimension of 'other-directed idea justification' in elementary student registers. The features on this dimension include second-person pronouns, conditional clauses, and prediction modals; these features commonly co-occur in certain kinds of student writing (e.g., "If you wanted to watch TV a lot you would not get very much done").

The factor analysis in Biber's (2006) study of university spoken and written registers identified four dimensions. Two of these are similar linguistically and functionally to dimensions found in other MD studies: dimension 1 (oral versus literate discourse) and dimension 3 (narrative orientation). However, the other two dimensions are specialized to the university discourse domain. Dimension 2 is interpreted as 'procedural versus content-focused discourse'. The co-occurring procedural features include modals, causative verbs, second-person pronouns, and verbs of desire + *to*-clause; these features are especially common in classroom management talk, course syllabi, and other institutional writing. The complementary content-focused features include rare nouns, rare adjectives, and simple occurrence verbs; these co-occurring features are typical of textbooks and especially common in natural science textbooks. Dimension 4, interpreted as 'academic stance', consists of features like stance adverbials (factual, attitudinal, likelihood) and stance nouns + *that*-clause; classroom teaching and classroom management talk is especially marked on this dimension.

A final example comes from Biber's (2008) MD analysis of conversational text types, which identified a dimension of 'stance-focused versus context-focused discourse'. Stance-focused conversational texts were marked by the co-occurrence of *that*-deletions, mental verbs, factual verbs + *that*-clause, likelihood verbs + *that*-clause, likelihood adverbs, and so on. In contrast, context-focused texts had high frequencies of nouns and *wh*-questions, which are used to inquire about past events or future plans. The text type analysis identified different sets of conversations characterized by one or the other of these two extremes.

In sum, MD studies of English registers have uncovered both surprising similarities and notable differences in the underlying dimensions of variation. Two parameters seem to be fundamentally important, regardless of the discourse domain: a dimension associated with oral versus literate discourse, and a dimension associated with narrative discourse.

At the same time, each of these MD analyses has identified dimensions that are unique to a discourse domain or language, reflecting the particular communicative priorities of that language, culture, or domain of use. For example, the MD analysis of Somali identified a dimension interpreted as 'distanced, directive interaction', represented by optative clauses, first- and second-person pronouns, directional preverbal particles, and other case particles. Only one register is especially marked for the frequent use of these co-occurring features in Somali: personal letters. This dimension reflects the particular communicative priorities of personal letters in Somali, which are typically interactive as well as explicitly directive.

Cross-linguistic comparisons further show that languages as diverse as English and Somali have undergone similar patterns of historical evolution following the introduction of written registers. For example, specialist written registers in both languages have evolved over time to styles with an increasingly dense use of noun phrase modification. Historical shifts in the use of dependent clauses are also surprising; in both languages, certain types of clausal embedding—especially complement clauses—turn out to be associated with spoken registers rather than written registers.

In sum, these synchronic and diachronic similarities raise the possibility of universals of register variation. The present paper has focused on the most important of these: a basic opposition between oral and literate discourse, associated with clausal versus nominal/phrasal grammatical styles.

REFERENCES

Berber-Sardinha, Tony. 2012. *Dimensions of Variation in Spoken and Written Brazilian Portuguese.* Unpublished manuscript.
Besnier, Niko. 1988. "The linguistic relationships of spoken and written Nukulaelae registers." *Language* 64: 707–36.
Biber, Douglas. 1988. *Variation across Speech and Writing.* Cambridge: Cambridge University Press.
———. 1995. *Dimensions of Register Variation: A Cross-Linguistic Perspective.* Cambridge: Cambridge University Press.
———. 2001. "Dimensions of variation among eighteenth-century speech-based and written registers." In *Multi-Dimensional Studies of Register Variation in English,* edited by S. Conrad and D. Biber, 200–214.
———. 2006. *University Language: A Corpus-Based Study of Spoken and Written Registers.* Amsterdam: John Benjamins.
———. 2008. "Corpus-Based analyses of discourse: Dimensions of variation in conversation." In *Advances in Discourse Studies,* 100–114, edited by V. Bhatia, J. Flowerdew, and R. Jones. London: Routledge.
———. 2009. "Are there linguistic consequences of literacy? Comparing the potentials of language use in speech and writing." In *Cambridge Handbook of Literacy,* 75–91, edited by David R. Olson and Nancy Torrance. Cambridge: Cambridge University Press.
Biber, Douglas, Ulla Connor, and Thomas A. Upton. 2007. *Discourse on the Move: Using Corpus Analysis to Describe Discourse Structure.* Amsterdam: John Benjamins.
Biber, Douglas, and Susan Conrad. 2009. *Register, Genre, and Style.* Cambridge: Cambridge University Press.
Biber, Douglas, Mark Davies, James K. Jones, and Nicole Tracy-Ventura. 2006. "Spoken and written register variation in Spanish: A multi-dimensional analysis." *Corpora* 1: 7–38.
Biber, D., and Bethany Gray. 2010. "Challenging stereotypes about academic writing: Complexity, elaboration, explicitness." *Journal of English for Academic Purposes* 9: 2–20.
———. 2013. *Discourse Characteristics of Writing and Speaking Responses on the TOEFL iBT.* Princeton, NJ: Educational Testing Service.
Biber, D., Bethany Gray, and Kornwipa Poonpon. 2011. "Should we use characteristics of conversation to measure grammatical complexity in L2 writing development?" *TESOL Quarterly* 45: 5–35.
Biber, D., and M. Hared. 1992. "Dimensions of register variation in Somali." *Language Variation and Change* 4: 41–75.
———. 1994. "Linguistic correlates of the transition to literacy in Somali: Language adaptation in six press registers." In *Sociolinguistic Perspectives on Register,* 182–216, edited by D. Biber and E. Finegan. Oxford: Oxford University Press.
Biber, Douglas, and James K. Jones. 2005. "Merging corpus linguistic and discourse analytic research goals: Discourse units in biology research articles." *Corpus Linguistics and Linguistic Theory* 1: 151–82.
Biber, D., and J. Kurjian. 2007. "Towards a taxonomy of web registers and text types: A multi-dimensional analysis." In *Corpus Linguistics and the Web,* 109–32, edited by M. Hundt, N. Nesselhauf, and C. Biewer. Amsterdam: Rodopi.
Biber, D., and N. Tracy-Ventura. 2007. "Dimensions of register variation in Spanish." In *Working with Spanish Corpora,* 54–89, edited by G. Parodi. London: Continuum.
Bloch, Maurice. 1993. "The uses of schooling and literacy in a Zafimaniry village." In *Cross-Cultural Approaches to Literacy,* 87–109, edited by Brian V. Street. Cambridge: Cambridge University Press.
Brown, Penelope, and Colin Fraser. 1979. "Speech as a marker of situation." In *Social Markers in Speech,* 33–62, edited by Klaus R. Scherer and Howard Giles. Cambridge: Cambridge University Press.
Conrad, Susan, and Douglas Biber, editors. 2001. *Multi-Dimensional Studies of Register Variation in English.* London: Longman.

Crossley, Scott A., and Max M. Louwerse. 2007. "Multi-dimensional register classification using bigrams." *International Journal of Corpus Linguistics* 12: 453–78.

Egbert, Jesse. 2012. "Style in nineteenth century fiction: A multi-dimensional analysis." *Scientific Study of Literature* 2.

Ervin-Tripp, Susan. 1972. "On sociolinguistic rules: Alternation and co-occurrence." In *Directions in Sociolinguistics*, 213–50, edited by J. J. Gumperz and D. Hymes. New York: Holt.

Friginal, Eric. 2008. "Linguistic variation in the discourse of outsourced call centers." *Discourse Studies* 10: 715–36.

———. 2009. *The Language of Outsourced Call Centers*. Amsterdam: John Benjamins.

Halliday, M. A. K. 1988. "On the language of physical science." In *Registers of Written English: Situational Factors and Linguistic Features*, 162–78, edited by M. Ghadessy. London: Pinter.

Halverson, John. 1991. "Olson on literacy." *Language in Society* 20: 619–40.

Hornberger, Nancy H. 1994. "Continua of biliteracy." In *Literacy across Languages and Cultures*, 103–39, edited by B. M. Ferdman, R. M. Weber, and A. G. Ramirez. Albany: State University of New York Press.

Hymes, Dell. 1974. *Foundations in Sociolinguistics: An Ethnographic Approach*. Philadelphia: University of Pennsylvania Press.

Jang, Shyue-Chian. 1998. "Dimensions of Spoken and Written Taiwanese: A Corpus-Based Register Study." PhD dissertation, University of Hawaii.

Kanoksilapatham, Budsaba. 2007. "Rhetorical moves in biochemistry research articles." In *Discourse on the Move: Using Corpus Analysis to Describe Discourse Structure*, 73–120, edited by D. Biber, U. Connor, and T. Upton. Amsterdam: John Benjamins.

Kim, YongJin, and Douglas Biber. 1994. "A corpus-based analysis of register variation in Korean." In *Sociolinguistic Perspectives on Register*, 157–81, edited by D. Biber and E. Finegan. New York: Oxford University Press.

Kodytek, Vilem. 2007. *On the Replicability of the Biber Model: The Case of Czech*. Unpublished manuscript.

Parodi, Giovanni. 2007. "Variation across registers in Spanish." In *Working with Spanish Corpora*, 11–53, edited by G. Parodi. London: Continuum.

Purvis, Tristan M. 2008. "A linguistic and discursive analysis of register variation in Dagbani." PhD dissertation, Indiana University.

Reppen, Randi. 2001. "Register variation in student and adult speech and writing." In *Multi-Dimensional Studies of Register Variation in English*, 187–99, edited by S. Conrad and D. Biber. London: Longman.

Sáiz, M. 1999. "A cross-linguistic corpus-based analysis of linguistic variation." PhD dissertation, University of Manchester.

Tognini-Bonelli, Elena. 2001. *Corpus Linguistics at Work*. Amsterdam: John Benjamins.

White, M. 1994. "Language in job interviews: Differences relating to success and socioeconomic variables." PhD dissertation, Northern Arizona University.

2

When Ethnicity Isn't Just about Ethnicity

PENELOPE ECKERT
Stanford University

The Seduction of Numbers

CORRELATIONS OVER LARGE DEMOGRAPHIC categories can be seductive. It is commonly found, for example, that women's speech is more standard than males'. But does this say something global about females and males, or is it a guide to speakers' use of standard grammar? Speculations about gender correlations have commonly relied on a view of women as upwardly mobile (Labov 1990), status conscious (Trudgill 1972), or socially vulnerable (Deuchar 1989). The fact that women commonly lead in sound change, thus having less standard phonology than men, has been said to constitute a "paradox" (Labov 2001). The problem, of course, is the underlying assumption that there will be a consistent male-female difference in standardness.

Figure 2.1 shows a typical gender correlation based on my ethnographic study of variation in a Detroit suburban high school (Eckert 2000). Overall, boys use negative concord at twice the rate of girls. This correlation holds up when local social categories are included to this, as shown in figure 2.2, which adds membership in class-based peer categories to the mix. Jocks (not necessarily athletes) are the kids who dominate the extracurricular sphere in the high school. Coming from predominantly middle-class families, jocks are college bound and base their social lives in and around school activities. Burnouts are the kids who reject the school as a basis of social life. Primarily from working-class families, burnouts are predominantly enrolled in a vocational curriculum and are bound for the local workforce after graduation. While the gender correlation holds up among both jocks and burnouts, it is considerably smaller among the burnouts. This corresponds to Labov's finding (1990) of a class crossover for certain variables, in which women at the upper end of the socioeconomic hierarchy are more standard than their male peers, while women at the lower end are less standard than their male peers.

Clearly, variation involves more than marking gender and class. At the very least, gender and class are interacting variables. But what exactly does that mean? Figure 2.3 breaks down the student body of Belten High even further, focusing on communities of practice (Lave and Wenger 1991; Eckert and McConnell-Ginet 1992), from the wildest "burned-out" burnout girls to the boys whose jock status is based on participation in nonsports school activities—what one might call the

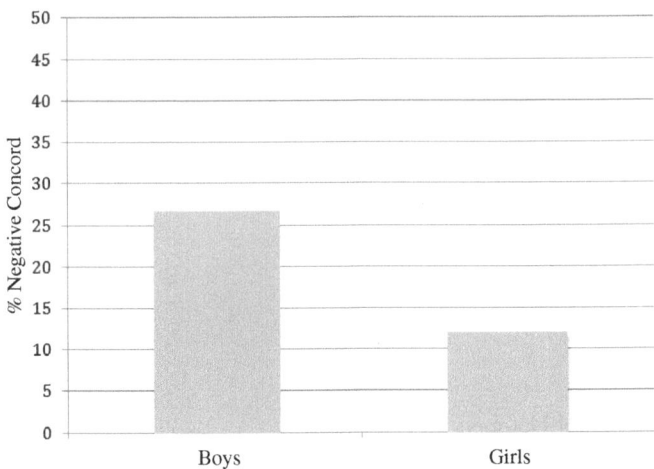

Figure 2.1 Negative Concord at Belten High (p=.000)

school's "corporate types." This picture suggests that negative concord is more about toughness and institutional stance than gender, although toughness and stance may be in turn part of the construction of gender—that is, negative concord can be said to index gender only indirectly (Ochs 1991). Our understanding of the indexical value of linguistic choices lies in the relation between social practice and the broader social categories. Categories like gender, age, and ethnicity are constructed in practice, and they in turn constrain practice. In using negative concord, the burned-out burnout girls are not claiming male identity, but instead indexing toughness; likewise,

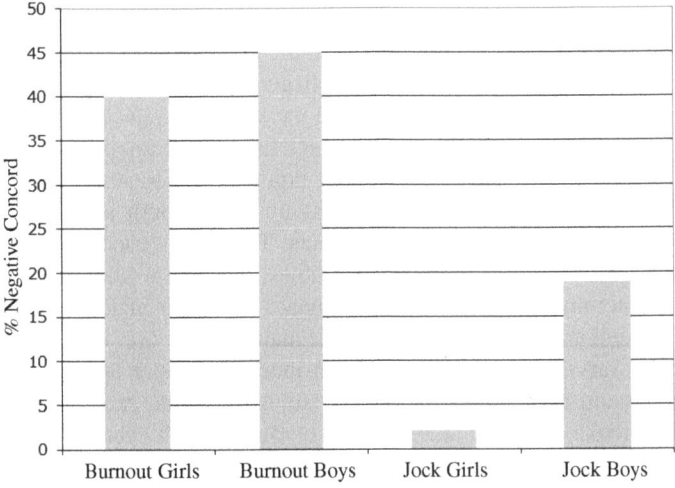

Figure 2.2 Negative Concord by Gender and Social Category

nonathlete jock boys are not claiming female identity, but instead constructing a corporate image.

These kids, in other words, have not passively inherited their patterns of variation from their social address, or from a desire to reflect that address. Rather, the broader correlations themselves are the result of accumulation of indexical activity at the local level. Males and working class people are more likely to construct tough personae, and gender and class are likely to create the conditions under which one might become tough or not. The relation between the two is a reproductive one, but not a determining one.

William Labov's (1963) study of Martha's Vineyard—the first quantitative community study of variation—showed this same dynamic. In this case, the most prominent Vineyard dialect feature, a central nucleus in /ay/ and /aw/, was recruited in a local fight against mainland incursion. Speakers on the island for some time had been gradually lowering the nucleus of these diphthongs to conform to mainland speech. But as the threat of mainland control of the island economy increased with growing tourism, those who had the most to lose from this incursion—primarily the people of English descent in the local traditional fishing trade—came to signal their local orientation by reversing the lowering trend. As Labov put it, "It is apparent that the immediate meaning of this phonetic feature is 'Vineyarder.' When a man says [rɐjt] or [hɐʊs], he is unconsciously establishing the fact that he belongs to the island: that he is one of the natives to whom the island really belongs" (198). In other words, this is a prime example of indexical order (Silverstein 2003) by which a feature that once simply indexed island origins came to index some quality or stance associated with the island. In this case, the centralized diphthongs index a particular

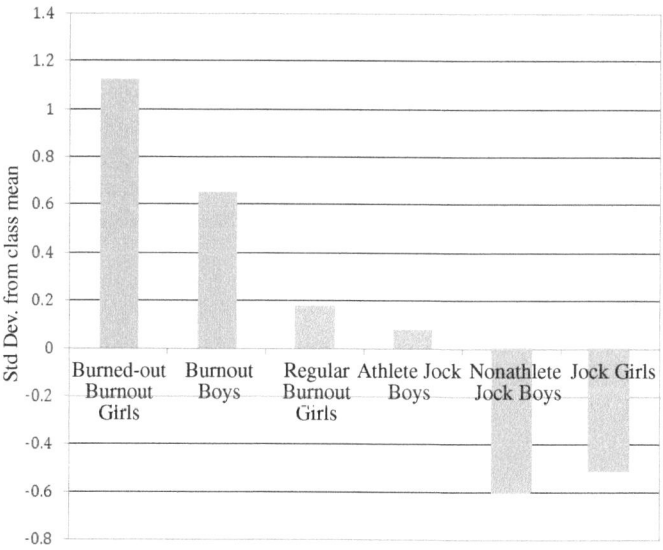

Figure 2.3 Negative Concord by Subgroups of Jocks and Burnouts

kind of Vineyard authenticity—that of the authentic fisherman. Presumably, there are other stances and qualities that are associated with the desired persona, such as being hard-working, hardy, seaworthy, and of original English settler stock. Scott Kiesling (2005) has argued that the indexical meaning of variation lies in stance, and, indeed, the social moves that established the status of the new authentic fisherman category involved stance-taking around ideological issues having to do with island life and the island economy. The use of centralization was an ideological move—a stance-taking that came to index the category of people who defined themselves by that stance. This stance-taking, including the linguistic move, actually constructs the category. In other words, if we intend to move past the macrosociological patterns to understand the indexical value of variation, we must go beyond the categories themselves to see who is creating these categories and why. What kinds of interests and ideologies are at work among members of the categories, and from whom are they distinguishing themselves? Macrosociological categories appear fixed because they are at a level of social structure that changes very slowly, but all social categories are continuously emerging, and indexing what underlies them is part of what helps them emerge.

In a similar case, Zhang (2005) has shown that the emerging economic differentiation resulting from China's entry into the global market has brought about a new social category, as young managers employed in the foreign-owned financial sector have differentiated themselves from their peers in state-owned financial institutions. The new yuppies' affluence affords them a distinctive cosmopolitan lifestyle complete with fancy apartments, cars, fashion, and electronics. To complete this cosmopolitan image, a style of Mandarin has emerged that downplays certain Beijing phonological features and adopts the distinctive full tone associated with Hong Kong and Taiwan Mandarin. In this case, the stylistic package is what brought the yuppie category into existence.

All this is to say that the social workings of variation take place at the local and personal level. Variation is the means by which people actively carve out a place for themselves in their immediate situations. Though speakers begin with what resources are available in their youth, stylistic practice allows them to forge new selves as they move through life. What they encounter as they move through life will be constrained by where they start and by the abstract categories that structure life as they move through it. However, more immediate to them is the everyday that unfolds from, and reproduces, that structure.

Ethnicity and Ethnolects

If the top-down approach to gender mistakes demographic categories for social meaning, it functions in this way even more intensely in the case of ethnic categories. The term "ethnolect" tends to evoke a notion of a linguistic monolith whose use unproblematically indexes ethnicity, but ethnic categories are not static. Their makeup, their social significance, and even their racial attributions (e.g., Brodkin 1998) change over time and space. This development represents an accumulation of changes that occur at a very local level, but with enough regularity to cause larger waves. By virtue of participation in broader communities, what may begin as purely ethnic features take on more complex indexical value as the members of the ethnic group articulate their experiences both within and beyond the group itself (see, particularly, Sharma 2011) and as others adopt ethnic features to index imagined ethnic characteristics (see, e.g., Bucholtz 2011). In what follows, I focus on one aspect of this dynamic in the speech of elementary school children in Northern California.

White Anglo-Americans are now the minority in California. Nonetheless, the public perception of the state often focuses on the young, white, affluent, urban coastal population and the popular stereotypes of the surfer and the valley girl. Perceptions of California speech focus on those two stereotypes, associating current sound changes in California with the laid-back dude or the catty mall crawler. Parts of the linguistic stereotypes associated with these social stereotypes represent sound changes in progress throughout California, which are possibly led by coastal speakers. Figure 2.4 shows the complete set of vowel changes that make up what one might call the Coastal California Shift. It has been common to define regional dialects on the basis of the speech of the regional white population, leaving other dialects with a kind of deterritorialized status and treating them as separate systems. The question often asked, then, is to what extent do members of particular ethnic groups participate in "regional" sound changes? Fought (1999) has argued against defining regional dialects against the baseline of regional white speech, showing that for Los Angeles Chicanos, participation and nonparticipation reflects conflicting norms within the Chicano community where the fronting of the GOOSE vowel indexes orientation to either mainstream or gang culture. The features of "ethnolects" in contact are part of everyone's linguistic landscape and must be seen not only as enregistered (Agha 2003) as "ethnic," but also as resources open to those who choose to adopt them.

While some elements of the Coastal California Shift are associated with surfer and valley girl stereotypes, they are by no means limited to people fitting these stereotypes or to Anglos more generally; for example, some features of Chicano English bleed into the speech of white Anglos. In what follows, though, I raise a different

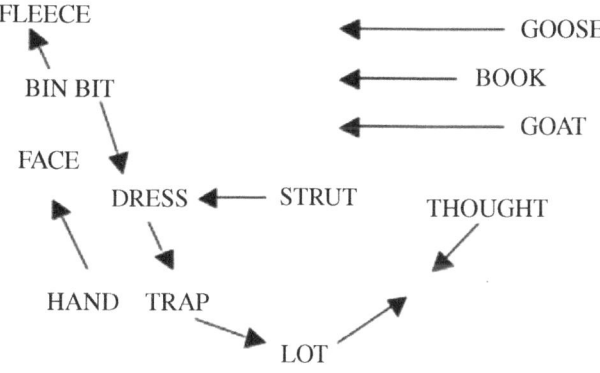

Figure 2.4 The Coastal California Shift

issue relating language and ethnicity, focusing on the range of meanings associated with the use of a group's own ethnic features. To do this, I draw on data from my ethnographic study of preadolescents in two Northern California elementary schools. Steps Elementary serves a catchment area that predominantly houses poor Latinos, Asian Americans, and a number of other nonwhite ethnic groups. Eight percent of the student body is white Anglo. Ten minutes away, Fields Elementary serves a financially stable catchment area, with an 80 percent white Anglo student body, and the remaining 20 percent mirroring the majority population at Steps. Kids in the two schools are aware of each other and recognize the relation between the neighboring schools and broader societal discourses of ethnicity. But despite differences between the schools, the kids in both are involved in the same central activity: the move from childhood to adolescence, and on the construction of the peer-based social order that defines adolescence. Language plays a central role in this process.

Variation and the Heterosexual Market

In each school, as in elementary schools across the United States, the last few years of elementary school bring about the emergence of a "popular crowd" at Fields and Steps—a coalescence of girls' and boys' networks into a community of practice centered around pioneering adolescent social practice. This coalescence involves merging friendship groups to create a significant mass that can dominate attention in the cohort, establish a base of power, and support its members in new potentially face-threatening activity. Central to this activity is the matching of boys and girls into couples. This is not a matter of individual choice, but an activity that occurs within the crowd as others decide who belongs with whom and negotiate the actual pairing up. Couples don't usually stay "together" for long, as this activity is not about individual relationships but instead about creating a social market. Rapid and repeated pairings construct social value for individuals based on whom they are paired with and on their ability to negotiate the pairing of others. This market of heterosexual desirability is at the center of an emerging status system in the cohort; desirability is based not only on perceived attractiveness, but on social knowledge—in short, coolness.

Ethnic differences between the two schools yield different preoccupations in the construction of coolness. While the crowd at Steps is ethnically diverse, the majority of participants are Chicano/a, and coolness is constructed with reference to the Chicano culture that surrounds the school. Orientation to gangs is a primary concern in this coolness. Gangs are an important part of the family and neighborhood life of many of the kids at Steps, and gang participation is recognized as part of the coming of age process associated with the young adult life stage. Gang orientation articulates social differences within the Latino population at the same time that it provides a visible and culturally rich form of opposition to mainstream culture. Specific to the life stage that the kids at Steps are going through is the Quinceañera—a coming of age celebration for fifteen-year-old girls with significant heterosexual significance. While the kids at Steps have a few years until their own celebrations, they often get leading roles in the festivities for their older relatives. These occasions—and the preparations leading up to them—are alive with cohort-based social meaning.

In contrast, the dominant culture of the crowd at Fields Elementary is middle class Anglo, and there is a clear sense that these kids consider themselves part of the mainstream. Sports—played both during recess and on teams outside of school hours—dominate the crowd's activities. In sixth grade, dances become a major preoccupation for the popular crowd. The fact that Steps doesn't hold dances points to perhaps the most telling difference between the two schools. Teachers and administrators at Steps are hyperaware of the dangers of their pupils' neighborhoods and work to keep the threat of gangs and early sexual engagement at bay. While the adults at Steps are fully engaged with their students, their stance is one of protection from the surrounding dangers, which puts the adults at odds with the crowd's maturational ambitions. At Fields, on the other hand, teachers view the crowd's engagement in heterosexual activity as harmless. This difference has far-reaching implications for education. For the purposes of the present study, it is relevant to point out that the indexical values associated with the resources of the two crowds' dominant linguistic varieties differ not only with respect to ethnicity, but also to such things as relation to the school institution. Be that as it may, the ethnic tone of each of the two popular crowds determines the kind of coolness they will seek and the linguistic resources they will use to construct themselves as cool.

As shown in figure 2.4, the Coastal California Shift involves the fronting of the back vowels GOOSE and GOAT. These two developments are associated with Anglo speakers and commonly cited in imitations of young California stereotypes (e.g., the fronting of the GOOSE vowel in the surfer pronunciation of *dude*). Fought (1999) has shown that, while most young Chicanos tend not to participate in this fronting, those who are more engaged in mainstream culture do front the GOOSE vowel. The Anglo nature of this fronting shows up clearly in the differences between Fields and Steps; while most kids at Fields front this vowel at least to some degree, most kids at Steps do not. The same is true of the fronting of the GOAT vowel. Fields speakers front both GOOSE and GOAT more than speakers at Steps, as measured by the second formant ($p < 0.001$ in both cases). But GOOSE and GOAT do not simply index ethnicity. At Fields, members of the popular crowd lead nonmembers in fronting the GOOSE vowel ($p < 0.05$) and the GOAT vowel ($p < 0.0015$). In other words, while these frontings index Anglo ethnicity at a higher demographic level, locally, they index a kind of social status among Anglos that has nothing to do with ethnicity.

Throughout North America, it is common for Anglo speakers to raise the TRAP vowel in a variety of environments. In the West quite generally, raising occurs only before nasal consonants (e.g., *stand*). This nasal pattern is enhanced in California Anglo speech by a concomitant lowering and backing of nonnasal occurrences of TRAP, leaving a considerable split between the two sets of occurrences. At Fields Elementary, the magnitude of this split has social significance—the crowd members show a significantly greater split, as measured by the distance between the means of the two sets of occurrences, than noncrowd members ($p < 0.001$). In Chicano English, however, there is no nasal pattern. Furthermore, all occurrences of the TRAP vowel are relatively low and considerably back. This ethnic pattern shows up in an overall difference between the two schools—the difference between nasal and nonnasal occurrences of TRAP is significantly greater at Fields than at Steps

($p < 0.001$). And, as at Fields, the school's pattern correlates locally with social status. At Steps, the magnitude of the split correlates inversely with crowd membership, with noncrowd members showing a greater split than crowd members ($p < 0.001$). In fact, no member of the crowd, regardless of ethnicity, shows a significant height difference between nasal and nonnasal occurrences, while most noncrowd members, once again, regardless of ethnicity, show a split with a significance ranging from 0.05 to 0.001. The dramatic differences between the patterns used by the crowds at Fields and Steps are shown in figures 2.5 and 2.6, which display F1-F2 plots of occurrences of TRAP in the speech of Rachel and Selena, prominent members of the crowd at Fields and Steps, respectively.

These cases all illustrate a single principle—that linguistic features that are associated with ethnicity take on meaning within the community that is orthogonal to ethnicity. Specifically, in each of these schools, phonological features that distinguish the ethnic community are deployed to index social status within the community. The Asian, African American, and Anglo members of the Steps crowd do not use Chicano features to lay claim to status as Chicanos. Likewise, the Chicana who is a prominent member of the Fields crowd does not use Anglo features to lay claim to Anglo status. Rather, in each school, locally current features are embraced by those laying claim to central local status. As the following example suggests, this central status is more specifically a claim to advanced maturational status: being a player in the heterosexual market.

Linda

Linda was a member of the Steps cohort with marginal status in the crowd. She had one Chicano parent and admired her older Chicano cousins for their coolness. While being Chicana was not a requirement for crowd membership, she resented the fact that her ethnic status was always in question. She was not paired up with any boys and was not considered cool. But things changed at the end of elementary school, when she began to "mess with" guys beyond her school. One day early in seventh grade, she said I should come with her with my recorder because she had something she wanted to tell me. Her friends rolled their eyes and said that I definitely had to hear what she had to tell me. As we walked to a quiet place to talk and record, she said she'd gotten into some serious and exciting stuff—she'd been "messing with" guys. She particularly wanted to tell me how she'd hooked up with a guy at her cousin's Quinceañera the previous weekend. Particularly noticeable in this long narrative was the importance of the audience to her actions. The boy himself, beyond the fact that he was a cholo and "so fine," was not the center of the story—rather, the story was built around the series of events that drew others' attention to the fact that she was daring and sexually engaged. She took on a completely different persona in this narrative; she became a "player" in stark contrast to her previous persona as a marginalized member of her sixth-grade crowd. Her speech suddenly showed a broad range of Chicano features and sounded radically different from her speech on other recent occasions. Figure 2.7 compares her pronunciation of the TRAP vowel in this conversation (black circles) with her pronunciation of the same vowel in a conversation a few months earlier (empty circles) when she was still in sixth grade. As this

WHEN ETHNICITY ISN'T JUST ABOUT ETHNICITY 29

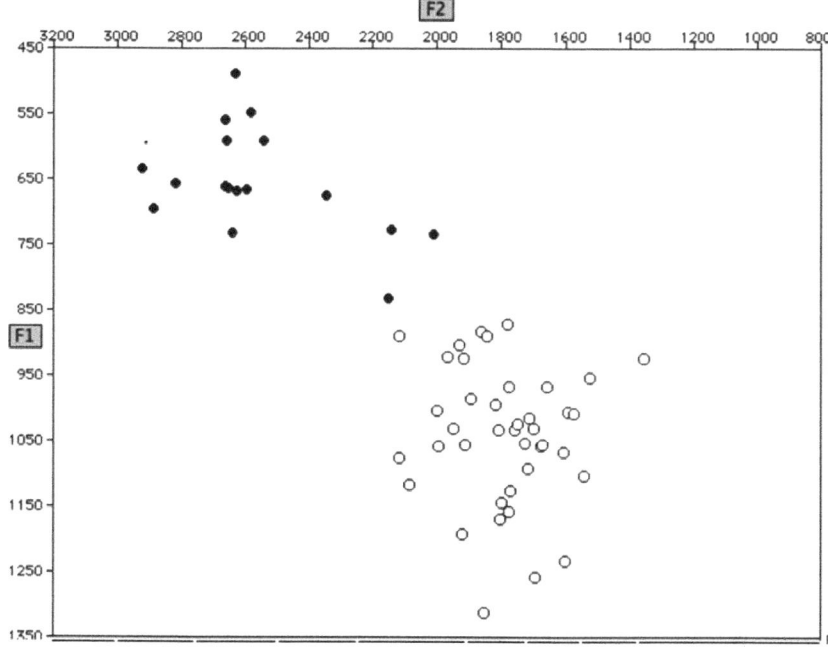

Figure 2.5 The Fields Pattern: Rachel's TRAP

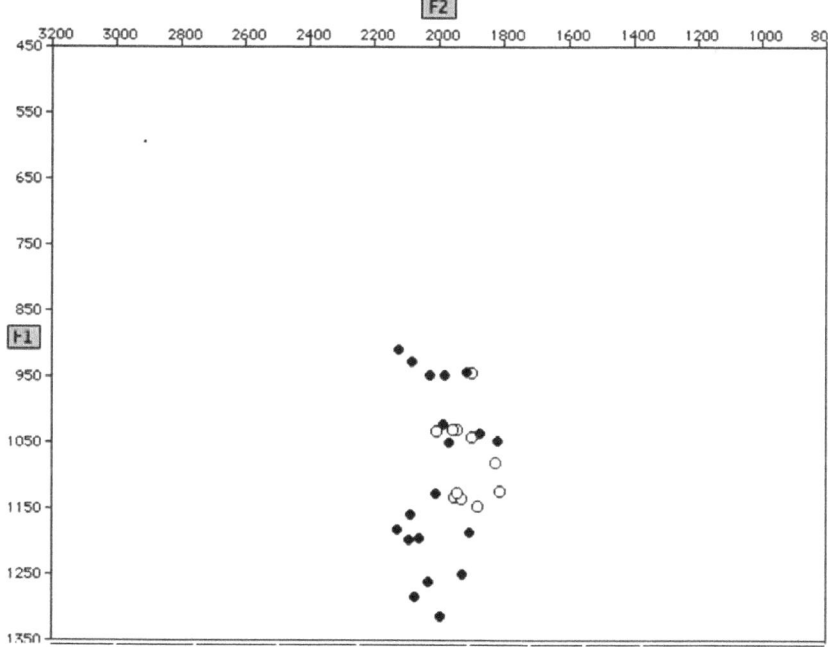

Figure 2.6 The Steps Pattern: Selena's TRAP

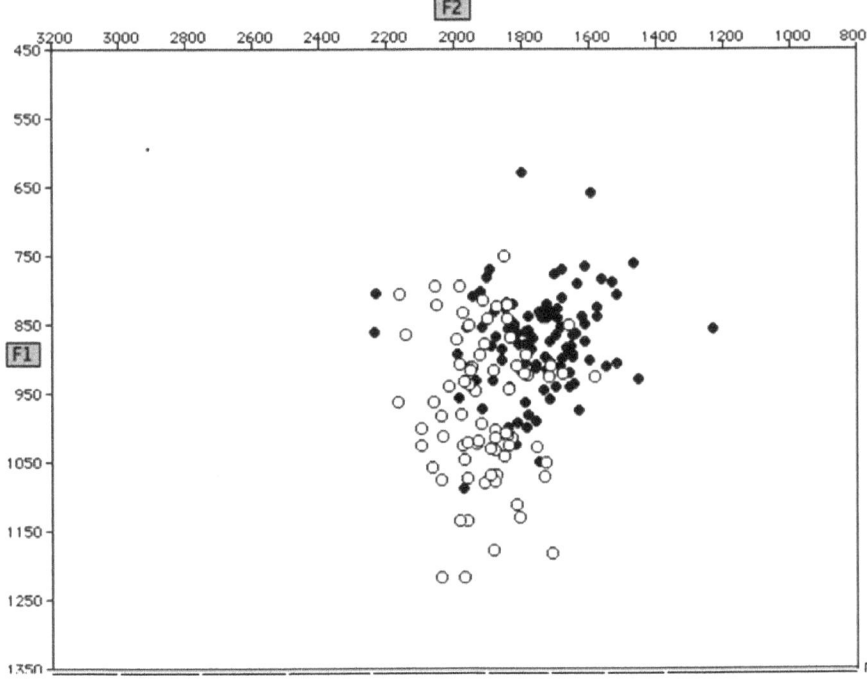

Figure 2.7 Linda's TRAP in Sixth and Seventh Grades

figure shows, her pronunciation of this vowel shows a dramatic difference between these two events, with her player pronunciation both farther back ($p < 0.001$) and higher ($p < 0.001$) than her sixth-grade pronunciation.

While Linda's speech conformed more to the Chicano pattern while telling this story, and while the events took place in a saliently Chicano context, the persona she was presenting was not laying claim to Chicano ethnicity so much as player status. Linda did not become "more Chicana" between sixth and seventh grade. She had been socially accepted in a Chicano setting outside of school before this incident. But, more importantly, if she ever wanted to be accepted as Chicana, it was for the sake of being a player in a Chicano-defined social market. In this case, she was no more Chicana than the Chicanas who were on the outs with the crowd in her elementary school. Indeed, she was not interested in a noncool Chicana identity; one might say that Chicano authenticity had no use to her if it was not the way to be cool.

Conclusion

We often miss the relation between linguistic and social practice by stopping at demographic categories. Though there is a statistically significant relation between ethnicity and one's use of linguistic variables, such as the nasal pattern, a focus on such correlations leads to a kind of essentialism that associates dialects passively with birthright. The Chicanos at Steps Elementary who show the nasal pattern are no less Chicano than those who do not. One could not reasonably say that they have become more "mainstream" than their peers in the crowd, or even that they have more Anglo friends. Rather, they are not engaged in the indexical work that associates Chicano features with coolness—perhaps they associate these features with completely different traits and practices. It is this indexical work that makes sociolinguistic variation what it is—a robust system for the construction of social meaning.

REFERENCES

Agha, Asif. 2003. "The social life of a cultural value." *Language and Communication* 23: 231–73.
Brodkin, Karen. 1998. *How Jews Became White Folks and What That Says about Race in America*. New Brunswick, NJ: Rutgers University Press.
Bucholtz, Mary. 2011. *White Kids: Language, Race, and Styles of Youth Identity*. Cambridge and New York: Cambridge University Press.
Charity, Anne H. 2007. "Regional differences in low SES African-American children's speech in the school setting." *Language Variation and Change* 19: 281–93.
Deuchar, Margaret. 1989. "A pragmatic account of women's use of standard speech." In *Women in Their Speech Communities*, 27–32, edited by Jennifer Coates and Deborah Cameron. London and New York: Longman.
Eckert, Penelope. 2000. *Linguistic Variation as Social Practice*. Oxford: Blackwell.
Eckert, Penelope, and Sally McConnell-Ginet. 1992. "Think practically and look locally: Language and gender as community-based practice." *Annual Review of Anthropology* 21: 461–90.
Fought, Carmen. 1999. "A majority sound change in a minority community /u/-fronting in Chicano English." *Journal of Sociolinguistics* 3: 5–23.
Kiesling, Scott. 2005. "Variation, stance and style." *English World-Wide* 26: 1–42.
Labov, William. 1963. "The social motivation of a sound change." *Word* 18: 1–42.
———. 1990. "The intersection of sex and social class in the course of linguistic change." *Language Variation and Change* 2: 205–51.
———. 2001. *Principles of Linguistic Change: Social Factors*. Cambridge: Blackwell.
Lave, Jean, and Etienne Wenger. 1991. *Situated Learning: Legitimate Peripheral Participation*. Cambridge: Cambridge University Press.
Ochs, E. 1991. "Indexing gender." In *Rethinking Context*, edited by A. Duranti and C. Goodwin. Cambridge: Cambridge University Press.
Sharma, Devyani. 2011. "Style, repertoire and social change in British Asian English." *Journal of Sociolinguistics* 15: 464–92.
Silverstein, Michael. 2003. "Indexical order and the dialectics of sociolinguistic life." *Language and Communication* 23: 193–229.
Trudgill, Peter. 1972. "Sex, covert prestige and linguistic change in the urban British English of Norwich." *Language in Society* 1: 179–95.
Zhang, Qing. 2005. "A Chinese yuppie in Beijing: Phonological variation and the construction of a new professional identity." *Language in Society* 34: 431–66.

3

Does Language Zipf Right Along?

Investigating Robustness in the Latent Structure of Usage and Acquisition

NICK C. ELLIS
University of Michigan

MATTHEW BROOK O'DONNELL
University of Michigan

UTE RÖMER
Georgia State University

EACH OF US AS language learners has had different language experiences, but somehow, we have converged on the same general language system. From diverse and often noisy samples, we end up with similar linguistic competence. How so? Do language form, language meaning, and language usage come together across scales to promote robust induction by means of statistical learning over limited samples? The research described here outlines an approach to this question with regard to English verb-argument constructions (VACs), their grammatical form, semantics, lexical constituency, and distribution patterns. Measurement and analysis of large corpora of language usage identifies Zipfian scale-free patterns in VAC type-token frequency and in the structure of their semantic networks. Using methods from cognitive linguistics, corpus linguistics, learning theory, complex systems, and network science, we explore how these latent structures of usage might promote the emergence of linguistic constructions in first and second language acquisition.

Literature Review
We seek an understanding of robust language acquisition. As a child, you engaged your parents and friends by talking about shared interests and using words and phrases that came to mind; this is how you learned language. None of the authors of this paper was privy to this system, but somehow, we have all converged on a similar-enough English to be able to communicate. How did this happen?

We take a two-pronged approach to this question. First, we consider the psychology of learning as applied to linguistic constructions. This is generally the approach to language acquisition as pursued within usage-based linguistics, cognitive linguistics, construction grammar, child language research, second language acquisition

(SLA), and psycholinguistics (Bybee 2010; Goldberg 2006; Robinson and Ellis 2008; Tomasello 2003). These views share the assumption that language acquisition is similar to the rest of cognition in that we learn language like we learn anything else. Of course, human cognition is not simple; there is much to the psychology of learning. The problem-space of language—mapping thoughts to serial sequences of sound—is particularly special, but it is parsimonious to assume that language is subject to the same learning mechanisms and cognitive constraints as the rest of our experience.

Second, for the factors that promote robust acquisition, we look to research within emergentism, dynamic systems theory, and complex adaptive systems (CAS). CAS are characterized by their robustness to different kinds of perturbations, by their scale-free properties, and by their structures emerging from the interactions of agents and components at many levels (Holland 1995; Page 2009), as shown by the recent explorations of *Language as a Complex Adaptive System* (Beckner et al. 2009; Ellis 1998; Ellis and Larsen-Freeman 2006, 2009b; Larsen-Freeman 1997; MacWhinney 1999; Solé et al. 2005).

A significant discovery in the early cognitive analysis of language involved how basic objects in natural categories underpinned the robust acquisition of nouns. Rosch et al. (1976) showed how basic categories—those that carry the most information in clustering the things of the world—are those whose members possess significant numbers of attributes in common, are visually imageable with similar shapes, and have similar associated motor programs. Basic natural categories are organized around prototypes. These prototype exemplars are most typical of the category, similar to many other category members, and not similar to members of other categories. People categorize prototype exemplars (like *robin* as *bird*) faster than those with less common features or feature combinations like *geese* or *penguins* (Rosch and Mervis 1975; Rosch et al. 1976). Basic categories are also those that are the most codable (faster naming), most coded, and most necessary in language (highly frequent in usage). Children acquire basic-category terms like *dog, bird, hammer,* and *apple* earlier than they do their superordinates *animal, tool,* and *fruit,* or subordinates *collie, wren, ball-peen hammer,* and *Granny Smith*. It is reliable visual and motor perceptual experience along with frequent and highly contingent labeling that makes these nouns reliably and robustly learnable, despite individual children experiencing different types of dogs and birds.

Cognitive linguistics, particularly construction grammar, has since extended these ideas to language as a whole. Nouns typically relate to the things of the world, but because language has emerged to describe our experiences, whole sentences are used to describe the doings of nouns. Linguistic constructions that correspond to basic sentence types encode as their prototypical senses events that are basic to human experience—those of something moving, something being in a state, someone causing something, someone possessing something, something causing a change of state or location, someone causing a change of possession, something undergoing a change of state or location, something having an effect on someone, and so on (Croft 2001, 2012; Goldberg 1995; Levin 1993).

Corpus and cognitive linguistics have shown that grammar and semantics are reliably associated, and, in turn, that grammatical patterns and their corresponding events jointly select particular lexical items. Syntax, lexis, and semantics are inextricably intertwined (Sinclair 2004). The meaning of the words of a language and how they can be used in combination depends on our perception and categorization of the world around us. Since we constantly observe and play an active role in this world, we know a great deal about it; this experience and familiarity is reflected in the nature of language. The differing degrees of salience, as well as the prominence of elements involved in situations that we wish to describe, will affect the selection of subjects, objects, adverbials, and other clause arrangements. Figure/ground segregation and perspective-taking—processes of vision and attention—are mirrored in language and have systematic relations with syntactic structure. In language production, what we express reflects which parts of an event attract our attention; depending on how we direct our attention, we can select and highlight different aspects of the frame, thus arriving at different linguistic expressions. The prominence of particular aspects of the scene and the perspective of the internal observer (i.e., the attentional focus of the speaker and the intended attentional focus of the listener) are key elements in determining regularities of association between elements of visuospatial experience and elements of phonological form. In language comprehension, abstract linguistic constructions (like locatives, datives, and passives) guide the listener's attention to a particular perspective on a scene while backgrounding other aspects (Langacker 1987; Talmy 2000; Taylor 2002).

By processes of syntactic and semantic bootstrapping, these associations of form and function could allow linguistic constructions to be learnable in an exemplar-by-exemplar fashion, with abstract schematic patterns induced from particular usage patterns and their interpretations. Researching this possibility requires interdisciplinary collaborations. The investigation of form involves structuralist, corpus linguistic, and computational linguistic approaches; the investigation of function involves functionalist, cognitive linguistic, and psycholinguistic analyses; and the study of embodied force dynamics involves an understanding of semantic organization and more. Their association requires quantitative linguistics for the statistical tallying of form and function as well as an understanding of the psychology of learning. The result of these collaborations should not be a dictionary, a grammar manual, or a frequency list. Rather, it should be a systemic network integrating the syntactic constructions of a language, the lexis they select, their meanings, and the distributions and mappings of these forms and functions.

In what follows, we sketch how we believe this work might progress, illustrating it with some preliminary findings of ongoing investigations of our own. We focus upon verb-argument constructions (VACs) in English, such as 'V *across* n' as in "she walked across the street." These initial studies convince us that learners do not acquire language from unstructured, unhelpful experience. Instead, the evidence of language usage is rich in latent structure. Learners' explorations of this problem-space are grounded and contextualized. There is much latent structure to scaffold development in the frequency distributions of exemplars of linguistic constructions and in the network structure of the corresponding semantic space. Furthermore, learners' investigations of the problem space of language usage are often directed, attentionally focused, and co-constructed in discourse interaction by an interlocutor as a helpful guide, although consideration of these aspects is beyond the scope of this chapter.

Our shared language understanding suggests that, just as for nouns, there is a basic variety of VACs, each with their own basic level verb prototype. For example, despite the fact that you and I have not heard the same input, our experience allows us similar interpretations of novel utterances like "it mandools across the ground" or "the teacher spugged the boy the book." You know that *mandool* is a verb of motion and have some idea of how mandooling works and its action semantics. You know that *spugging* involves transfer, that the teacher is the donor, the boy the recipient, and the book the transferred object. How is this possible, given that you have never previously heard these verbs? Each word of the construction contributes individual meaning, and the verb meanings in these VACs are usually at the core. But the larger configuration of words as a whole also carries meaning. The VAC, as a category, has inherited its schematic meaning from the conspiracy of all of the examples you have heard. *Mandool* inherits its interpretation from the echoes of the verbs that occupy this VAC—words like *come, walk, move, . . . , scud, skitter,* and *flit*.

As you read these utterances, you parse them and identify their syntagmatic form: "it mandools across the ground" as a verb locative (VL) construction; "the teacher spugged the boy the book" as a double-object (VOO) construction. Then the paradigmatic associations of the types of verb that fill these slots are awakened: for the VL 'V *across* n' pattern, you associate *mandool* with *come, walk, move, . . . , scud, skitter,* and *flit*; for the VOO construction, you associate *spugged* with *give, send, pass, . . . , read, loan,* and *fax*. Knowledge of language is based on these types of inference of syntactic and semantic bootstrapping. Verbs are the cornerstone of the syntax-semantics interface, which is why we focus upon VACs in our research.

In the rest of this chapter we consider the nature of VACs and the psychology of their learning before turning to a complex systems analysis of the dynamic structure of language usage and how it might support robust language learning.

Constructions and Their Acquisition
Construction Grammar
We take the Saussurian (1916) view that the units of language are constructions—form-meaning mappings, conventionalized in the speech community, and entrenched as language knowledge in the learner's mind. They are the symbolic units of language that relate the defining properties of their morphological, lexical, and syntactic form with particular semantic, pragmatic, and discourse functions (Goldberg 1995, 2006). Construction grammar argues that all grammatical phenomena can be understood as learned pairings of form (from morphemes, words, and idioms to partially lexically filled and fully general phrasal patterns) and their associated semantic or discourse functions: "the network of constructions captures our grammatical knowledge *in toto*, i.e., it's constructions all the way down" (Goldberg 2006, 18). Such beliefs, increasingly influential in the study of child language acquisition, emphasize

data-driven, emergent accounts of linguistic systematicities (e.g., Ambridge and Lieven 2011; Ellis 2011; Tomasello 2003).

The Psychology of Learning

Usage-based approaches hold that we learn linguistic constructions while engaging in communication (Bybee 2010). Psycholinguistic research provides the evidence of usage-based acquisition in its demonstrations that language processing is exquisitely sensitive to usage frequency at all levels of language representation—from phonology, through lexis and syntax, to sentence processing (Ellis 2002). Since language users are sensitive to the input frequencies of these patterns, they must have registered their occurrence in processing. Therefore, these frequency effects are compelling evidence for usage-based models of language acquisition that emphasize the role of input. Language knowledge involves statistical knowledge, so humans more easily learn and process high frequency forms and regular patterns, which are exemplified by many types and have few competitors (e.g., Ellis 2006a; MacWhinney 2001).

Constructionist accounts of language learning involve the distributional analysis of the language stream and the parallel analysis of contingent perceptuo-motor activity. Abstract constructions are often learned as categories from the integrated experience of concrete exemplars of usage that follow statistical learning mechanisms relating input and learner cognition (Bybee and Hopper 2001; Christiansen and Chater 2001; Ellis 2006b; Jurafsky and Martin 2009).

Determinants of Construction Learning

Psychological analyses of the learning of constructions as form-meaning pairs are informed by the literature on the associative learning of cue-outcome contingencies. The usual determinants include: (1) form frequency in the input (type-token frequency, Zipfian distribution), (2) function (prototypicality of meaning), and (3) interactions between these (contingency of form-function mapping) (Ellis and Cadierno 2009).

Construction Frequency. Frequency of exposure promotes learning and entrenchment (e.g., Anderson 2000; Ebbinghaus 1885). Learning, memory, and perception are all affected by frequency of usage; the more times we experience something, the stronger our memory for it, and the more fluently it is accessed. The more times we experience conjunctions of features, the more they become associated in our minds and the more these subsequently affect perception and categorization (Harnad 1987; Lakoff 1987; Taylor 1998).

Type and Token Frequency. Token frequency counts how often a particular form appears in the input. The greater the token frequency of an exemplar, the more it contributes to defining the category, and the greater the likelihood it will be considered the prototype. On the other hand, type frequency refers to the number of distinct lexical items that can be substituted in a given slot in a construction, whether it is a word-level construction for inflection or a syntactic construction specifying the relation among words. For example, the regular English past tense *-ed* has a very high type frequency because it applies to thousands of different types of verbs, whereas the vowel change exemplified in *swam* and *rang* has much lower type frequency. The productivity of phonological, morphological, and syntactic constructions is a function of type rather than token frequency (Bybee and Hopper 2001).

Zipfian Distribution. In natural language, Zipf's law (Zipf 1935) describes how the highest frequency words account for the most linguistic tokens. Zipf's law states that the frequency of words decreases as a power function of their rank in the frequency table. Thus, in English, the most frequent word (*the* with a token frequency of about 60,000 occurrences per million words) occurs approximately twice as often as the second most frequent word, three times as often as the third most frequent word, and so on. If P_f is the proportion of words whose frequency in a given language sample is f, then $P_f \sim f^{-\gamma}$, with $\gamma \approx 1$. Zipf showed that this scaling law holds across a wide variety of language samples. Subsequent research provides support for this law as linguistically universal. Many language events across scales of analysis follow his power law, including words (Evert 2005), collocations (Bannard and Lieven 2009; Solé et al. 2005), formulaic phrases (O'Donnell and Ellis 2009), morphosyntactic productivity (Baayen 2008), grammatical constructs (Ninio 2006; O'Donnell and Ellis 2010), and grammatical dependencies (Ferrer i Cancho and Solé 2001, 2003; Ferrer i Cancho, Solé, and Köhler 2004). Zipfian covering, which involves splitting concepts hierarchically (e.g., animal, canine, dog, retriever, Labrador, and so on) in order to communicate clearly, determines basic categorization, the structure of semantic classes, and the language form-semantic structure interface (Manin 2008; Steyvers and Tennenbaum 2005). Scale-free laws pervade language structure and usage.

However, this does not apply solely to language structure and usage; power law behavior like this has since been shown to apply to a wide variety of structures, networks, and dynamic processes in physical, biological, technological, social, cognitive, and psychological systems of various kinds (e.g., magnitudes of earthquakes, populations of cities, citations of scientific papers, number of hits received by websites, sizes of airline hubs, perceptual psychophysics, memory, categorization, etc.) (Kello et al. 2010; Newman 2005). It has become a hallmark of complex systems theory. It is tempting to think of Zipfian scale-free laws as universals. Complexity theorists suspect them to be fundamental and are beginning to investigate how they might underlie language processing, learnability, acquisition, usage, and change (Beckner et al. 2009; Ellis and Larsen-Freeman 2009b; Ferrer i Cancho and Solé 2001, 2003; Ferrer i Cancho, Solé, and Köhler 2004; Solé et al. 2005).

Various usage-based linguists (e.g., Boyd and Goldberg 2009; Bybee 2008, 2010; Ellis 2008a; Goldberg 2006; Goldberg, Casenhiser, and Sethuraman 2004; Lieven and Tomasello 2008; Ninio 1999, 2006) suspect that it is the Zipfian coming together of linguistic form and function that makes language robustly learnable despite learners' idiosyncratic experience. For example, in first language acquisition, Goldberg, Casenhiser, and Sethuraman (2004) demonstrated that there is a strong tendency for VL, verb object locative (VOL), and double object ditransitive (VOO) VACs to be occupied by one single verb with very high frequency in comparison to other verbs used, a profile that closely mirrors that of the mothers' speech to their children. They argue that this promotes language acquisition because the low variance sample allows learners to discern what will account for most of the category members, with the category defined later with experience of the full breadth of exemplar types.

Function (Prototypicality of Meaning). Categories have graded structure; some members are better exemplars than others. In the prototype theory of concepts (Rosch and Mervis 1975; Rosch et al. 1976), the prototype as the central ideal is the best example of the category, appropriately summarizing the most representative attributes of a category. As the typical instance of a category, it serves as the benchmark against which less representative instances are classified.

In child language acquisition, a small group of semantically general verbs (e.g., *go, do, make, come*) are learned early (Clark 1978; Goldberg 2006; Ninio 1999; Pinker 1989). Ellis and Ferreira-Junior (2009a) show the same is true of the second language acquisition of VL, VOL, and VOO constructions. These first verbs are prototypical and generic in function (*go* for VL, *put* for VOL, and *give* for VOO). In the early stages of learning categories from exemplars, acquisition might thus be optimized by the introduction of an initial low-variance sample centered upon prototypical exemplars.

Contingency of Form-Function Mapping. Psychological research into associative learning has long recognized that, while frequency of form is important, more so is contingency of mapping (Shanks 1995). For example, when looking at exemplars of birds, though eyes and wings are equally frequently experienced features, wings are the distinctive feature that differentiates birds from other animals. Wings are important features because they are reliably associated with class membership; eyes are a more universal and less reliable trait. Raw frequency of occurrence is less important than the contingency between cue and interpretation (Rescorla 1968). Contingency, reliability of form-function mapping, and associated aspects of predictive value, information gain, and statistical association are driving forces of learning. They are also central in psycholinguistic theories of language acquisition (Ellis 2006a, 2006b, 2008b; Gries and Wulff 2005; MacWhinney 1987).

Usage-Based Acquisition

The primary motivation of construction grammar involves bringing together linguistic form, learner cognition, and usage. Constructions cannot be defined purely on the basis of linguistic form, semantics, or frequency of usage alone. All three factors are necessary in their operationalization and measurement. Psychology theory relating to the statistical learning of categories suggests that constructions are robustly learnable when they are: (1) Zipfian in their type-token distributions in usage, (2) selective in their verb form occupancy, (3) coherent in their semantics, and (4) similar in form and function.

Taking this into account, it is important to measure whether language usage provides experience of this type. If it does, then VACs as linguistic constructions should be robustly learnable. Is language, which is shaped by the human brain (Christiansen and Chater 2008), consequently shaped *for* the human brain, in that the structures latent in language usage make language robustly learnable?

Language Use as a Complex Adaptive System

This fundamental claim that Zipfian distributional properties of language usage help to make language learnable has just begun to be explored for a small number of VACs in first (Goldberg 2006; Goldberg, Casenhiser, and Sethuraman 2004; Ninio 2006, 2011) and second language acquisition (Ellis and Ferreira-Junior 2009a, 2009b; Ellis and Larsen-Freeman 2009a). It remains a priority to explore its generality across the wide range of English verbal grammar. In order to do this, we need: (1) an integrative analysis of the VACs of a language, the lexis they select, their meanings, and the distributions and mappings of these forms and functions; (2) to determine if the latent structures therein are of the type that would promote robust learning; (3) and to measure corpora of learner language (L1 and L2) to see if learning is shaped by the input. These steps are no small task. Here, we describe some of our pilot work and suggestions for further research.

A Usage-Based Grammar of English Verbs and Verb-Argument Constructions

A Catalogue of VACs. In order to avoid circularity, the determination of the semantic associations of particular linguistic forms should start from structuralist definitions of VACs defined by bottom-up means that are semantics-free. No one in corpus linguistics trusts the text more than Sinclair (2004) in his operationalizations of linguistic constructions on the basis of repeated patterns of words in collocation, colligation, and phrases. We therefore use the patterns presented in the *Grammar Patterns: Verbs* (Hunston and Francis 1996) that arose out of the COBUILD project (Sinclair 1987) for our initial analyses. There are over seven hundred patterns of varying complexity in this volume. The form-based patterns described in the COBUILD Verb Patterns volume (Francis, Hunston, and Manning 1996) take the form of word class and lexis combinations, such as the 'V *across* n' pattern:

> The verb is followed by a prepositional phrase which consists of *across* and a noun group.
>
> This pattern has one structure:
> * Verb with Adjunct.
> *I cut across the field.*

Our initial research (for further details see Ellis and O'Donnell 2012; Römer, O'Donnell, and Ellis, in press) describes the methods and findings for an initial convenience sample of twenty-three VACs, most of which follow the verb-preposition-noun phrase structure, such as 'V *into* n', 'V *after* n', 'V *as* n' (Goldberg 2006). We also include other classic examples, such as the 'V n n' ditransitive and the *way* construction.

A Large Corpus of English. To get a representative sample of usage, one needs a large corpus. We investigate the verb type-token distribution of these VACs in the one hundred million word British National Corpus (BNC 2007), parsed using the XML version of the BNC and the RASP parser (Briscoe, Carroll, and Watson 2006). For each VAC, we translate the formal specifications from the COBUILD patterns into queries to retrieve instances of the pattern from the parsed corpus. Using a combination of part of speech, lemma, and dependency constraints, we formulate queries for each of the construction patterns. For example, the 'V *across* n' pattern is identified by looking for sentences that have a verb form within three words of an instance of *across* as a preposition, where there is an indirect object relation holding between *across* and the verb, and where the verb does not have any other object or complement relations to following words in the sentence.

The Lexical Constituency of Verbs in VACs. The sentences extracted using this procedure produced verb type frequency distributions like the following one for the 'V *across* n' VAC:

come	483				
walk	203				
cut	199	...			
run	175	veer	4		
...		slice	4	...	
			...	navigate	1
				scythe	1
				scroll	1

These distributions appear to be Zipfian, exhibiting the characteristic long-tail in a plot of rank against frequency. We generated logarithmic plots and linear regressions to examine the extent of this trend using logarithmic binning of frequency against log cumulative frequency following Adamic and Huberman (2002). Figure 3.1 shows such a plot for verb type frequency of the 'V *across* n' construction alongside the same plot for verb type frequency of the ditransitive 'V n n' construction. In these graphs, we randomly selected one verb from each frequency bin for illustration. Both distributions produce a good fit of Zipfian type-token frequency with $r^2 > 0.97$ and slope (γ) around 1. Inspection of the construction verb types, ranked from most frequent to least frequent, also demonstrates that the lead member is prototypical of the construction and generic in its action semantics.

Since Zipf's law applies across language, the Zipfian nature of these distributions is potentially trivial. But they are more interesting if the company of verb forms occupying a construction is selective—in other words, if the frequencies of the particular VAC verb members cannot be predicted from their frequencies in language as a whole. We measure the degree to which VACs are selective by using measures of association and the statistic '1-tau', where Kendall's tau measures the correlation between the rank verb frequencies in the construction and in language as a whole. For the VACs studied so far, 1-tau is typically about 0.7, showing that the rankings of

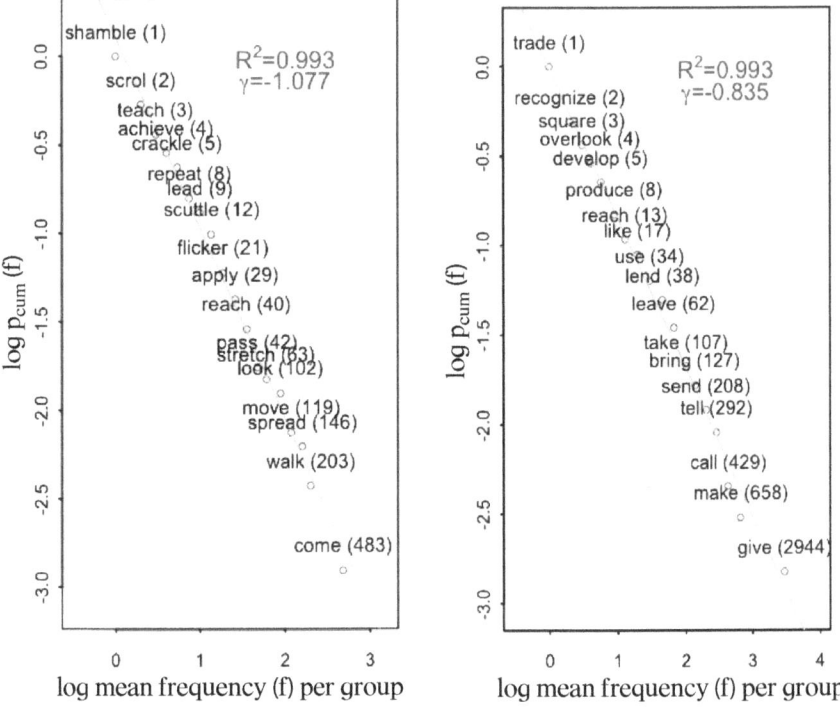

Figure 3.1 BNC Verb Type Distribution for 'V across n' and for 'V n n'

verbs in particular VACs differ markedly from the rankings of verbs in the language as a whole. VACs are selective in their verb constituency.

Verb-VAC Contingency. Another way of looking at this is to assess verb-VAC contingency. Some verbs are closely tied to a particular construction; for example, *give* is highly indicative of the ditransitive construction, whereas *leave*, although it can form a ditransitive, is more often associated with other constructions, such as the simple transitive or intransitive. The more reliable the contingency between a cue and an outcome, the more readily an association between them can be learned (Shanks 1995). Thus, constructions with more faithful verb members should be more readily acquired and higher contingency verbs should be learned first in a VAC and should come to mind first when processing that VAC. The measures of contingency we adopt are: (1) faithfulness—the proportion of tokens of total verb usage that appear in this particular construction (e.g., the faithfulness of *give* to the ditransitive is approximately 0.40; that of *leave* is 0.01); (2) directional mutual information (MI Word → Construction: *give* 16.26, *leave* 11.73 and MI Construction → Word: *give* 12.61 *leave* 9.11); and (3) the one-way dependency statistic ΔP (Allan 1980) used in the associative learning literature (Shanks 1995) and in other studies of form-function contingency in construction usage, knowledge, and processing (Ellis 2006a;

Ellis and Ferreira-Junior 2009b; Ellis, O'Donnell, and Römer, in press). Our analyses for the twenty-three VACs studied so far show a general pattern in which individual verbs tend to select particular constructions (MI_{wc}, ΔP_{wc}) and particular constructions select particular verbs (MI_{cw}, ΔP_{cw}) (for details see Ellis and O'Donnell 2012; Ellis, O'Donnell, and Römer, in press).

VAC Meanings and Coherence. Our semantic analyses use WordNet, a distribution-free semantic database based on psycholinguistic theory that has been in development since 1985 (Miller 2009). WordNet places words into a hierarchical network. At the top level, the hierarchy of verbs is organized into 559 distinct root synonym sets (synsets such as *move1* expressing translational movement, *move2* expressing movement without displacement, etc.) which is then split into over 13,700 verb synsets. Verbs are linked in the hierarchy according to relations such as hypernym (verb Y is a hypernym of the verb X if the activity X is a type of Y—to *perceive* is a hypernym of to *listen*), and hyponym (verb Y is a hyponym of the verb X if the activity Y is doing X in some manner—to *lisp* is a hyponym of to *talk*). Various algorithms to determine the semantic similarity between WordNet synsets have been developed that consider the distance between the conceptual categories of words, as well as the hierarchical structure of the WordNet (Pedersen, Patwardhan, and Michelizzi 2004). We take the lists of verbs occupying each VAC using the methods described earlier and compare the verbs pairwise on these metrics. We then apply networks science, such as graph-based algorithms (de Nooy, Mrvar, and Batagelj 2010) to build semantic networks in which the nodes represent verb types and the edges show strong semantic similarity for each VAC. Standard measures of network density, average clustering, degree centrality, transitivity, and so on are used to assess the cohesion of these semantic networks; we also apply algorithms for the detection of communities within the networks representing different semantic sets (Clauset, Newman, and Moore 2004; Danon et al. 2005). The network for 'V *across* n' is shown as an example in figure 3.2. The network is fairly dense. The hubs, shown here as larger nodes, are those that are most connected, meaning they have the highest degree. They are *go*, *move*, and *travel*—the prototypical 'V *across* n' senses. However, there are also subcommunities, shown in different colors. For example, one relating to vision includes *look, stare, gaze, face*; another relating to speeded movement with unspecified action semantics includes *shoot, skud, race, rush*, etc.; and another emphasizing flat contact includes *lay, lie, sprawl*, etc. Note that degree in the network is unrelated to token frequency in the corpus; it simply reflects verb type connectivity within the network. This also applies to betweenness centrality, which was developed as a measure quantifying the control of a human on the communication between other humans in a social network. Betweenness centrality is a measure of a node's centrality in a network equal to the number of shortest paths from all vertices to all others that pass through that node. In semantic networks, central nodes are those which are prototypical of the network as a whole.

Across the VACs we have investigated to date (O'Donnell, Ellis, and Corden 2012), the semantic networks are coherent, with short path-lengths between the nodes and degree distributions which approximate a Zipfian power function. Satisfaction of

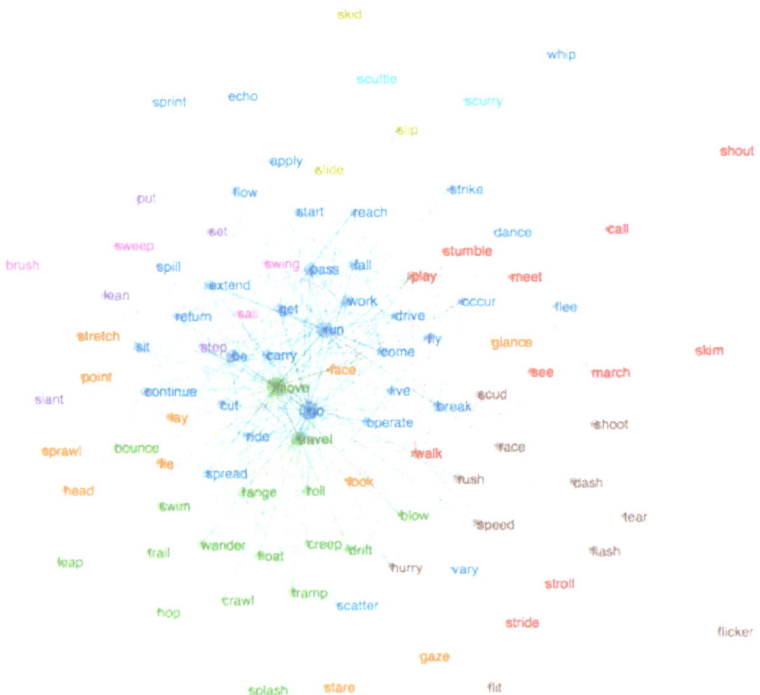

Figure 3.2 A Semantic Network for 'V *across* n' from the BNC Using WordNet as a Base

these two criteria classifies them as small-world networks (Barabási 2002). Steyvers and Tennenbaum (2005) show more generally across semantic networks—such as Roget's thesaurus and WordNet—that the distributions of the number of connections as a whole follow power laws that indicate a scale-free pattern of connectivity, with most nodes having relatively few connections joined together through a small number of hubs with many connections. Small-world networks are interesting because they are more robust to perturbations than other network architectures (Barabási 2002). They achieve this through the high connectivity of their hubs.

Is the Latent Structure of VACs of the Type That Would Promote Robust Acquisition following the Proposed Learning Principles?

Our core research questions concern the degree to which VAC form, function, and usage might promote robust learning. As we explained, the psychology of learning as it relates to these psycholinguistic matters suggests, in essence, that learnability will be optimized for constructions that are: (1) Zipfian in their type-token distributions in usage, (2) selective in their verb form occupancy, and (3) coherent in their semantics. The findings we summarized earlier confirm that these factors apply.

Remember that the two Zipfian distributions described earlier are different. The first relates to type-token frequency distribution in the language. The second relates to node connectivity (degree distribution and betweenness centrality) in the semantic network, and it has no regard of corpus frequencies. Nevertheless, the high-degree items in the semantic distribution also tend to be the high-token frequency items in the corpus. We believe that it is this coming-together of the two Zipfian distributions that makes language robustly learnable. The VAC pattern is seeded by a high-token frequency exemplar that is also prototypical in the action-dynamic construal of events to which it relates. Thereafter, the forms and functions of verbs added to the VACs resonate with the category itself. "(T)his process is actually the organization of exemplars of utterances and of verb-specific constructions into clusters of greater or lesser size, with greater or lesser semantic coherence" (Croft 2012, 393).

Further Directions and Conclusions

These initial investigations make it clear that usage is intricately structured in ways typical of complex adaptive systems in that there are scale-free distributions in verb usage frequency within constructions and scale-free connectivity patterns within semantic networks. This latent structure could potentially scaffold robust development.

Note that these results are preliminary, as they are based on an analysis of only about twenty constructions to date. There are over seven hundred patterns of varying complexity in the *Grammar Patterns #1: Verbs* (Francis, Hunston, and Manning 1996).

There is a considerable amount of additional statistical analysis and modeling to be done, as well as analyses of longitudinal corpora of language acquisition (and the matching child directed speech or NS interlocutor language) to test out the predictions of learning. Experimental psycholinguistic research is also necessary to test the psychological validity of VACs.

We identify the following priorities:

- Learning theory makes *relative* predictions as well, and these should inform our understanding of language acquisition and processing. VACs that are higher frequency in the language, with more verb types and greater semantic cohesion, should be acquired earlier and accessed more readily in speakers' minds. Similarly, verbs that are more frequent constituents of a VAC, more faithful to that VAC, and closer to the VAC semantic prototype should be acquired earlier in that VAC and accessed more readily in speakers' minds when they consider that VAC schema. A considerable amount of statistics and modeling remains necessary to test these hypotheses. We report some initial findings in Ellis, O'Donnell, and Römer (in press).
- This work needs to be done for second language acquisition, too. We have made a start (Ellis and Ferreira-Junior 2009a, 2009b), but there is an imperative for larger L2 corpora.
- The psychological reality of VACs needs further work. In various studies we use free association tasks to have people think of the first word that comes to

mind to fill the V slot in a particular VAC frame. The responses of adult native and fluent L2 learners are highly predicted by corpus frequencies, showing that users have implicit knowledge of the occupancy and frequencies of verbs in VACs (Ellis and O'Donnell 2011; Römer, O'Donnell, and Ellis, in press). We are particularly excited that we have identified separable influences—(1) the frequency of the verb in the language, (2) VAC-verb contingency (ΔP_{cw}), and (3) the prototypicality of the verb in the semantic network (as indexed by its betweenness centrality)—as factors in the determination of the verbs freely associated with skeletal VAC frames.

- The semantic analyses here are crude; other distributional measures could be well applied alongside techniques for investigating network growth (O'Donnell, Ellis, and Corden 2012).
- The acquisition data here are basically correlational. There need to be experimental studies comparing the relative learnability of Zipfian skewed input compared with languages with flatter frequency profiles. Casenhiser and Goldberg (2005) and Goldberg, Casenhiser, and Sethuraman (2004) have made important steps in doing this in children and adults, but they investigate the learning of just one construction from a small number of trials, and there is need for larger causal studies of the effects of combined Zipfian frequency distributions and Zipfian semantic connectivity upon more complete approximations to natural language.
- To better understand the processes of how these latent structures of usage affect robust acquisition and stable usage, there is need for modeling, both connectionist (Ellis and Larsen-Freeman 2009a) and agent-based (Beckner et al. 2009).

Meanwhile, we can at least say that the input from which learners acquire language is far from unstructured, unhelpful, or barren. The evidence of language usage is rich in latent structure. We believe that, with language as with other cognitive realms, our experiences conspire to give us competence. In the spirit of GURT 2012, such beliefs become either firmer or falsified, dependent upon the extent to which we can measure and test them.

ACKNOWLEDGMENTS

We thank Katie Erbach, Mary Smith, Lucy Zhao, Gin Corden, Danny Tsu-yu Wu, Liam Considine, Jerry Orlowski, and Sarah Garvey for help in the design, data collection, and analysis of these data. We also thank the University of Michigan LSA Scholarship/Research funding opportunity for supporting the project "Piloting the development of an inventory of usage of English verb grammar."

REFERENCES

Adamic, L. A., and B. A. Huberman. 2002. "Zipf's law and the Internet." *Glottometrics* 3: 143–50.

Allan, L. G. 1980. "A note on measurement of contingency between two binary variables in judgment tasks." *Bulletin of the Psychonomic Society* 15: 147–49.

Ambridge, B., and E. Lieven. 2011. *Child Language Acquisition: Contrasting Theoretical Approaches*. Cambridge: Cambridge University Press.

Anderson, J. R. 2000. *Cognitive Psychology and Its Implications*, fifth edition. New York: W. H. Freeman.
Baayen, R. H. 2008. "Corpus linguistics in morphology: morphological productivity." In *Corpus Linguistics: An International Handbook*, edited by A. Ludeling and M. Kyto. Berlin: Mouton De Gruyter.
Bannard, C., and E. Lieven. 2009. "Repetition and reuse in child language learning." In *Formulaic Language Volume Two: Acquisition, Loss, Psychological Reality, and Functional Explanations*, 299–321, edited by R. Corrigan, E. A. Moravcsik, H. Ouali, and K. M. Wheatley. Amsterdam: John Benjamins.
Barabási, A. L. 2002. *Linked: The New Science of Networks*. Cambridge, MA: Perseus Books.
Beckner, C., R. Blythe, J. Bybee, M. H. Christiansen, W. Croft, N. C. Ellis, J. Holland, J. Ke, D. Larsen-Freeman, and T. Schoenemann. 2009. "Language is a complex adaptive system." Position paper. *Language Learning, 59 Supplement 1*, 1–26.
BNC. 2007. BNC XML Edition. www.natcorp.ox.ac.uk/corpus/.
Boyd, J. K., and A. E. Goldberg. 2009. "Input effects within a constructionist framework." *Modern Language Journal* 93 (2): 418–29.
Briscoe, E., J. Carroll, and R. Watson. 2006. "The second release of the RASP system." Paper presented at the Proceedings of the COLING/ACL 2006 Interactive Presentation Sessions, Sydney, Australia.
Bybee, J. 2008. "Usage-based grammar and second language acquisition." In *Handbook of Cognitive Linguistics and Second Language Acquisition*, edited by P. Robinson and N. C. Ellis. London: Routledge.
———. 2010. *Language, Usage, and Cognition*. Cambridge: Cambridge University Press.
Bybee, J., and P. Hopper, editors. 2001. *Frequency and the Emergence of Linguistic Structure*. Amsterdam: John Benjamins.
Casenhiser, D., and A. E. Goldberg. 2005. "Fast mapping between a phrasal form and meaning." *Developmental Science* 8: 500–508.
Christiansen, M. H., and N. Chater. 2008. "Language as shaped by the brain." *Behavioral & Brain Sciences* [target article for multiple peer commentary] 31: 489–509.
Christiansen, M. H., and N. Chater, editors. 2001. *Connectionist Psycholinguistics*. Westport, CO: Ablex.
Clark, E. V. 1978. "Discovering what words can do." In *Papers from the Parasession on the Lexicon*, 34–57, edited by D. Farkas, W. M. Jacobsen, and K. W. Todrys. Chicago Linguistics Society, April 14-15, 1978. Chicago: Chicago Linguistics Society.
Clauset, A., M. E. J. Newman, and C. Moore. 2004. "Finding community structure in very large networks." *Physical Review E* 70: 066111.
Croft, W. 2001. *Radical Construction Grammar: Syntactic Theory in Typological Perspective*. Oxford: Oxford University Press.
———. 2012. *Verbs: Aspect and Causal Structure*. Oxford: Oxford University Press.
Danon, L., A. Díaz-Guilera, J. Duch, and A. Arenas. 2005. "Comparing community structure identification methods." *Journal of Statistical Mechanics* 29: P09008.
de Nooy, W., A. Mrvar, and V. Batagelj. 2010. *Exploratory Social Network Analysis with Pajek*. Cambridge: Cambridge University Press.
Ebbinghaus, H. 1885. *Memory: A Contribution to Experimental Psychology*. Translated by H. A. R. C. E. B.: 1913. New York: Teachers College, Columbia.
Ellis, N. C. 1998. "Emergentism, connectionism and language learning." *Language Learning* 48 (4): 631–64.
———. 2002. "Frequency effects in language processing: A review with implications for theories of implicit and explicit language acquisition." *Studies in Second Language Acquisition* 24 (2): 143–88.
———. 2006a. "Language acquisition as rational contingency learning." *Applied Linguistics*, 27 (1): 1–24.
———. 2006b. "Selective attention and transfer phenomena in SLA: Contingency, cue competition, salience, interference, overshadowing, blocking, and perceptual learning." *Applied Linguistics* 27 (2): 1–31.
———. 2008a. "Optimizing the input: Frequency and sampling in usage-based and form-focused learning." In *Handbook of Second and Foreign Language Teaching*, edited by M. H. Long and C. Doughty. Oxford: Blackwell.

---. 2008b. "Usage-based and form-focused language acquisition: The associative learning of constructions, learned-attention, and the limited L2 endstate." In *Handbook of Cognitive Linguistics and Second Language Acquisition*, 372–405, edited by P. Robinson and N. C. Ellis. London: Routledge.
---. 2011. "The emergence of language as a complex adaptive system." In *Handbook of Applied Linguistics*, 666–79, edited by J. Simpson. London: Routledge/Taylor Francis.
Ellis, N. C., and T. Cadierno. 2009. "Constructing a second language." *Annual Review of Cognitive Linguistics* 7 (special section): 111–290.
Ellis, N. C., and F. Ferreira-Junior. 2009a. "Construction learning as a function of frequency, frequency distribution, and function." *Modern Language Journal* 93: 370–86.
---. 2009b. "Constructions and their acquisition: Islands and the distinctiveness of their occupancy." *Annual Review of Cognitive Linguistics*: 111–39.
Ellis, N. C., and D. Larsen-Freeman. 2006. "Language emergence: implications for applied linguistics." *Applied Linguistics* 27 (4).
---. 2009a. "Constructing a second language: Analyses and computational simulations of the emergence of linguistic constructions from usage." *Language Learning* 59 (Supplement 1): 93–128.
---. 2009b. "Language as a complex adaptive system (special issue)." *Language Learning* 59 (Supplement 1).
Ellis, N. C., and M. B. O'Donnell. 2011. "Robust language acquisition—an emergent consequence of language as a complex adaptive system." In *Proceedings of the 33rd Annual Conference of the Cognitive Science Society*, 3512–17, edited by L. Carlson, C. Hölscher, and T. Shipley. Austin, TX: Cognitive Science Society.
---. 2012. "Statistical construction learning: Does a Zipfian problem space ensure robust language learning?" In *Statistical Learning and Language Acquisition*, 265–304, edited by J. Rebuschat and J. Williams. Berlin: Mouton de Gruyter.
Ellis, N. C., M. B. O'Donnell, and U. Römer. 2012. "Usage-Based language: Investigating the latent structures that underpin acquisition." *Currents in Language Learning* 1, 63: Suppl. 1, pp. 25–51.
---. In press. "The processing of verb-argument constructions is sensitive to form, function, frequency, contingency, and prototypicality." *Cognitive Linguistics* 25 (1).
Evert, S. 2005. *The Statistics of Word Cooccurrences: Word Pairs and Collocations*. Stuttgart: University of Stuttgart.
Ferrer i Cancho, R., and R. V. Solé. 2001. "The small world of human language." *Proceedings of the Royal Society of London* 268: 2261–65.
---. 2003. "Least effort and the origins of scaling in human language." *PNAS* 100: 788–91.
Ferrer i Cancho, R., R. V. Solé, and R. Köhler. 2004. "Patterns in syntactic dependency networks." *Physical Review* E69: 0519151–58.
Francis, G., S. Hunston, and E. Manning, editors. 1996. *Grammar Patterns 1: Verbs. The COBUILD Series*. London: Harper Collins.
Goldberg, A. E. 1995. *Constructions: A Construction Grammar Approach to Argument Structure*. Chicago: University of Chicago Press.
---. 2006. *Constructions at Work: The Nature of Generalization in Language*. Oxford: Oxford University Press.
Goldberg, A. E., D. M. Casenhiser, and N. Sethuraman. 2004. "Learning argument structure generalizations." *Cognitive Linguistics* 15: 289–316.
Gries, S. T., and S. Wulff. 2005. "Do foreign language learners also have constructions? Evidence from priming, sorting, and corpora." *Annual Review of Cognitive Linguistics* 3: 182–200.
Harnad, S, editor. 1987. *Categorical Perception: The Groundwork of Cognition*. New York: Cambridge University Press.
Holland, J. H. 1995. *Hidden Order: How Adaption Builds Complexity*. Reading: Addison-Wesley.
Hunston, S., and G. Francis. 1996. *Pattern Grammar: A Corpus Driven Approach to the Lexical Grammar of English*. Amsterdam: John Benjamins.
Jurafsky, D., and J. H. Martin. 2009. *Speech and Language Processing: An Introduction to Natural Language Processing, Computational Linguistics, and Speech Recognition*, second edition. Englewood Cliffs, NJ: Prentice Hall.

Kello, C. T., G. D. A. Brown, R. Ferrer i Cancho, J. G. Holden, K. Linkenkaer-Hansen, T. Rhodes, and G. C. Van Orden. 2010. "Scaling laws in cognitive sciences." *Trends in Cognitive Science* 14: 223–32.

Lakoff, G. 1987. *Women, Fire, and Dangerous Things: What Categories Reveal about the Mind.* Chicago: University of Chicago Press.

Langacker, R. W. 1987. *Foundations of Cognitive Grammar: Volume One. Theoretical Prerequisites.* Stanford, CA: Stanford University Press.

Larsen-Freeman, D. 1997. "Chaos/complexity science and second language acquisition." *Applied Linguistics* 18: 141–65.

Levin, B. 1993. *English Verb Classes and Alternations: A Preliminary Analysis.* Chicago: Chicago University Press.

Lieven, E., and M. Tomasello. 2008. "Children's first language acquisition from a usage-based perspective." In *Handbook of Cognitive Linguistics and Second Language Acquisition*, edited by P. Robinson and N. C. Ellis. New York and London: Routledge.

MacWhinney, B. 1987. "The competition model." In *Mechanisms of Language Acquisition*, 249–308, edited by B. MacWhinney. Hillsdale, NJ: Erlbaum.

———. 2001. "The competition model: The input, the context, and the brain." In *Cognition and Second Language Instruction*, 69–90, edited by P. Robinson. New York: Cambridge University Press.

MacWhinney, B, editor. 1999. *The Emergence of Language.* Hillsdale, NJ: Erlbaum.

Manin, D. Y. 2008. "Zipf's law and avoidance of excessive synonymy." *Cognitive Science* 32: 1075–98.

Miller, G. A. 2009. "WordNet—about us." Princeton University. Accessed March 1, 2010. http://wordnet.princeton.edu

Newman, M. 2005. "Power laws, Pareto distributions and Zipf's law." *Contemporary Physics* 46: 323–51.

Ninio, A. 1999. "Pathbreaking verbs in syntactic development and the question of prototypical transitivity." *Journal of Child Language* (26): 619–53.

———. 2006. *Language and the Learning Curve: A New Theory of Syntactic Development.* Oxford: Oxford University Press.

———. 2011. *Syntactic Development, Its Input and Output.* Oxford: Oxford University Press.

O'Donnell, M. B., and N. C. Ellis. 2009. "Measuring formulaic language in corpora from the perspective of language as a complex system." Paper presented at the Fifth Corpus Linguistics Conference, University of Liverpool, July 20–23.

———. 2010. "Towards an inventory of English verb argument constructions." Proceedings of the 11th Annual Conference of the North American Chapter of the Association for Computational Linguistics, Los Angeles.

O'Donnell, M. B., N. C. Ellis, and G. Corden. 2012. "Exploring semantics in verb argument constructions using community identification algorithms." Paper presented at the Language and Network Science Symposium at the International Conference on Network Science NETSCI 2012, Northwestern University.

Page, S. E. 2009. Understanding Complexity [DVD-ROM]. Chantilly, VA: The Teaching Company.

Pedersen, T., S. Patwardhan, and J. Michelizzi. 2004. "WordNet: Similarity—Measuring the relatedness of concepts." Paper presented at the Proceedings of Fifth Annual Meeting of the North American Chapter of the Association of Computational Linguistics (NAACL 2004).

Pinker, S. 1989. *Learnability and Cognition: The Acquisition of Argument Structure.* Cambridge, MA: Bradford Books.

Rescorla, R. A. 1968. "Probability of shock in the presence and absence of CS in fear conditioning." *Journal of Comparative and Physiological Psychology* 66: 1–5.

Robinson, P., and N. C. Ellis, editors. 2008. *A Handbook of Cognitive Linguistics and Second Language Acquisition.* London: Routledge.

Römer, U., M. O'Donnell, and N. C. Ellis. In press. "Using COBUILD grammar patterns for a large-scale analysis of verb-argument constructions: Exploring corpus data and speaker knowledge." In *Corpora, Grammar, Text and Discourse: In Honour of Susan Hunston*, edited by M. Charles, N. Groom, and S. John. Amsterdam: John Benjamins.

Rosch, E., and C. B. Mervis. 1975. "Cognitive representations of semantic categories." *Journal of Experimental Psychology: General* 104: 192–233.

Rosch, E., C. B. Mervis, W. D. Gray, D. M. Johnson, and P. Boyes-Braem. 1976. "Basic objects in natural categories." *Cognitive Psychology* 8: 382–439.

Saussure, F. D. 1916. *Cours de Linguistique Générale*, translated by Roy Harris. London: Duckworth.

Shanks, D. R. 1995. *The Psychology of Associative Learning*. New York: Cambridge University Press.

Sinclair, J. 2004. *Trust the Text: Language, Corpus and Discourse*. London: Routledge.

Sinclair, J, editor. 1987. *Looking Up: An Account of The COBUILD Project in Lexical Computing*. London: Collins ELT.

Solé, R. V., B. Murtra, S. Valverde, and L. Steels. 2005. Language Networks: Their Structure, Function and Evolution. *Trends in Cognitive Sciences* 12.

Steyvers, M., and J. Tennenbaum. 2005. "The large-scale structure of semantic networks: Statistical analyses and a model of semantic growth." *Cognitive Science* 29: 41–78.

Talmy, L. 2000. *Toward a Cognitive Semantics: Concept Structuring Systems*. Cambridge, MA: MIT Press.

Taylor, J. R. 1998. "Syntactic constructions as prototype categories." In *The New Psychology of Language: Cognitive and Functional Approaches to Language Structure*, 177–202, edited by M. Tomasello. Mahwah, NJ: Erlbaum.

———. 2002. *Cognitive Grammar*. Oxford: Oxford University Press.

Tomasello, M. 2003. *Constructing a Language*. Boston, MA: Harvard University Press.

Zipf, G. K. 1935. *The Psycho-Biology of Language: An Introduction to Dynamic Philology*. Cambridge, MA: The MIT Press.

4

Subjectivity and Efficiency in Language Assessment

Explorations of a Compensatory Rating Approach

STEVEN J. ROSS
University of Maryland

QUANTIFICATION IN LANGUAGE ASSESSMENT is so pervasive that it seems a bit odd to reconsider what is now so commonly seen as the default way of analyzing and describing language proficiency and achievement. The currently standard quantitative methods of analyzing language assessment outcomes are a recent development relative to the much longer history of subjectivity, and are the culmination of a number of issues motivating a shift from hermeneutics to quantification in language assessment. The trend toward quantification began in the late nineteenth century, soon after a number of discoveries about interrelated phenomena in the physical world were hypothesized to also apply to cognitive phenomena and, eventually, to the assessment of language.

Bernard Spolsky's (1995) account of the history of language testing traces the evolution of applications of measurement concepts to cognitive phenomena into mental testing. Spolsky traces the milestones in testing theory and the influence of technology on the eventual industrialization of language testing in particular. Essential to the evolution of modern language testing has been the concurrent development of quantitative methods that have made complex scoring and the assessment of validity arguments possible, which have largely been the products of technological changes. Advances in the technology of language testing have at times created pressure points between what technology can do and what types of language can be sampled with that technology. There has always been a temptation to fit the measurement of language into the newest technology available to score it; the once ubiquitous multiple-choice machine-scorable test has long been recognized—and often criticized—as the most obvious example.

Many modern practitioners of language assessment may be unfamiliar with the history of the ideas that form the conceptual cornerstones supporting inferences about the fundamentals of reliability and validity. It may be surprising that some of the key criteria we use to evaluate modern language tests and assessments have been with us for more than a century. One of the fundamental quantitative concepts is measurement consistency. The conceptual basis for measurement consistency, known in modern times as reliability, originated in the 1880s when Francis Galton, building on Mill's (1843) method of concomitant variation, postulated that there were systematic linear relations among phenomena in the natural world. Not a decade later, Karl Pearson, Galton's protégé, formulated the now familiar correlation coefficient, which made Galton's ideas about linear relations systematically calculable. The logic of correlation was soon applied to both reliability and validity. In its simplest form, reliability was conceptualized as the stability of relative scores if the same test instrument was administered twice to the same persons without any intervening factor to change their scores (Spearman 1904, 1910). Criterion validity was assumed to be the correlation between a test score and an interval measure of some other outcome of interest. It was soon recognized that simple correlation evidence is ambiguous at best (Rodgers and Nicewander 1988), considering all other possible extraneous sources of covariance with both the variables involved in the simple product-moment correlation.

It was Francis Edgeworth (1888) who realized that the newly conceptualized quantitative methods could be applied to practical problems in assessment. Edgeworth observed that methods used to mark academic performances at universities were often wildly variable and subjective. He called for a more systematic approach to assessment, proposing a system of measurement that would at least provide consistency in the assessment process. Edgeworth deduced that a candidate's true ability would be derived from the mean of ratings by expert judges; this method sowed the seeds of the classical test theory that developed decades later. Most significant was Edgeworth's observation that subjective judgments of performances can be inaccurate and that the observed scores could be partitioned into true and error components.

The issue Edgeworth noticed still presents a challenge to modern-day language assessment policymaking. It is the ongoing struggle between efficient objectivity and subjective interpretation (Moss 1994, 2004; cf Mislevy 2004). Subjective assessments are known to be influenced by the interactions between the candidate, the assessor, and task sampling. Performances are thus seen to be the joint product of all participants and conditions (McNamara 1996). Objective assessments aim to isolate the latent constructs that are hypothesized to generate overt performance abilities. By repeated sampling of the domain of skill or knowledge, a systematic picture of an individual's abilities is thought to emerge. Instead of a few lengthy performance samples assessed by content area specialists, the objective approach typically requires multiple measures scored to optimize consistency and efficiency.

Sources of Score Variation

Performance assessments usually involve an expert judge who subjectively assesses the quality of the performance. Whenever subjective judgments are involved, an immediate influence on the observed score can obscure the picture of candidate ability. An examination of oral proficiency interview ratings should illustrate this point. In interactive oral proficiency interviews, discrete speaking tasks are formulated by interviewers to test base levels of proficiency and to probe to higher ranges until the candidate shows evidence of his limits in proficiency. In this framework, the tasks are organized in Interagency Language Roundtable (ILR) base level sets. In figure 4.1, a

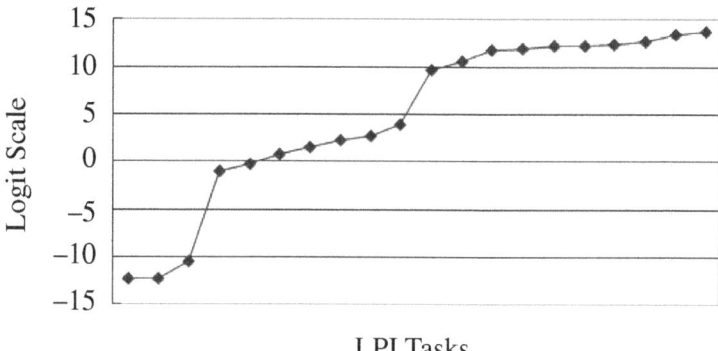

Figure 4.1 OPI Task Difficulties

calibration of over one thousand interviews and the corresponding tasks shows that tasks are, indeed, arrayed across the three base levels of the ILR, though particular tasks within each level vary in difficulty.

Of particular note is the fact that ILR level 2 (limited working proficiency) tasks, in fact, span five logits of difficulty, ranging from slightly below the midpoint (zero) on the logit scale up to nearly a logit of five. This variation in task difficulty is possibly compounded by variation across raters in their idiosyncratic severity in rating any particular level 2 task. On OPI rating outcomes, which are reported on the ILR scale, it is usually not possible to identify which particular tasks are passed or failed unless a task scoring sheet is available for analysis. If task scoring sheets are available for post hoc analysis, it is possible to analyze rater variation at the task level. Relative rater leniency or severity can be estimated from a matrix of task rating outcomes collected over many interview rating instances. Using a Rasch calibration approach, it is possible to derive a rater's tendency to rate any particular type of interview task leniently or severely.

It is also possible to derive an overall rater severity metric from the cumulative record of rating outcomes for each rater. Assuming that candidates are randomly assigned to raters, the expectation is that raters averaged over many rating events will gravitate to a group norm with a small amount of variation. Rater severity calibration can also be accomplished with a Rasch model. By using the leniency/severity metric as a characteristic of the rater, it is then possible to estimate the probability of raters disagreeing on rating outcomes, while controlling for other candidate factors in a multilevel logistic regression model (Raudenbush and Bryk 2002).

As an illustration of such a model, the rater severity logits of 23 OPI raters who had rated a total of 2,923 OPIs were estimated. The probability that raters will assign a divergent ILR rating across a base level category boundary (e.g., ILR 2 versus 1+) is the object of the analysis. Initial raters (the interviewers) who have in the past tended to be lenient are likely to differ from a second rater of an OPI if the second rater has shown an overall tendency to be less lenient. The probability of a categorical rating disagreement is expressed as a mixed regression model:

$$\log[\varphi/1-\varphi]=\gamma_{00}+\gamma_{01}*liberal+\gamma_{10}*TOEIC+u_0$$

where *TOEIC* is a continuous covariate attributable to the OPI candidate and is unobserved by the interviewer or rater. *Liberal* is a dichotomous code denoting whether a rater is above or below the mean leniency logit derived from the Rasch analysis of rater severity. The dependent variable in the logistic model is a binary code for any rating outcome where the first and second raters yield ratings that cross an ILR rating category (CAT) boundary. For instance, a first rating of 2+ and a second rating of 2 would not involve a categorical boundary; a first rating of 2 and a second rating of 1+ would cross an ILR category boundary and would be coded as a categorical difference in this analysis.

Figure 4.2 illustrates the differences in the probability of rating disagreement attributable to the overall classification of raters' tendency toward leniency. It is important to note that as the centered covariate score (TOEIC) increases relative to its mean, the probability of a rating disagreement increases for both liberal (lenient) and less lenient raters. This may be because candidates with higher reading and listening scores on the TOEIC proficiency measure have often resided in an English-speaking environment and have atypical patterns of fluency and accuracy, which may be the source of faulty ratings by interviewers and raters. Lenient raters, for instance, may attend to fluent speech in the interview without monitoring for systematic accuracy, while less lenient raters attend to both aspects of candidate speech in the interview. Figure 4.2 also shows that raters with a higher than average logit of leniency are increasingly likely to give an OPI rating different from another rater in a double-blind rating system. Expressed as an odds ratio, differences in leniency lead to a 1.8 times larger chance of an OPI rating disagreement ($p < 0.001$). Indeed, if we calibrate rater severity as a proclivity to rate task performances liberally or severely, the probability that any particular pairing of raters will disagree on an OPI performance is consistently a function of their leniency metric. The issue of subjectivity in language assessment has spawned much research and has driven the search for alternatives favoring objectivity and automation free from the influence of fickle human judgment.

Dealing with Subjectivity

A persistent issue in language assessment has been how to deal with the effects of subjectivity in performance assessment. As performance assessments strive to sample demonstrations of language proficiency in realistic simulations, the influence of subjective differences in rating those performances has loomed large as a practical problem. Two main strategies for dealing with subjectivity in assessment have emerged over the last twenty five years. The first approach estimates the extent of variation attributable to tasks and raters of the task performances and optimizes the task sampling and rating system to get the maximum reliability under the most efficient rating design scheme. This approach estimates sources of variance in judgments, simulates

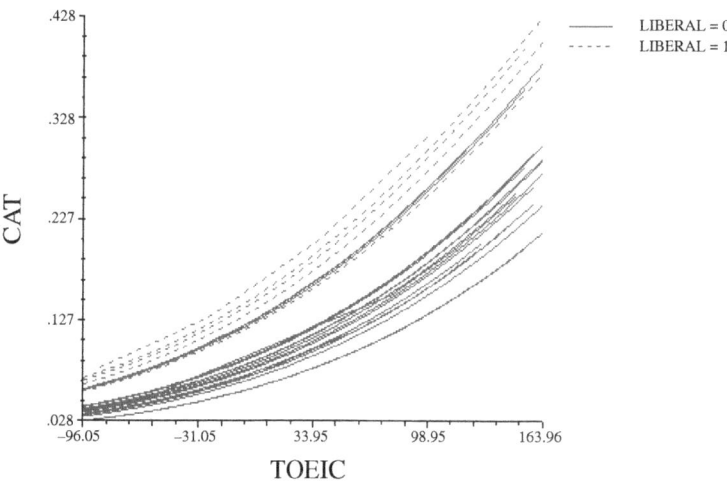

Figure 4.2 Probability of Rating Difference by Rater Severity

the degree of their influence, and spreads out their effects through randomization of the measurement error. All test takers are at equal risk of being rated by the more severe or exacting judges on tasks assumed to be randomly sampled from the universe of possible tasks. A second approach, to be explicated later in this paper, aims for maximal authenticity but provides a compensatory adjustment for variation in task difficulty and rater severity factors that can be expected to influence observed outcomes. The first strategy maximizes efficiency, while the second prioritizes fairness.

The first strategy is based on Generalizability Theory (Cronbach, Nageswari, and Gleser 1963; Shavelson and Webb 1991; Brennan 2001). Here, the variance attributable to individual differences in ability, the usual object of interest, is partitioned from the variance attributable to raters and tasks. All of the possible facets of measurement are tested for their interaction. The goal is to maximize person variance and minimize variance attributable to all other facets of the measurement process. This is typically done with a Decision Study simulation. Here, the number of tasks, raters, and occasions can be simulated to identify the most efficient and generalizable measurement system. This method assumes in practice complete randomization of persons to tasks and performances to raters. The working assumption is that rater differences in severity and task difficulty will be maximally dispersed. However, it is possible that some unlucky people will get the severest raters and the most difficult tasks, though the aim is to find the most cost-efficient and generalizable assessment system.

A preference for efficient scoring of performance assessments has emerged in large-scale language tests. Sawaki (2007) and Lee (2006) are examples of how Generalizablity Theory has been applied to TOEFL IBT performance assessments in order to justify the number of tasks and the minimal number of raters needed to arrive at acceptable levels of reliability. Given the logistical difficulties associated with rapid scoring and reporting of large-scale tests such as the TOEFL, the premium has been placed on efficiency and, increasingly, on automated scoring procedures. Generalizability studies have been done to rationalize scoring systems that are optimally cost-efficient, perhaps at the expense of optimal fairness in the scoring process. The size of the tradeoff has not been thoroughly investigated.

An alternative to the Generalizability Theory approach is to calibrate influences on the person measurement and provide compensatory weights to adjust for observed differences. The use of the Many-Facet Rasch model (Linacre 1996a; McNamara 1996) estimates person measurement uncontaminated by task and rater differences. By use of the "fair average" metric, which adjusts the observed rating to reflect what the candidate would get if rated by an average severity judge on a task of average difficulty, the ultimate assessment decision can account for the tasks and raters assigned to any particular candidate.

A fairly large number of language assessment studies have been conducted using the Many-Facet Rasch model. Some salient examples are Engelhard (1994, 2002), which focused on rater effects in scoring writing. Bonk and Ockey (2003) assessed the effects of different sources of variance on a group oral assessment. Eckes (2005) investigated rater effects on a German as a second language test used for admissions screening. More recently, Kim (2009) compared native and nonnative teachers as raters of oral assessments, finding considerable comparability in ranges of severity. To date, very few studies have compared Generalizability and the Many-Facet Rasch approach directly. A notable example is the study done by Lynch and McNamara (1998). Their study examined performances on a test for immigrants to Australia and concluded that Generalizability Theory and the Many-Facet Rasch approach can play different and complementary roles. The former was found useful for identifying the optimal sampling of tasks and raters, and the latter for diagnosing rater inconsistencies and possible criteria for enhanced rater training. The Lynch and McNamara study did not examine the possibility of a difference in the rank order of candidates scored under these two methods. Rank-ordered outcomes are typically used in norm-referenced decision making such as norm-referenced admissions testing. When the assessment goals involve monitoring change and improvement, the influence of subjective ratings becomes more complicated because the sources of the observed changes may reflect authentic growth in a candidate's ability or may be an artifact of inter-rater differences that co-occur with observed score changes. In order to untangle such ambiguities, the Rasch approach is considered preferable (Linacre 1996b).

Modeling Change in Speaking Proficiency

If the assessment goal is to determine if test takers have, in fact, improved over time, such as a period of months, evidence of growth may be obscured by variation in rater severity differences. This fact can prove vexing for examining the validity of incentive-driven language assessment policies such as those used to motivate foreign language specialists to maintain and improve their proficiency over time. Periodic retesting may show gains and losses of proficiency that do not reflect genuine learning or attrition, but rather shifts in the rater severity facet when performance assessments such as the OPI are the method of assessment.

To test this possibility, rater severity difference is here modeled as a covariate in an event history analysis (Singer and Willet 2003) where the "event" is defined as a test taker showing improvement in speaking proficiency over time between test events. The assumption made for this analysis is based on the hypothesis that time between OPI measures for active learners and users of a foreign language will be filled with experiences and learning activities that should stimulate increased language acquisition and thus improvement on the subsequent OPI.

For the influence of the OPI rater to be modeled, it is necessary to estimate the severity of each rater, know which raters were assigned to any particular interviewee's performance, and know the rating outcomes. With this information in hand, it is then possible to construct a matrix with all interview outcomes and rater identification for use in a rater severity calibration for both the pretest OPI and the posttest OPI. For each assessment, the probability of candidate (B) receiving a particular rating on an ordered rating scale (F) is contingent on the severity of the particular rater (C) involved in the assessment (Linacre 1996a; Lunz and Stahl 1993). The rater severity logit (C_j) is derived from a Many-Facet Rasch model:

$$P_{nkj} = \frac{e^{(B_n + F_k + C_j)}}{1 + e^{(B_n + F_k + C_j)}}$$

Each rater's severity is estimated on all cumulative rating records in addition to the pretest interview ratings, and again cumulatively on all posttest interview ratings. Thus, it is possible to calculate the severity difference between the pretest and posttest OPI raters for each candidate, as raters are randomly assigned to rate recorded interviews. For the analysis to follow, the pre- to posttest rater severity logit difference metric is used as a covariate in differentiating test candidates who show improvement in speaking proficiency over time and those who do not. The severity logit is dichotomized to reflect a standard deviation difference between the severity of the pretest rater and the posttest rater.

In an event history analysis, the time to the occurrence of the event of interest is the object of analysis. In the present case, the event is defined as improving on a retested OPI after a lapse of time that is measured in months. The range of time between testing events varies for each person. Cases registering a gain in speaking proficiency are coded as experiencing the gain event, while all other cases are censored cases. Cases that remain the same or decline in proficiency are considered censored and remain in the population of repeated OPI cases ($n = 756$). The gain event is defined as the difference between the posttest OPI outcome on the ILR scale relative to the pretest OPI rating outcome. The OPI rater severity difference, $C_{j2} - C_{j1}$, is included in the Cox regression model:

$$H(t_{ij}) = H_0(t_j) e^{(B_1 C_j)}$$

The event is expressed as a hazard ratio (H) for each case (i) at time (j). At the beginning of time H_o, the pretest OPI, and over time thereafter, the chances of improving are expected to increase. The dichotomized severity difference C_j covariate tests the hypothesis that rater severity differences constrain OPI growth over time. The significance of the severity difference covariate, $W = 16.7$, $p < 0.001$, supports the inference that cases with the largest differences in rater severity between the pretest and posttest are at risk of not showing improvement as time goes on. Inverted to express a hazard function over time in figure 4.3, a greater rater severity difference is associated with a larger hazard of *not* gaining proficiency, thus injecting ambiguity into the measurement of gains from pretest to posttest OPIs.

As stated above, the usual prediction is that active learners of a foreign language should improve over time and should, in general, show small incremental gains in speaking proficiency from pretest to posttest. That is, as time between testing events increases, it is assumed there is more time to learn the target language between the test events. An analysis of the residuals from the Cox regression (figure 4.4) suggests there are many posttest cases that did not improve. When plotted against the difference in severity between the pretest rater and the posttest rater, it is apparent that a considerable cluster of cases above the trend line would have been expected to have shown OPI gains given the period of time between interviews. The cases labeled with '0' below the trend line in figure 4.4 are delayed in their gains, and would have been expected to fall into the gain '+' categorization.

When holistic ratings of proficiency are used on performance assessments such as the OPI, some rather bold assumptions have to be made. One is that training and certification makes interviewers and raters completely interchangeable. Rasch analysis calibrations of raters often suggest that there is considerable variation, even after certification.

A possible solution to the problem of rater severity differences is to co-calibrate raters in order to compensate candidates via the Rasch model for the rater severity facet. Such a scheme would require a rather complex and carefully planned judgment design (Linacre 1996a). With a finite pool of certified raters, independent double

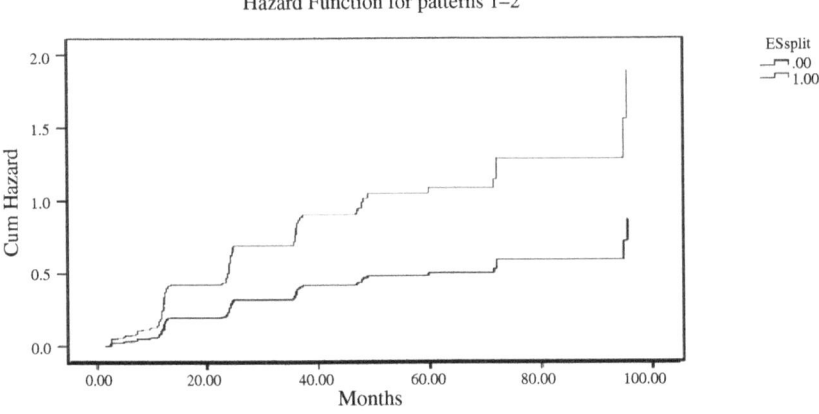

Figure 4.3 Risk of Not Improving over Time Attributable to Severity Differences

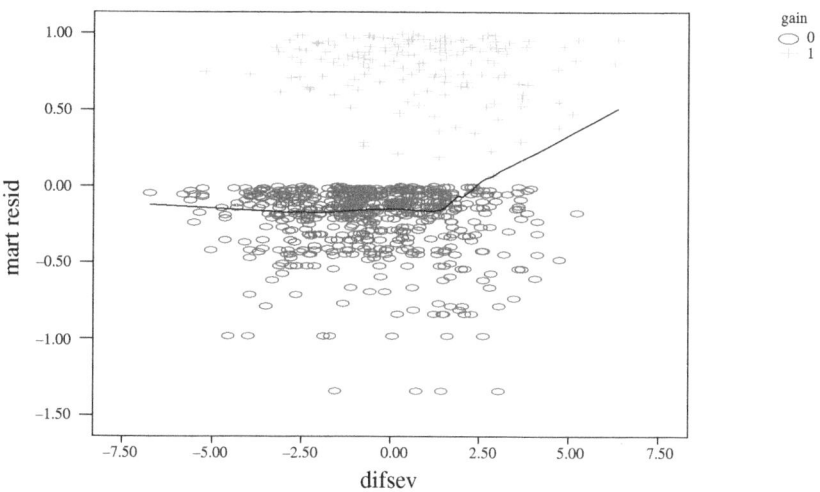

Figure 4.4 Martingale Residuals for Rater Severity Differences

ratings would be required in a judgment plan designed such that each possible pair of raters is matched at least once in a cumulative database of rating outcomes. Once an archive of rating outcomes has been built, it would be possible to design a compensatory rating model, either by estimation of abilities relative to rater severity differences recalibrated after each test administration, or perhaps more efficiently, by basing the estimation on rater anchors from earlier cumulative records of rater severity metrics. Figure 4.5 illustrates how a rater co-calibration system might look.

In figure 4.5, the left panel shows a pretest and posttest OPI judging design for a sample of candidates. For Person 001, Raters B and G rated the pretest OPI, and Raters H and P rated the posttest. The right panel shows pre- and posttest OPI ratings stacked with all four rater records available for co-calibration. In the separate calibration, each candidate would get two different estimates of ability reflecting the severity of the raters involved in the two isolated OPI administrations. Under the cumulative calibration scheme, the posttest interview outcome would be scaled to reflect the severity of all current and previous raters involved with any particular candidate. Based on co-calibrations or rater anchors, interview candidate ratings would be adjusted and reported on a log odds unit scale. As the OPI is designed to be criterion-referenced, the logit scale would have to be converted back to the original scale used for reporting. The additional conversion step would not be problematic and, through periodic standard setting checks, could retain a consistency that would be much less susceptive to gains and losses resulting from rater variation.

Preliminary research on rater equating through Rasch co-calibration suggests that the assessment of speaking proficiency growth could, in principle, be made independent of the rater severity difference effect. As a case in point, the matrix of data in this study was restructured to stack all candidate and rater records suitable as input to the Many-Facet Rasch model (i.e., the cumulative calibration panel of figure 4.5).

Separate Calibration

Person	Rater 1	Rater 2
P001	B	G
P002	F	A
P003	C	A
P004	G	C
P005	B	C
Etc.		

Person	Rater 3	Rater 4
P001	H	F
P002	A	C
P003	B	D
P004	F	A
P005	A	D
Etc.		

VERSUS

Cumulative Calibration

Person	Rater	Rater
P001	B	G
P001	H	P
P002	F	A
P002	A	C
P003	C	A
P003	B	D
P004	G	C
P004	F	A
P005	B	C
P005	A	D

Pretest   Posttest   Pre- & Posttests

Figure 4.5 Rater Co-Calibration Scheme

Candidate ability logits were generated as measures that take rater severity into account in the compensatory manner that the Rasch model affords. Defining gain in the same manner described above, the rater severity difference metric was replaced in a follow-up event history analysis. Here, the covariate is the severity difference between the pretest and posttest raters after co-calibration. As figure 4.6 suggests, the risk of not gaining on the posttest OPI is no longer mediated by the differences in rater severity, as made evident by the decreased hazard attributable to rater severity differences.

After controlling for rater severity, the effect of the rater difference is no longer significant ($W = 2.3, p > 0.05$). This outcome suggests that when growth on a performance assessment such as the OPI is the object of interest, the ambiguity attendant with simple comparisons of holistic ratings can be reduced with the use of a compensatory model such as that provided with the Many-Facet Rasch model.

A question one might ask is "Why hasn't a compensatory Rasch approach penetrated high stakes testing?" The answer to this question entails the consideration of a number of factors involving logistics, cost, and practicality. Test reporting time is truncated due to the wide availability of information technology among test users, who increasingly demand test results soon after administration. The processes associated with a variety of factors such as transmission of interview results to raters, collation of results, calibration, reconversion to a familiar scale, and banding along a proficiency continuum present substantive barriers to implementation and quick turnaround time for reporting. Another salient factor is the investment needed in managing rater assignment and fairly involved calibrations needed for a compensatory model.

Particularly in large-scale standardized testing, even with the recent introduction of internet-delivered performance assessments in writing and speaking, the

SUBJECTIVITY AND EFFICIENCY IN LANGUAGE ASSESSMENT

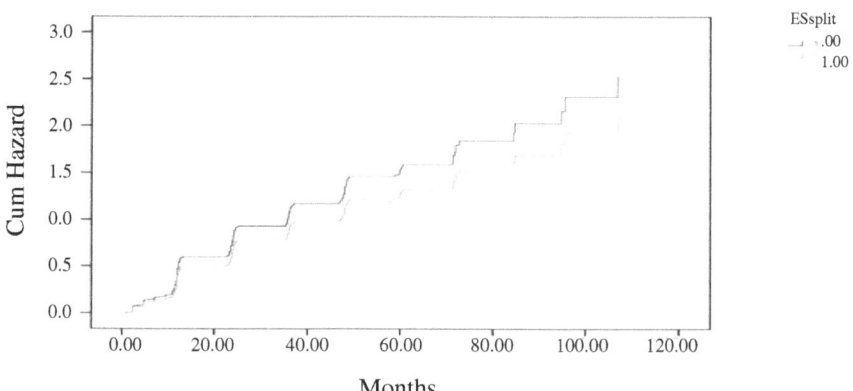

Figure 4.6 Risk of Not Improving over Time after Rating Co-Calibration

potential for the Rasch model to make performance assessment "rater free" has not been widely realized. This may be attributable to the lack of a strong consensus that a compensatory model would be, in the end, demonstrably more equitable to test candidates. It is recognized that neither Generalizability Theory nor Rasch analysis is equipped to compensate test takers for erratic or overtly biased raters—the best the Rasch model can do is identify such raters for retraining, and the Generalizability Theory approach spreads error randomly so that all candidates are equally at risk. Further, large-scale testing faces increased time pressure to score and report assessment outcomes to client institutions and individual test users.

While the study outlined above suggests that a compensatory approach to making oral proficiency interview gains less susceptive to rater severity is possible, it entails considerable initial effort and management of test records. The feasibility of reducing rater effects would have to be weighed against the cumulative benefits before a policy change would be considered viable.

REFERENCES

Bonk W. J., and G. Ockey. 2003 "A many-facet Rasch analysis of the second language group oral discussion task." *Language Testing* 20 (1): 89–110.

Brennan, R. L. 2001. *Generalizability Theory*. New York: Springer-Verlag.

Cronbach, L. J., R. Nageswari, and G. C. Gleser. 1963. "Theory of generalizability: A liberation of reliability theory." *The British Journal of Statistical Psychology* 16: 137–63.

Eckes, T. 2005. "Examining rater effects in TestDaF writing and speaking performance assessments: A many-facet Rasch analysis." *Language Assessment Quarterly* 2 (3): 197–221.

Edgeworth, F. Y. 1888. "On a new method of reducing observations relating to several quantities." *The London, Edinburgh, and Dublin Philosophical Magazine and Journal of Science* 25 (154): 184–91.

Engelhard, G., Jr. 2002. "Monitoring raters in performance assessments." In *Large-Scale Assessment Programs for All Students: Validity, Technical Adequacy, and Implementation*, 261–87, edited by G. Tindal and T. M. Haladyna. Mahwah, NJ: Lawrence Erlbaum Associates.

———. 1994. "Examining rater errors in the assessment of written composition with a many-faceted Rasch model." *Journal of Educational Measurement*. 31(2): 93–112.

Kim, Y. H. 2009. "An investigation of native and non-native teachers' judgments of oral English performance: A mixed methods approach." *Language Testing* 26 (2): 187–217.

Linacre, J. 1996a. *Many-Facet Rasch Measurement*. Chicago: MESA.

———. 1996b. "Generalizability theory and many-facet Rasch measurement." In *Objective Measurement: Theory into Practice Volume Three*, edited by G. Engelhard Jr. and M. Wilson. Norwood NJ: Ablex.

Lee, Y. W. 2006. "Dependability of scores for a new ESL speaking assessment consisting of integrated and independent tasks." *Language Testing* 23 (2): 131–66.

Lunz, M. E., and J. A. Stahl. 1993. "The effect of rater severity on person ability measure: A Rasch model analysis." *The American Journal of Occupational Therapy* 47 (4): 311–17.

Lynch, B., and T. McNamara. 1998. "Using generalizability theory and many facet Rasch measurement in the development of performance assessments of the speaking skills of immigrants." *Language Testing* 15 (2): 158–80.

McNamara, T. 1996. *Measuring Second Language Performance*. New York: Oxford University Press.

Mill, J. S. 1843, 2002. *A System of Logic*. Honolulu: University Press of the Pacific.

Mislevy, R. J. 2004. "Can there be reliability without 'reliability'?" *Journal of Educational and Behavioral Statistics* 29 (2): 242–44.

Moss, P. A. 1994. "Can there be validity without reliability?" *Educational Researcher* 23 (2): 5–12.

———. 2004. "The meaning and consequences of 'reliability'." *Journal of Educational and Behavioral Statistics* 29 (2): 245–49.

Raudenbush, S., and A. Bryk. 2002. *Hierarchical Linear Models: Applications and Data Analysis Methods, second edition*. Thousand Oaks, CA: Sage.

Rodgers, J. L., and W. A. Nicewander. 1988. "Thirteen ways to look at the correlation coefficient." *The American Statistician* 42 (1): 59–66.

Sawaki, Y. 2007. "Construct validation of analytic ratings scales in a speaking assessment: Reporting a score profile and a composite." *Language Testing* 24 (3): 355–90.

Shavelson, R. J., and N. M. Webb. 1991. *Generalizability Theory: A Primer*. Thousand Oaks, CA: Sage.

Singer, J., and J. Willet. 2003. *Applied Longitudinal Data Analysis: Modeling Change and Event Occurrence*. New York: Oxford University Press.

Spearman, C. E. 1904. "The proof and measurement of association between two things." *American Journal of Psychology* 15: 72–101.

———. 1910. "Correlation calculated from faulty data." *British Journal of Psychology* 3: 271–95.

Spolsky, B. 1995. *Measured Words: The Development of Objective Language Testing*. New York: Oxford University Press.

5

Subgrouping in Nusa Tenggara

The Case of Bima-Sumba

EMILY GASSER
Yale University

THE AUSTRONESIAN LANGUAGE FAMILY is one of the largest and most diverse in the world, but despite extensive historical work by scholars over the past century, much of its internal structure remains poorly understood. The Bima-Sumba (Bi-Su) subgroup, consisting of roughly twenty-seven Central Malayo-Polynesian (CMP) languages (Lewis 2009), was first proposed in 1938 by the Dutch language officer S. J. Esser as part of an atlas of colonial Indonesia. Although it has since been repeatedly cited in the linguistic literature, the first paper to investigate Bima-Sumba's validity as a subgroup was by Robert Blust (2008), who concluded that this particular collection of languages is not in fact monophyletic; that is, they cannot be traced back to a single exclusive common ancestor. Here, I return to the question of Bima-Sumba's existence as a legitimate and cohesive subgroup, using Bayesian phylogenetic tools to reconstruct a likely family tree using lexical data. These methods have not been uncontroversial (see, e.g., Eska and Ringe 2004), but have repeatedly been shown to be accurate and useful in historical linguistics (e.g., Dunn et al. 2008; Greenhill, Drummond, and Gray 2010; Greenhill and Gray 2009) and have recently been used to investigate historical hypotheses on a number of language families (e.g., Bowern and Atkinson, in press; Gray and Atkinson 2003; Gray and Jordan 2000; Rexová, Bastin, and Frynta 2006). The analysis presented here shows that when the Flores-Lembata (FL) languages are included, Bima-Sumba does indeed constitute a single clade (i.e., a branch of the tree), contradicting Blust's finding. Based on this result, I propose the recognition of a new subgroup, Bima-Sumba-Flores (BSF), encompassing all of the Bima-Sumba and Flores-Lembata languages.

Subgrouping Hypotheses within CMP

Figure 5.1 illustrates schematic trees that show a simplified version of the four main subgrouping hypotheses discussed below. Tree (a) represents Esser's original classification; (b) represents the current standard classification, as listed in the Ethnologue; (c) is Blust's proposed classification; and (d) shows the Bima-Sumba-Flores hypothesis presented here.[1] Tree (e) is a simplified excerpt of the Austronesian family tree produced by Gray, Drummond, and Greenhill (2009), which constitutes independent

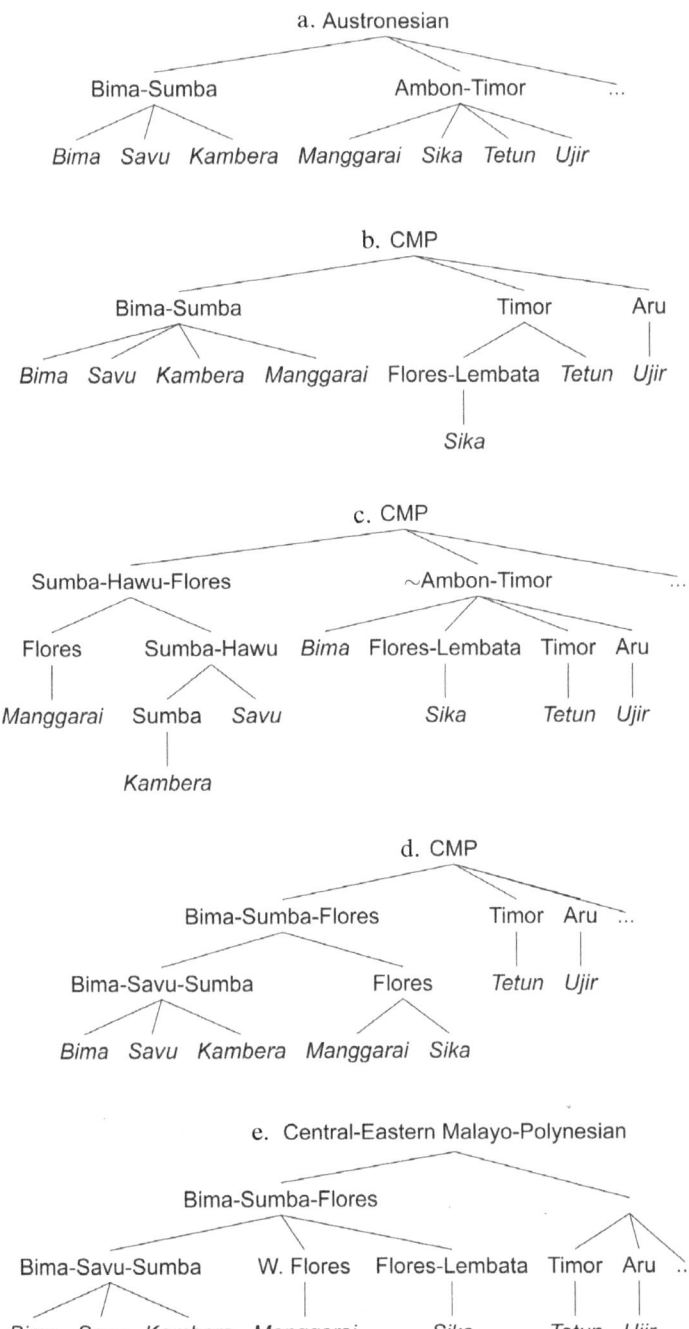

Figure 5.1 Five Subgrouping Hypotheses

corroboration of the Bima-Sumba-Flores hypothesis. Further differences in higher-level structure between their tree and the other modern hypotheses are discussed below.

The Bima-Sumba-Flores languages belong to the Central Malayo-Polynesian branch of Austronesian. The first Bima-Sumba proposal appeared in 1938, when the Dutch colonial government in Indonesia published their *Atlas van Tropisch Nederland*. This volume included Esser's categorization of a number of the languages of Indonesia into nineteen implicitly genetic groupings: seventeen Austronesian and two non-Austronesian (Esser 1938). The languages currently recognized as part of the CMP were divided by Esser into the Sula-Bacan, Ambon-Timor, and Bima-Sumba groups. It is unclear how Esser arrived at his classification, as he presents no supporting evidence for his decisions. His accounting of the languages of Indonesia was far from exhaustive, and his list of the Bima-Sumba languages includes six of the twenty-seven classified as such in the Ethnologue (Lewis 2009).

Several conflicting subgrouping hypotheses regarding the Sula-Bacan and Ambon-Timor groups have been proposed since Esser (e.g., Blust 1981; Campbell 2004; Collins 1983; Dyen 1965; Hughes 1987; Mills 1991). As these proposed groupings are not mutually compatible, in this analysis I sample from the subgroups of CMP as listed in the Ethnologue, though the source of these groupings is not clear and they may well fail to hold up to further investigation. Nevertheless, sampling from this classification ensures wide genetic and geographical coverage in the languages used here.

Investigations of Bima-Sumba

Bima-Sumba, however, has not received such scrutiny. Bima-Sumba has been generally accepted as a classification for Bima[2], Savu, and the languages of Sumba and western Flores (e.g., Forth 1988; Klamer 1994; Musgrave 2008), but little evidence has been presented to support its existence. Blust (2008), using the comparative method, was the first to examine Bima-Sumba. He compares four Bi-Su languages representative of the geographic span of the family and fails to find sufficient numbers of exclusively shared innovations to support the existence of the subgroup, concluding that it must be paraphyletic: there is no single common ancestor language from which these languages and no others descend. He does, however, propose a Sumba-Hawu subgroup, consisting of Savu and all of the languages of Sumba. Based on lexicostatistic evidence showing high levels of shared vocabulary with the Timor language Tetun, Blust asserts that Bima can only be included in a single subgroup with the other Bi-Su languages if a number of other members of Esser's Ambon-Timor family are added to the group as well.

Conflicting evidence comes from Gray, Drummond, and Greenhill (2009), who present a phylogenetic analysis of the entire Austronesian family. They fail to find a single node exclusively denoting CMP, confirming the proposals of several linguists (e.g., Blust 1993) that the group descends from a network of overlapping dialects rather than a single discrete language. Their tree supports the existence of BSF as a subgroup with all of the constituent languages proposed here, though their paper focuses on the geographic origins of Austronesian and large-scale patterns of migration and settlement in the Pacific, rather than questions of low-level language subgrouping. As such, Bima-Sumba goes entirely unmentioned in the text of this and subsequent articles by these authors and alternative hypotheses for the region go unexamined. That their tree and the one presented here should resemble each other is unsurprising, as they were based on similar methods applied to largely the same set of lexical data, though the dataset was expanded and cognate coding decisions revised somewhat for use here.

The Bima-Sumba-Flores Hypothesis
The analysis presented here differs from Blust's (2008) in its methodology and from Gray, Drummond, and Greenhill (2009) in scope and aim. Instead of four representative languages, I included seventeen Bi-Su varieties in my sample. Blust hypothesized that a number of other Ambon-Timor languages must be included if a monophyletic clade descended from a single ancestor language is to be found; to test this claim I have included a number of languages from that now-discredited group, spoken both in close geographic proximity to Bima-Sumba and farther afield. My results support Blust's proposal of a single clade containing all of the languages of Sumba. However, the tree groups Bima with Savu and the Sumba languages with high levels of support—therefore, rather than being a distant cousin of the other Bi-Su languages, Bima is deeply embedded in the subgroup and must be included if any of the Flores languages are to be considered part of the group.

One point of revision suggested by these results concerns the Flores-Lembata languages. These were not listed by Esser (1938) as belonging to Bima-Sumba, and the Ethnologue classifies Flores-Lembata as one of the primary branches of the Timor subgroup of CMP. The trees produced by this analysis show the FL languages grouping closely with the Bi-Su languages of Flores rather than the other Timor languages. In this respect, Blust was right; some Ambon-Timor languages must be included if a single ancestor node is to be found that dominates all of the traditional Bima-Sumba languages. However, by leaving out these Ambon-Timor languages, the languages of Flores are excluded from the subgroup, not Bima. It is on this basis that I propose Bima-Sumba-Flores as a monophyletic subgroup.

Data and Methods
Geographic and Classificational Orientation
The phylogenic analyses on which this paper is based were conducted on data drawn from 29 of the 169 Central Malayo-Polynesian languages of eastern Indonesia (Lewis 2009), as well as two Western Malayo-Polynesian languages, Cebuano and Dayak Ngaju. These were included here as an outgroup to further illuminate the internal structure of CMP and BSF. The seventeen traditionally Bima-Sumba languages included in the sample represent the full geographic range of the subgroup. Twelve languages from Esser's Ambon-Timor phylum were included as well, falling into the modern Timor and Aru subgroups. In all, this sample includes approximately 63 percent of the Bima-Sumba languages recognized in the Ethnologue, and 17 percent of the total linguistic diversity of Central Malayo-Polynesian. Table 5.1 lists the languages investigated in this paper. Unless otherwise noted, the data in this

table comes from the Ethnologue. Speaker counts may be up to twenty-five years old and are intended as approximations only. Figure 5.2 shows the approximate positions of these languages on a map of eastern Indonesia.

The Choice of Languages
In order to produce as clear a picture as possible of the internal structure of the Bima-Sumba subgroup, it was necessary to include data from as many Bi-Su languages as feasible; therefore, all Bi-Su varieties with sufficient available data were used. These seventeen varieties include fifteen individual languages, of which two, Kodi and Kambera, are represented by two dialects each. Within the Timor and Aru subgroups, languages were chosen to ensure the geographic and genetic breadth of the sample. Once the final list was compiled, only three languages were missing data for 5 percent or more of the 191 word meanings included: Erai (7 percent), Ujir (9 percent), and Mambai (15 percent). Cebuano and Dayak Ngaju were chosen as outgroups because they were well-attested and, while sufficiently closely related to CMP to be illuminating, are clearly not a part of the family. These languages' geographical distance from the CMP group means they are unlikely to share traits as a result of contact, and that they did not participate in local trading and political networks, another possible source of transmission. In particular, Cebuano is unlikely to show unidentified loans from Standard Indonesian, as it is spoken outside of Indonesia.

Wordlist Compilation
The data used in this analysis was retrieved with permission from the Austronesian Basic Vocabulary Database (ABVD) (Greenhill, Blust, and Gray 2008), a collection of lexical data from languages of the Pacific. The word list for each language includes 210 basic vocabulary items from a range of semantic fields; the level of

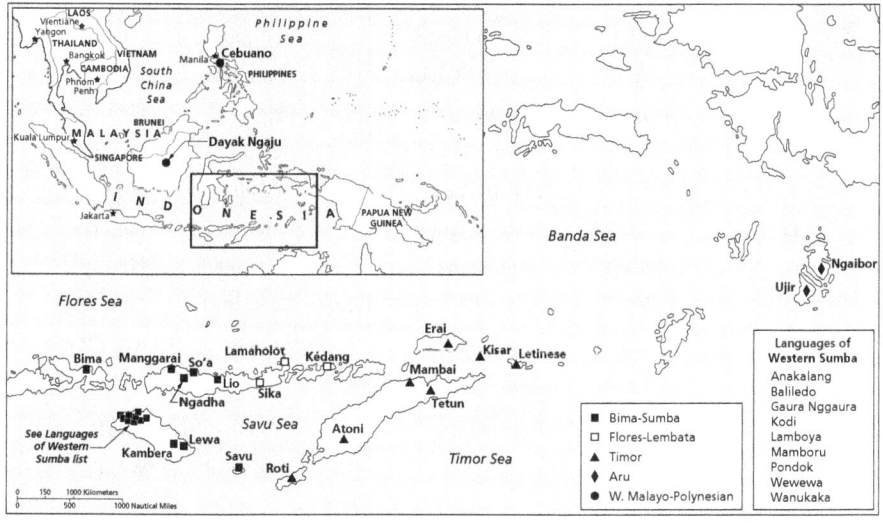

Figure 5.2 Language Map

Table 5.1.
Languages analyzed

Language	ISO	Location	Speakers	Classification
1. Anakalang	AKG	southwestern Sumba Island	~14,000	Bima-Sumba
2. Baliledo[1]	n/a	west-central Sumba Island	?	Bima-Sumba
3. Bima	BHP	eastern Sumbawa Island	~500,000	Bima-Sumba
4. Gaura Nggaura[2]	KOD	western Sumba Island	?	Bima-Sumba
5. Kambera	XBR	eastern Sumba Island	~235,000	Bima-Sumba
6. Kodi	KOD	coastal western Sumba Island	~40,000	Bima-Sumba
7. Lamboya	LMY	southwest Sumba Island	~25,000	Bima-Sumba
8. Lewa[3]	XBR	eastern Sumba Island	?	Bima-Sumba
9. Lio	LJL	central Flores	~130,000	Bima-Sumba
10. Mamboru	MVD	northwest Sumba Island	~16,000	Bima-Sumba
11. Manggarai	MQY	western Flores	~500,000	Bima-Sumba
12. Ngadha	NXG	south-central Flores	~60,000	Bima-Sumba
13. Pondok[4]	n/a	central Sumba	?	Bima-Sumba
14. Savu	HVN	Hawu & Raijua Islands, eastern Sumba	~20,000	Bima-Sumba
15. So'a	SSQ	central Flores	~10,000	Bima-Sumba
16. Wanukaka	WNK	southwest Sumba	~10,000	Bima-Sumba
17. Wewewa[5]	WEW	interior western Sumba	~65,000	Bima-Sumba
18. Kédang	KSX	Lembata Island	~30,000	Timor (FL)
19. Lamaholot[6]	SLP	eastern Flores, west Solor Island	150,000	Timor (FL)
20. Sika	SKI	eastern Flores	~175,000	Timor (FL)
21. Atoni[7]	AOZ	western Timor	~586,000	Timor
22. Erai[8]	ILU	Wetar Island	~1,400	Timor
23. Kisar	KJE	Kisar Island	~20,000	Timor
24. Letinese	LTI	Leti Island	~7,500	Timor
25. Mambai	MGM	eastern Timor	~80,000	Timor
26. Roti[9]	TWU	Rote Island	~30,000	Timor
27. Tetun	TET	eastern & central Timor	~400,000	Timor
28. Ngaibor[10]	n/a	Aru Islands	?	Aru (?)
29. Ujir	UDJ	Aru, Ujir, & Wokam Islands	~980	Aru
30. Cebuano	CEB	Philippines	~15,800,000	WMP
31. Dayak Ngaju	NIJ	Kalimantan	~890,000	WMP

Table 5.1. (continued) **Languages analyzed**

1. Not listed in the Ethnologue, location from Greenhill, Blust, and Gray (2008).
2. A dialect of Kodi.
3. A dialect of Kambera.
4. Not listed in the Ethnologue, little information provided in Greenhill, Blust, and Gray (2008). Also known as Buawa.
5. Tana Righu dialect.
6. Ile Mandiri dialect.
7. Listed in the Ethnologue as Uab Meto.
8. Listed in the Ethnologue as Ili'uun.
9. Listed in the Ethnologue as Termanu.
10. Not listed in the Ethnologue, little information provided in Greenhill, Blust, and Gray (2008). Classification is geographical.

completeness varies from language to language. These entries are coded for cognacy with the other languages of the database. Here again, the level of completeness varies. Known loanwords are marked as such.

Within each of the languages sampled for this analysis, synonyms were removed so that each list had only one entry per English meaning. While some researchers prefer to include multiple entries for a single lexical meaning, doing so raises issues concerning how exact synonymy must be to include more than one entry per meaning in a language, which it is impossible to address given the data available here. Furthermore, the number of synonymous forms varies greatly language-to-language, from Anakalang, with one or no entries attested per meaning, to Lewa, with 289 total entries for the 210 lexical meanings. Therefore, all synonyms were excluded to ensure consistency. Those meanings with entries in less than half of the languages or with more than half of their entries not already coded for cognacy were also excluded. Entries that were removed across all languages included the words for *if, to count, branch*, and numbers over four.

Likely loanwords were coded as unique states rather than shared traits. Undetected loanwords can confuse a phylogenetic analysis by creating the appearance of shared descent where no such relationship exists. The appearance of loans in the data set is minimized by using basic vocabulary items, such as words for body parts, basic kinship terms, simple verbs, colors, and low numbers, as basic vocabulary is slower to evolve and more resistant to borrowing than other parts of the lexicon (Swadesh 1952). Additionally, failure to recognize some loans will not prove fatal. Bowern et al. (2011) demonstrated that, cross-linguistically, loan rates in basic vocabulary are low, with a median of 2.49 percent of items for the languages in their sample. Greenhill, Currie, and Gray (2009) have shown that Bayesian phylogenetic analyses are able to reliably estimate tree topology on datasets with a borrowing rate of up to 30 percent per thousand years. Based on Bowern et al.'s (2011) results and the fact that loans were explicitly identified in this dataset and coded as unique states rather than shared features, it is unlikely that enough unidentified loans remain in the data to have a significant effect on the analysis.

Coding Decisions

The majority of entries were already coded for cognacy in the ABVD. Cognates are homologous words descended from a common form in an ancestor language, and their existence can be deduced based on the existence of regular sound correspondences between multiple forms in the languages in question.[3] With few exceptions, the existing cognate judgments from the ABVD were retained in this analysis. A small number of items had been miscoded: some noncognate forms were labeled as cognate despite the lack of regular sound correspondences to support their common descent, while other cognate groups failed to be identified. These were identified based on the sound correspondences observable in the wordlists and corrected. I coded items that remained uncoded in the ABVD so that a full word list could be analyzed. In all, coding was changed or added for 24 percent of lexical entries.[4]

To determine the existence of a cognate relationship, sound changes were deduced from the list itself, with stringent standards for deciding that two forms were cognate. The regularity of correspondence is a fact independent of the subgrouping inferred from those correspondences; the purpose of the phylogenetic algorithms is to deduce the most likely direction of change from the correspondence sets found in the data. Where a plausible potential relationship existed between forms, the lists were checked for evidence (i.e., regular sound correspondences) to support the existence of a regular correspondence between the differing segments. Ideally, all segments in a word should follow the regular correspondence pattern in order to be deemed part of a cognate set. Sometimes this was not possible, due to an opaque, environment-driven history of sound changes, sporadic irregular developments, or because the limited dataset did not yield sufficient comparable examples of a given sound, in general or in a specific environment, to establish what the expected corresponding phoneme should be. In these borderline cases, the vast majority of segments had to fit with the established correspondence set for the form to be deemed cognate. Where the supporting evidence was insufficient, the forms were coded as unrelated.

A small sample of the final coded data is included for illustrative purposes in table 5.2. Words in the same row marked with the same number are judged to be cognate. For example, the words for "old" here are judged to be cognate in Bima and Tetun, as well as in Sika and Ngadha, while Kambera has an unrelated form. All five languages share cognate forms for "egg," while none do for "to grow." The Ngadha word for "feather" is a loan from Dutch and thus coded as a unique state even if other

Table 5.2.
Sample data (cognate judgments)

Word	Bima	Sika	Ngadha	Kambera	Tetun
"old"	tua 1	blupur 2	bupu 2	kawiada 3	tuan 1
"to vomit"	lohi 1	muta 2	muta 2	mutta 2	muta 2
"egg"	dolu 1	telo 1	telo 1	tilu 1	tolun 1
"feather"	kere 1	wuluŋ 2	feder 3 [loan]	wulu 2	rahun 4
"to grow"	mori 1	tawa 2	mézé 3	tumbu 4	-- X

languages in the set have also borrowed that word. There is no word listed in the dataset for "to grow" in Tetun.

Only presence or absence of each cognate in each language is passed on to the computational model, as opposed to the words themselves or the sound changes involved. To encode this information, the original multistate cognate coding was next converted into a binary matrix. Table 5.3 shows the coding for the meaning "old" for the same five languages, converted into binary. Unlike table 5.2, in which each row of the table is a lexical meaning and each cognate set is represented by a different number within the row, here each row is a single cognate set. A "1" in a language's column indicates the presence of that cognate in the language; a "0" indicates its absence.

Analysis

The word list codings were then converted to binary and analyzed using two methods: NeighborNet, as implemented in SplitsTree (Huson and Bryant 2006) and a stochastic Dollo model, implemented in BEAST (Drummond and Rambaut 2007). The resulting structures are reproduced below as figures 5.3 and 5.4, respectively. These models are discussed below.

NeighborNet

The NeighborNet agglutinative hierarchical clustering algorithm, implemented in SplitsTree (Huson and Bryant 2006), was used to give a network representation of relationships between the languages in question. Unlike Bayesian methods, NeighborNet is distance-based, taking into account the degree of similarity between languages rather than the possible evolutionary paths necessary to produce the attested state of affairs. A split is a division of the taxa under analysis into two (nontrivial) subsets, as when the proto-language A divides into two daughter languages B and C, each of which in turn may have several descendant languages. In NeighborNet, as with other split networks, splits in the tree are represented not by single branches but by parallel edges. The weight of each split is reflected by the length of the associated edges, similar to branch length in a tree diagram. The resulting network gives only an implicit representation of the evolutionary history of the associated taxa rather than an explicit one, as a tree model does. Individual nodes in the network may well not represent discrete ancestor languages, only possible splits. Such models are useful in representing inconsistent or ambiguous signals in the data set; the more compact and tree-like the structure of the network, the less conflicting data is present in the analysis. The network produced by the NeighborNet algorithm is shown in figure 5.3.

Table 5.3.
Sample data for "old", with coding converted to binary

Word	Bima	Sika	Ngadha	Kambera	Tetun
Cognate set 1: *tua/tuan*	1	0	0	0	1
Cognate set 2: *blupur/bupu*	0	1	1	0	0
Cognate set 3: *kawiada*	0	0	0	1	0

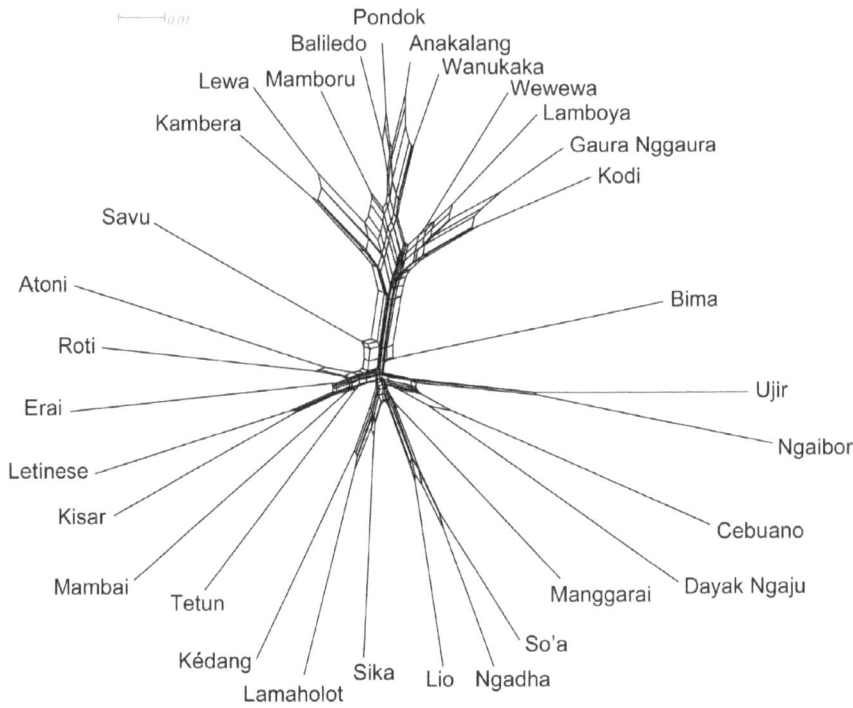

Figure 5.3 Unrooted Distance-Based Network

MCMC Phylogenetic Models

Phylogenetic models such as the ones used here were originally developed to test evolutionary models in biology. These models, which use Bayesian methods to infer the most likely evolutionary history leading to the attested state of affairs, have been used in linguistics to test a range of historical hypotheses (see, e.g., Bowern and Atkinson, 2012; Gray and Atkinson 2003; Gray, Drummond, and Greenhill 2009; Holden and Gray 2006; Kitchen et al. 2009; Rexová, Bastin, and Frynta 2006; Ringe, Warnow, and Taylor 2002). Dunn et al. (2008) and Greenhill, Drummond, and Gray (2010) have shown that phylogenetic methods can faithfully reproduce generally accepted trees constructed using the comparative method, proving their usefulness for inferring linguistic as well as genetic evolution. For a more extensive discussion of the use of phylogenetic methods to reconstruct cultural traits such as language, see Nunn (2011).

Once the data are coded, the analysis begins by specifying a stochastic model of evolution. The set of parameters describing the model specifies the rates of cognate gain and loss over time, represented as transition probabilities for each character. Rather than requiring a single constant rate, a distribution of rates may be used to account for the differences in rates of change between specific cognate sets and between branches of the tree (Greenhill and Gray 2009). Additional parameters may be used to specify rates of speciation or to describe other aspects of the evolutionary process (Dunn et al. 2008). These parameters are not presumed by the method; it is up to the researcher to determine appropriate parameters to use in an analysis.

The aim of the analysis is to determine the set of trees that best explains the observed data under the given model of evolution. If the set of languages being evaluated is of nontrivial size, it is impossible to directly inspect and evaluate every possible family tree, as their numbers quickly balloon with each added language. Assuming a strictly binary-branching tree structure, the number of possible trees for a set of n languages can be calculated by the following formula (Graham and Foulds 1982):

$$\frac{-(2n-2)!}{2^{n-1}(n-1)!}$$

For example, the number of possible trees for a set of five languages is 105; if there are 50 languages being considered, the number of possible trees is larger than the number of atoms in the universe (Greenhill and Gray 2009). For the set of 31 languages analyzed here, there are 2.9×10^{40} possible trees.

To avoid the computationally intractable problem of trying to complete a search over such an impossibly large number of states, a Bayesian Markov Chain Monte Carlo method is used instead to sample the space of possible trees and return those with the highest likelihood scores. The process begins with a single random tree. At each step, some small change or changes are made, altering for example the topology of the tree, its branch lengths, or the model parameters. The likelihoods of the new and old trees are compared, with the search algorithm preferentially selecting the tree with the higher likelihood. This process is iterated many times, so that trees are sampled in proportion to the posterior probability distribution. In contrast to the network produced by NeighborNet, Bayesian trees contain temporal information, and each node represents a hypothetical ancestor language. Sampled trees are recorded only intermittently in order to avoid the auto-correlation that comes from the Markov chain aspect of the procedure and make the recorded samples statistically independent. As the early trees are highly dependent on the starting parameters of the model, approximately the first 20 percent of sampled trees are discarded as burn-in (Greenhill and Gray 2009). These trees can be examined as a set, or a consensus tree can be constructed from them.

For this analysis, a stochastic Dollo model (Nicholls and Gray 2006, 2008) was implemented using the BEAST program (Drummond and Rambaut 2007). This model allows each trait (i.e., cognate set) to arise only once in the tree, such that the only possible progression of a trait is from absence to presence to absence. Since the total number of distinct traits generated by the model is random, this number is informative of the relative rates of cognate birth and death. A Bayes Factor Comparison (Suchard, Weiss and Sinsheimer 2001) shows the stochastic Dollo model to fit the data 176 times better than a covarion model and 259 times better than a binary simple model.

The data was processed with a chain length of fifty million iterations, sampling every one thousand trees. The derivation was set to begin from a UPGMA distance-based tree using a Yule prior (Yule 1925). Based on Greenhill and Gray's (2009) estimate of the age of Proto Malayo-Polynesian at about 4,300 years before present, which is consistent with an age of roughly 5,500 years for Proto-Austronesian (Blust 1995; Greenhill and Gray 2009; Pawley 2002), a root age of 4,500 years was set for the initial tree in the chain. Because of their extremely high rate of lexical divergence from the rest of the languages, preliminary analyses had placed the Aru clade outside the WMP outgroup on the tree, in a position more appropriate to the Austronesian languages of Taiwan. Therefore, the CMP languages were enforced as a monophyletic group in this analysis to reflect our existing knowledge of the history. The maximum clade credibility tree constructed from the resulting distribution is given in figure 5.4, with the number at each node representing the posterior probability for that split.

Results

The network produced by NeighborNet, which is presented here as figure 5.3, shows a treelike structure with a delta score of 0.284 (a lower delta score indicates a more treelike structure). This is an unrooted structure, and so does not explicitly show branchings in the tree nor include any temporal information, but the major subgroups clearly cluster together; the three Flores-Lembata languages, the western/

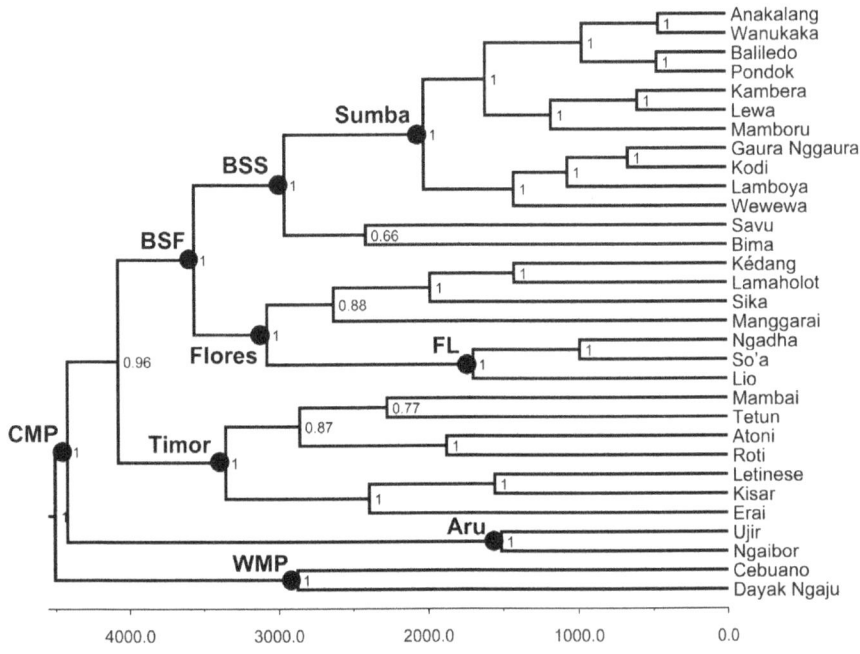

Figure 5.4 Stochastic Dollo Maximum Clade Credibility Tree

central Flores languages, and the Sumba languages each appear grouped together, with the Sumba languages further dividing geographically into far-eastern, central-eastern, and western groups. The Timor (minus Flores-Lembata) and Aru groups also receive support. The Western Malayo-Polynesian outgroups, Cebuano and Dayak, appear grouped together beside Aru. The highest level of conflicting signal is among the Sumbanese languages, which may in some cases more accurately be considered members of a dialect network. These languages developed in dense geographical proximity with intense continuing contact and multilingualism.

The Bayesian tree, shown in figure 5.4, shows a geographic split within the traditional Bima-Sumba subgroup, with Bima, Savu, and the Sumbanese languages comprising one clade and the languages of Flores, including the Flores-Lembata languages, forming another. The inclusion of the FL languages within BSF rather than the Timor subgroup is a novel result, though no argument has been made to date for their inclusion within Timor. Bima, found on the island of Sumbawa, does not fall clearly in one group or another on geographic grounds. Savu is also relatively geographically isolated; it is spoken mainly on Hawu Island to the east of Sumba, as well as in small enclaves on the eastern coast of Sumba and on small neighboring islands (Lewis 2009). Again, see figure 5.2 for a map of these languages. These patterns closely resemble those found in the tree produced by Gray, Drummond, and Greenhill (2009), as discussed above.

Based on these structures, it is more accurate to refer to a Bima-Sumba-Flores subgroup, encompassing all of the current Bima-Sumba and Flores-Lembata languages. This newly recognized subgroup has two primary branches: Bima-Savu-Sumba (BSS), including Bima, Savu, and the languages of Sumba; and Flores, including all of the languages of Flores and its satellite islands.

Finally, a Bayes Factor Comparison (Suchard, Weiss, and Sinsheimer 2001) was conducted using the Tracer program (Drummond and Rambaut 2003) to compare the likelihoods under the stochastic Dollo model of the four proposals represented in figure 5.1. The tree representing the Bima-Sumba-Flores proposal was shown to be 40.1 times more likely than Blust's proposal, 11.9 times more likely than the classification presented in the Ethnologue, and 11.2 times more likely than Esser's proposal. That is, under the model that, as shown above, best fits the data, the BSF proposal is an order of magnitude better than its next most likely competitor.

Conclusion

This paper has presented the results of a Bayesian phylogenetic analysis of twenty-nine Central-Malayo-Polynesian languages, which supports the existence of a single monophyletic subgroup encompassing Bima, Savu, the languages of Sumba, and the languages of Flores. Bima is not, as has previously been argued, only a distant cousin of these languages, and groups much more closely with the languages of Sumba and Hawu than those of Timor. As the Flores-Lembata languages appear in the resulting trees embedded within Bima-Sumba, I propose renaming the group Bima-Sumba-Flores to reflect its full geographical range. Contrary to Blust's findings, the remaining Ambon-Timor languages tested here are shown not to be a part of the subgroup.

Bayesian methods have already shown their utility in other subfields of linguistics; for example, in modeling aspects of grammar such as morphology (Johnson, Griffiths, and Goldwater 2007) and word segmentation (Johnson and Goldwater 2009); child language acquisition (Kemp, Perfors, and Tenenbaum 2007) and human sentence processing (Narayanan and Jurafsky 2004); and for use in natural language processing applications such as sentence parsing and machine translation (Finkel, Manning, and Ng 2006). Within historical linguistics, Bayesian phylogenetic tools have proven a valuable complement to the traditional comparative method. By quantifying the uncertainty implicit in any linguistic family tree and presenting it overtly as the set of posterior probabilities, these methods make explicit the status of the family tree as a hypothesis, and show clearly which aspects of the classification are highly certain and which are less so. Further uses include dating the resulting trees, locating the homeland for a language family, and tracing routes of migration (Bouckaert et al. 2012), as well as investigating relative rates of change between languages, subgroups, and lexical items or other linguistic features (Pagel, Atkinson, and Meade 2007). Used in combination with traditional techniques, Bayesian phylogenetics can shed new light on standing questions of language change.

Acknowledgments

Many thanks to Claire Bowern, Russell Gray, Simon Greenhill, E-Ching Ng, and Bob Frank for their invaluable feedback and insights. This research was funded in part by the National Science Foundation under grant no. 1209597.

Notes

1. While these trees include the Timor and Aru subgroups, the hypothesis presented here claims only that they are distinct from Bima-Sumba-Flores. Any other details of their structure and relative positions are beyond the scope of this paper. Similarly, the cohesion of Central Malayo-Polynesian itself is also debated (see Gray, Drummond, and Greenhill 2009); its existence as a single node in the tree is not at all crucial to this hypothesis.
2. Many of these languages have several alternate names and are referred to differently across the available sources. Here I call the languages by the names used in the ABVD, with ISO codes listed in table 5.1 for reference.
3. For further discussion of the comparative method and identification of lexical cognates, see, for example, Crowley and Bowern (2010).
4. This number is somewhat misleading, as items judged to be unique states (those lacking cognates in other languages) are generally left uncoded in the ABVD, as they are uninformative to the analysis. Coding was added for those items here, whether or not they were revealed to be cognate with others in the sample.

REFERENCES

Blust, Robert. 1981. "The Soboyo reflexes of Proto-Austronesian *S." In *Historical Linguistics in Indonesia, Volume One,* 21–30, edited by Robert Blust. *NUSA 10.* Jakarta: Lembaga Bahasa, Universitas Katolik Indonesia Atma Jaya.
———. 1993. "Central and Central–Eastern Malayo-Polynesian." *Oceanic Linguistics* 32: 241–93.
———. 1995. "The prehistory of the Austronesian-speaking peoples: The view from language." *Journal of World Prehistory* 9: 453–510.
———. 2008. "Is there a Bima-Sumba subgroup?" *Oceanic Linguistics* 41(1): 45–113.

Bouckaert, Remco, Philippe Lemey, Michael Dunn, Simon J. Greenhill, Alexander V. Alekseyenko, Alexei J. Drummond, Russell D. Gray, Marc A. Suchard, and Quentin D. Atkinson. 2012. "Mapping the origins and expansion of the Indo-European language family." *Science* 337: 957–60.

Bowern, Claire, and Quentin Atkinson. 2012. "Computational phylogenetics and the internal structure of Pama-Nyungan." *Language* 88 (4): 817–45.

Bowern, Claire, Patience Epps, Russell Gray, Jane Hill, Keith Hunley, Patrick McConvell, and Jason Zentz. 2011. "Does lateral transmission obscure inheritance in hunter-gatherer languages?" *PLOS ONE* 6 (9).

Campbell, Lyle. 2004. *Historical Linguistics: An Introduction, second edition*. Edinburgh: Edinburgh University Press.

Collins, James. 1983. *The Historical Relationships of the Languages of Central Maluku, Indonesia*, Pacific Linguistics D-47. Canberra: The Australian National University.

Crowley, Terry, and Claire Bowern. 2010. *An Introduction to Historical Linguistics*. New York: Oxford University Press.

Drummond, Alexei, and Andrew Rambaut. 2003. *Tracer* [computer program]. http://beast.bio.ed.ac.uk/tracer.

———. 2007. "BEAST: Bayesian evolutionary analysis by sampling trees." *BMC Evolutionary Biology* 7: 214.

Dunn, Michael, Stephen C. Levinson, Eva Lindström, and Ger Reesink. 2008. "Structural phylogeny in historical linguistics: Methodological explorations applied in Island Melanesia." *Language* 84 (4): 710–59.

Dyen, Isadore. 1965. *A Lexicostatistical Classification of the Austronesian Languages*. International Journal of American Linguistics, Memoir 19. Supplement to *International Journal of American Linguistics* 31 (1). Baltimore.

Eska, Joseph, and Don Ringe. 2004. "Recent work in computational linguistic phylogeny." *Language* 80: 569–82.

Esser, S. J. 1938. "Talen." *Atlas van Tropisch Nederland*. Het Koninklijk Aardrijkskundig Genootschap in Samenwerking met den Topografischen Dienst in Nederlandsch Indië. The Hague: Nijhoff.

Finkel, Jenny Rose, Christopher D. Manning, and Andrew Y. Ng. 2006. "Solving the problem of cascading errors: Approximate Bayesian inference for linguistic annotation pipelines." *Proceedings of the 2006 Conference on Empirical Methods in Natural Language Processing*. Association for Computational Linguistics, 618–26.

Forth, Gregory. 1988. "Komodo as seen from Sumba: Comparative remarks on eastern Indonesian relationship terminology." *Bijdragen tot de Taal-, Land- en Volkenkunde* 144 (1): 44–63.

Graham, R. L., and L. R. Foulds. 1982. "Unlikelihood that minimal phylogenies for a realistic biological study can be constructed in reasonable computational time." *Mathematical Biosciences* 60: 133–42.

Gray, Russell, and Quentin Atkinson. 2003. "Language-tree divergence times support the Anatolian theory of Indo-European origin." *Nature* 426: 435–39.

Gray, Russell, Alexei Drummond, and Simon Greenhill. 2009. "Language phylogenies reveal expansion pulses and pauses in Pacific settlement." *Science* 323: 479–83.

Gray, Russell, and Fiona Jordan. 2000. "Language trees support the express-train sequence of Austronesian expansion." *Nature* 405: 1052–55.

Greenhill, Simon, Robert Blust, and Russell Gray. 2008. "The Austronesian basic vocabulary database: From bioinformatics to lexomics." *Evolutionary Bioinformatics* 4: 271–83.

Greenhill, Simon, Thomas Currie, and Russell Gray. 2009. "Does horizontal transmission invalidate cultural phylogenies?" *Proceedings of the Royal Society B: Biological Sciences* 276: 2299–2306.

Greenhill, Simon, Alexei Drummond, and Russell Gray. 2010. "How accurate and robust are the phylogenetic estimates of Austronesian language relationships?" *PLOS ONE* 5 (3).

Greenhill, Simon, and Russell Gray. 2009. "Austronesian language phylogenies: Myths and misconceptions about Bayesian computational methods." In *Austronesian Historical Linguistics and Culture History: A Festschrift for Robert Blust*, edited by Alexander Adelaar and Andrew Pawley. Canberra: Pacific Linguistics.

Holden, Clare, and Russell Gray. 2006. "Rapid radiation, borrowing and dialect continua in the Bantu languages." In *Phylogenetic Methods and the Prehistory of Languages*, 19–31, edited by P. Forster and C. Renfrew. Cambridge: McDonald Institute for Archaeological Research.

Hughes, Jock. 1987. "The languages of Kei, Tanimbar and Aru: A lexicostatistical classification." 12 *NUSA* 27: 71–111.

Huson, Daniel, and David Bryant. 2006. "Application of phylogenetic networks in evolutionary studies." *Molecular Biology and Evolution* 23 (2): 254–67.

Johnson, Mark, and Sharon Goldwater. 2009. "Improving nonparameteric Bayesian inference: Experiments on unsupervised word segmentation with adaptor grammars." *Proceedings of Human Language Technologies: The 2009 Annual Conference of the North American Chapter of the Association for Computational Linguistics*, 317–25.

Johnson, Mark, Thomas Griffiths, and Sharon Goldwater. 2007. "Bayesian inference for PCFGs via Markov chain Monte Carlo." *Proceedings of Human Language Technologies: The 2007 Annual Conference of the North American Chapter of the Association for Computational Linguistics*, 139–46.

Kemp, Charles, Amy Perfors, and Joshua B. Tenenbaum. 2007. "Learning overhypotheses with hierarchical Bayesian models." *Developmental Science* 10: 1467.

Kitchen, Andrew, Christopher Ehret, Shiferaw Assefa, and Connie J. Mulligan. 2009. "Bayesian phylogenetic analysis of Semitic languages identifies an Early Bronze Age origin of Semitic in the Near East." *Proceedings of the Royal Society B: Biological Sciences* 276: 2703–10.

Klamer, Marian. 1994. "Kambera: A Language of Eastern Indonesia." PhD thesis, Vrije Universiteit, Amsterdam.

Lewis, M. Paul, editor. 2009. *Ethnologue: Languages of the World*. Dallas: SIL International, sixteenth edition. Online version: www.ethnologue.com.

Mills, Roger. 1991. "Tanimbar-Kei: An eastern Indonesian subgroup." In *Currents in Pacific Linguistics. Papers on Austronesian Languages and Ethnolinguistics in Honour of George W. Grace*, Pacific Linguistics C-117, 241–63, edited by Robert Blust. The Australian National University.

Musgrave, Simon. 2008. "Typology and geography in eastern Indonesia." In *Selected Papers from the 2007 Conference of the Australian Linguistic Society*.

Narayanan, Srini, and Daniel Jurafsky. 2004. "Bayesian models of human sentence processing." *Proceedings of the Twelfth Annual Meeting of the Cognitive Science Society*.

Nicholls, Geoff, and Russell Gray. 2006. "Quantifying uncertainty in a stochastic model of vocabulary evolution." In *Phylogenetic Methods and the Prehistory of Languages*, 161–71, edited by P. Forster and C. Renfrew. Cambridge: McDonald Institute for Archaeological Research.

———. 2008. "Dated ancestral trees from binary trait data and its application to the diversification of languages." *Journal of the Royal Statistical Society: Series B (Statistical Methodology)* 7 (3): 545–66.

Nunn, Charles L. 2011. *The Comparative Approach in Evolutionary Anthropology and Biology*. Chicago: The University of Chicago Press.

Pagel, M., Quentin Atkinson, and A. Meade. 2007. "Frequency of word-use predicts rates of lexical evolution throughout Indo-European history." *Nature* 449: 717–20.

Pawley, Andrew. 2002. "The Austronesian dispersal: Languages, technologies and people." In *Examining the Farming/Language Dispersal Hypothesis*, 251–74, edited by P. Bellwood and C. Renfrew. Cambridge: McDonald Institute for Archaeological Research.

Rexová, Kateřina, Yvonne Bastin, and Daniel Frynta. 2006. "Cladistic analysis of Bantu languages: A new tree based on combined lexical and grammatical data." *Naturwissenschaften* 93: 189–94.

Ringe, Don, Tandy Warnow, and Ann Taylor. 2002. "Indo-European and computational cladistics." *Transactions of the Philological Society* 100: 59–129.

Suchard, Marc, Robert Weiss, and Janet Sinsheimer. 2001. "Bayesian selection of continuous time Markov Chain evolutionary models." *Molecular Biology and Evolution* 18: 1001–13.

Swadesh, Morris. 1952. "Lexico-statistic dating of prehistoric ethnic contacts." *Proceedings of the American Philosophical Society* 96: 452–63.

Yule, George U. 1925. "A mathematical theory of evolution, based on the conclusions of Dr. J. C. Willis, F. R. S." *Philosophical Transactions of the Royal Society B: Biological Sciences* 213: 21–87.

6

Young Learners' Storytelling in Their First and Foreign Languages

YUKO GOTO BUTLER AND WEI ZENG
University of Pennsylvania

MANY FOREIGN LANGUAGE PROGRAMS at elementary schools (FLES), placing a strong emphasis on children's development of oral communicative abilities in the target language as an instructional goal, are increasingly employing picture-book reading and storytelling as part of their classroom activities. Narrative speech requires a substantial transition in children's language skills because narratives often involve "there-and-then" events as opposed to "here-and-now." Narrative performance is also found to be related to children's later reading performance (Griffin et al. 2004).

There is substantial research on narrative development among young children in their first language (L1) (e.g., Bamberg 1997; Berman and Slobin 1994; Hickmann 2003). Discourse organization is considered to be a relatively late development; narrative structure continues to be reorganized throughout a student's school years and beyond (Viberg 2001). However, most studies on narrative development in L1 have concentrated on children up to ten years old. Narrative development in students beyond that age has not been fully understood, but there seem be substantial differences in narrative construction between ten-year-olds and adults. For example, the proportion of past or perfective markers with predicates in English gradually increases up to ten years old; however, this proportion drops drastically among adults, who frequently use the historical present (Hickmann 2003). Precise developmental changes between ten-year-olds and adults are not yet clear even in L1 acquisition due to scarce data on narratives among older school-age learners.

Though attention to narrative development among bilingual children is growing (e.g., Minami 2011; Verhoeven and Strömqvist 2001), we still have little information about narrative development among school-age children and adolescents in their foreign language (FL). This paucity of research is unfortunate because, as we mentioned above, storytelling activities have increased in popularity in FLES worldwide, and researchers and educators have repeatedly emphasized the importance of multilingual competence.

The present study investigates elementary- and middle-school students' narratives in both their L1 and FL and how these narratives differ across different age groups. It focuses on coherence and content in narratives in very typologically and oral-culturally different languages: namely, Chinese (L1) and English (FL).

Models to Analyze Narrative Structure

The structure of narrative content, or coherence, has been extensively studied as one of the critical features of narrative development among children. Various methods have been used to analyze coherence in children's narratives, depending on researchers' theoretical foundations and the types of narratives being examined (e.g., personal or fictional narratives). Bamberg (1997) classified major methods into six different approaches: cognitive, interactive, constructive, cross-cultural, sociocultural, and contextual approaches. These approaches differ with respect to how to define a narrative and its coherence, how to conceptualize the goals and course of development, and what methodological frameworks to use to analyze narrative coherence.

Although researchers do not agree on how best to capture narrative coherence, the vast majority have adopted a cognitive approach called story grammar, which assumes that narratives have underlying common components. In particular, a story grammar framework proposed by Nancy Stein and her colleagues (e.g., Stein 1988; Stein and Albro 1997) is perhaps "some of the most careful, systematic, conceptually self-conscious, and broadly influential investigation of narrative coherence in developmental research" (Nicolopoulou 2008, 301). Their model is based on the assumption that story coherence is achieved not simply by having temporal relations among episodes, but by having causal connections among goals, actions, and outcomes. According to this model, a well-formed story is composed of episodes that rest on human intentionality and goal-oriented actions taken by a major protagonist. In constructing the model, Stein and her colleagues identified a sequence of dimensions that should be incorporated in goal-directed actions. These dimensions are, in the order of the sequence, temporal relations, causal relations, goals, obstacle, and ending. Based on these dimensions, the model classifies stories into eight levels that are assumed to increase in cognitive complexity (Stein and Albro 1997, 9):

1. No structure
2. Descriptive sequence
3. Action sequence (with temporal relations but no causal relations)
4. Reactive sequence (with causal relations but not goal-based episode)
5. Goal-based episode without either an obstacle to goal attainment or an ending
6. Goal-based episode with an ending but no obstacle
7. Goal-based episode with an obstacle but no ending
8. Goal-based episode with both an obstacle and an ending

In this model, a person's narrative structure gains increasing coherence along with his/her other cognitive abilities such as memory, logical reasoning, and language, while various educational, cross-cultural, and other environmental factors play a minor role in the course of development.

Challenges for Analyzing Narratives

Many studies have applied Stein and colleagues' framework, or its modifications, as well as similar story-grammar approaches. Such studies, done mostly among

English-speaking children, have often reported that the majority of children already exhibit a high level of story grammar in their narratives by seven to nine years old. After reviewing these studies, however, Heilmann, Miller, and Nockerts (2010) concluded that "these existing story grammar measures may be too easy and potentially insensitive for preschool and young school-age children" (608). Indeed, their analyses of narratives among five- to seven-year-old English-speaking children indicated that "the majority of the scores were closely bunched together near the ceiling" (614).

In addition to the potential issue of measurement insensitivity among story-grammar approaches, particularly when analyzing school-age children, some researchers have questioned the assumption that there is a common underlying story grammar at all. While acknowledging that goal-directed actions can surely capture some aspects of children's narrative development, Nicolopoulou (2008) claims that framing the well-formed story solely based on this criterion is "simply too restrictive and one-sided" and that "it misses a good deal of what is interesting and complex about children's stories" (305). In comparing Korean and American preschoolers' narratives, Lee et al. (2011) found that the coherence of the children's fictional narratives measured by Stein (1988) was significantly different between the two groups; the mean score among American children was higher than that of Korean children. The authors attributed the result to differences in teachers' attitudes toward literacy practice between the two cultures; the American teachers embraced narrative activities more explicitly, spent more time reading stories aloud, and had more books in the classrooms. If narrative coherence is largely influenced by different socialization experiences with the given narrative practice, it may also be possible that the story-grammar scale used in this particular approach did not capture the children's narrative development equally across cultures and languages.

Not only does the structure of narratives differ between cultures, but the content expressed in children's narratives may differ by culture as well. For example, Chinese families tend to use storytelling to convey morality and social norms (Miller et al. 1997). Domino and Hannah (1987) reported that eleven- to thirteen-year-old Chinese students' narratives contained more emotional states than the narratives of their American counterparts. Similarly, Wang and Leichtman (2000) found that six-year-old Chinese children expressed more moral correctness, more emotional states, and more situational details than their American counterparts.

Aksu-Koç (1996) found differences in narrative content depending on the children's social economic status (SES) within a language community. Lower-SES children's narratives focused on themes and contained more subjective information, while higher-SES children's narratives focused on sequences of events and included more objective information.

Bilingual/multilingual children who are socialized into more than one language environment exemplify the idea that narrative development is indeed a complicated interplay among various factors (Verhoeven and Strömqvist 2001). In examining bilingual/multilingual children, we may be able to sort out which narrative features are age-related and which are cross-linguistic or second/foreign language-related. However, such investigation is still in the infant stage and we have very limited information. In one pioneering work, Viberg (2001) examined Swedish and Finnish bilingual children's narratives, reporting that the bilingual children tended to exhibit similar narrative structures to one another and to have similar numbers of propositions (i.e., a similar amount of information) in both of their languages. They tended to provide more concrete and detailed information in both languages than did their monolingual counterparts, who, in contrast, tended to have more condensed information. However, the similarities and differences Viberg found may result from complex interplay among various factors embedded in a particular context, such as the students' learning experiences, language combinations (typological relationship between the learners' L1 and L2/FL), vocabulary levels and language proficiencies, and so forth.

Research Questions

The present study aims to understand how young FL-learning students' narratives in their L1 and FL develop in terms of coherence and content. Young FL-learning students may learn differently than simultaneous and/or early bilingual children in that they start exposure to their FL later in childhood in a formal instructional setting and, thus, tend to have very different proficiency levels in their L1 and FL. We focus on Chinese children who are learning English as their FL; two languages that are very different typologically and oral-culturally. More specifically, the study investigates the following questions:

1. How does young learners' structural coherence in FL relate to that in L1? How does young learners' structural coherence in FL also relate to their SES background as well as their vocabulary level in FL? How may such relationships differ across grade levels?
2. How do the contents of young learners' narratives in FL relate to L1? How may such relationships differ across grade levels?

The "contents" in the second question refer to the amount of information conveyed in narratives, as well as the amount of content that overlaps between the narratives in L1 and FL. As part of an ongoing longitudinal project, the present study reports the results of an analysis of the baseline data employing a cross-sectional design.

Participants

The participants were fourth-, sixth-, and eighth-grade students (thirty-two students for each grade level, ninety-six total) who were enrolled in public elementary schools and middle schools in a medium-sized eastern city in China. They were focus group students in a larger project with 572 students in total. Stratified random sampling was used to select the focus group students. They were chosen from twelve participating classes from four schools in the original study. The study was controlled for gender and general English proficiency level; the same number of boys and girls were selected and the students' general English proficiency, measured by the schools' in-house written exam scores, was roughly evenly distributed.

All the participating students had received English instruction from the third grade onward at school based on the uniform curriculum implemented in the city. The participants' schools all used a textbook series approved by the local government.

The textbook aimed to enhance the students' oral and written communicative competence. Various oral activities including story-reading and storytelling were employed in English classes, especially at the elementary school level. Story-reading and storytelling were also implemented regularly as an extracurricular activity at the participating elementary schools.

According to the participants' teachers, storytelling activities in Chinese were popular in kindergarten and during the first one or two years in elementary school, but they were no longer practiced in class in the upper elementary school grades. A parental survey (described below) indicated that some parents with relatively higher SES had English as well as Chinese books at home. At the time of the study, no parents read to their children in Chinese or English at home.

Instruments and Procedures

The students were asked to tell a story to a researcher based on a wordless picture book, *The Chicken Thief* (Rodriguez 2005), first in their L1 and then in their FL. We used a wordless picture book because we believed that it would be easier for the students to tell a story if they had visual aids, and that it would be easier to compare the stories in both languages. Though Mayer's (1969) *Frog, Where Are You?* has been widely used in narrative developmental studies in the literature (e.g., Berman and Slobin 1994), we decided not to use it because our pilot study indicated that the book was too difficult for our students to tell a story in their FL. *The Chicken Thief* begins with a chicken stolen by a fox from her home. The chicken's friends (Bear, Rabbit, and Rooster) go on an adventure to chase the fox, but in the end they find, to their surprise, that the fox is not a villain. We chose this story for its relatively simple storyline with a clear goal, cute and colorful pictures, and its potential for rich description. We found from the pilot study that the original story was slightly too long for our students, so we chose ten pictures while keeping the original storyline.

None of the participating students had seen the book before; however, they could spend as much time as they wanted to start telling a story. The students were allowed to ask for help with vocabulary and expressions from the researcher if they needed it. Some fourth-graders asked the researcher about vocabulary, but few sixth- or eighth-graders did so. After the students finished their stories in both languages, the researcher asked them some comprehension questions. All of the stories and exchanges between the students and the researcher were recorded and transcribed.

As an indicator of the students' English proficiency level, we used the Peabody Picture Vocabulary Test (PPVT), a standardized receptive vocabulary measure. The students took the PPVT between telling the story in L1 and in FL. All the above activities took thirty minutes per student on average. Finally, information on the participants' SES, their literacy, and other educational practice at home was collected through a questionnaire sent to their parents. Since the measures employed in the survey to obtain the students' SES (i.e., parental household income, the mother's education level, and the father's education level) were all highly correlated with one another at all three grade levels, the mother's educational level was used in the following analysis as it has been reported that a mother's education level plays a particularly significant role in children's literacy development in general (Burchinal et al. 2002).

Analyses

To analyze structural coherence, we used Stein's story-grammar approach, described above (Stein 1988; Stein and Albro 1997). Two trained research assistants initially coded five randomly chosen narratives independently. Any discrepancies were discussed, and then they coded the rest of the narratives independently again. The inter-rater reliabilities, based on percentage agreement of 96 narratives in each language, were 96.8 percent for Chinese and 93.7 percent for English.

To analyze content, we first examined the amount of information conveyed in the narratives and then the extent to which such information was shared between the narratives in L1 and FL. To choose the unit of analysis, we decided to use idea units because they are considered to be more suitable for capturing oral data than other structural units such as T-units and C-units. While idea units can be defined semantically, structural-based definitions have generally been used in practice, including Carrell (1985) who considered a clause an essential unit:

> Basically, each idea unit consists of a single clause (main or subordinate, including adverbial and relative clauses). Each infinitival construction, gerundive, nominalized verb phrase, and conjunct was also identified as a separate idea unit. In addition, optional and/or heavy prepositional phrases were designated as separate idea units (Carrell 1985, 737).

However, using a clause as an essential unit has proved to be unsuitable for analyzing oral data among less-proficient learners because a clause-based unit does not accurately represent learners' fragmented speech. In response to this problem, Sakai (2005, 54) modified Carrell's definition to include units smaller than clauses and considered "adverbials and non-heavy prepositional phrases as adverbials" as independent idea units. Since FL proficiency among the students in the present study was assumed to be low in general, we adopted Sakai's definition. For example, the following utterance is composed of four idea units based on Sakai's definition:

> [Long long ago]$_1$, uh(::) [some chicken and a bear, uh some chicken and rabbit and a bear lived [together]$_2$ [in a small house]$_3$]$_4$.

1. Time Adverbial Phrase: *long long ago*
2. Manner Adverbial Phrase: *together*
3. Location Adverbial Phrase: *in a small house*
4. Main Clause: *some chicken and rabbit and a bear lived (together in a small house)*

We calculated the number of idea units contained in the two languages, as well as the overlap in content among idea units in both languages. Two raters initially coded twelve randomly selected students' narratives individually. The inter-rater reliabilities were 92.5 percent for Chinese based on percentage agreement of 848

Table 6.1.
Descriptive statistics (means and standard deviations) of structural coherence scores in L1 and FL

	Fourth graders (N=32)	Sixth graders (N=32)	Eighth graders (N=32)
Chinese (L1)	5.45 (1.41)	5.75 (1.55)	5.47 (1.18)
English (FL)	2.02 (0.79)	3.56 (1.59)	4.31 (1.66)

units, and 95.1 percent for English based on percentage agreement of 346 units. Differences in coding were then discussed until 100 percent agreement was reached. One of the raters then coded the rest of the data set.

Results and Discussion
Narrative Structural Coherence in L1 and FL

Table 6.1 summarizes the result of the descriptive statistics of the coherence scores in L1 and FL for the three grade levels. Figures 6.1–6.3 are scatterplots showing the relationship between the coherence scores in L1 and FL, and table 6.2 shows the result of the regression analyses (predicting the coherence scores in English from those in Chinese).

First, we note substantial variability in coherence scores in students' L1, far from the ceiling effect reported previously among English-speaking younger children. Interestingly, this variability did not seem to change significantly across the grade levels. The mean coherence scores in Chinese also did not show any significant differences across grade level [$F(2, 93) = 0.46, p = 0.63$]. The variability we observed may reflect specific sociocultural experiences, as Lee et al. (2011) suggest. However, it may also indicate a possibility that the assumed story-grammar sequence in Stein (1988) did not best capture the development of narrative structures among Chinese-speaking children.

Second, as figures 6.1–6.3 show, the linear regression slopes become steeper as the grade level increases. This resulted primarily from the fact that the coherence scores in English among fourth-grade students were clustered around levels 1 to 3, while the older students showed greater variability in their English scores. The correlation coefficient between the scores in Chinese and English was substantially higher among the eighth-grade students than among the younger students.

However, when a loess (locally weighted scatterplot smoothing) method was used in order to best fit a curve to the data, an interesting tendency emerged. Namely,

Table 6.2.
Regression analyses predicting the story grammar scores in FL from those in L1

	B	SE B	β	r	R^2	adjusted R^2
Fourth graders (N=32)	.28	.09	.51*	.51*	.26	.23
Sixth graders (N=32)	.51	.15	.52*	.52*	.27	.25
Eighth graders (N=32)	1.11	.16	.79*	.79*	.62	.61

* $p < .01$

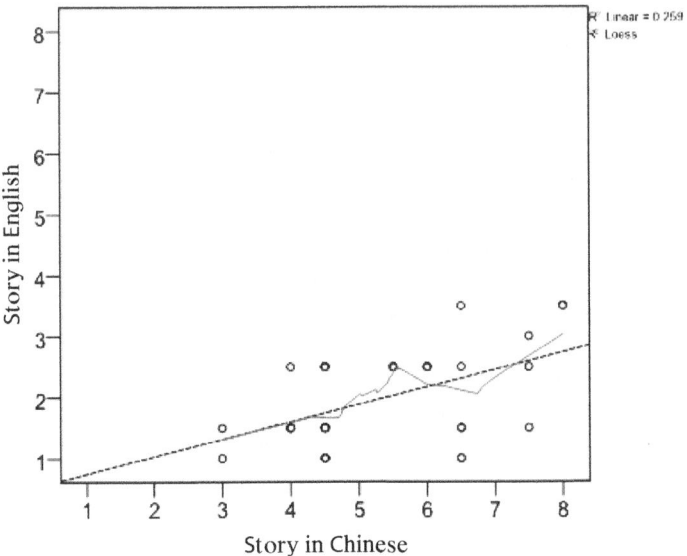

Figure 6.1 Structural Coherence in L1 and L2 and FL Fourth Graders (N = 32)

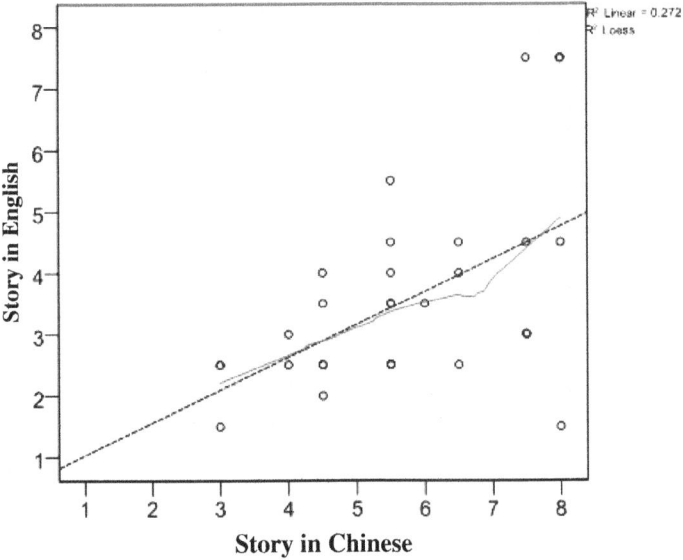

Figure 6.2 Structural Coherence in L1 and FL Sixth Graders (N = 32)

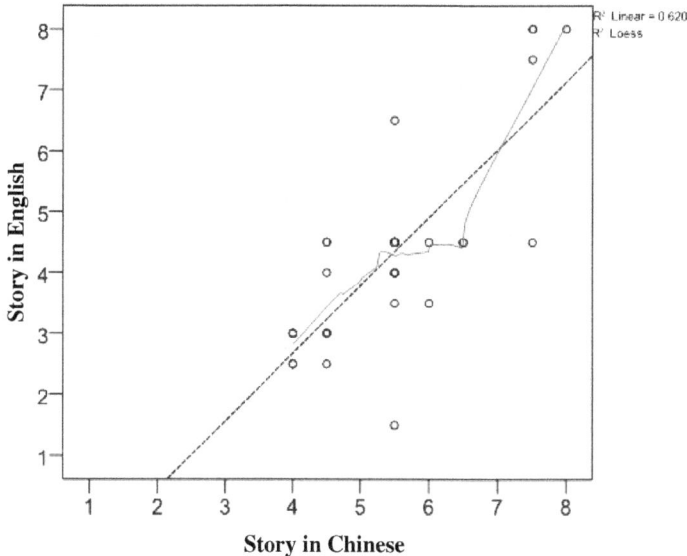

Figure 6.3 Structural Coherence in L1 and FL Eighth Graders (N = 32)

one can see changes in the slope somewhere between 6 and 7 in the Chinese scores. Such changes were barely noticeable among the fourth graders, but were increasingly evident among the older students. Levels 6–7 in Stein (1988) mean that the story has at least either an obstacle or an ending and thus requires much more structural complexity. According to Stein and Albro (1997), stories at these levels are evaluated as "good stories" by adults (in this case, English-speaking adults). If the students' Chinese narratives contained at least these story-grammar components (i.e., an obstacle and/or ending), their English scores tended to be higher among the sixth- and eighth-grade students.

Relationships between Narrative Coherence and other Variables

Table 6.3 shows correlations between the students' narrative coherence and their mothers' educational level as well as their PPVT performance. The mother's education level showed significant correlations with the coherence scores in both L1 and FL among the fourth graders, but not among the older groups. The reason for this result is unknown; however, it may relate to the fact that among the older children, storytelling was no longer practiced at home.

When it comes to relationships with vocabulary level, the PPVT in English showed significant correlations with the coherence scores in English, and higher correlations were obtained particularly among sixth- and eighth-grade students. The PPVT in English also showed a significant correlation with coherence scores in Chinese among eighth graders. This result is not surprising, given the fact that

Table 6.3.
Correlations among variables

	Fourth (N=32)			Sixth (N=32)			Eighth (N=32)		
	1	2	3	1	2	3	1	2	3
1 Story in English									
2 Story in Chinese	.56**			.52**			.79**		
3 Mother's education	.59**	.52**		.26	-.02		.06	.05	
4 PPVT in English	.37*	.18	.15	.67**	.29	.29	.57**	.50**	.21

* $p<.05$
** $p<.01$

eighth-grade students' coherence scores in English were highly correlated with those in Chinese.

However, when the relationship between the coherence scores in English and the PPVT in English is plotted (see figure 6.4), we see interesting individual differences. Though the coherence scores among the fourth graders appear to be largely constrained by their limited vocabulary level in English, two interesting groups of students were identified among the sixth and eighth graders: a group of students whose PPVT performance was high but whose coherence scores were low, and another group of students who had the reverse profile (indicated in figure 6.4 as Group A and Group B, respectively).

The students in Group A used a wider variety of vocabulary, more action verbs, and their narratives were much more fluent, reflecting their generally higher proficiency in English. However, the Group A students tended to describe events simply in a temporal linear fashion, as in the example below. (Pseudonyms are used in the following excerpts.)

Excerpt 1 (David, Group A):

Hmm fox ran to the sea. And uh(::) three animals find him. And fox (.) find a boat and uh (2.0) and uh he drove it into the sea. And the three animals followed him.

The coherence scores in Chinese among Group A students were around 5 to 6. In contrast, the students in Group B all obtained high coherence scores in Chinese (7.5 to 8) as well as in English. Compared with the Group A students, however, the Group B students were less fluent, and they sometimes had to pause to organize words and sentences. Excerpt 2 below describes the penultimate scene, which is the story's twist: when the three animals break into the fox's house and are about to save the chicken, they find their friend and the fox close to/friendly with each other.

Excerpt 2 (Lilly, Group B)

They were very angry and uh the fox was very (.) surprised at them. The chicken, uh, then the chicken help … then the chicken uh (.) say . . . said some words to (.) help the fox. Hmm they meant the fox isn't . . . the fox (.) doesn't

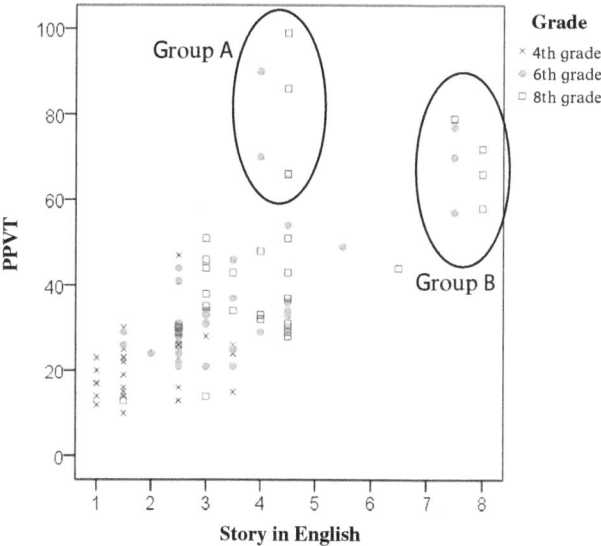

Figure 6.4 Structural Coherence in FL and PPVT in FL

want to . . . ah didn't want to eat . . . eat it and they were very good friends, so the fox took (.) him (.) to his house. Uh (1.0) the . . . the other animals under . . . understood the chickens . . . understood the chickens and then they (.) uh (.) they sat in the . . . they sat in the fox home and talked very happily.

Despite her struggle to find words and expressions, Lilly's success in explaining the unexpected ending to the listener is evident. She clearly constructs the obstacles and effectively describes the animals' reactions. This contrasts with David's description of the same scene. His narrative in English was delivered in a more fluent and condensed fashion but lacked a clear indication of an obstacle or a coherent transition from the initial event of the scene to the unexpected ending.

Excerpt 3 (David, Group A)
Uh. They find the fox and the white chicken was talking happily. Uh(::) after they asked the fox, the the chicken, they they know, they knew they were good friends now.

Different characteristics observed in the students' narratives above suggest the complex nature of the development of narratives in L1 and FL in relation to general language proficiency among young learners.

Narrative Contents in L1 and FL

Figures 6.5–6.7 show the number of idea units contained in the students' narratives in Chinese and English, as well as the number of idea units that overlapped in both languages. The content analysis is conducted on the narratives of half of the participants

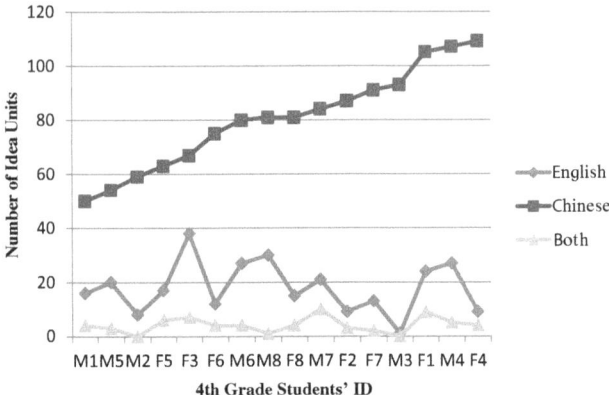

Figure 6.5 Number of Idea Units Fourth Grade (N = 16)

while controlling for gender and general English proficiency, which is measured by the schools' in-house written exam; we had sixteen students for each grade level for this part of the analysis. The x-axis in the figures indicates each participant with his/her gender and ID number indicated (F refers to a female student and M refers to a male).

First, we see substantial variability in the number of idea units in Chinese. Such variability was observed across the grade levels; the numbers roughly ranged from 30–40 to 100–110 at the all three grade levels. With respect to the English version, the numbers of idea units generally increased as the grade level increased.

What is striking in these data is that there is little overlap in idea units between Chinese and English. This result appears to differ from Viberg (2001), who identified propositions in a video story and calculated the number of propositions contained in narratives produced by Finnish-Swedish speaking bilingual children based on the video. While a direct comparison between Viberg and our study is not possible

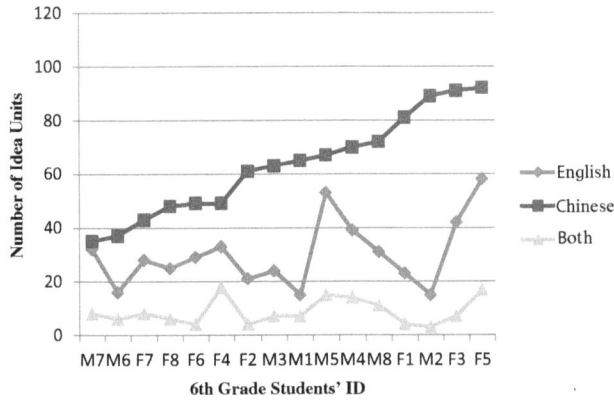

Figure 6.6 Number of Idea Units Sixth Grade (N = 16)

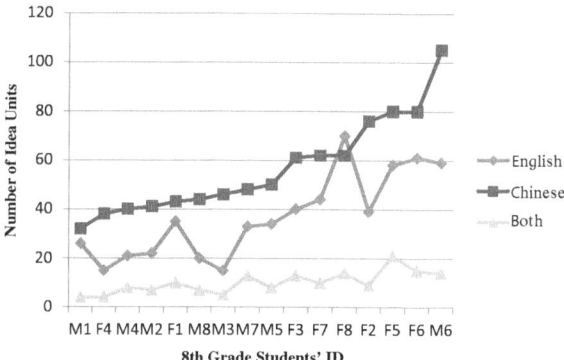

Figure 6.7 Number of Idea Units Eighth Grade (*N* = 16)

because the method of analysis was different in the two studies, Viberg found substantial overlap between the Finnish and Swedish versions. This led him to conclude that "narrative structure belongs to a general conceptual level which is relatively independent of individual languages" (97). However, the bilingual children in Viberg received lessons at a school that was "relatively evenly distributed between the L1 and Swedish L2" (91). Their L2 learning experiences can be assumed to be very different from those of the students in our study (i.e., students whose FL was English and thus were assumed to have substantially different exposure to the two languages, both qualitatively and quantitatively).

The small overlap between the narratives in Chinese and English observed in our study may perhaps still be due to the students' relatively limited linguistic resources in English, as Viberg (2001) suggested. Through a detailed qualitative comparison, we generally observed that although the students tended to use a variety of action verbs and expressions in Chinese, their narratives in English tended to be limited to basic verbs and expressions. This difference appeared to be largely due to the students' limited linguistic knowledge in English, as this example of an eighth-grade student's narrative shows:

Excerpt 4 (Sue, Chinese):
［它们［推开树洞的门］］₁发现［狐狸和鸡，呃，［它偷的］₂鸡都［在(.)那里面］₃］₄°［然后］₅，呃，嗯，［小熊和兔子就在，［就］₆［跟狐狸］₇开始(2.5)［争论］₈］₉°［最后］₁₀［它们，［一起］₁₁(.)围着火堆］₁₂，［聊了［起来］₁₃］₁₄°

(Translation) They pushed open the hollow tree house's door and found the fox and the chicken, uh, the chicken it had stolen were both in there. Then, uh, hmm, little bear and the rabbit began to argue with the fox. At last they sat together around the fire and started chatting.

Excerpt 5 (Sue, English):

[They uh opened the door]$_1$ and [asked the fox]$_2$, uh, "[Why do you uh stole our (.) chicken?]$_3$," [The chi-chicken said]$_4$, "uh, [the fox was very lonely]$_5$. [I want [to stay [with (.) him]$_6$]$_7$]$_8$." [The rabbit uh and uh the bear uh (.) say]$_9$, "[That's OK.]$_{10}$"

Sue produced fourteen idea units in Chinese and ten in English, but there was little overlap in content between the two versions. The above narratives were based on the same scene as those in excerpts 2 and 3, which indicates a complicated episode and can be explained as multiple events. For her Chinese version, Sue described the sequence of events one by one: the three animals entering the house, seeing the fox and the chicken inside, arguing with the fox, and sitting around the fireplace and chatting together at the end. In her English version, however, her idea units mostly took the form of a dialogue between the three animals and the chicken. As a result, the student told the two narratives from different perspectives. In general, such dialogue forms were frequently observed in the English narratives among our students. Telling a story in the form of "here and now" in the first person is also popular among L1-learning younger children (e.g., Tomasello 2003). This may have been a compensation strategy among our FL-learning young students if they had limited vocabulary and linguistic knowledge in FL.

While the students' limited FL knowledge may largely explain the low overlap between the content of the L1 and FL narratives in our study, it is possible that there may be additional reasons. The role of figurative and poetic expressions in narrative appeared to be one such possibility. Figurative and poetic expressions were frequently observed in the Chinese narratives, particularly among sixth- and eighth-grade students. Examples of such figurative expressions included 像落汤鸡一样 (someone as soaking wet as a drenched chicken), 来龙去脉 (originally used to describe the direction of mountain ranges, but now used more often in its figurative sense, meaning the beginning, development, and results of an event), and 图谋不轨 (planning to do something violating laws or regulations). These are traditionally considered to be important components of "good stories" in Chinese. By using these expressions, narratives in Chinese can be told in a condensed manner, allowing narrators to leave the details untold because they can assume that the readers share background stories from which the figurative expressions originally came.

Conclusions

We examined school-age FL learners' narratives in their L1 and FL with respect to structural coherence and content. We chose a combination of two languages that are very typologically and oral-culturally different: Chinese (the students' L1) and English (their FL). As part of a larger, ongoing longitudinal project, we used cross-sectional data to examine possible differences in the students' narratives across grade levels. Structural coherence was examined using Stein's (1988) widely adopted story-grammar framework and narrative content was examined using idea units as the unit of analysis.

The study was limited in terms of both methodology (e.g., the limited number of participants and the cross-sectional research design) and the analytical tools for examining the data (e.g., the limited ways of analyzing the data). However, as one of the first attempts to examine narrative development among young school-age learners in both their L1 and FL, the study reveals some of the complex relationships in narrative development in students' L1 and FL, which are not yet fully understood.

With respect to narrative coherence, there was substantial variability even in the students' L1. Their performance in L1 and FL showed increasingly higher correlations among older students, although a nonlinear analysis also indicated that there appeared to be a threshold level in L1 to obtain higher coherence in FL. Moreover, the study identified different patterns of coherence in L1 and FL in relation to the students' proficiency level (measured by the vocabulary level) and in addition to the age factor. It appeared that the students' story-grammar scores did not necessarily increase in tandem with their vocabulary growth, although we need longitudinal data to confirm this definitively.

Regarding content, as with coherence, the study found that there was substantial diversity in the amount of information mentioned in the narratives in the students' L1. Most strikingly, we found very little overlap in the content conveyed in both languages; the students shed light on different aspects of the story and/or told the story from different perspectives. Such differences may in part result from strategies that the students came up with in their FL to compensate for their limited linguistic knowledge in the target language. They may also partially result from their effort to tell a "good story," which may mean something different in the two languages.

Storytelling activities are increasingly popular in FLES programs. When implementing storytelling activities in FLES, we need to keep in mind that young learners' storytelling abilities in their L1 cannot be expected simply to transfer to their FL, nor can they be expected to directly translate from their L1. As the results of our study suggest, multiple factors (e.g., FL proficiency, vocabulary size, SES, age, and narrative convention) seem to contribute to the L1 and FL narratives. Considering the substantial individual differences in narrative performance found in this study (in both L1 and FL), it is also advisable that teachers employ multiple and flexible approaches to storytelling activities depending on the students' individual styles of developing narrative skills in both their L1 and FL.

As we have demonstrated, the development of children's narratives in both L1 and FL appear to be greatly influenced by multiple factors and in complicated ways. Therefore, it is unrealistic to assume that any single measure is sensitive enough to capture the same thing equally across languages and contexts. One of the implications of the present study is that methods of quantification need to be contextualized when they are applied in cross-linguistic and cross-cultural studies. Moreover, it is necessary to combine multiple methods (e.g., using multiple quantification methods and combining qualitative and quantitative methods) to capture complicated phenomena such as bilingual/multilingual language development.

REFERENCES

Aksu-Koç, Ayhan. 1996. "Frames of mind through narrative discourse." In *Social Interaction, Social Context, and Language: Essays in Honor of Susan Ervin-Tripp*, 309–28, edited by Dan Issac Sloban, Julie Gerhardt, Amy Kyratzis, and Jiansheng Guo. Mahwah, NJ: Lawrence Erlbaum Associates.

Bamberg, Michael. 1997. *Narrative Development: Six Approaches*. Mahwah, NJ: Lawrence Erlbaum Associates.

Berman, Ruth A., and Dan I. Slobin. 1994. *Relating Events in Narrative: A Crosslinguistic Developmental Study*. Hillsdale, NJ: Lawrence Erlbaum Associates.

Burchinal, Margaret R., Ellen Peisner-Feinberg, Robert Pianta, and Carollee Howes. 2002. "Development of academic skills from preschool through second grade: Family and classroom predictors of developmental trajectories." *Journal of School Psychology* 40 (1): 415–36.

Carrell, Patricia L. 1985. "Facilitating ESL reading by teaching text structure." *TESOL Quarterly* 19: 727–52.

Domino, George, and Mo Therese Hannah. 1987. "A comparative analysis of social values of Chinese and American children." *Journal of Cross-Cultural Psychology* 18 (1): 58–77.

Griffin, Terri M., Lowry Hemphill, Linda Camp, and Dennis Palmer Wolf. 2004. "Oral discourse in the preschool years and later literacy." *First Language* 24 (2): 123–47.

Heilmann, John, Jon F. Miller, and Ann Nockerts. 2010. "Sensitivity of narrative organization measures using narrative retells produced by young school-age children." *Language Testing* 27 (4): 603–26.

Hickmann, Maya. 2003. *Children's Discourse: Person, Space and Time across Languages*. Cambridge: Cambridge University Press.

Lee, Young-ja, Jeehyun Lee, Myae Han, and Judith A. Schickedanz. 2011. "Comparison of preschoolers' narratives, the classroom book environment, and teacher attitudes towards literacy practices in Korea and the United States." *Early Education and Development* 22 (2): 234–55.

Mayer, Mercer. 1969. *Frog, Where Are You?* New York: Dial Press.

Miller, Peggy J., Angela R. Wiley, Heidi Fung, and Chung-Hui Liang. 1997. "Personal storytelling as a medium of socialization in Chinese and American families." *Child Development* 68: 557–68.

Minami, Masahiko. 2011. *Telling Stories in Two Languages: Multiple Approaches to Understanding English-Japanese Bilingual Children's Narratives*. Charlotte, NC: Information Age Publishing.

Nicolopoulou, Ageliki. 2008. "The elementary forms of narrative coherence in young children's storytelling." *Narrative Inquiry* 18 (2): 299–325.

Rodriguez, Béatrice. 2005. *The Chicken Thief*. Wellington, New Zealand: Gecko Press.

Sakai, Hideki. 2005. "An examination of free written recall tasks as listening comprehension test." *The Journal of the Japan-Britain Association for English Teachers (JABAET Journal)* 9: 46–62.

Stein, Nancy. 1988. "The development of children's storytelling skills." In *Child Language: A Reader*, 282–97, edited by Margery B. Franklin and Sybil Barten. Oxford: Oxford University Press.

Stein, Nancy L., and Elizabeth R. Albro. 1997. "Building complexity and coherence: Children's use of goal-structured knowledge in telling stories." In *Narrative Development: Six Approaches*, 5–44, edited by Michael Bamberg. Mahwah, NJ: Erlbaum.

Tomasello, Michael. 2003. *Constructing a Language: A Usage-Based Theory of Language Acquisition*. Cambridge, MA: Harvard University Press.

Verhoeven, Ludo, and Sven Strömqvist, editors. 2001. *Narrative Development in a Multilingual Context*. Amsterdam: John Benjamins.

Viberg, Åke. 2001. "Age-related and L2-related features in bilingual narrative development in Sweden." In *Narrative Development in a Multilingual Context*, 87–128, edited by Ludo Verhoeven and Sven Strömqvist. Amsterdam: John Benjamins.

Wang, Qi, and Michelle D. Leichtman. 2000. "Same beginnings, different stories: A comparison of American and Chinese children's narratives." *Child Development* 71 (5): 1329–46.

7

Measuring Quechua to Spanish Cross-Linguistic Influence

MARILYN S. MANLEY
Rowan University

WHILE MUCH RESEARCH HAS been carried out to describe Andean Spanish (Cusihuaman 2001; de Granda 2001; Escobar 1978; Feke 2004; Hurley 1995; Lee 1997; Lipski 1996; Mamani and Chávez 2001; Manley 2007; Odlin 1989; Romero 1993; Sánchez and Camacho 1996; Zavala 2001; Zúñiga 1974), this work is the first to quantify the presence of a broad range of Quechua to Spanish cross-linguistic influence (CLI) features.[1] Additionally, this contribution is unique in its approaches to measuring speakers' overall degree of CLI, with a wide variety of CLI features being taken into account. The quantitative methods described here may also be applied to the measurement of CLI among other languages in contact.

Specifically, this paper examines three different methods utilized to quantify the presence of thirty-one Quechua to Spanish phonetic, morphosyntactic, and calque (translations from Quechua into Spanish) CLI features in the speech of seventy members of two bilingual Quechua-Spanish communities in the city of Cuzco, Peru. These thirty-one CLI features have been described previously in the literature by the authors listed above. For each of the seventy speakers, a (1) Total Cross-Linguistic Feature Score (Total CLF Score), a (2) Calque-Weighted Total Cross-Linguistic Feature Score (Calque-Weighted Total CLF Score), and an (3) Implicational-Weighted Total Cross-Linguistic Feature Score (Implicational-Weighted Total CLF Score) were calculated in order to measure the overall degree of Quechua influence in his/her Spanish. In the sections that follow, each of these three measures is described in detail and compared for the purpose of determining which is the most representative of these speakers' degree of Quechua to Spanish CLI.

The creation of both the Calque-Weighted Total CLF Score and the Implicational-Weighted Total CLF Score was motivated by the desire to improve upon the Total CLF Score. While the Total CLF Score weighs each of the thirty-one features equally, the Calque-Weighted Total CLF Score weighs the presence of calques of Quechua language structures produced in Spanish more heavily than other features. Eleven of the thirty-one CLI features are calques. The only explanation for the occurrence of calque features is that they were the result of influence from Quechua. This is not so for the noncalque features, whose presence might be explained as resulting from factors such as internal language change, which may include general processes of simplification, and the use of a universal interlanguage for those learning Spanish as a second language. With the Implicational-Weighted Total CLF Score, each of the thirty-one features was weighted differently based on the results of a Guttman procedure, also referred to as "implicational scaling" (Hatch and Lazaraton 1991, 204–16). In order to create an implicational scale for the thirty-one cross-linguistic features, both the number of features utilized by each participant as well as the number of participants who used each of the thirty-one features were taken into account.

To determine which of the three measures is the most representative of the speakers' degree of Quechua to Spanish CLI, a variety of statistical tests were carried out. Reliability analyses using Cronbach's alpha, a measure of internal consistency, in addition to a Guttman procedure, lend support to the Total CLF Score and indicate that it is a more representative measure than both the Calque-Weighted Total CLF Score and the Implicational-Weighted Total CLF Score.

Participants and Data Collection

The data presented here were collected in 2003 from two communities of bilingual, Quechua-Spanish speakers living in the city of Cuzco, Peru: forty-two male participants from the *Asociación Civil, 'Gregorio Condori Mamani' Proyecto Casa del Cargador* (CdC) (Gregorio Condori Mamani Civil Association, House of the Carrier Project) and twenty-eight female participants from *El Centro de Apoyo Integral a la Trabajadora del Hogar* (CAITH) (Center for the Integral Support of the Female Home Worker). Both the CdC and CAITH are nonprofit, nongovernmental agencies that serve as temporary homes for their inhabitants. Primarily, adolescent males live at the CdC, the majority of whom earn a living as *cargadores* (carriers) by transporting agricultural goods within the large market places of Cuzco. The objective of the CdC is to improve the quality of life of the peasant migrant carriers, thereby allowing them to attain respectable levels of health, education, and familial well-being. The main goal of CAITH is to offer educational support and assistance to female adolescent domestic servants who come from rural areas outside of the city of Cuzco (Rofes 2002).

Table 7.1 lists some relevant characteristics of the seventy participants, including their first language, the age at which they claimed to have started Spanish language acquisition, and the age at which they claimed to have arrived in Cuzco for the first time. The participants ranged in age from eleven to fifty-eight years old at the time of data collection. Given this demographic profile, one might expect relatively less Quechua influence in these speakers' Spanish, since the majority was younger than thirteen upon arrival in Cuzco and also when Spanish acquisition began.

The data presented here were collected from the seventy participants through a Language Attitudes Interview carried out in Spanish. Hornberger (1989) and Vassberg (1993) served as the main references for the creation of the interview, an English translation of which is included in the appendix.

Table 7.1.
Participant Characteristics

Characteristic	No. of Participants
First language:	
Quechua	68
Quechua/Spanish	2
Started Spanish acquisition:	
0–13 years	54
14–18 years	16
Arrived in Cuzco:	
0–13 years	40
14–21 years	30

Total CLF Score

After completion of a detailed transcription of the seventy Language Attitudes Interviews, the participants' usage of the thirty-one different cross-linguistic features was analyzed and is presented in table 7.2.

If these cross-linguistic features appeared in the speech of the participants during their interviews, they received a score of 1 for each of these features. Therefore, it was possible for participants to receive Total CLF Scores ranging from 0 to 31. The Total CLF Scores of the seventy participants examined here ranged from 9 to 26. Therefore, the speech of all participants was found to contain CLI from Quechua to Spanish to varying degrees.

To assess the robustness of the Total CLF Score, a reliability analysis was carried out. In this case, the Total CLF Score was used to measure the Quechua to Spanish CLI present in the participants' Spanish speech. If the reliability coefficient were 1.00, that would mean that the participants' Total CLF Scores perfectly reflected the varying levels of Quechua influence in their speech. However, "all test scores have some degree of measurement error" due to such things as variations in participants' health, motivation, anxiety, attitude, and attention change (Gay and Airasian 2003, 141).

Here, a Cronbach's alpha reliability measure was carried out. In this case, this measure of internal consistency quantifies the extent to which each of the thirty-one features similarly measures Quechua to Spanish CLI. As Gay and Airasian explain, "Kuder Richardson (KR) and Cronbach's alpha estimate internal consistency reliability by determining how all items on a test relate to all other test items and to the total test. When its items or tasks are measuring similar things, they are internally consistent" (2003, 144). In this case, the internal consistency of the Total CLF Score was determined by examining how each of the thirty-one cross-linguistic features relates to each of the other features and to the Total CLF Score. Including all of the thirty-one features resulted in a Cronbach's alpha of 0.65, which is a moderately reliable result.

■ Table 7.2.
Classification of thirty-one cross-linguistic features

	Phonetic Features
1	vowel raising
2	nonstandard realization of /f/
3	stress shift
4	consonant cluster simplification
5	metathesis
6	diphthong simplification
7	nonstandard palatalization
8	nonstandard realization of /b/, /d/, or /g/
	Morphosyntactic Features
9	nonstandard gerund use
10	avoiding the subjunctive
11	nonstandard verb conjugation
12	nonstandard number agreement
13	nonstandard gender agreement
14	nonstandard person agreement
15	nonstandard article agreement
16	nonstandard preposition agreement
17	*hay veces* (there are times) preposition avoidance
18	nonstandard object pronoun agreement
19	double possessive
20	nonstandard word order
	Calque Features
21	diminutive calque
22	*no más* calque
23	*ya* calque
24	*pues* calque
25	*dice* calque
26	*sí* calque
27	*así* calque
28	elongated /s/ calque
29	*siempre* calque
30	voiceless [r] calque
31	pluralization calque

While a Cronbach's alpha coefficient of 0.65 may be quite low for some applications, it may be considered to constitute an acceptable level of reliability given explanations such as that of Gay and Airasian (2003, 145):

> What constitutes an acceptable level of reliability is to some degree determined by the type of test, although very high reliability coefficients would be acceptable for any test. The question really is concerned with what constitutes the minimum level of acceptability. This will differ among test types. For example, standardized achievement and aptitude tests should have high reliability, often higher than 0.90. On the other hand, personality measures do not typically report such high reliabilities ... and one would therefore be satisfied with a reliability somewhat lower than expected from an achievement test. Moreover, when tests are developed in new areas, reliability is often low initially.

Calque-Weighted Total CLF Score

As an alternative to the Total CLF Score, a Calque-Weighted Total CLF Score was calculated to measure the CLI in the speech of the seventy participants. Similar to the Total CLF Score, in calculating the Calque-Weighted Total CLF Score, it was noted which of the thirty-one cross-linguistic features each of the seventy participants produced. However, rather than assigning a score of 1 for each of the thirty-one features, a score of 2 was assigned for each of the calque features present; each of the non-calque features present received a score of 1. Of the thirty-one features examined, eleven were calques. Therefore, possible Calque-Weighted Total CLF Scores could range from 0 to 42. The Calque-Weighted Total CLF Scores of the seventy participants ranged from 12 to 36. Of the eleven calques, participants produced as few as three and as many as ten in their speech.

Motivation for weighing the eleven calque features more heavily came from the fact that many of the twenty non-calque cross-linguistic features may appear in dialects of Spanish that are not Andean and have not been influenced by any indigenous language, possibly due to general simplification processes or natural changes in these other Spanish dialects (i.e. Gutiérrez (2003) for US Spanish and Santoro (2007) for Puerto Rican Spanish). Also, many of the twenty non-calque features may appear in the interlanguage of those learning Spanish as a nonnative language, regardless of the learners' native language (Cuza 2010; Martinez-Gibson 2011; Montrul, Foote, and Perpiñán 2008; Montrul 2011; Santoro 2011). The presence of each of the twenty non-calque features is considered as contributing to an overall measure of Quechua to Spanish CLI for these participants because, while the occurrence of these twenty non-calque features may not be solely due to Quechua influence, there is evidence and reasoning to explain the presence of each of these features in Andean Spanish as resulting from CLI from Quechua. This evidence and reasoning is presented in Feke (2004). As the use of calques of Quechua expressions in Andean Spanish may be explained only as resulting from CLI from Quechua and a Quechua mindset, weighing the presence of the eleven calque features more heavily could produce a more accurate representation of the level of CLI from Quechua present in the Spanish of each of the participants.

In this case, a reliability analysis was also carried out for the Calque-Weighted Total CLF Score, resulting in a Cronbach's alpha coefficient of 0.62. This result is slightly less reliable than that calculated for the Total CLF Score.

Implicational-Weighted Total CLF Score

A third alternative to the Total CLF Score and the Calque-Weighted CLF Score, the Implicational-Weighted Total CLF Score, was calculated for each of the seventy participants. As for the first two measures, it was noted which of the thirty-one cross-linguistic features each of the participants produced. However, rather than assigning scores of 1 or 2 for each of the features, a Guttman procedure, also referred to as implicational scaling (Hatch and Lazaraton 1991, 204–16), was performed to determine the weights of each of the thirty-one features. In order to create an implicational scale for the thirty-one cross-linguistic features, it was first necessary to count how many participants used each of the features at least once in their speech. Figure 7.1 orders the cross-linguistic features from those produced by the fewest number of participants to those produced by the greatest number of participants. Having already calculated a Total CLF Score for each of the participants, the seventy participants and thirty-one features were then sorted by Total CLF Score and by the number of participants producing each feature, as shown in figure 7.2.

The right-most column of figure 7.2, the sum column, displays the sums of the features produced by each of the seventy participants (i.e., the sums contained in this column are the participants' Total CLF Scores). The sum column along the bottom of figure 7.2 displays the total number of participants that produced each of the thirty-one features.

In general, the lower right-hand section of figure 7.2 contains mostly patterned cells, indicating the presence of these features in the speech of the participants, whereas the upper left-hand portion of the figure contains mostly empty cells, indicating the absence of those features. A general diagonal line separates the patterned and empty cells, starting from the upper right and progressing toward the lower left. The thick black line drawn through the table displays where this diagonal line would fall were the division between the patterned and empty cells to form a perfect idealized matrix. To place the diagonal line, one counts the number of cells equal to the sum in the right-most column from the right to the left side of the figure. For example, in the first two rows at the top of figure 7.2, which have sums of 9, the division line falls on the left edges of the ninth cells counting from the right edge of figure 7.2 to the left. The fact that there are many empty cells to the right of the idealized diagonal line (212 errors) and many patterned cells to the left of this line (also 212 errors) indicates that these data do not represent a perfectly idealized implicational hierarchy.

To determine the level of scalability for this data, it was necessary to calculate a variety of statistics, including the coefficient of reproducibility (Hatch and Lazaraton, 1991, 210–12), which reveals how reliably one can predict a participant's performance based on that participant's position in the matrix.

Here, a coefficient of reproducibility of 0.805 indicates that it is possible to accurately predict which features the participants will produce based on their position in the matrix roughly 80 percent of the time. Hatch and Lazaraton explain, "By

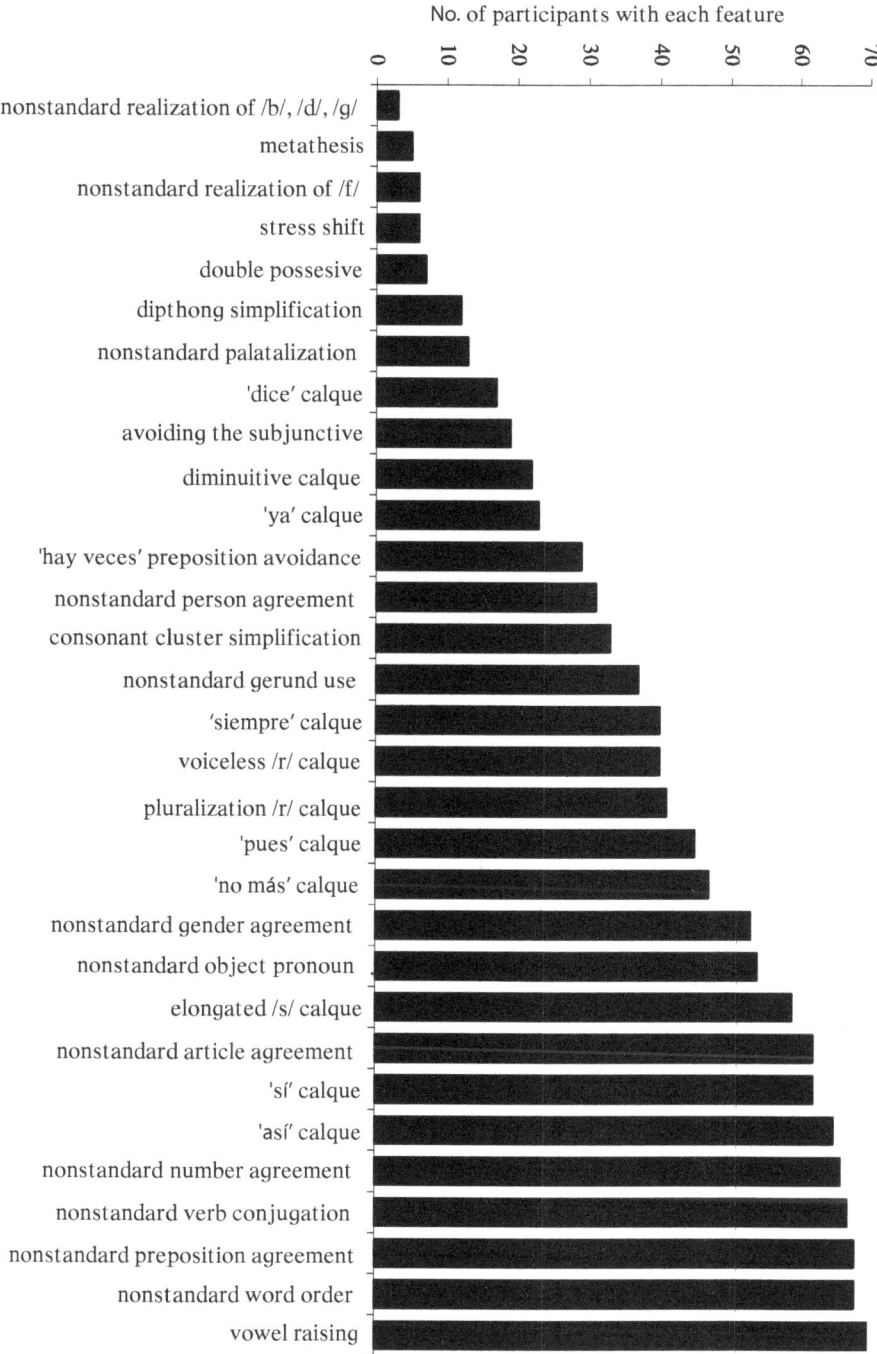

Figure 7.1 Number of Participants Using the Thirty-One Features

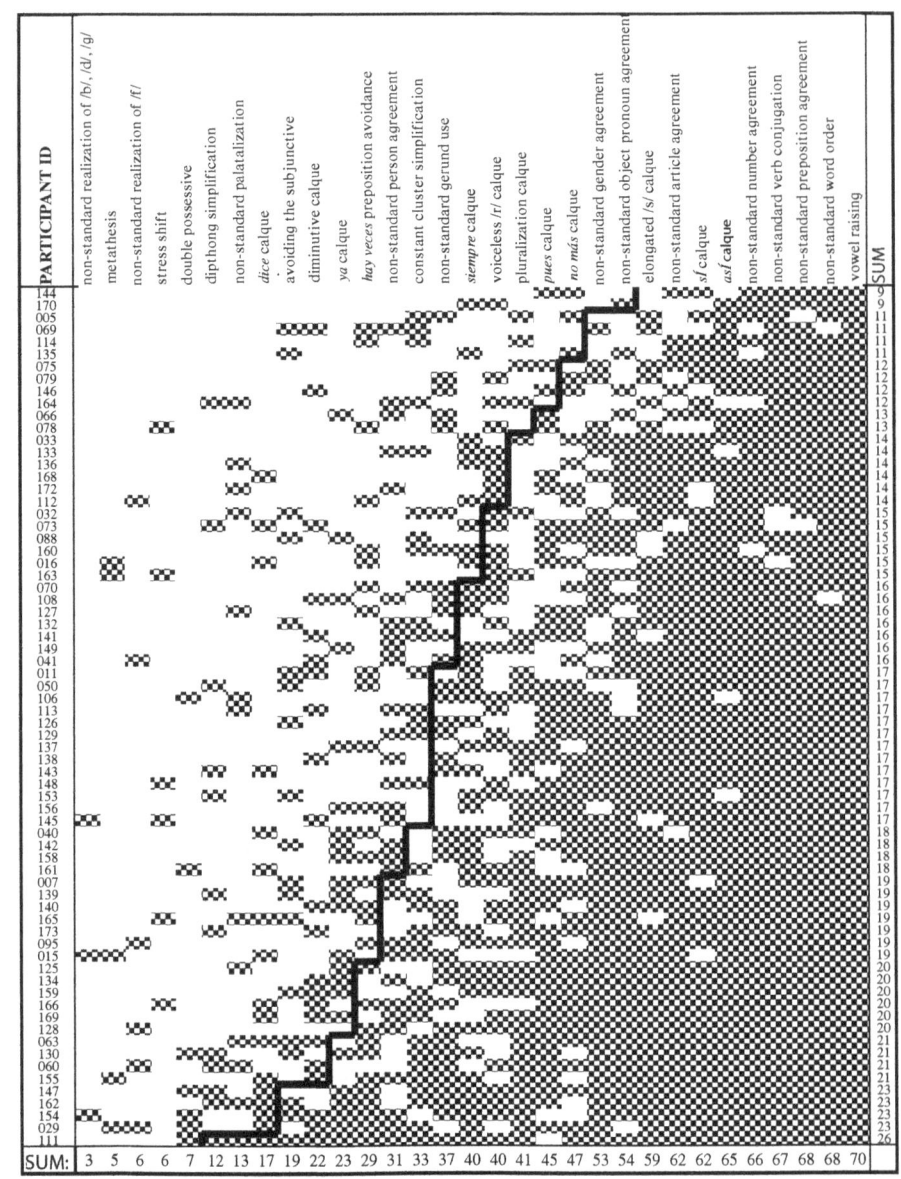

Figure 7.2 Cross-Linguistic Feature Implicational Scale

convention, mathematicians have determined that the value of the coefficient of reproducibility should be over .90 before the scale can be considered 'valid'" (1991, 210). Therefore, mathematically, this implicational scale would not be considered valid.

The minimum marginal reproducibility is a measure of how well one can predict the participants' performance without considering the errors that occur when the participants behave in ways not predicted by the model (Hatch and Lazaraton 1991, 211). For valid implicational scales, the minimum marginal reproducibility must be less than the coefficient of reproducibility. Here, the minimum marginal reproducibility of 0.783 was less than the coefficient of reproducibility.

The coefficient of scalability " . . . indicates whether a given set of features are truly scalable (and unidimensional)" (Hatch and Lazaraton 1991, 212). The coefficient of scalability for these data is 0.102. As Hatch and Lazaraton explain, "Statisticians have determined that the coefficient of scalability must be above .60 before we claim scalability" (1991, 212). Therefore, the current data do not show a clear unidimensional scale and it is not possible to claim scalability.

While it is true that it is not statistically possible to claim scalability, based on the appearance of the data in figure 7.2 and the fact that the coefficient of reproducibility, 0.805, is quite close to the 0.90 threshold, it is proposed here that there is an implicational trend in the data, such that participants who manifest a particular feature 'A' will also generally manifest those features ordered to the right of 'A' in figure 7.2. Therefore, an Implicational-Weighted CLF Score was calculated for comparison to the previous two CLF Scores.

Based on the Guttman procedure, different weights were determined for each of the thirty-one features, which were then summed in order to calculate an Implicational-Weighted Total CLF Score for each of the seventy participants. In order to determine the weight for each feature, the following equation was employed:

$$\text{Implicational weight for each feature} = 100\left(1 - \frac{\text{number of subjects with each feature}}{70}\right)$$

The following example demonstrates the use of this equation. In figure 7.2, it is possible to observe that three participants (4 percent of the total sample) manifested alternate realizations of the Spanish phonemes, /b/, /d/, or /g/. One minus 0.04 is equal to 0.96. For ease of calculation, 0.96 is multiplied by 100, resulting in 96. Therefore, 96 is the implicational-weighted value for the alternate realization of /b/, /d/, /g/ feature. In order to find each participant's Implicational-Weighted Total CLF Score, the implicational-weighted values of all features produced by that participant were added together. Possible Implicational-Weighted Total CLF Scores could range from 0 to 1,430. The Implicational-Weighted Total CLF Scores of the seventy participants ranged from 108 to 1,023.

A reliability analysis was carried out for the Implicational-Weighted Total CLF Score as well, resulting in a Cronbach's alpha coefficient of 0.58. This result is less reliable than those calculated for the Total CLF Score and the Calque-Weighted Total CLF Score.

Conclusion

Although both the Calque-Weighted and Implicational-Weighted Total CLF Scores were conceived of as possible improvements upon the Total CLF Score, the robustness of the Total CLF Score was supported as an adequate measure of the Quechua to Spanish CLI present in the speech of the seventy participants. Reliability analyses using Cronbach's alpha indicated that the Total CLF Score was the most reliable of the three measures with a coefficient of 0.65, compared with a coefficient of 0.62 for the Calque-Weighted Total CLF Score and a coefficient of 0.58 for the Implicational-Weighted Total CLF Score.

In assessing the robustness of the Implicational-Weighted Total CLF Score, it was determined that although the data do not show a clear, unidimensional scale and it is not possible to mathematically claim scalability, the coefficient of reproducibility of 0.805 indicates that it is possible to accurately predict which features the participants will produce based on their position in the matrix roughly 80 percent of the time. For this reason, it is proposed that there is a general implicational trend in the data such that participants who manifest a particular feature 'A' will also often produce those features ordered to the right of 'A' in figure 7.2. Therefore, it is possible to assume that two participants with equal Total CLF Scores generally produce similar sets of features and so may be treated as having similar levels of Quechua influence present in their Spanish. Furthermore, a higher Total CLF Score may indeed indicate more Quechua influence than a lower Total CLF Score, as generally the higher Total CLF Score will include the features that make up the lower Total CLF Score.

Limitations and Suggestions for Future Research

It is important to note that each of the three measures of Quechua to Spanish CLI presented here has the same limitation; namely, that a single instance of each of the thirty-one features in the speech of the participants is interpreted as indicating CLI. Therefore, although the participants generally produced the majority of the thirty-one features numerous times throughout the course of their speech, the relative prevalence of the thirty-one features in the Spanish of the seventy participants was not determined. In other words, frequencies of the thirty-one features were not calculated; rather, it was noted whether the participants produced each of the features at least once.

Consequently, there is an assumption here that single instances of the features are not simply flukes or mistakes but rather do indicate that the thirty-one features are present in the Quechua-influenced Spanish grammars of the participants. While this assumption may appear problematic, language contact scholars, such as Escobar (1997, 2000), Klee and Ocampo (1995), Lee (1997), Lipski (1996), Odlin (1989), and Zavala (2001), often make no claims regarding the frequencies of cross-linguistic features present in their subjects' speech but instead cite specific examples as indicating the presence of CLI. Clyne's (2003, 76) definition of transfer also supports the approaches presented here: "A 'transfer' is an instance of transference, where the form, feature or construction has been taken over by the speaker from another language, whatever the motives or explanation for this." Therefore, according to this definition, even a single instance of transfer may be taken as indicating CLI. Since Andean Spanish includes pervasive influence from Quechua at all levels of the linguistic hierarchy, a measure of CLI that takes into account a broad range of features, like the Total CLF Score, may be more representative than other measures that include the frequency of use of a more limited range of CLI features.

An additional limitation of the approaches presented here is that they do not take into account the fact that some participants produced more speech than others in response to the interview questions. Participants who spoke more overall had more opportunities than those who spoke less to demonstrate their use of the thirty-one cross-linguistic features. In response to this limitation, one future direction for this research could be to determine the total number of words spoken by the participants during the interview and present their level of CLI as a ratio of the number of different features that they produced to their total number of words produced. In their examination of CLI as measured through the use of borrowings and lexical inventions by Catalán-Spanish learners of English, in addition to calculating the total number of instances of borrowings and lexical inventions, Navés, Miralpeix, and Celaya (2005, 120) determine percentages per total number of words and state, "The percentage of borrowings per total number of words is seldom reported in the literature but is highly revealing (of the participants' degree of CLI)." Although determining the total number of words spoken by participants appears straightforward, this task would not be trivial, as this method would require some important decision-making regarding what constitutes a word; for example, false starts, stuttering, and repetition of words may or may not be considered as unique words. In their case study of a Hong Kong, Cantonese-English bilingual child, Yip and Matthews (2000, 197) acknowledge that the problem of deciding what constitutes a word has not been resolved in general or with specific regard to Chinese.

With respect to the limitation of not taking into account the different amounts of speech produced by the participants, another possible avenue for future investigation could be to find the frequency of each feature produced by each participant and then to determine the ratio of these frequencies to the number of total possible environments in which each of the features could have been produced. Nakahama uses this approach to investigate CLI on referent introduction and tracking in oral narratives in Japanese as a second language and states, "Due to differences in the length of narratives, average percentages of the proportional use of the forms in context, instead of the raw number of their occurrences, were used as the dependent variables to ensure fair comparisons" (2009, 246). In the case of this work, while establishing possible environments for the production of the cross-linguistic features might be straightforward for some features (for example, counting each instance where /f/ would be produced in standard Spanish), this may prove more difficult in the case of other features. For example, regarding the calques for the Quechua evidential markers, it may not always be possible to know when a speaker is describing an event in Spanish that was witnessed directly or became known to the speaker second-hand. A difference in terms of information source is one factor that may lead Quechua speakers to choose one evidential marker over another and, therefore, to choose one evidential calque in Spanish over another.

In general, as CLI due to language contact is a worldwide phenomenon, improving methods for measuring CLI is of widespread importance for linguistic research as well as for a variety of possible applications. For example, having a measure of the degree of CLI among speakers may aid in the development of appropriate pedagogical tools for second language acquisition. Also, by improving methods for measuring CLI, sociolinguistic studies of identity construction and maintenance may be supported, since, with a reliable measure of CLI, it is possible to investigate correlations with social characteristics and language attitude. Whether the presence of CLI features is due to a deliberate decision on the part of speakers or to processes beyond their conscious control, CLI features serve to index speakers' identity. In the case of this work, when Quechua speakers exhibit influence from Quechua in their Spanish, they index their identity as Quechua speakers. If these speakers do purposefully incorporate CLI features from Quechua into their Spanish, rather than demonstrating a lack of skill in Spanish, these features may instead be taken as indicating skillful use of the speakers' linguistic repertoire in order to express their identity and group membership in much the same way as has been suggested for the use of intentional code-switching (De Fina 2007; Thompson 2011).

APPENDIX
Language Attitudes Interview (English translation)

True/False

1. I can express myself better in Quechua.
2. I speak more in Quechua than in Spanish.
3. Young people speak less Quechua than adults.
4. Young people don't speak Quechua well.
5. Quechua is used more in the city.
6. Spanish is used more in the countryside.
7. All students in Peru should learn Quechua.
8. All children in Peru should have the opportunity to receive their educations through the means of Quechua.
9. Spanish is more important than Quechua.
10. I can always say the same things in Spanish and in Quechua.
11. Spanish is more useful than Quechua.
12. Knowledge of Quechua can be important at work.

Narrative Questions

13. Which language do you prefer? Why?
14. Which language do you use more on a daily basis? Why?

15. Which language is more important? Why?
16. Which language is more beautiful? Why?
17. Do you listen to Quechua on the radio? How often?
18. Do you read the newspaper or anything else in Quechua? How often?
19. What is the Quechua culture like?
20. Do you identify yourself with the Quechua culture? Why?
21. If you didn't speak Quechua, do you feel that you would still be able to identify yourself with the Quechua culture? Why?
22. What will your future job be?
23. Are you going to use Spanish in the future in your work? How?
24. Are you going to use Quechua in the future in your work? How?
25. Why do some Quechua speakers deny that they speak their language?
26. Is it important to speak Spanish? Why?
27. Have you ever denied that you speak Quechua? Why?
28. When are you proud of speaking Quechua?
29. Would you vote for a Quechua-speaking candidate? Why?
30. Do Spanish-speakers hold prejudices against Quechua speakers? Why?
31. Do people value that which has to do with the Incas? Why?
32. Are Quechua-speakers of a different race than Spanish speakers? Why?
33. Which aspects of the Quechua culture are bad?
34. Which aspects of the Quechua culture are good?

Note
1. This work draws from the author's doctoral dissertation (Feke 2004).

REFERENCES
Clyne, Michael. 2003. *Dynamics of Language Contact.* Cambridge, UK: Cambridge University Press.
Cusihuaman, Antonio. 2001. *Gramática quechua, Cuzco Collao, segunda edición.* Cuzco, Peru: Centro de Estudios Regionales Andinos "Bartolomé de Las Casas."
Cuza, Alejandro. 2010. "The L2 acquisition of aspectual properties in Spanish." *Canadian Journal of Linguistics* 55 (2):181–208.
De Fina, Anna. 2007. "Code-switching and the construction of ethnic identity in a community of practice." *Language in Society* 36: 371–92.
de Granda, Germán. 2001. *Estudios de lingüística andina.* Lima, Perú: Pontificia Universidad Católica del Perú.
Escobar, Alberto. 1978. *Variaciones sociolingüísticas del castellano en el Perú.* Lima, Perú: Instituto de Estudios Peruanos.
Escobar, Anna María. 1997. "Contrastive and innovative uses of the present perfect and the preterite in Spanish in contact with Quechua." *Hispania, American Association of Teachers of Spanish and Portuguese* 80: 859–70.
———. 2000. *Contacto social y lingüístico, el español en contacto con el quechua en el Perú.* Lima, Perú: Pontificia Universidad Católica del Perú Fondo Editorial.
Feke, Marilyn S. 2004. "Quechua to Spanish Cross-linguistic Influence among Cuzco Quechua-Spanish Bilinguals: The Case of Epistemology." PhD dissertation, University of Pittsburgh.

Gay, L. R., and Peter Airasian. 2003. *Educational Research*. Upper Saddle River, NJ: Merrill Prentice Hall.
Gutiérrez, Manuel J. 2003. "Simplification and innovation in US Spanish." *Multilingua* 22: 169–84.
Hatch, Evelyn, and Anne Lazaraton. 1991. *The Research Manual: Design and Statistics for Applied Linguistics*. Newbury House.
Hornberger, Nancy. 1989. *Haku Yachaywasiman: la educación bilingüe y el futuro del quechua en Puno*. Lima/Puno: Programa de Educación Bilingüe de Puno.
Hurley, Joni Kay. 1995. "The impact of Quichua on verb forms used in Spanish requests in Otavalo, Ecuador." In *Spanish in Four Continents: Studies in Language Contact and Bilingualism*, 39–51, edited by Carmen Silva-Corvalán. Washington DC: Georgetown University Press.
Klee, Carol, and Alicia Ocampo. 1995. "The expression of past reference in Spanish narratives of Spanish-Quechua bilingual speakers." In *Spanish in Four Continents: Studies in Language Contact and Bilingualism*, 52–70, edited by Carmen Silva-Corvalán. Washington DC: Georgetown University Press.
Lee, Tae Yoon. 1997. *Morfosintaxis amerindias en el español americano, Desde la perspectiva del quechua*. Madrid: Ediciones Clásicas, Universidad Complutense de Madrid.
Lipski, John M. 1996. *El español de América*. Madrid: Ediciones Cátedra.
Mamani P., Mario, and Virginia Chávez P. 2001. *Contacto lingüístico, Converge diverge el préstamo lexical del castellano en el quechua*. La Paz, Bolivia: Universidad Mayor de San Andrés.
Manley, Marilyn. 2007. "Cross-linguistic influence of the Cuzco Quechua epistemic system on Andean Spanish." In *Spanish in Contact: Policy, Social, and Linguistic Inquiries*, 191–209, edited by Kim Potowski and Richard Cameron. Amsterdam: John Benjamins.
Martinez-Gibson, Elizabeth. 2011. "A comparative study on gender agreement errors in the spoken Spanish of heritage speakers and second language learners." *Porta Linguarum* 15: 177–93.
Montrul, Silvina, Rebecca Foote, and Silvia Perpiñán. 2008. "Gender agreement in adult second language learners and Spanish heritage speakers: The effects of age and context of acquisition." *Language Learning* 58 (3): 503–53.
Montrul, Silvina. 2011. "Morphological errors in Spanish second language learners and heritage speakers." *Studies in Second Language Acquisition* 33: 163–92.
Nakahama, Yuko. 2009. "Cross-linguistic influence on referent introduction and tracking in Japanese as a second language." *The Modern Language Journal* 93 (2): 241–60.
Navés, Teresa, Immaculada Miralpeix, and M. Luz Celaya. 2005. "Who transfers more . . . and what? Cross-linguistic influence in relation to school grade and language dominance in EFL." *International Journal of Multilingualism* 2 (2): 113–34.
Odlin, Terrence. 1989. *Language Transfer: Cross-linguistic Influence in Language Learning*. Cambridge Applied Linguistics: Cambridge University Press.
Rofes Chávez, Maite. 2002. *¿Estás bien? CAITH: La cultura del afecto con trabajadoras del hogar*. Cuzco, Perú: CAITH.
Romero, Francisco Carranza. 1993. *Resultados lingüísticos del contacto quechua y español*. Trujillo, Perú: Editorial Libertad EIRL.
Sánchez, Liliana, and José Camacho. 1996. "'*De mi padre, su padre*': The syntax of word order transfer and person agreement in Andean L2 Spanish." *Proceedings of the Annual Boston University Conference on Language Development* 20 (1): 155–66.
Santoro, Maurizio. 2007. "Puerto Rican Spanish: A case of partial restructuring." *Hybrido: arte y literatura* 9: 47–57.
———. 2011. "L2 acquisition of Spanish clitic case morphology: A generative approach." *Journal of Language and Culture* 2 (4): 56–66.
Thompson, Gregory L. 2011. "Coding-switching as style-shifting." *International Journal of Language Studies* 5 (4): 1–18.
Vassberg, Liliane M. 1993. *Alsatian Acts of Identity: Language Use and Language Attitudes in Alsace*. Multilingual Matters LTD, Clevedon.
Yip, Virginia, and Stephen Matthews. 2000. "Syntactic transfer in a Cantonese-English bilingual child." *Bilingualism: Language and Cognition* 3: 193–208.

Zavala, Virginia. 2001. "Borrowing evidential functions from Quechua: The role of *pues* as a discourse marker in Andean Spanish." *Journal of Pragmatics*. 33: 999–1023.

Zúñiga, Madeleine. 1974. "La educación bilingüe y la enseñanza de pronunciación castellana a niños quechua-hablantes." PhD dissertation, Universidad Nacional Mayor de San Marcos Centro de Investigación de Lingüística Aplicada, Lima, Perú.

8

Speedup versus Automatization

What Role Does Learner Proficiency Play?

JESSICA G. COX AND ANNE M. CALDERÓN
Georgetown University

THE TRANSITION FROM CONTROLLED processing to automatized processing in L2 acquisition is characterized by moving from slow, effortful processing to quicker processing outside of conscious control. However, this has been difficult to operationalize since it is not reportable. The current work builds on Hulstijn, van Gelderen, and Schoonen's (2009) attempt to operationalize and quantify the two. The distinction between automatization and speedup is important within the SLA field because it reflects a change in the learner's mind.

Phillips et al. (2004) reported that the more proficient the learner, the higher the level of automatization; however, Hulstijn, van Gelderen, and Schoonen (2009) failed to find the same result in a longitudinal study. Previous studies, however, have not included independent assessments of L2 proficiency nor have they controlled for lexical knowledge.

The present study investigated the role played by L2 proficiency in the transition from speedup of controlled processes to automatization. One hundred and three L1 English university students enrolled in either intermediate, advanced, or advanced+ Spanish, completed L1 and L2 semantic decision tasks that recorded speed and accuracy (based on Segalowitz and Freed 2004). Proficiency groups were determined by class level and justified with an independent measure (*Diploma de Español como Lengua Extranjera*) taken by a subset of participants. Speedup and automatization were operationalized following Hulstijn, van Gelderen, and Schoonen (2009). Results showed evidence of both speedup and automatization at all proficiency levels; Fisher's z analyses revealed that both automatization and speedup decreased in the advanced+ group. We conclude that there are significant amounts of automatization and speedup at all levels, though we hint at a change between advanced and advanced+ proficiencies.

Theoretical Foundation

The acquisition of a first (L1) and second language (L2), although different in many ways, are both examples of the acquisition of skills occurring in a gradual manner.

Automatization, or the routinization and restructuring of component processes, is a key element of skilled behavior.

There are two main theories that attempt to define automaticity as it relates to skill acquisition in psychology literature. Both consider automatic processing to be effortless. Anderson's (1983) adaptive control of thought theory posits that automatization begins with controlled and conscious processes of declarative knowledge and slowly proceeds to processing of routines without attention. In contrast, Logan (1998) views automatization as starting off with rules of thumb that eventually progress to higher order "instances." These instances finally become strong enough to cause a bypass of rule application and the learner depends solely on the retrieval of the stored instances.

Fast processing, as coined by Segalowitz and Segalowitz (1993), is a concept central to skill acquisition. While automatization involves the "bypassing of serial execution of component processes" (Hulstijn, van Gelderen, and Schoonen 2009, 557), fast processing (speedup) is the "speeding up of essentially all component processes that make up the execution of a task in the earliest stage of skill acquisition" (Hulstijn, van Gelderen, and Schoonen 2009, 557).

Measuring automaticity and speedup requires an understanding of the measurement of skill acquisition, which can be demonstrated empirically by a decrease in time required to perform an acquired action as practice in the skill increases (Hulstijn, van Gelderen, and Schoonen 2009). Accuracy and speed (reaction time [RT]) on speeded linguistic tasks such as lexical and semantic decision tasks are used to measure linguistic skill. The relationship between mean RT and the standard deviation of the mean (SD_{RT}) is, in most cases, linear: with practice, participants reduce their RT and reduce the variability in their RT (i.e., SD_{RT}) (Hulstijn, van Gelderen, and Schoonen 2009). Given this, Segalowitz and Segalowitz (1993) distinguished between automatization and speedup by proposing that in the case of speedup, mean RT and SD_{RT} will each be reduced without a change in the coefficient of variance (CV_{RT}), calculated as SD divided by mean RT. CV_{RT} is a measure of the variability at each level of latency (RT); in other words, it measures the efficiency of processing. In contrast, since automatization is characterized by the routinization or elimination of component processes (Hulstijn, van Gelderen, and Schoonen 2009), in this case processing is more efficient, so mean RT, SD_{RT}, and CV_{RT} will all be reduced. This also yields an increasing correlation between mean RT and CV_{RT}. Research investigating speedup and automatization can be cross-sectional (individuals at differing levels of skill tested at one time) or longitudinal (same participants tested at various points in time as their skill increases).

The distinction between automatization and speedup is important for L2 skill acquisition and skill assessment. For example, automatization implies that word recognition moves directly from a printed word to meaning activation without passing through translation into the L1 or stages of phonological encoding (Hulstijn, van Gelderen, and Schoonen 2009).

Empirical Evidence for the Disassociation between Automaticity and Speedup

Several investigators have documented both automaticity and speedup; the majority of the results support a dissociation between the two. As Hulstijn, van Gelderen, and Schoonen (2009) stated, "The crucial test for whether there is a difference between speedup and automatization . . . is whether, longitudinally, a decrease in mean RT produced a significant decrease in CV with an accompanying increase in CV-RT correlation" (563).

Segalowitz and Segalowitz (1993) tested the ability of sixty-six L1 French students—whose English proficiency ranged from beginner to near-fluent—to complete two tasks. The nonlinguistic signal detection task required participants to press a button as soon as they saw a square on a computer screen; a simple RT task such as this one was not expected to show differential use of effortful processes. The lexical decision task contained English words (baseline words and repetition words), as well as pronounceable nonwords, and it required subjects to determine whether each item was in fact a word. Latency to respond to baseline words was the indicator of level of word-recognition skill. Latency to repeated words was used to investigate the relationship between RT and CV when practice effects were present. Given that making a lexical decision is a more cognitively complex task than the first task, it was expected that less-skilled participants would be more dependent on effortful processes. This, in turn, would result in CV correlating significantly with RT across individuals. Results from the signal detection task showed that the standard deviation correlated significantly with RT ($r = 0.61$) but CV did not, thereby showing evidence of speedup but not automatization. An analysis of the baseline items in the lexical decision task showed that the standard deviation correlated significantly with RT, thus supporting the linearity assumption, and CV correlated significantly with RT. The authors concluded that skilled (faster) participants used fewer slower processes. Repetition data from initially skilled and less-skilled participants were analyzed separately. Given that CV correlated significantly with RT for the skilled participants at the first and last presentations, the authors interpreted this as evidence for differential use of effortful processes among skilled participants. Data from less-skilled participants at the first presentation did not show a differential use of effortful processes (i.e., RT did not correlate with CV); however, the last presentation among less-skilled participants did show a positive correlation between CV and RT, thus providing support for the idea that the less-skilled participants showed gains in perceptual fluency with repeated items.

Segalowitz, Watson, and Segalowitz (1995) looked again at automaticity versus speedup in a study of a single native Turkish learner of English with a moderate-to-high reading level in his L2. As in Segalowitz and Segalowitz (1993), a positive correlation between CV and RT defined automatization. The participant performed a visual lexical decision task including previously viewed words and control words (words he had not seen before) four times over three weeks. CV of previously viewed words decreased significantly but CV of control words did not. The authors concluded that purposeful reading of selected words resulted in greater automaticity in an L2 learner with a moderate-to-high reading level.

Segalowitz, Segalowitz, and Wood (1998) tested the performance of 105 L1 English learners of French on a visual lexical decision task spanning six sessions over one year. Participants' fluency, as determined by a self-rating questionnaire, ranged from beginning to near-fluent. Participants performed a visual lexical decision task; the RT of baseline words was used to divide them into an initially fast group and an initially slow group. Automaticity was defined as a change in RT accompanied by a change in CV_{RT}. The residual RT and residual CV were correlated for both the initially fast and initially slow groups. The stability of reaction time increased (i.e., CV decreased) as participants repeated the task, showing evidence of automatization.

Segalowitz and Freed (2004) used CV to measure L2 skill acquisition by comparing a study abroad group ($n = 22$) and an at-home group ($n = 18$) of L1 English learners of Spanish. Although they considered several dependent variables, only the measure of lexical efficiency is reported here. Participants completed a two-option, forced-choice animacy judgment task in the L1 and the L2, both before and after a semester during which the study abroad group was in Spain and the at-home group continued studying Spanish in the US. Both reaction time and accuracy were recorded. The English words were high-frequency; the task in Spanish consisted mostly of translations of the English words. Two Spanish instructors judged the Spanish words as likely to be known by lower-level Spanish learners. Data from participants with an error rate greater than 21 percent were excluded from the analyses. Lexical access was measured via a residualized gain score for each participant. Efficiency of processing was operationalized by CV_{RT}. Results showed significant Language × Time interactions for response time (lexical access speed) and CV (lexical access efficiency). The significant interaction for response time indicated an overall gain in speed of L2 lexical access over time. The significant interaction for CV showed an overall gain in L2 processing efficiency. Unfortunately, correlations between CV and mean RT were not reported. No significant main effects were found for context.

Akamatsu (2008) studied practice effects on a lexical decision task and the resultant RTs and CVs. ESL participants ($n = 49$) were trained on a set of vocabulary items and then tested on a lexical decision task with these items (and fillers). Training consisted of presentation of strings of words without spaces between them in which participants marked word boundaries. Testing consisted of pre- and posttreatment lexical decision tasks separated by seven weeks. Analyses showed a weak positive correlation between RT and CV for low-frequency items at both testing times, but no correlation for high-frequency items. Also, CV scores significantly decreased from pre- to posttest for low frequency words, suggesting that processing low-frequency items is automatized, while processing high-frequency items is merely sped up.

An experiment from Hulstijn, van Gelderen, and Schoonen (2009) failed to find concrete evidence for automatization. Participants ($n = 41$) were eighth-grade students in Amsterdam with an average of three and a half years of English instruction who completed a visual lexical decision task in English before and after training aimed at automatization. Automatization was operationalized as a reduction in mean RT, SD_{RT}, and CV_{RT}. Results showed that participants achieved greater accuracy after the training, but only two of six analyses showed a significant reduction in CV: one that excluded data from participants with more than two misses and one that additionally replaced the highest and lowest outliers from each participant. Other experiments reported in Hulstijn, van Gelderen, and Schoonen (2009) are discussed in the next section.

In summary, there seems to be little doubt that automatization occurs in L2 learning; moreover, Segalowitz and Segalowitz (1993), Segalowitz, Watson, and Segalowitz (1995), Segalowitz, Segalowitz, and Wood (1998), and Segalowitz and Freed (2004) all found quantified evidence for automatization. Only results from Hulstijn, van Gelderen, and Schoonen (2009) failed to support a dissociation between automatization and speedup. Furthering research in this area can help identify ways in which quantified automatization can be used to measure L2 learning in a more fine-grained way than traditional test scores or percentage of target-like use.

Empirical Evidence for the Role of Proficiency in Automaticity

Previous studies have found some support that L2 proficiency level may be associated with the extent of automatization in the interlanguage.

Phillips et al. (2004) found convincing evidence for automatization at higher proficiency levels. Their two experiments consisted of thirty-seven and thirty L1 English participants (for Experiments 1 and 2, respectively) who were more proficient and less proficient users of L2 French. A semantic decision task in Experiment 1 asked participants to make living or nonliving judgments to English and French nouns, all of which were presented twice: once primed by a semantic association and once unprimed. RTs and CVs revealed that regardless of proficiency level, participants had lower CVs in L1 than in L2, showing that they had greater automaticity in their L1 than in their L2. Furthermore, there was a significant interaction between language and proficiency, indicating that only the more proficient participants had similar CVs in L1 and L2. The second experiment examined electrophysiological correlates of semantic priming by looking at electrical brain activity; more specifically, it examined N400 amplitude, latency, and variability, as reflected in a CV analysis of the N400 waveform. The procedure and design were otherwise nearly the same as the first experiment. Experiment 2 mirrored the results of Experiment 1. The authors concluded that learners with higher levels of L2 proficiency have more automatic semantic associations in the L2 than learners with lower proficiency. Harrington (2006) investigated automaticity in L2 English students of intermediate and advanced proficiency (n = 32 and 36, respectively) and native English speakers (n = 42). The L2 English participants were of varied Asian L1s. Results from a visual lexical decision task in English with four word frequency classes showed that accuracy and speed increased with proficiency level and was the highest in the native English group. Correlations between CV and RT were significant in the intermediate group for only the most frequent word class, in the advanced group for the three most frequent word classes, and in the native English group for all four word frequency classes. These results indicate greater automaticity as proficiency increases, with native speakers having higher levels of automaticity in a lexical decision task than L2 speakers.

Hulstijn, van Gelderen, and Schoonen (2009) obtained longitudinal data on automatization and speedup by following a group of 397 secondary school students over three years. Participants came from homes with a variety of non-English L1s; however, the authors declared Dutch the dominant language and English the most important L2. At the time of the first data collection, participants had an average of three and a half years of English instruction. Each year, participants completed twenty-one tests, nine of which measured RT, and, therefore, also CV. The tests included lexical decision tasks, lexical retrieval tasks, sentence verification tasks, and sentence production tasks, all in both English and Dutch, along with a language-neutral typing fluency task. Although results showed that participants became faster in both languages over time, there was a significant decrease in CV over time in only two of the nine tasks measuring CV. Contrary to what was expected based on Segalowitz and Segalowitz (1993), widespread automaticity was not documented in this study.

In summary, definitive conclusions cannot yet be made regarding the relationship between proficiency in automatization: while Harrington (2006) and Phillips et al. (2004) documented greater automatization at higher L2 proficiency levels, Hulstijn, van Gelderen, and Schoonen (2009) did not find conclusive evidence of the same.

Limitations of Previous Studies
Although a considerable amount of research has investigated automaticity as operationalized by Segalowitz and Segalowitz (1993), many of these previous studies have methodological limitations that make it difficult to compare findings across studies and reach a conclusion regarding the relationship between L2 proficiency and developing automatization as compared to speedup.

The main limitation in previous studies is the lack of an independent assessment of L2 proficiency. Many studies used the preexisting L2 proficiency levels in which students were placed at their academic institution (Harrington 2006; Hulstijn, van Gelderen, and Schoonen 2009; Segalowitz and Freed 2004; Segalowitz and Segalowitz 1993) or a self-rating scale (Phillips et al. 2004; Segalowitz, Segalowitz, and Wood 1998; Segalowitz, Watson, and Segalowitz 1995) without using an independent assessment to verify L2 proficiency level. Furthermore, proficiency was not taken into account in the majority of the previous studies (Segalowitz and Segalowitz 1993; Segalowitz, Watson, and Segalowitz 1995; Segalowitz, Segalowitz, and Wood 1998; Segalowitz and Freed, 2004; study no. 2 in Hulstijn, van Gelderen, and Schoonen 2009), even though all discussed participant L2 proficiency as it relates to automaticity. For example, Segalowitz, Segalowitz, and Wood (1998) used a five-point self-rating scale to distinguish between low and high fluency, but they did not separate their data to consider proficiency as an independent variable.

Furthermore, previous research has not always used both measures of automatization: Segalowitz and Segalowitz (1993) considered only the correlation between CV and RT, while many (Segalowitz, Watson, and Segalowitz 1995; Segalowitz and Freed 2004; Philips et al. 2004; Harrington 2006) reported significant decreases in CV without considering the relationship of CV to RT. Segalowitz, Segalowitz, and Wood (1998) found a decrease in CV within subjects across time, but did not state whether the change was significant. While Akamatsu (2008) considered both measures, the results did not follow the proposal of Segalowitz and Segalowitz (1993): although CV significantly decreased over time as expected, the CV-RT correlation also decreased when it would be expected to increase.

In addition, previous studies such as Segalowitz and Freed (2004) have seldom controlled for participant knowledge of the lexical items presented in the semantic decision tasks. This can be a limitation because a lack of knowledge of a lexical item may result in slower RT or higher error rates. Without a test of the lexical items used in the semantic decision task, the researcher cannot determine whether slower RTs are caused by this lack of knowledge or simply a slower response due to other factors.

Finally, participants' L1 was not always controlled in previous studies. For example, Harrington (2006) stated that participants had a variety of L1s; additionally, while the first study in Hulstijn, van Gelderen, and Schoonen (2009) used participants who reported speaking Dutch as their L1, the authors acknowledged that 29 percent of participants came from homes in which another language was spoken.

Rationale and Research Questions

In summary, the majority of previous studies (Segalowitz and Segalowitz 1993; Segalowitz, Watson, and Segalowitz 1995; Segalowitz, Segalowitz, and Wood 1998; Segalowitz and Freed 2004; study no. 2 in Hulstijn, van Gelderen, and Schoonen 2009) report a dissociation between automaticity and speedup in L2 learners; however, additional studies investigating learner L2 proficiency and the automaticity/speedup disassociation have failed to provide definitive conclusions. Regardless, previous research is limited by methodological issues, such as the lack of independent assessments of L2 proficiency and the use of learners with a variety of L1s. These past findings and limitations highlight the need for further investigation into the dissociation between automatization and speedup, especially as related to learner L2 proficiency. The present study therefore addresses issues raised in previous research by determining the relationship between L2 proficiency in developing speedup and automatization by asking the following research questions:

1. Is there evidence for speedup in each proficiency level as operationalized by significant correlations of L2RT with L2SD when L1RT and L1SD are partialled out?
2. Is the amount of speedup different in each proficiency level as operationalized by significantly different correlation coefficients for each proficiency group?
3. Is there evidence for automatization in each proficiency level as operationalized by significant correlations of L2RT with L2CV when L1RT and L1CV are partialled out?
4. Is the amount of automatization different in each proficiency level:
   a. as operationalized by significantly different correlation coefficients by each proficiency group?
   b. as operationalized by a decrease in L2CV when proficiency increases?

Method
Participants
This study used a cross-sectional design to investigate speedup and automatization at different levels of L2 proficiency. Participants were recruited from third- (intermediate level), fifth- (advanced level), and seventh- (advanced+ level) semester Spanish language classes at a northeastern US university. All participants were native speakers of English and had learned Spanish in the classroom. Seventeen reported having spent time in a Spanish-speaking country for the purpose of learning Spanish. Participants received extra credit for participation. Although 154 students initially reported to the data acquisition lab, only data from 103 participants were included in analyses. Participants' data were excluded from analyses if they were native speakers of a language other than English, did not complete all parts of the study, or had error rates of 20 percent or higher in at least one of the semantic decision tasks. Table 8.1 reports participant characteristics for each proficiency level. Most participants were women, reflecting the tendency for women to outnumber men in advanced-level foreign language classes and in L2 research. As such, results may not be fully extendable to male learners.

Materials
Diploma de Español como Lengua Extranjera (DELE). The DELE was used as the independent assessment of L2 Spanish proficiency. It serves as the official accreditation of expertise in the Spanish language, and it is issued and recognized by the Ministry of Education, Culture, and Sport of Spain (www.dele.org). There are six tests, each corresponding to a different level as described by the Common European Framework of Reference for Languages. The current study used the Grammar and Vocabulary section of the B2-level Grammar and Vocabulary test. L2 learners placing at this level show sufficient linguistic ability to perform in communication circumstances that do not require specialized use of the language. This part of the test consists of sixty multiple choice questions. For each question, the test-taker chooses the correct word to fill in the blank in the context of either a two-line dialogue or an expository text on the history of salsa music.

The B2-level Grammar and Vocabulary test was chosen to verify participants' existing proficiency groups because two instructors of Spanish judged it able to distinguish well between intermediate and advanced proficiency levels.

Table 8.1.
Participant characteristics by proficiency level

Level	N (women)	Mean age (min, max)	Mean days abroad (min, max)
Intermediate	23 (16)	19.1 (18, 21)	2.6 (0, 60)
Advanced	49 (31)	19.0 (18, 26)	8.9 (0, 90)
Advanced +	36 (25)	19.2 (18, 21)	8.0 (0, 96)
Total	103 (70)	19.1 (18, 26)	7.1 (0, 96)

Semantic decision tasks. This task was adapted from Segalowitz and Freed (2004); their stimuli were balanced for frequency and similarity between L1 and L2 and had been used with a similar sample. Stimuli were presented with an appropriate definite or indefinite article (half with indefinite articles and half with definite) to highlight which language the word belonged to and to mark English words as nouns and not verbs. The task consisted of two blocks: one in English and one in Spanish, with the order of blocks counterbalanced between participants. The English block formed the baseline for analysis and the Spanish block functioned as the experimental block. This allowed for within-subject controls rather than resorting to comparisons to likely monolingual native speakers as controls (as in Harrington 2006), as well as controlling for individual differences that stem from causes other than L2 processing, such as handedness, fine motor skills, and working memory capacity. Two native English speakers rejected both "the maple" and "a maple" as stand-alone nouns, so this item was removed from the stimulus list. This resulted in ninety-nine items forming the English task (forty-nine animate and fifty inanimate). Due to a technical error, the Spanish animate noun *la abeja* ("the bee") had to be removed from analyses, resulting in ninety-nine items in the Spanish block (forty-nine animate and fifty inanimate). Each language block was preceded by a six-item practice session. The task was administered using SuperLab 4.0 and participants had 1500 ms to respond to each item by pressing the appropriate key on the keyboard. Items were interspersed with a hash mark focal point that stayed on the screen for 500 ms. In each block, participants indicated their response by pressing either "a" with the left index finger for "animate" or ";" with the right index finger for "inanimate." The experimental stimuli provided two measures in each language: speed of lexical accesses (RT and SD_{RT}) and efficiency of lexical access (CV).

While Segalowitz and Freed did not control for vocabulary knowledge and thus lost nearly 28 percent of their data due to high error rates, the current study included a vocabulary familiarization stage prior to the semantic decision task. This stage consisted of item-by-item PowerPoint presentation of the Spanish words with an image of their referents. Each screen was presented for two seconds and appeared three times. Presentation was followed by a quiz in which the participant had to choose the correct Spanish word from two options to match each image. These tasks served as a vocabulary refresher to participants and as a way to teach any lexical items that were not familiar.

Language Contact Profile (LCP). The Language Contact Profile (Freed et al. 2004) consists of seventeen multiple-choice and fill-in-the-blank questions in English, and gathered data from participants on demographics, language-learning history, contact with native speakers, and use of language outside the classroom.

Procedure

This study consisted of one session. Each participant first read and signed an informed consent form and then completed the DELE and LCP with paper and pencil. Next, the participant completed the Familiarization Task, Familiarization Quiz, and the semantic decision tasks on the computer.

Coding and Operationalizations

DELE and Familiarization Quiz. The DELE test was scored by hand by the researchers. Scoring was dichotomous for thirteen items and polytomous for the remaining forty-seven items, all of which had either three or four options to choose from. One point was assigned for each correct answer and zero points for each incorrect answer for a possible sixty total points. The Familiarization Quiz was also scored by hand; correct answers were awarded one point and incorrect answers were awarded zero points.

Semantic decision tasks. Only RTs for accurate responses were included in analyses (i.e., when the participant responded correctly with "animate" or "inanimate"). The average L1 RT for each participant was assumed to be the baseline for that participant, and L2 performance was analyzed while controlling for L1 performance. Participants who had incorrect or no responses to more than twenty items in a language block (that is, an error rate greater than 20 percent) were not included in the final analyses; this affected seventeen participants (approximately 11 percent of the original data pool) in the L2 task. No participants had error rates above 20 percent in the L1 task.

CV was calculated as the quotient of the SD_{RT} divided by the mean RT for each participant in L1 and L2. Presence of speedup was operationalized as a significant correlation between L2RT and L2SD. Presence of automatization was operationalized as an additional significant correlation between L2RT and L2CV, when the significant correlation of L2RT and L2SD was obtained. Quantitative differences in speedup were then determined by significant differences in correlation coefficients by proficiency group; quantitative differences in automatization were determined by the same as well as by significantly different L2CV's by proficiency group.

Results

A subset of intermediate ($n = 12$) and advanced ($n = 24$) participants completed the DELE. Scores ranged from seventeen to forty-eight out of a possible sixty points ($M = 32.08$). Results from a non-parametric Spearman's correlation test between class level (intermediate or advanced) and DELE score showed a statistically significant high correlation between the two in this subset: $r_s = 0.78$, $p < 0.00$. Therefore, class level was the operationalization of proficiency in the remaining analyses.

The highest possible score on the Familiarization Quiz was 106 points, and mean scores in each proficiency level were between 105 and 106 points (Intermediate $M = 105.78$, $SD = 0.42$; Advanced $M = 105.83$, $SD = 0.52$, Advanced+ $M = 105.52$, $SD = 1.52$). Thus, all participants had comparable lexical knowledge prior to completing the semantic decision task. Descriptive statistics of RT, SD_{RT}, CV_{RT}, and error rates in the L1 and L2 are reported in table 8.2.

To answer research question 1 (RQ1), whether there was evidence of speedup at each proficiency level, correlations of L2 RT and L2 SD_{RT} were run while partialling out L1 RT and L1 SDRT. Partial correlations were large and significant at each proficiency level: for Intermediate, $r(21) = 0.94$, $p < .001$; for Advanced, $r(47) = 0.94$, $p < 0.001$; for Advanced+, $r(34) = 0.69$, $p < 0.001$. Thus, speedup was documented at all proficiency levels.

Table 8.2.
Mean RT (ms), *SD*RT, *CV*RT, and error rate for L1 and L2 (standard deviations in parentheses)

Proficiency level	L1RT	L1SD	L1CV	L1 error	L2RT	L2SD	L2CV	L2 error
Intermediate	1241.90 (63.22)	190.48 (45.31)	.14 (.04)	5.79 (3.19)	1432.88 (208.55)	219.89 (79.81)	.15 (.03)	15.67 (3.76)
Advanced	3597.87 (16553.31)	190.41 (41.98)	.15 (.04)	6.63 (4.25)	1418.84 (238.32)	209.48 (75.00)	.14 (.03)	11.57 (4.20)
Advanced+	1233.32 (64.55)	180.42 (41.28)	.15 (.03)	6.19 (4.49)	1315.48 (70.05)	166.46 (39.63)	.13 (.03)	8.00 (4.21)
All groups	2338.74 (11307.95)	187.38 (42.39)	.15 (.04)	6.30 (4.08)	1390.55 (199.55)	198.75 (70.37)	.14 (.03)	11.42 (4.93)

To answer research question 2 (RQ2), whether the extent of speedup differed by proficiency level, Fisher's *z* scores were used to compare the correlation coefficients from RQ1. The correlation coefficient of the Advanced+ group was found to be significantly lower than that of the Advanced group ($p < 0.05$) and significantly lower than that of the Intermediate group ($p < 0.05$). Intermediate and Advanced correlation coefficients did not differ significantly from each other ($p > 0.05$). This shows that while the Intermediate and Advanced conditions did not differ significantly from each other in their amount of speedup, the Advanced+ participants demonstrated less speedup than the other two proficiency groups.

Research question 3 (RQ3) asked whether automatization would be present in each proficiency level. Analyses from RQ1 already showed that L2 RT and *SD* were correlated at each level. Additional correlations of L2 RT and CV that partialled out L1 RT and CV were also significant at each proficiency level: for Intermediate, $r(21) = 0.78$, $p < 0.001$; for Advanced, $r(74) = 0.94$, $p < 0.001$; for Advanced+, $r(34) = 0.59$, $p < 0.01$. Thus, automatization was present at all proficiency levels.

Research question 4 (RQ4) asked whether the extent of automatization would differ between proficiency levels. We investigated this question in two ways: first, by using Fisher's *z* scores to compare the correlation coefficients found in answering RQ3, and second, with a L2 CV × Proficiency ANOVA. As in RQ2, Fisher's *z* showed that the correlation coefficient in the Advanced+ group was significantly smaller than that in the Advanced ($p < .05$) or Intermediate ($p < 0.05$) groups, while the latter two did not differ significantly from each other ($p > 0.05$). The one-way ANOVA confirmed that there was a significant difference between groups, $F(2, 102) = 5.89$, $p = 0.004$. A planned post-hoc Scheffé comparison indicated that the significant difference was that CV in the Advanced+ group was significantly lower than in the Intermediate group ($p = .009$) and the Advanced group ($p = 0.02$). Intermediate and Advanced groups did not have significantly different CVs ($p > 0.05$). In other words, the Intermediate and Advanced groups did not significantly differ from each other in amount of automatization, but each showed more automatization than the Advanced+ group did.

Discussion

This study aimed to investigate speedup and automatization in three levels of L2 Spanish proficiency. In response to RQ1, results showed that there was speedup at each of the three proficiency levels. However, since the increasing correlation between RT and SD_{RT} also figures into the operationalization of automatization, this finding does not preclude the use of automatized processes at these levels.

Results from RQ2 indicate that Advanced+ participants showed less evidence of speedup than the lower proficiency groups. This suggests that they are able to employ quicker processing outside of conscious control instead of depending on the more effortful processing associated with speedup.

In response to RQ3, the current investigation shows automatization at all proficiency levels tested. This contradicts findings of previous studies such as Hulstijn, van Gelderen, and Schoonen (2009), which failed to find widespread support for automatization. These results, along with the evidence for speedup at all proficiency levels as documented above, indicate that lower proficiency learners do not exclusively use speedup and higher proficiency learners do not use only automatization. Rather, both speedup and automatization seem to occur within one learner while performing one task, regardless of proficiency. It may be that the automatization threshold for lexical access occurs before the Intermediate proficiency level. In other words, since all proficiency groups evidenced automatization, it is possible that automatization first appears at an even earlier stage in L2 learning. If this is the case, including a beginner proficiency group in future studies could provide additional information regarding the possibility of a low threshold for the presence of automatization in L2 lexical access. It is also possible that the lexical familiarization task boosted knowledge of these items to a higher proficiency level than there would be for other lexical items, although this explanation is unlikely since familiarization was relatively short, entirely receptive in nature, and proficiency groups did not have equivalent accuracy on the experimental task.

The fourth research question asked whether the extent of automatization would differ by proficiency level. While the Intermediate and Advanced groups did not significantly differ in amount of automatization, there were significant differences from Advanced to Advanced+ and from Intermediate to Advanced+ as shown by both ways of measuring automatization. However, the significant difference is a decrease in correlation between L2RT and CV at the Advanced+ level compared to the two lower levels of proficiency. While not predicted by Segalowitz and Segalowitz (1993), this result does have precedent in the literature: Akamatsu (2008) found a decrease in the RT-CV correlation of low-frequency words over time, although its implications are not explored in the discussion. One possible explanation for the current finding may be due to the more sophisticated processing that only more advanced learners have, such as noticing more subtle lexical and morphological features, which may slow them down. The effects of proficiency level on automatization were investigated in two different ways: first, by using Fisher's z scores to compare the correlation coefficients found in answering RQ3 (thus operationalizing automaticity as an increase in correlation between RT and CV), and second, with a L2 CV × Proficiency ANOVA that operationalized automatization as a decrease in CV. Given that both operationalizations revealed the same group differences, it appears that for the participants in the current study, both are accurate in determining automatization. Most importantly, this finding provides greater validation of past attempts to operationalize automatization by a decrease in CV accompanied by an increase in the correlation between RT and CV (e.g., Segalowitz and Segalowitz 1993), as well as a decrease solely in CV (e.g., Segalowitz, Watson, and Segalowitz 1995; Segalowitz, Segalowitz, and Wood 1998; Segalowitz and Freed 2004; Philips et al. 2004; Harrington 2006). Our study also improves on previous research by using an outside measure of L2 proficiency with a subset of participants to justify groups; this could be further improved by using it with all participants.

In conclusion, the current study provides strong evidence for the presence of both speedup and automatization at all three proficiency levels tested. Furthermore, there were significant differences in the amount of automatization and speedup between the Advanced and Advanced+ groups. This hints at the possibility of changes in both automatization and speedup between these two proficiency groups.

The results of the current study highlight the need for future research that tests an even wider range of L2 proficiencies. More specifically, including beginner L2 learners could provide valuable information regarding automatization early in the learning process. Furthermore, including longitudinal, within-subject data could provide a more complete picture of the processes involved in L2 learning. Finally, the current study is limited to the automatization and speedup of lexical access in L2 development. As Hulstijn, van Gelderen, and Schoonen (2009) noted, there are many other linguistic domains to be considered. Further work in this paradigm is vital for SLA researchers because the distinction between speedup and automatization at different proficiency levels is an important piece in the puzzle of demarcating L2 development in learners, which in the past has been difficult to research since learners cannot self-report this part of development.

The questions of how to analyze and interpret learner RT also has implications for research on implicit L2 learning (often characterized by learners' "fast" speed) and L2 research on instructional conditions, which is moving away from reliance solely on the coarse measure of accuracy to include finer-grained measures. Researchers should capitalize on the information they can gleam from RT by including *SD* and CV calculations in their analyses.

REFERENCES

Akamatsu, Nobuhiko. 2008. "The effects of training on automatization of word recognition in English as a foreign language." *Applied Psycholinguistics* 29: 1–19.

Anderson, John R. 1983. *The Architecture of Cognition*. Mahwah, NJ: Erlbaum Associates.

Freed, Barbara F., Dan P. Dewey, Norman Segalowitz, and Randall Halter. 2004. "The language contact profile." *Studies in Second Language Acquisition* 26: 349–56.

Harrington, Michael. 2006. "The lexical decision task as a measure of L2 proficiency." *EUROSLA Yearbook* 6: 147–68.

Hulstijn, Jan H., Amos van Gelderen, and Rob Schoonen. 2009. "Automatization in second language acquisition: What does the coefficient of variation tell us?" *Applied Psycholinguistics* 30: 555–82.

Logan, Gordon D. 1998. "Toward an instance theory of automatization." *Psychological Review* 95: 492–527.

Phillips, Natalie A., Norman Segalowitz, Irena O'Brien, and Naomi Yamasaki. 2004. "Semantic priming in a first and second language: Evidence from reaction time variability and event-related brain potentials." *Journal of Neurolinguistics* 17: 237–62.

Segalowitz, Norman, and Barbara F. Freed. 2004. "Context, contact, and cognition in oral fluency acquisition: Learning Spanish in at home and study abroad contexts." *Studies of Second Language Acquisition* 26: 173–99.

Segalowitz, Norman S., and Sidney J. Segalowitz. 1993. "Skilled performance, practice, and the differentiation of speed-up from automatization effects: Evidence from second language word recognition." *Applied Psycholinguistics* 14: 369–85.

Segalowitz, Norman S., Vivien Watson, and Sidney Segalowitz. 1995. "Vocabulary skills: Single case assessment of automaticity of word recognition in a timed lexical decision task." *Second Language Research* 11: 121–36.

Segalowitz, Sidney J., Norman S. Segalowitz, and Anthony G. Wood. 1998. "Accessing the development of automaticity in second language word recognition." *Applied Psycholinguistics* 19: 53–67.

9

Frequency Effects, Learning Conditions, and the Development of Implicit and Explicit Lexical Knowledge

PHILLIP HAMRICK
Georgetown University

PATRICK REBUSCHAT
Lancaster University

FREQUENCY EFFECTS IN LANGUAGE are robust, but they interact in complex ways with other internal and external factors. An experiment investigated such an interaction between frequency, awareness (internal), and learning conditions (external) in adult lexical development. Participants were exposed to pseudowords and images under either incidental or intentional conditions and were then given a picture-matching task with subjective measures of awareness (Rebuschat 2008). We report two primary findings: first, frequency effects in lexical development are similar for implicit and explicit knowledge, consistent with theories of SLA proposing a single memory system for implicit and explicit lexical knowledge. Second, frequency effects were larger under incidental than intentional learning conditions. Overall, the results suggest complex interactions between frequency, learning conditions, and awareness.

Decades of psycholinguistic research have shown that input frequency and the probabilistic quality of natural language impact language acquisition at all levels (see, e.g., Ellis 2002; Lieven 2010; Rebuschat and Williams 2012; Saffran 2003). Humans are sensitive to how often words, phrases, and syntactic constructions co-occur in the input. Indeed, language is rich with such statistical information. For example, in English, the probability that a noun will occur immediately after *the* is very high, while the probability that *the* is followed by an adjective is lower, and the probability that it is followed by an adverb even lower. However, humans do not develop sensitivity to such frequencies and probabilities in a vacuum. They do not simply tally frequency information. Rather, their knowledge of natural language frequencies is modulated by other factors. For example, Goldschneider and DeKeyser (2001) showed that frequency interacts with perceptual salience to predict 71 percent of the variance in second language (L2) morpheme acquisition order, which is more than frequency contributes when isolated. Likewise, frequency interacts with attentional processing. Higher frequency of surface forms makes attentional processing during learning more likely and influences the subsequent strengthening of that knowledge (Perruchet and Vinter 2002). Thus, although frequency is an independent variable in learners' input with its own characteristics, it nevertheless interacts with other variables. However, despite an increasing consensus that frequency effects are a crucial aspect of language acquisition, many questions about them remain unexplored. In the present experiment, we investigated two of these questions. The first has implications for second language acquisition (SLA) theory: Is there any relationship between implicit and explicit knowledge and input frequency? That is, are implicit and explicit knowledge subserved by mechanisms with the same or different underlying sensitivities to frequency? This question is important, as it addresses fundamental assumptions of Emergentist and neurocognitive approaches to language (Ellis 2002; Ullman 2005). The second question has implications for research methodology: Are frequency effects on learning the same or different under incidental and intentional learning conditions? In other words, does frequency impact learning differently under different learning conditions?

Before describing our investigation of these questions, we briefly review theories of frequency effects, implicit and explicit knowledge, and learning conditions. We first review measures of implicit and explicit knowledge as they are a central element of our experimental design. We then report our experiment and the relevance of our findings for SLA theory and methodology, and, briefly, other language-related fields, in particular, corpus linguistics.

Frequency, Implicit and Explicit Knowledge, and Learning Conditions

Frequency-based mechanisms, often termed statistical learning mechanisms, are often argued to underlie the development of implicit knowledge—knowledge that is unconscious and generally difficult to verbalize. Some researchers assume that implicit learning and statistical learning are the same phenomenon (Conway and Christiansen 2006; Ellis 2002, 2005; Perruchet and Pacton 2006); however, elsewhere it has been argued that frequency-driven statistical learning appears to give rise to both implicit and explicit knowledge (Hamrick and Rebuschat 2012). There is general agreement that learners do not simply count up instances of use in language (Ellis 2002). The actual processing of frequency information in learning is implicit, but the acquired knowledge is not necessarily also implicit, which is to say that implicit brain processes might result in conscious knowledge (Perruchet and Vinter 2002). Moreover, it is unclear to what extent the resulting implicit and explicit knowledge veridically reflects the frequencies processed by the learning mechanisms (Shanks 1995).

Likewise, it is not clear to what extent frequency effects are modulated by learning conditions. Many studies purporting to show the effects of frequency and other statistical information in language learning have varied in their use of incidental and intentional learning conditions. For present purposes, we consider incidental learning conditions to be those in which participants are not informed of a test or that they should be learning. Intentional learning, on the other hand, refers to informing participants of a subsequent test phase, as well as possibly telling participants to try to learn the regularity or pattern in the stimulus material.

Frequency-driven learning has been clearly demonstrated under intentional learning conditions. Yu and Smith (2007) found that adults were sensitive to word-referent co-occurrence frequencies when told to try to learn. Likewise, Kachergis, Yu, and Shiffrin (2009) found more fine-grained evidence of frequency effects in intentional word learning, with increasing frequency leading to incrementally better performance. However, other studies on frequency-based and statistical learning have relied on strictly incidental learning conditions. For example, Saragi, Nation, and Meister (1978) and Pellicer-Sánchez and Schmitt (2010) found incidental learning of novel vocabulary that appeared to be driven in part by frequency. Incidental learning based on frequency and statistical cues has been shown in other language domains as well, (e.g., Hasher et al. 1987; Saffran et al. 1997; Romberg and Saffran 2010). For example, Saffran et al. (1997) showed that children and adults were equally good at extracting words from a speech stream when the only cues to speech segmentation were probabilistic. In sum, while many studies have shown robust frequency-driven learning effects, there has been little in the way of a systematic investigation of whether incidental or intentional learning conditions constrain or promote frequency effects.

One notable exception is Kachergis, Yu, and Shiffrin (2010, experiment 2), who compared incidental and intentional cross-situational word learning using a within-subjects design in order to investigate implicit learning. Cross-situational word learning requires participants to track pseudoword-referent co-occurrence frequencies across training trials (this paradigm is explained further in the methods section below). Kachergis, Yu, and Shiffrin (2010) found that participants were able to learn some pseudoword-referent pairs under incidental conditions, but that the same participants performed much better when instructed to search for word meanings. Thus, there is some evidence that learning conditions modulate frequency-based learning. However, despite their claims to be investigating implicit learning, no measures of awareness were included—it is unclear whether the acquired knowledge was implicit or explicit. There were also no manipulations of individual pseudoword-referent pairing frequency. Therefore, the interactions between frequency, learning conditions, and awareness were not assessed.

The present study sought to investigate these gaps in the literature. Humans aquire both implicit and explicit knowledge about language, and language acquisition appears to be, at least in part, the consequence of frequency-based learning mechanisms. But it is unclear to what extent implicit and explicit knowledge reflect the statistical properties of the input. Further complicating matters is the fact that frequency-based learning effects are often reported without reference to learning conditions, making the role of frequency difficult to interpret. It is possible that the amount of learning in these studies is the result not just of frequency effects, but also of their interaction with learning conditions. Before discussing how our experiment addressed these issues, we briefly review the measures of awareness we used in order to assess the conscious status of learners' knowledge in our study.

Measuring Implicit and Explicit Knowledge
Whether the knowledge acquired during incidental learning is actually implicit is a controversial issue. Several measures of awareness have been proposed (see Dienes and Seth 2010; Rebuschat, in press), and here we review those used in the present study.

Verbal reports. A common way of distinguishing implicit and explicit knowledge is to prompt subjects to verbalize anything they might have noticed while doing the experiment (e.g., Reber 1967). Knowledge is considered to be unconscious if subjects perform above chance despite being unable to verbalize the knowledge that underlies their performance. But this operationalization has been criticized for a variety of reasons (Perruchet 2008). For one, participants may only be able to verbalize knowledge after a long exposure period. Another problem is that verbal reports are a relatively insensitive and incomplete measure of implicit and explicit knowledge. For example, subjects may not verbalize knowledge because low-confidence knowledge retrieval may be difficult.

Subjective measures. Dienes (2008) advocated the use of subjective measures in order to assess whether the knowledge acquired during Artificial Grammar Learning (AGL) tasks is implicit or explicit. One way of dissociating implicit and explicit knowledge is to collect confidence ratings (e.g., Dienes et al. 1995). In AGL tasks, for example, participants can be asked to report how confident they were for each grammaticality decision. Dienes et al. (1995) suggested two ways in which confidence judgments could index implicit knowledge. First, knowledge can be considered unconscious if participants believe they are guessing when their classification performance is, in fact, significantly above chance. This is called the guessing criterion. Second, knowledge is unconscious if participants' confidence is unrelated to their accuracy. This is known as the zero correlation criterion. Several studies have shown that performance on standard AGL tasks can result in unconscious knowledge according to these criteria (e.g., Dienes et al. 1995).

Structural knowledge and judgment knowledge. Confidence judgments have been criticized because of the type of knowledge that is assessed by this measure, especially regarding the case of natural language acquisition (Dienes 2008). Language acquisition is often considered a prime example of implicit learning. All cognitively unimpaired adults are able to discern grammatical sentences of their native language from ungrammatical ones, even though they are unable to report the underlying rule system. However, when asked how confident they are in their grammaticality decisions, most native speakers will report high confidence levels; for example, they might say, "'John bought an apple in the supermarket' is a grammatical sentence, and I am 100% confident in my decision, but I do not know what the rules are or why I am right." In these cases, confidence judgments and accuracy will be highly correlated, but does this mean that language acquisition is not an implicit learning process after all? Probably not. Dienes (2008) and Dienes and Scott (2005) proposed a convincing explanation for this phenomenon based on Rosenthal's (2005) Higher-Order Thought Theory.

Dienes argued that when participants are exposed to letter sequences in an AGL experiment, they learn the structure of the sequences. This structural knowledge can consist, for example, of knowledge of associations, exemplars, fragments, or rules. In the testing phase, participants apply their structural knowledge to construct a different type of knowledge: knowledge of whether the test items shared the same structure as the training items. Dienes labeled this judgment as knowledge. Both structural and judgment knowledge can be implicit or explicit. For example, a structural representation about letter repetition is only conscious if it is explicitly represented—in other words, if there is a corresponding higher-order thought such as "I {know/think/believe, etc.} that a letter can repeated several times." Likewise, judgment knowledge is only conscious if there is a corresponding higher-order thought (e.g., "I {know/think/believe, etc.} that this item has the same structure as the training sequences.") The guessing criterion (i.e., participants believe they are guessing, but they perform above chance) and the zero correlation criterion (i.e., confidence is unrelated to accuracy) measure the conscious status of judgment knowledge, not structural knowledge.

Moreover, Dienes and Scott (2005) posit that conscious structural knowledge leads to conscious judgment knowledge. However, if structural knowledge is unconscious, judgment knowledge could still be either conscious or unconscious, which explains why, in the case of natural language, people can be very confident in their grammaticality decisions without knowing why. Here, structural knowledge of the language is implicit while metalinguistic judgment knowledge is explicit. This leads to the phenomenology of intuition: knowing that a judgment is correct, but not knowing why. However, if both structural and judgment knowledge are implicit, the phenomenology is that of guessing. In both cases, the structural knowledge acquired during training is implicit. To assess the conscious status of both structural and judgment knowledge, source attributions can be added to the confidence ratings in the testing phase. Thus, after asking participants how confident they were in their grammaticality judgments, one also prompts the participants to report the basis of their judgments.

Method

The following experiment had two objectives. The first objective was to investigate a theoretical question: Do implicit and explicit knowledge reflect input frequency in similar ways, or do implicit and explicit knowledge reflect different sensitivities to frequency? The second objective was to address a methodological question: Are frequency effects differentially influenced by incidental and intentional learning conditions? In order to address these questions, we employed the cross-situational word learning paradigm, which has been widely used in the investigation of frequency-driven learning and statistical learning (e.g., Hamrick and Rebuschat 2012; Yu and Smith 2007; Kachergis, Yu, and Shiffrin 2010).

Participants

Thirty native speakers of English (19 women and 11 men, M_{age} = 19.3) were recruited from introductory linguistics classes randomly assigned to incidental or intentional learning conditions (fifteen in each group). There were no significant differences between the two groups in terms of age or number of other languages spoken, $ps > 0.05$.

Stimuli

An artificial lexicon consisting of twenty-seven auditory pseudowords was created for this experiment. All pseudowords were bisyllabic, stressed on the first syllable, and obeyed English phonotactics. The pseudowords were read aloud by a female native speaker of English and digitally recorded by means of sound processing software (Audacity, version 1.2.4). Each pseudoword was then matched with one or more black-and-white drawings from the International Picture-Naming Project website (Szekely et al. 2004).

The lexicon was divided into twelve target and fifteen filler items. All filler items were unambiguous and only occurred once each in the input during the exposure phase. The target items were subdivided into six lexically ambiguous pseudowords (i.e., one word with three matching referents) and six lexically unambiguous pseudowords (i.e., one word with one matching referent). All target words were manipulated in terms of their pseudoword-referent co-occurrence frequencies. Some pseudowords co-occurred with their matching referents six times, other pseudowords co-occurred with their appropriate referents four times, and others co-occurred with their appropriate referents twice (see table 9.1). For example, the pseudoword *houger* occurred twelve times: six times with an elephant, four times with a glass, and two times with a pear.

Table 9.1.
Ambiguous and unambiguous target items and their referents

Pseudoword	Referents (Co-Occurrence Frequency)		
dobez	backpack (6),	arrow (4),	bathtub (2)
paylig	wheelchair (6),	towel (4),	bandage (2)
femod	bench (6),	thumb (4),	bridge (2)
Whoma	comb (6),	crib (4),	fan (2)
Houger	elephant (6),	glass (4),	pear (2)
Jillug	ladder (6),	leaf (4),	mixer (2)
Keemuth	mop (6)		
Nengee	panda (6)		
Zomthos	radio (4)		
Loga	stethoscope (4)		
Shrama	robot (2)		
Thueek	tank (2)		

EFFECTS, CONDITIONS, AND DEVELOPMENT OF LEXICAL KNOWLEDGE

Exposure phase. In the exposure phase, subjects in both conditions were presented with the same fifty-seven trials. In each trial, a fixation cross was first displayed for two seconds. Then two images were displayed on the screen at the same time, one on the left side and the other on the right side (see figure 9.1). The two images were displayed for six seconds. While the images were on display, two pseudowords were played once each. For example, subjects might see an image of a panda on the left and an image of a glass on the right, while hearing first the pseudoword *houger*, followed by the pseudoword *nengee*. Importantly, the presentation order of the pseudowords was not related to the location of the images on the screen. That is, each word could refer either to the image on the left or to the image on the right. The only way for participants to learn the artificial vocabulary was to use the pseudoword-object co-occurrence frequencies across trials. The order of trials was randomized for each participant.

Procedure

The experiment was presented on a PC with a 15.6-inch screen using Microsoft Power Point 2007 running a randomization macro. Instructions were displayed in black text (Arial font sizes 20–24) on a white background. Pseudowords were played through headphones. The experiment consisted of an exposure phase and a testing phase. The content of the exposure and testing phases was the same for both groups. The groups only differed in how they interacted with the fifty-seven exposure trials.

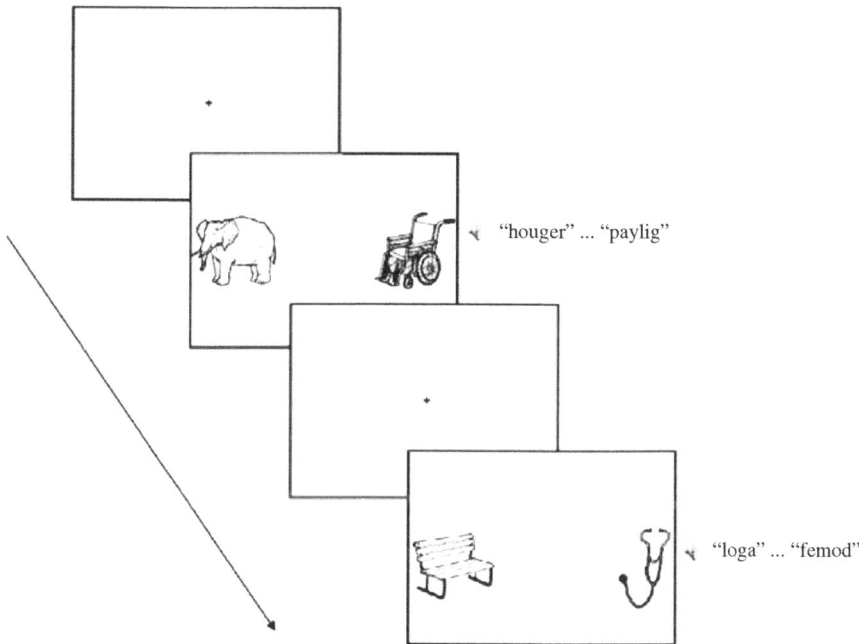

Figure 9.1 Simple Screenshot Sequence from the Exposure Phase

Exposure phase. Subjects in the intentional learning condition ($n = 15$) were told that they were participating in a word-learning experiment and were instructed to "learn the meanings of the words." They were also told that they would be tested afterwards. In contrast, subjects in the incidental learning condition ($n = 15$) were not informed about the true purpose of the experiment, nor did they know that they would be tested after the exposure phase. Moreover, participants were given a deliberately misleading task. They were told that the objective of the study was to investigate how people with different language experience perceive and categorize objects. Their task during the exposure phase was to indicate how many objects on each slide were animate. There were three possible responses per trial (zero, one, or two animate objects) and participants were instructed to enter 0, 1, or 2 on their keypads. This task was made more difficult by the presence of pictures that were not easily classifiable as animate or inanimate (e.g., a thumb, a leaf). They were informed that they would have to do the task while hearing "nonsense" words through their headphones.

In sum, all experimental subjects were exposed to the same fifty-seven trials. The key difference between subjects in the intentional and incidental groups is how they interacted with the stimuli. Subjects in the former group were instructed to learn the meanings of words, whereas subjects in the latter group were asked to perform an irrelevant task and to treat the auditory pseudowords as nonsense.

Test phase. After the exposure phase, all participants completed a four-alternative forced-choice (4AFC) picture matching task. The 4AFC task consisted of thirty trials. In each trial, participants were presented with four pictures, one in each corner of the screen, and a spoken pseudoword. Their task was to select the appropriate referent as quickly and accurately as possible.

For each trial, the screen contained one correct referent and three foils. Each picture was numbered and participants indicated the best match by writing down their answers on an answer sheet. Additionally, subjects were asked to report how confident they were in their decision and what the basis of their decision was. Subjects were asked to place their confidence on a continuous scale, ranging from 50 percent (complete guess) to 100 percent (complete certainty). We emphasized that subjects should only use 50 percent when they believed they were truly guessing—in other words, they might as well have flipped a coin. In the case of the source attributions, there were three response options: guess, intuition, and memory. The guess category indicated that subjects believed the classification decision to be based on a true guess. The intuition category indicated that they were somewhat confident in their decision but did not know why it was right—they simply had a "gut feeling." The memory category indicated that the judgment was based on the recollection of pseudoword-referent mappings from the exposure phase. All participants were provided with these definitions before starting the testing phase.

At the end of the test phase, all subjects completed a debriefing questionnaire which asked them to report if they had learned any of the pseudoword-referent mappings during exposure, whether or not they had used any specific learning strategies, and, if so, what kind of strategies.

Results

Performance on the 4AFC task served as the measure of learning. Awareness was measured by means of confidence ratings and source attributions.

Four-Alternative Forced-Choice Task

The analysis of the 4AFC task showed that both the incidental group ($M = 44.4\%$, $SD = 7.5\%$) and the intentional group ($M = 73.3\%$, $SD\ 10.7\%$) performed significantly above chance (chance = 25%), $t_{incidental}(14) = 9.99, p < 0.05, t_{intentional}(14) = 17.53$, $p < 0.05$. Performance in the intentional group was also significantly above that of the incidental group, $t(28) = 8.54, p < 0.001$. The results indicate that there was a clear learning effect for both groups, with a greater learning effect under intentional learning conditions.

Measuring the Conscious Status of the Acquired Knowledge

Confidence ratings. The average confidence level was 61.3 percent ($SD = 7.2\%$) in the incidental group and 80.6 percent ($SD = 6.3\%$) in the intentional group. The difference was significant: $t(28) = 7.79, p < 0.05$. Further analysis showed that accuracy and confidence were significantly correlated in the intentional group ($r = 0.77$, $p < 0.05$), but not in the incidental group ($r = 0.45, p > 0.05$). When intentional learners were confident in their decision, they tended to be accurate. This suggests that subjects in the intentional group had acquired conscious judgment knowledge; these participants were partially aware that they had acquired some knowledge during the exposure phase. In contrast, subjects in the incidental group were not consistently aware of having acquired knowledge, despite the fact that their performance on the 4AFC task clearly indicates that they did. The zero correlation criterion was thus met in the case of the incidental group.

We then analyzed all classification decisions for which subjects gave a 50 percent rating, meaning that they believed they had guessed when deciding on the appropriate referent for the pseudoword. Incidental participants indicated that they were guessing on 44.2 percent of test trials, while intentional participants indicated that they were guessing on only 9.9 percent of trials. A one-sample t-test indicated that participants' accuracy on the test when they gave a 50 percent confidence rating was 33.5 percent ($SD = 17.2\%$), which trended toward significance, $t(14) = 1.92$, $p = 0.07$. In the case of the intentional group, when subjects gave a confidence rating of 50 percent, their mean classification performance was 44.1 percent ($SD = 18.9\%$), which was significantly above chance: $t(14) = 2.95, p < 0.05$. Thus, the guessing criterion for unconscious judgment knowledge was satisfied in the intentional group, while there was trending evidence for unconscious judgment knowledge in the incidental group.

The confidence ratings indicate that the incidental group was largely unaware of having acquired knowledge during the exposure phase. In the case of the intentional group, subjects were clearly aware of having acquired knowledge (see correlation between confidence and accuracy), though some of their judgment knowledge did remain unconscious (as indicated by the guessing criterion).

Source attributions. In terms of proportion, the incidental group most frequently believed their classification decisions to be based on a guess or intuition (86 percent of judgments). The memory category was selected least frequently (only 14 percent of all judgments). That is, during the 4AFC task, subjects in the incidental group generally based their decisions on the more implicit categories. In the case of the intentional group, the memory category was selected most frequently (61 percent of judgments), followed by guessing and intuition. In terms of accuracy, the analysis showed that the incidental group scored highest when reporting that their classification was based on memory, followed by the intuition and guess categories (table 9.2). The same pattern was observed in the intentional group; these subjects were most accurate when attributing their classification decision to memory. They were, however, considerably more accurate, performing close to 90 percent accuracy.

Repeated measures ANOVAs with Source Attribution (three levels: guess, memory, and intuition) as a within subjects factor and accuracy as the dependent variable revealed significant effects of Source Attribution in both the incidental group $[F(2, 14) = 8.25, p < 0.05]$ and the intentional group $[F(2, 14) = 5.59, p < 0.05]$. In the case of the incidental group, the difference between decisions based on guessing and decisions based on intuition was significant ($p < 0.05$), as was the difference between decisions based on guessing and those based on memory ($p < 0.05$). In the intentional group, the differences between decisions based on guessing and intuition, guessing and memory, and intuition and memory were all significant ($p < 0.05$).

Interestingly, subjects in both groups performed significantly above chance across categories, regardless of whether they attributed their decision to guessing, intuition, or memory. The guessing criterion was therefore satisfied in both groups: when subjects believed the source of their judgment to be a guess, their actual classification performance suggests that they had acquired the knowledge to make that decision. This suggests that subjects in both groups acquired at least some unconscious structural knowledge. Table 9.2 shows the classification performance for the different attributions.

Verbal reports. Analysis of the verbal reports showed that only learners in the intentional condition became aware of many pseudoword-referent pairs and were able to name a few. When prompted for strategies, the most commonly reported strategies were repeating the pseudowords, making a link between pseudowords and prior knowledge (e.g., "that sounded like something in French"), and hypothesis testing. In contrast, subjects in the incidental group reported deliberately trying to block out the pseudowords. Indeed, many interpreted the pseudowords to be a distraction and consequently tried to ignore them.

Frequency Effects and Interactions

To investigate the effects of frequency and ambiguity on learning outcomes, a 2×2×3 mixed design ANOVA was performed with group (two levels: incidental and intentional) as a between-subjects variable, frequency (three levels: high, mid, and low), and ambiguity (two levels: ambiguous and unambiguous) as within-subjects variables. Accuracy on the 4AFC was the dependent variable. The ANOVA revealed

EFFECTS, CONDITIONS, AND DEVELOPMENT OF LEXICAL KNOWLEDGE

Table 9.2.
Accuracy and proportions (%) across source attributions

		Guess	Intuition	Memory
Incidental	Accuracy	35.8*	48.5**	61.4**
	Proportion	44.2	41.7	14.1
Intentional	Accuracy	54.2**	61.9**	88.9**
	Proportion	23.2	27.9	48.9

Significantly different from chance (25%): *$p < .01$, **$p < .001$

a significant effect of group [$F(1, 28) = 53.02$, $p < 0.001$, partial $\eta^2 = 0.65$], which simply replicated the earlier finding of a significant difference in accuracy between the two groups. There was no effect of ambiguity ($p > 0.05$), which indicated that ambiguity alone was not a significant factor in participants' accuracy. There was an effect of frequency: $F(2, 28) = 17.06$, $p < 0.001$, partial $\eta^2 = 0.38$. This indicates that input frequency influenced accuracy at test (figure 9.2). Finally, a significant interaction was found between group, ambiguity, and frequency [$F(2, 28) = 3.56$, $p < 0.05$, $\eta^2 = 0.11$], which indicates that participants in the incidental and intentional conditions were differentially influenced by frequency and ambiguity combined.

Further investigations of frequency effects were conducted on each group separately (see figure 9.2). There was a significant effect of frequency on the incidental group [$F(2, 28) = 12.52$, $p < 0.001$], and on the intentional group (Greenhouse-Geisser corrected) [$F(1.38, 19.42) = 5.86$, $p < 0.05$]. To investigate the effect size for frequency in the incidental and intentional groups, we conducted correlation analyses between accuracy on the 4AFC task and input frequencies for the test pseudowords. There were significant relationships between accuracy and frequency for participants

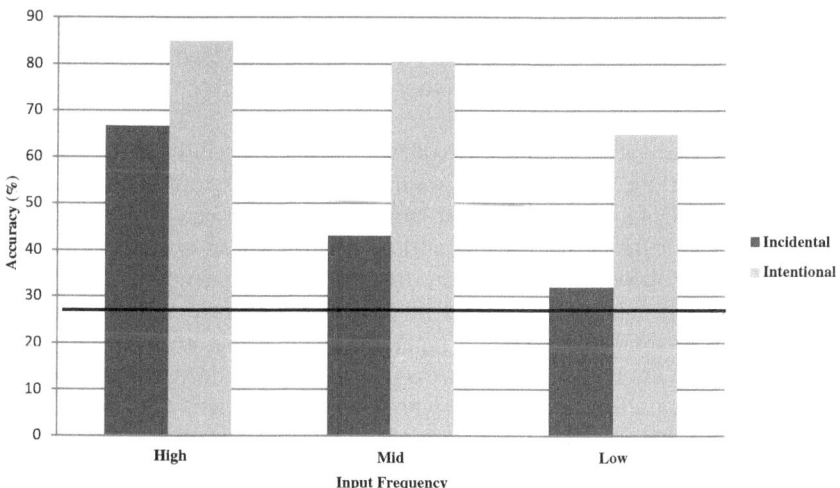

Figure 9.2 Accuracy at Test by Input Frequency When Using Implicit and Explicit Knowledge

in the incidental condition ($\rho = 0.51$, $p < 0.01$) and intentional condition ($\rho = 0.26$, $p < 0.05$). Thus, the effect size of frequency on accuracy at test was larger for the incidental group than the intentional group.

We also wondered to what extent the implicit and explicit knowledge that participants developed was sensitive to input frequency. Correlation coefficients were computed between participants' accuracy when using implicit or explicit knowledge at test and input frequency. There were significant relationships between accuracy and frequency when participants used both implicit knowledge ($\rho = 0.45$, $p < 0.01$) and explicit knowledge ($\rho = 0.46$, $p < 0.05$).

Discussion

Results of the present experiment show that adult learners can learn pseudoword-referent mappings using co-occurrence frequencies under both incidental and intentional learning conditions. The results also show that adult learners can acquire implicit and explicit lexical knowledge. In terms of our research questions, our first question asked if implicit and explicit knowledge differentially reflect input frequency. The current evidence suggests that the answer is no, at least in the case of lexical knowledge. Participants showed frequency effects equally whether using implicit or explicit knowledge. This finding fits the view that frequency effects are ubiquitous and not restricted to implicit knowledge (Ellis 2002; Hamrick and Rebuschat 2012; Perruchet and Vinter 2002). More importantly for theories of SLA, these results are consistent with single-mechanism views of language learning, which posit that implicit and explicit knowledge stem from a single underlying memory system (e.g., Shanks 1995). However, the results are also consistent with the dual-mechanism view in the declarative/procedural model of language (Ullman 2005), which posits that both implicit and explicit lexical knowledge are supported by declarative memory. Our present results do not allow us to make further distinctions between these memory-based models, but this may prove to be an important avenue for further research. At the least, our results are consistent with theories of L2 vocabulary acquisition involving a common memory system that subserves both implicit and explicit lexical knowledge.

Our second question asked if frequency effects were different in incidental and intentional learning conditions. Our results suggest that the answer is yes. Accuracy levels of incidental learners showed larger frequency effects than accuracy levels of intentional learners, but intentional learners had higher overall accuracy. Thus, we make the following interpretation: frequency-based intentional learning results in significantly higher accuracy, but frequency-based incidental learning results in accuracy more veridically related to input frequency. Therefore, incidental and intentional learning are both sensitive to frequency; however, increased sensitivity does not entail increased accuracy. This finding is methodologically important because it demonstrates that learning conditions constrain frequency effects in different ways. Also, this finding is consistent with that of Kachergis, Yu, and Shiffrin (2010) and many others who have found that intentional learning conditions often result in more robust learning than incidental learning conditions (e.g., Rebuschat 2008).

Consequently, future research on frequency effects should indicate clearly the learning conditions under which participants are exposed to their input and consider the possibility that their results may not stem from frequency effects alone, but also from the learning conditions themselves. One likely solution would be for researchers to use different exposure conditions in order to assess the learning process. It should be noted that another possible explanation for the results comes from the fact that intentional learning participants performed so well that there might have been some ceiling effects. High accuracy would reduce the variation needed to find larger correlations. Teasing apart these explanations remains an issue for future research.

Finally, this study also constitutes another demonstration of the usefulness of subjective measures of awareness (cf. Rebuschat 2008, in press). Although verbal reports provided important insights into learners' thought processes and to their general levels of awareness, they would not have been fine-grained enough to permit detailed analysis of the relationship between frequency effects and implicit and explicit knowledge. Since the subjective measures provided a trial-by-trial indication of the conscious status of learners' knowledge, we were able to assess the relationship between frequency and awareness with more precision. We recommend the use of subjective measures in conjunction with other measures of awareness any time researchers are considering looking for specific relationships between test item performance, awareness, and other factors.

Conclusion

To summarize, our experiment yielded two important results, the first theoretical and the second methodological. First, frequency effects in adult language learning are not limited to implicit knowledge, but also are evident in explicit knowledge. This finding supports theories of SLA that assume a common underlying memory system for implicit and explicit lexical knowledge. Second, we showed that the ubiquity of frequency effects does not necessarily lead to the same learning results. That is, the extent to which learners develop and mirror their input is largely a result of the interaction between frequency and their learning conditions. Thus, researchers should take into account the role of task instructions in modulating learning effects. Finally, our results have implications for other areas of linguistics, such as corpus linguistics. For example, if frequency-driven learning interacts with other mechanisms and learning conditions, then researchers designing corpus-based language models may want to include analogous mechanisms in their models. Likewise, our findings are consistent with researchers working on exemplar-based approaches to variation who argue that frequency effects on mental representation are mediated by other cognitive and contextual factors. In sum, the role of frequency in language learning is mediated by learning conditions, and it is important for researchers to carefully consider this issue when conducting future investigations on frequency and language.

Acknowledgments

The authors would like to thank Nick Ellis, John Williams, Ron Leow, Katie Kim, Julie Lake, and Kaitlyn Tagarelli for their feedback on this project.

REFERENCES

Conway, Christopher, and Morten Christiansen. 2006. "Statistical learning within and between modalities." *Psychological Science* 17: 905–12.

Dienes, Zoltan. 2008. "Subjective measures of unconscious knowledge." *Progress in Brain Research* 168: 49–64.

Dienes, Zoltan, and Ryan Scott. 2005. "Measuring unconscious knowledge: Distinguishing structural knowledge and judgment knowledge." *Psychological Research* 69: 338–51.

Dienes, Zoltan, and Anil Seth. 2010. "The conscious and the unconscious." In *Encyclopedia of Behavioral Neuroscience*, volume 1, 322–27, edited by George Koob, Michel Le Moal, and Richard Thompson. Oxford: Academic Press.

Dienes, Zoltan, Gerry Altman, Liam Kwan, and Alastair Goode. 1995. "Unconscious knowledge of artificial grammars is applied strategically." *Journal of Experimental Psychology: Learning, Memory, and Cognition* 21: 1322–38.

Ellis, Nick. 2002. "Frequency effects in language processing: A review with implications for theories of implicit and explicit language acquisition." *Studies in Second Language Acquisition* 24: 143–88.

———. 2005. "At the interface: Dynamic interactions of explicit and implicit language knowledge." *Studies in Second Language Acquisition* 27: 305–52.

Goldschneider, Jennifer, and Robert DeKeyser. 2001. "Explaining the 'natural order of L2 morpheme acquisition' in English: A meta-analysis of multiple determinants." *Language Learning* 51: 1–50.

Hamrick, Phillip, and Patrick Rebuschat. 2012. "How implicit is statistical learning?" In *Statistical Learning and Language Acquisition*, edited by Patrick Rebuschat and John Williams. Berlin: Mouton de Gruyter.

Hasher, Lynn, Rose Zacks, Karen Rose, and Henrianne Sanft. 1987. "Truly incidental encoding of frequency information." *American Journal of Psychology* 100: 69–91.

Hulstijn, Jan. 2003. "Incidental and intentional learning." In *The Handbook of Second Language Research*, 349–81, edited by Catherine Doughty and Michael Long. London: Blackwell.

Kachergis, George, Chen Yu, and Richard Shiffrin. 2009. "Frequency and contextual diversity effects in cross-situational word learning." In *Proceedings of the 31st Annual Conference of the Cognitive Science Society*, edited by Niels Taatgen, Hedderik van Rijn, John Nerbonne, and Lambert Schomaker. Austin, TX: Cognitive Science Society.

———2010. "Cross-situational statistical learning: Implicit or intentional?" In *Proceedings of the 32nd Annual Conference of the Cognitive Science Society*, edited by Richard Cambtrabone and Stellan Ohlsson. Austin, TX: Cognitive Science Society.

Lieven, Elena. 2010. "Input and first language acquisition: Evaluating the role of frequency." *Lingua* 120: 2546–56.

Pellicer-Sánchez, Anna, and Norbert Schmitt. 2010. "Incidental vocabulary acquisition from an authentic novel: Do *Things Fall Apart*?" *Reading in a Foreign Language* 22: 31–55.

Perruchet, Pierre. 2008. "Implicit learning." In *Learning and Memory: A Comprehensive Reference*, volume two, 597–621, edited by John Byrne. Oxford: Elsevier.

Perruchet, Pierre, and Sebastien Pacton. 2006. "Implicit learning and statistical learning: One phenomenon, two approaches." *Trends in Cognitive Sciences* 10: 233–38.

Perruchet, Pierre, and Annie Vinter. 2002. "The self-organizing consciousness." *Behavioral and Brain Sciences* 25: 297–388.

Reber, Arthur. 1967. "Implicit learning of artificial grammars." *Journal of Verbal Learning and Verbal Behavior* 6: 317–27.

Rebuschat, Patrick. 2008. "Implicit Learning of Natural Language Syntax." Unpublished PhD dissertation, University of Cambridge.

———. In press. "Measuring implicit and explicit knowledge in second language research: A review." *Language Learning*.

Rebuschat, Patrick, and John Williams. 2012. *Statistical Learning and Language Acquisition*. Berlin: Mouton de Gruyter.

Romberg, Alexa, and Jenny Saffran. 2010. "Statistical learning and language acquisition." *Wiley Interdisciplinary Reviews: Cognitive Science*. doi:10.1002/wcs.78.

Rosenthal, David. 2005. *Consciousness and Mind*. Oxford: Oxford University Press.

Saffran, Jenny. 2003. "Statistical language learning: Mechanisms and constraints." *Current Directions in Psychological Science* 12: 110–14.

Saffran, Jenny, Elissa Newport, Richard Aslin, Rachel Tunick, and Sandra Barrueco. 1997. "Incidental language learning: Listening (and learning) out of the corner of your ear." *Psychological Science* 8: 101–5.

Saragi, Thomas, I. S. Paul Nation, and G. Meister. 1978. "Vocabulary learning and reading." *System* 6: 72–78.

Shanks, David R. 1995. *The Psychology of Associative Learning*. Cambridge: Cambridge University Press.

Szekely, Anna, Thomas Jacobsen, Simona D'Amico, Antonella Devescovi, Elena Andonova, Daniel Herron, and E. Bates. 2004. "A new on-line resource for psycholinguistic studies." *Journal of Memory and Language* 51: 247–50.

Ullman, Michael T. 2005. "A cognitive neuroscience perspective on second language acquisition: The declarative/procedural model." In *Mind and Context in Adult Second Language Acquisition*, 141–78, edited by Cristina Sanz. Washington, DC: Georgetown University Press.

Yu, Chen, and Linda Smith. 2007. "Rapid word learning under uncertainty via cross-situational statistics." *Psychological Science* 18: 414–20.

10

The Differential Role of Language Analytic Ability in Two Distinct Learning Conditions

NADIA MIFKA PROFOZIC
University of Zadar, Croatia

THIS PAPER EXAMINES WHETHER the role of language analytic ability in L2 acquisition may change relative to different types of corrective feedback provided in a communicative language classroom. Two groups of high school students in New Zealand ($n = 18$ in each group) that were learning French as a foreign language were subjected to different learning conditions while working on three communicative tasks over two weeks. In one group, learners were asked to self-correct following the teacher's request for clarification whenever they committed an error in the production of the target structures; the other group received recasts as a type of input-based corrective feedback. The target structures were the French *passé composé* and *imparfait,* which are past-tense structures. Along with language tests, the participants completed a test designed to measure language analytic ability (Ottó 2004). Correlations between gain scores of accurate production and analytic ability were different for the two groups. Analytic ability was significantly correlated with oral and written production gains for the group that received clarification requests, whereas the learners who received recasts had to rely on their analytic ability only to retain long-term gains of passé composé in oral production. Lack of correlation with gains for the recasts group suggests that recasts assisted all learners irrespective of their ability, whereas strong correlation of analytic ability with gains in the clarification requests group means that these students learned no more than their analytic ability would predict.

Language analytic ability has been identified as a component of language aptitude, which refers to a person's "capacity to analyze or process language input" (Skehan 1986, 202). Analytic ability correlates with general intelligence (Sasaki 1996), particularly with those aspects of intelligence known as fluid intelligence (Ehrman and Oxford 1995; Sternberg 2002). Analytic ability is essential for making inferences and generalizations, and thus contributes to all aspects of abstract, formal, logical, or mathematical thinking. In the most complex and widely used aptitude battery to date, the Modern Languages Aptitude Test (Carroll and Sapon 1959), language analytic ability is partially measured by the grammatical sensitivity subtest (the words in sentences section of the MLAT). As a counterpart to the top-down processing associated with grammatical sensitivity, the bottom-up types of analyses assisted by inductive language learning ability also contribute to language processing. Hence, inductive learning ability is also considered to be part of language aptitude (Carroll 1962), although it is not measured by the MLAT. In Skehan's (1998) framework of his information processing model, grammatical sensitivity and inductive language learning ability together constitute language analytic ability, which may facilitate analyses performed during the processing phase of language learning.

Language Aptitude
As repeatedly emphasized in literature on individual differences in language learning (Ellis 2004; Robinson 2001; Sawyer and Ranta 2001; Skehan 1989; Sparks and Ganschow 2001; Sternberg 2002), analytic ability is only one component of language aptitude; the other parts are related to memory and phonemic coding ability. It has been suggested that different components of aptitude may be linked to specific areas of language learning. For example, Nagata, Aline, and Ellis (1999) examined how different aspects of aptitude influenced different areas of L2 learning, and showed that analytic ability as measured by the MLAT grammatical sensitivity subtest was closely related to comprehension but not to vocabulary learning. Harley and Hart (1997) found stronger correlations with memory measures for early starters in L2 immersion settings, whereas for late starters, there was a significant correlation with analytic ability.

Strong support for the claim that the role of analytic ability is clearly related to the age of L2 onset has been provided by DeKeyser (2000), who was able to show that analytic ability as measured by the MLAT grammatical sensitivity subtest correlated significantly with scores on a grammaticality judgment test (GJT) for those L2 speakers who arrived in the United States after the age of seventeen. The GJT scores of young arrivals—those who arrived in the United States before they reached the age of puberty—did not correlate with their analytic ability, thus providing further evidence for the critical period hypothesis (Johnson and Newport 1989). However, adults are different from young learners who still have access to their implicit learning mechanisms; when faced with the challenge of learning an L2, adult learners have to rely on their general cognitive resources, and, therefore, their analytic ability becomes central to L2 learning. Harley and Hart's (2002) second study—confirming that the L2 age of onset, rather than the learning setting, allowed the more able learners to achieve higher levels of L2 proficiency—is crucial to understanding why analytic ability plays such an important role in L2 learning.

Analytic Ability and Learning Conditions
Although there is strong evidence that language aptitude, particularly in regards to analytic ability, is a factor in adult foreign language learning (de Graaff 1997; DeKeyser 2000; Ehrman and Oxford 1995), the question of whether particular learning conditions and instructional approaches might trigger language aptitude and language analytic ability to a greater or lesser extent has not been completely resolved.

As a response to Krashen's (1981, 1985) objections that aptitude may be related only to conscious learning that takes place in schools, Skehan (1986, 1989) argued that informal learning environments may be even more challenging for L2 learners than structured formal settings; therefore, there is no reason to minimize the role of individual processing abilities in less formal learning conditions. Ranta's (2002) study, conducted in Quebec with young L1 French speakers in an intensive ESL program, has often been cited in support of claims that analytic ability is equally important in communicative as well as formal classroom settings. It is noteworthy, however, that the task used to measure analytic ability in French L1 children in this study tested grammatical knowledge in written French rather than analytic ability, and thus only showed a close relationship between L2 proficiency and mastery of L1 knowledge. This test did not tap the learners' ability to analyze novel sentences or to generalize, both of which are essential components of language analytic ability (Grigorenko, Sternberg, and Ehrman 2000; Sternberg 2002).

On the other hand, Robinson's (1996, 1997) experimental study examined four types of instructional conditions for learning both difficult and easy grammatical rules in English: explicit (with clear presentation of the grammar rule), implicit (as memorization of the text with the in-built rule), rule-searching, and incidental (with an orientation to meaning). In the first three conditions, gains in acquisition correlated strongly with participants' aptitude scores, whereas incidental learning did not relate to aptitude measured by the MLAT subtests. In this condition, the participants were given a meaning-related task with the rule built into the material. This study was replicated (Robinson 2002) using another language (Samoan) and the same four conditions. Once again, the gains indicated no significant correlation with aptitude in the group that was assigned to the incidental learning condition.

Erlam (2005) also provided evidence of a nonuniform relationship between analytic ability and gains in learning French direct object pronouns. Fourteen-year-old learners were given three distinct conditions: structured input instruction, inductive instruction, and deductive instruction. Deductive instruction was the only condition that benefited all learners irrespective of their abilities, meaning that in the deductive group, there was no evidence of a significant correlation between the learners' individual differences in language aptitude and their gain scores. However, the deductive instruction group received explicit explanation of the rule, as well as a chart that classified the use of pronouns and was available at all times, so this may have affected the results.

These findings suggest that there might be situations and learning conditions—such as incidental, meaning-focused learning—in which language analytic ability is not central to L2 learning. Additional conditions may involve the frequency and length of exposure to an L2 (Ross, Yoshinaga, and Sasaki 2002; Skehan 1986), as well as the selection of language structures more or less susceptible to abstraction. Particular conditions may involve types of corrective feedback.

Although there has recently been more research concerned with the effects of corrective feedback relative to memory measures, few researchers have been interested in the relationship between corrective feedback and the analytic ability component of aptitude. In one of the earliest studies on classroom error correction and individual differences, DeKeyser (1993) found that grammatical sensitivity was a significant predictor of grammar test scores, but the hypothesis that students with strong grammatical sensitivity would benefit most from error correction was not confirmed.

More recently, Sheen's (2007) research revealed that analytic ability scores correlated significantly with the gains of those participants who received explicit metalinguistic correction (written and oral). In contrast, the gains of the group that received oral recasts were not related to the learners' level of analytic ability. Although these results were not seen as particularly interesting, they actually corroborate Robinson and Yamaguchi's (1999) findings as reported in Robinson (2005), where, at the end of a five-week period in which students received recasts in task-based instruction, learning gains were not associated with the scores on the grammar sensitivity subtest of MLAT.

Clearly, there is a need for more research that clarifies how different learning conditions and instructional approaches induce learning processes in which language analytic ability and aptitude are not of equal importance.

Research Questions

The current study was undertaken to address this issue by looking at the role of analytic ability in two distinct conditions that were determined by the type of corrective feedback provided. The study attempted to answer the following research questions:

1. Is there a positive relationship between analytic ability and gains in language learning during communicative tasks involving oral corrective feedback in the form of recasts?
2. Is there a positive relationship between analytic ability and gains in language learning during communicative tasks involving oral corrective feedback in the form of clarification requests?

Method

The study was conducted with sixteen-year-old students from a New Zealand secondary school. The thirty-six students used in the study were learning French as a foreign language. The structures used in the study were two past-tense structures in French: the passé composé and the imparfait. The students came from two classes taught by the same teacher and had experienced around five hundred hours of French instruction. The two classes were comparable in terms of their use of French past tenses prior to the beginning of the study: no significant differences were found between the classes on oral and written production pretests.

Each of the two groups worked on three communicative tasks over two weeks. One group of learners ($n = 18$) received recasts (RE group) as an input-providing type of feedback; the other group ($n = 18$) was asked to self-correct, following the teacher's clarification requests (CR group) whenever they made an error in the production of the two past tenses. Phrases used to ask for clarification were "Comment?" (How?), "Pardon?" (Excuse me?), "Tu peux répéter?" (Can you repeat?). Other errors were ignored. The treatment tasks were picture-based, designed to encourage communication and to elicit the use of the target structures. The following are examples of a recast and a clarification request from the current study:

L2: ummm les deux garçons un garçon acheté et . . . (**trigger**)
umm the two boys one boy buy (PP) and . . .
"Umm two boys one boy buy/bought and . . ."

T: ils <u>ont acheté</u>? (**recast**)
they have (AUX) buy (PP)
"They bought?"

L34: . . . il faisait très chaud donc ils <u>ont</u> très soif (**trigger**)
. . . it do (IMP) very warm therefore they have very thirst
"It was hot so they are very thirsty"

T: comment ?tu peux répéter? (**clarification request**)
how? you can to repeat?
"How? Can you repeat?"

Target Structures
The two target structures in the study usually present considerable challenges to French L2 learners (Bardovi-Harlig 2000; Harley 1989). The difficulties arise from both formal and functional complexity. The formal complexity of the French passé composé (PC) and the imparfait (IMP) lies in the nature of the rules governing their form, as well as the numerous items that must be learned. The passé composé employs two different auxiliaries (*avoir* and *être*) in a structure consisting of the auxiliary and the past participle, which requires agreement with the subject according to relatively complex grammar rules. Imparfait, by comparison, has a simple form, with fixed person- and number-related inflections for all verb groups.

The passé composé has one basic meaning: perfective—or completed—action. On the other hand, the imparfait has three semantic meanings: imperfective (ongoing), iterative, and durative. Harley (1989) has shown that learners first start by using the passé composé; this is followed by the imparfait, but only with certain state verbs (e.g., *être, avoir*, and modals). Beginner students usually experience more problems with the accuracy of passé composé forms than with the imparfait forms (using only a limited number of verbs with inherent state lexical aspect), whereas at later stages, the use of the imparfait presents considerably more difficulties to L2 learners (Kaplan 1987).

Data Collection and Data Analysis
All participants completed a pretest, immediate posttest, and delayed posttest for oral and written production. The immediate posttest took place after the last of the three treatment tasks, and the delayed posttest was four to five weeks later. All tests were of the same format as the treatment tasks, but each of them involved a different story and included a range of verbs. The tests were scored and the percentage of accuracy was obtained using Pica's (1983) target-like use analysis, based on the established

obligatory contexts and taking into consideration the overuse of the target forms. The following formula was used:

$$\frac{\text{N correct suppliance in context (including correct form)}}{\text{N obligatory contexts + oversuppliance in non-obligatory contexts}} \times 100 = \% \text{ accuracy}$$

The passé composé and the imparfait were coded and scored separately by the author. The number of obligatory use contexts was established for PC and IMP, and all instances of overuse were identified. The tests in oral production elicited a range of five to fifteen obligatory occasions for the use of PC, with an average of ten uses per student per test. The same tests elicited a range of three to thirteen obligatory occasions for IMP, with an average of six uses per student per test. In written production, a range of three to fifteen obligatory occasions for PC were identified, with an average of eight uses per student per test, and a range of three to eleven obligatory occasions for IMP, with an average of six uses per student per test.

Another rater, a French native teacher, rated 15 percent of all the tests so that 16 randomly chosen oral production and 15 written production tests—involving in total 383 items of verb structure (218 of PC and 165 of IMP)—were co-rated. Agreement was calculated in percentage: the obtained agreement in oral production was 95 percent for PC and 97 percent for IMP. In written production agreement was 96 percent for PC and 98 percent for IMP.

Along with the narrative tasks/tests, the participants were asked to complete the language analysis test (LAT) developed by Ottó (2002) and published in Schmitt et al. (2004). The test is based on an artificial language and consists of fourteen multiple-choice items. It requires the participants to analyze the grammatical markers supplied in the glossary, deduce the rule, and select the correct equivalent English sentence. The LAT was scored by awarding one point for each correct answer. The total possible score was fourteen points and the final scores were calculated in percentages. The descriptive statistics of the LAT for each group were calculated (table 10.1) and an independent samples t-test was used to establish that the two groups were comparable: $t(32) = 0.92$. Reliability of the test was estimated by calculating internal consistency using the Cronbach alpha coefficient: $\alpha = 0.82$.

A mixed design repeated measures ANOVA with post hoc paired samples t-tests was used to establish if learning over time was above the chance level. Effect sizes were calculated using Cohen's d. An ANCOVA, with the pretest scores as a covariate,

Table 10.1
Descriptive statistics for language analysis test

Group	Mean	SD	Md	Min	Max
RE (N=16)	71.43	23.18	82.14	28.57	100
CR (N=18)[1]	64.28	21.64	71.43	14.28	92.86

Note: Two participants in RE group did not complete LAT, so all subsequent correlations with gains in this group were based on N=16. In CR group 18 participants completed LAT but one of them missed the language tests, so subsequent analyses are based on N=17.

was used to examine between group differences; even though there was no statistical difference on pretests, some variation was evident (tables 10.2 and 10.3), which must be taken into account (Miller and Chapman 2001).

To see if there was a relationship between acquisition gains and language aptitude, correlations between the LAT scores and the gain scores for each target structure (in oral and written modes) were computed. Gains were calculated by subtracting the pretest scores from the immediate posttest scores (short-term, Gain 1) and from the delayed posttest scores (long-term, Gain 2). A Pearson product moment coefficient was used if the data were normally distributed and Spearman coefficient if the data were not normally distributed. A one-tailed correlation was chosen since research so far has established that there is a generally positive correlation between aptitude and language acquisition.

Results

The results indicate that the two different types of corrective feedback had differential effects on the acquisition of the two target structures (tables 10.2, 10.3 and 10.4); this feedback also had differential effects on the involvement of language analytic ability in the participants' learning (table 10.5). In oral production (table 10.2), the results of repeated measures ANOVA for PC $[F(2, 66) = 5.12, p = 0.009]$ indicate that only the learners in the RE group showed statistically significant gains in target-like use of PC from pretest to immediate posttest $[t(17) = 5.6, p = 0.000, d = .76]$ and from pretest to delayed posttest $[t(17) = 6.9, p = 0.002, d = 0.67]$. Repeated measure ANOVA for IMP $[F(2, 64) = 4.35, p = 0.017]$ also shows that target-like use of IMP in oral production by the RE group improved significantly from pretest to immediate posttest $[t(17) = 3.2, p = 0.002, d = .76]$ and from pretest to delayed posttest $[t(17) = 5.6, p = 0.000, d = 1.05]$. In the CR group no statistically significant gains were observed in oral production, and the effect sizes were small.

In written production (table 10.3), again the results of repeated measures ANOVA for PC $[F(2, 64) = 3.52, p = 0.036]$ indicate that only the RE group showed gains above the chance level in target-like use of PC, both between the pretest and the immediate posttest $[t(16) = 3.5, p = 0.038, d = 0.46]$ and between the pretest and the delayed posttest $[t(16) = 4.3, p = 0.000, d = 0.89]$. However, for IMP in written

Table 10.2
Descriptive statistics for test scores in oral production

	Pretest		Posttest 1		Posttest 2	
Group	Mean	SD	Mean	SD	Mean	SD
Passé composé						
RE (N=18)	29.4	26.4	50.8	30.1	48.5	30.9
CR (N=17)	37.4	27.2	38.1	22.9	39.6	23.0.
Imparfait						
RE (N=18)	15.8	19.5	35.2	31.6	47.7	29.2
CR (N=17)	16.5	23.2	22	26.1	23.8	29.6

Table 10.3
Descriptive statistics for test scores in written production

		Pretest		Posttest 1		Posttest 2	
Group		Mean	SD	Mean	SD	Mean	SD
Passé composé							
RE	(N=17)	35.0.	30.0.	50.2	35.7	61.9	30.3
CR	(N=17)	45.5	28.1	47.0.	33.7	49.8	32.1
Imparfait							
RE	(N=17)	25.5	26.2	54.3	35.7	65.0.	26.9
CR	(N=17)	16.0.	20.7	29.2	23.4	37.8	26.0.

production, group over time effect was not significant [$F(2, 64) = 1.91, p > 0.05$], indicating that there was no difference in group behavior over time. In other words, both groups significantly improved in target-like use of IMP: the RE group improved from pretest to immediate posttest [$t(16) = 4.1, p = 0.000, d = 0.93$] and to delayed posttest [$t(16) = 5.5, p = 0.000, d = 1.49$], whereas the CR group showed gains in the use of IMP in written production above the chance level only between the pretest and the delayed posttest [$t(16) = 3.2, p = 0.003, d = 0.93$].

Comparison of the two groups, as shown by repeated measures ANOVA, followed by an ANCOVA with the pretest scores as a covariate (table 10.4), also indicates that recasts were significantly more effective than clarification requests for acquisition of both target structures. In short, the results demonstrate that the learners who received recasts—making them aware of an error and providing a corrected model of the problematic form—were able to show greater gains than the learners who received only clarification requests, which point to an error but do not provide a corrected model of the form.

The relationship between analytic ability and gain scores, as shown in table 10.5, is significantly different between the two learning conditions (recast or clarification request). In the RE group, there is a significant positive correlation only between the long-term oral PC gains and the language analysis scores ($r = 0.62, p < 0.01$). The negative correlation between LAT scores and IMP long-term written gains indicates that learners with lower LAT score achieved greater written IMP gains.

Table 10.4
Between group differences on each posttest: RE and CR group

Oral production	PC	IMP
Posttest 1	$F(1,32)= 8.08, p= .008$	$F(1,32)= 3.03, p= .09$
Posttest 2	$F(1,32)= 4.51, p= .042$	$F(1,31)= 6.88, p= .013$
Written production	PC	IMP
Posttest 1	$F(1,31)= 1.63, p= .05$	$F(1,31)= 4.17, p= .05$
Posttest 2	$F(1,31)= 4.20, p= .049$	$F(1,31)= 7.04, p= .012$

Table 10.5
Correlations between gains and LAT scores
Language analysis test score (r)

Test	Gains	RE (N=16)	CR (N=17)
Oral PC	Short-term	0.41	.44* (p=.040)
	Long-term	.62** (p=.005)	.43* (p=.044)
Oral IMP	Short-term	0.41	.58** (p=.008)
	Long-term	0.07	.71** (p=.001)
Written PC	Short-term	0.07	.67** (p=.001)
	Long-term	0.06	.77** (p<.000)
Written IMP	Short-term	−0.05	0.14
	Long-term	−.58* (p=.02)	0.35

* Significant p<.05.
** Significant p<.01.

In contrast, the results for oral production in the CR group indicate a significant positive correlation between language analytic ability and both short- and long-term gains for both structures (for PC: $r = 0.44$, $p < 0.05$, $r = 0.43$, $p < 0.05$; for IMP: $r = 0.58$, $p < 0.01$, $r = 0.71$, $p < 0.01$). The results for written production of the CR group show significant correlations between LAT scores and both short-term ($r = 0.67$, $p < 0.01$) and long-term gains ($r = 0.77$, $p < 0.01$) in target-like use of PC. No significant correlation was found between analytic ability and gains in target-like use of IMP in written production in the CR group.

Discussion

This study investigated whether there is a relationship between learning gains and learners' individual differences in analytic ability. The data incorporate two corrective feedback conditions provided during communicative tasks. The results show that the correlations between target-like use gains and language analytic ability exhibit different patterns for the recast and clarification request groups. Clearly, the link between analytic ability and learning gains is much stronger in the clarification request group, with statistically significant correlations between target-like use gains and language analytic ability for both language structures (PC and IMP) in oral production, and for only PC in written production.

The significant correlations in the CR group suggest that focus on form via requests for clarification required the learners to fully employ their cognitive resources when attempting to produce the target-like grammatical structures of PC and IMP in context. In the case of learners figuring out how to repair their own errors, the use of the target structures in both written and oral production tests (with the exception of IMP in written production) clearly presented highly demanding cognitive tasks for L2 learners. Since they received only implicit negative feedback with no corrected model of the target form, they had to employ general problem-solving and abstract reasoning skills. As a consequence, more capable students with higher levels of analytic ability exhibited greater gains in target-like use, whereas learners with lower analytic ability gained less. The results in the CR group correspond to most of the studies investigating the influence of language analytic ability on L2 learning (e.g., Carroll 1962; de Graaff 1997; DeKeyser 2000; Ehrman and Oxford 1995), confirming its important role for L2 learning. Clearly, the fact that L2 attainment depends heavily on analytic ability and aptitude may explain large differences among L2 learners, most of whom fail to acquire full linguistic competence in L2.

A different pattern of correlations characterizes the recast group's results. In the RE group, the learners' gains in target-like use of both structures show far less of a close relationship with LAT scores. These results correspond to Robinson's (1996, 1997, 2002) findings, which showed that in incidental learning during a task oriented to meaning, language analytic ability might not be a significant factor. This can be further linked to those studies (e.g., Sheen 2007) that found a positive relationship between learning gains and analytic ability in regard to the type of treatment using explicit metalinguistic feedback, but not for recasts.

The present study demonstrates that the use of recasts during communicative tasks may benefit all learners irrespective of their analytical abilities, whereas the use of clarification requests favors the more capable learners. Because recasts provide a corrected model of the problematic target form, learners are exposed to a greater number of target structures. Clarification requests, on the other hand, although challenging, certainly limit students' opportunities to hear more target-like language forms, particularly if their attempts to self-correct are not successful. In the current study, the RE group received significantly more target structures than the CR group; including learners' uptake during the treatment tasks, sixty-three tokens of PC and sixty-six tokens of IMP were recorded in the RE group, compared to seventeen tokens of PC and nineteen tokens of IMP in the CR group (Mann-Whitney independent samples test: Assymp.sig = 0.008 for PC, 0.007 for IMP).

The differences observed between the correlations relating to the acquisition of the two past-tense structures may be explained by their nature and by the level of the participants' interlanguage development. As already pointed out, at the interlanguage level of the current participants, the morphological complexity of PC presents more difficulties than IMP used only with a limited number of verbs. Therefore, the retention of morphological variety, characteristic of PC, poses higher cognitive demands on L2 learners. To maintain and use PC forms in semi-constrained (picture related), unplanned oral production, greater reliance on language analytic ability may be needed; in such situations, higher levels of analytic ability may help produce a better, more target-like performance on oral tasks. This is demonstrated in the RE group's only correlation between LAT scores and oral PC long-term gains. On all other measures, the RE group's gains were unrelated to their LAT scores. However, the use of IMP may have been simpler for this study's participants. Because of the limited number of verbs used in IMP, their acquisition may be reduced to the acquisition of lexical 'chunks'. This observation has been supported by a number of French L2 classroom studies (e.g., Harley 1989, 1993; Kaplan 1987). Interestingly, only the written IMP gains of the CR group did not correlate significantly with their LAT scores. Moreover, the long-term written IMP gains were the only significant within-group gains for the CR group. It seems that the use of IMP in written modality, at the level of current participants' interlanguage, does not pose high cognitive demands on learners. Therefore, all learners in the CR group, irrespective of their abilities, were able to learn from clarification requests and demonstrated significant gains. Surprisingly, however, in the RE group, there was a significant negative correlation between written IMP gains and LAT scores, suggesting that the learners of lower analytic ability showed significantly greater gains than learners of higher ability. This result is unexpected, but it might be explained by the slow development of imparfait (Bardovi-Harlig 2000; Shirai and Andersen 1995) and the fact that full acquisition of imperfective aspect takes place, if at all, only at later stages of language development. It is possible that recasts assisted the learners of lower ability so they could achieve their maximum for the given interlanguage level; on the other hand, recasts may have been ineffective for the more capable learners to move to the next level, further from the stage limited by the acquisition of imperfective aspect for verbs with inherent lexical aspect of state.

Recasts seem to be particularly effective when involving morphologically more complex forms. Since they provide both negative feedback and positive evidence, recasts can reduce the cognitive load on learners and, thus, not only assist in achieving more target-like accuracy, but also make more "space" available to be used for complexity and fluency development (Skehan 1998). In such conditions, the acquisition of grammar and improvement of accuracy may not be seen as a cognitively demanding task. Higher frequency of certain forms in the input, condensed into a short time span, might correspond to more time spent on learning, and therefore the benefits are twofold—in terms of accuracy gains and in terms of neutralizing the need for analytic ability. As Skehan (1986) argued when pointing to the value of Carroll's 1962 model of school learning, the role of language aptitude increases in conditions determined by pressure and shortage of time. Conversely, if there is more time available, including higher frequency of input, the role of aptitude may become less important.

Limitations and Conclusion

The sample size was rather small, involving eighteen participants in each group. Moreover, in one of the groups, two learners did not complete the LAT, so the number was even smaller. However, this is the average size of a foreign language class in the New Zealand secondary school, so the study has ecological validity, even if the conclusions cannot be generalized to other groups outside of the study.

Another sampling limitation is the fact that the participants were recruited from one of the top schools in the country, so the sample may not represent a larger population of foreign language learners.

Additionally, only language analytic ability was investigated, although it is only one of several components of language aptitude. However, the aim of this study was to focus on analytic ability exclusively, since this component—involving both grammatical sensitivity and inductive language learning ability—has been shown to play the major role in adult acquisition of L2 grammar.

In summary, the present study demonstrates how different learning conditions affect the type of learning that takes place in a foreign language classroom. The results provide further evidence that adult L2 acquisition may not always be dependent on analytic ability and language aptitude. For at least one structure under investigation, PC verbal morphology, the use of recasts resulted not only in greater accuracy gains, but in a qualitatively different type of learning, evidenced by online production and available to all learners irrespective of their analytic ability. The correlations to LAT scores explain the gains in the two groups; the use of recasts provided opportunities for increasing the frequency of target forms in the input by supplying the corrected model immediately and simultaneously with the implicit negative feedback, while learners' attention was focused on meaning. Hence, this study of incidental learning at the beginner stages of tense-aspect verbal morphology lends tentative support to those theories which argue that frequency, saliency, recency, and context are key factors (Ellis 2002; Ellis and Collins 2009) guiding L2 acquisition.

Acknowledgments

The findings reported in this paper are based on part of my PhD thesis completed at the University of Auckland. I would like to thank my supervisors Rod Ellis and Helen Basturkmen, as well as the students who contributed data to this study. I am sincerely grateful to the anonymous reviewers, and particularly to the editors of this volume, whose comments on the previous version of this paper were extremely helpful.

REFERENCES

Bardovi-Harlig, Kathleen. 2000. *Tense and Aspect in Second Language Acquisition: Form, Meaning, and Use*. Oxford: Blackwell.

Carroll, John B. 1962. "The prediction of success in foreign language training." In *Training Research and Education*, 87–136, edited by Robert Glaser. Pittsburgh: University of Pittsburgh Press.

Carroll, John B., and Stanley M. Sapon. 1959. *Modern Language Aptitude Test (MLAT): Manual*. San Antonio, TX: Psychological Corporation.

de Graaff, Rick. 1997. "The EXperanto experiment." *Studies in Second Language Acquisition* 19: 249–76.

Dekeyser, Robert. 1993. "The effect of error correction on L2 grammar knowledge and oral proficiency." *The Modern Language Journal* 77: 501–14.

———. 2000. "The robustness of critical period effects in second language acquisition." *Studies in Second Language Acquisition* 22 (4): 499–533.

Ehrman, Madeline E., and Rebecca L. Oxford. 1995. "Cognition plus: Correlates of language learning success." *The Modern Language Journal* 79: 67–89.

Ellis, Nick C. 2002. "Frequency effects in language processing." *Studies in Second Language Acquisition* 24: 143–88. doi:10.1017/S0272263102002024.

Ellis, Nick, and Laura Collins. 2009. "Input and second language acquisition: The roles of frequency, form, and function, introduction to the special issue." *The Modern Language Journal* 93: 329–36.

Ellis, Rod. 2004. "Individual differences in second language learning." In *The Handbook of Applied Linguistics*, 525–51, edited by Alan Davies and Catherine Elder. Malden, MA: Blackwell Publishing.

Erlam, Rosemary. 2005. "Language aptitude and its relationship to instructional effectiveness in second language acquisition." *Language Teaching Research* 9: 147–71. doi:10.1191/1362168805lr161oa.

Grigorenko, Elena L., Robert J. Sternberg, and Madeline E. Ehrman. 2000. "A theory-based approach to the measurement of foreign language learning ability: The Canal-F theory and test." *The Modern Language Journal* 84: 390–405.

Harley, Birgit. 1989. "Functional grammar in French immersion: A classroom experiment." *Applied Linguistics* 10: 331–60. doi:10.1093/applin/10.3.331.

———. 1993. "Instructional strategies and SLA in early French immersion." *Studies in Second Language Acquisition* 15: 245–59. doi:doi:10.1017/S0272263100011980.

Harley, Birgit, and Doug Hart. 1997. "Language aptitude and second language proficiency in classroom learners of different starting ages." *Studies in Second Language Acquisition* 19: 379–400.

———. 2002. "Age, aptitude and second language learning on a bilingual exchange." In *Individual Differences and Instructed Language Learning*, 301–30, edited by Peter Robinson. Amsterdam: John Benjamins.

Johnson, Jacqueline S., and Elissa L. Newport. 1989. "Critical period effects in second language learning: The influence of maturational state on the acquisition of English as a second language." *Cognitive Psychology* 21: 60–99. doi:10.1016/0010-0285(89)90003-0.

Kaplan, Marsha A. 1987. "Developmental patterns of past tense acquisition among foreign language learners of French." In *Foreign Language Learning: A Research Perspective*, 52–60, edited by Bill VanPatten, Trisha R. Dvorak, and James F. Lee. New York: Newbury House.

Krashen, Steven D. 1981. *Second Language Acquisition and Second Language Learning*, first edition. New York: Oxford University Press.

———. 1985. *The Input Hypothesis: Issues and Implications*. New York: Longman.

Miller, Gregory A., and Jean P. Chapman. 2001. "Misunderstanding analysis of covariance." *Journal of Abnormal Psychology* 110: 40–48.

Nagata, Hirota, David Aline, and Rod Ellis. 1999. "Modified input, language aptitude and the acquisition of word meanings." In *Learning a Second Language Through Interaction*, 133–49, edited by Rod Ellis. Amsterdam: John Benjamins.

Ottó, Istvan. 2004. "Language analysis test." In *Formulaic Sequences: Acquisition, Processing, and Use*, 75–76, edited by Norbert Schmitt. Amsterdam: John Benjamins.

Pica, Teresa. 1983. "Methods of morpheme quantification: Their effect on the interpretation of second language data." *Studies in Second Language Acquisition* 6: 69–78. doi:10.1017/S0272263100000309.

Ranta, Leila. 2002. "The role of learners' language analytic ability in the communicative classroom." In *Individual Differences and Instructed Language Learning*, 159–80, edited by Peter Robinson. Amsterdam: John Benjamins.

Robinson, Peter. 1996. *Consciousness, Rules, and Instructed Second Language Acquisition*. New York: Peter Lang.

———. 1997. "Individual differences and the fundamental similarity of implicit and explicit adult second language learning." *Language Learning* 47: 45–99. doi:10.1111/0023-8333.21997002.

———. 2001. *Cognition and Second Language Instruction*. Cambridge: Cambridge University Press.

———. 2002. "Effects of individual differences in intelligence, aptitude and working memory on adult incidental SLA: A replication and extension of Reber, Walkenfield and Hernstadt." In *Individual Differences and Instructed Language Learning*, 211–66, edited by Peter Robinson. Amsterdam: John Benjamins.

———. 2005. "Aptitude and second language acquisition." *Annual Review of Applied Linguistics* 25: 46–73. doi:10.1017/S0267190505000036.

Robinson, P., and Y. Yamaguchi. 1999. Cited in Robinson, P., 2005. "Aptitude and second language acquisition." *Annual Review of Applied Linguistics* 25: 46–73.

Ross, Steven, N. Yoshinaga, and M. Sasaki. 2002. "Aptitude-exposure interaction effects on Wh-movement violation detection by pre-and-post-critical period Japanese bilinguals." In *Individual Differences and Instructed Language Learning*, 267–97, edited by Peter Robinson. Amsterdam: John Benjamins.

Sasaki, Miyuki. 1996. *Second Language Proficiency, Foreign Language Aptitude, and Intelligence: Quantitative and Qualitative Analyses*. New York: Peter Lang.

Sawyer, Mark, and Leila Ranta. 2001. "Aptitude, individual differences, and instructional design." In *Cognition and Second Language Instruction*, 319–53, edited by Peter Robinson. Cambridge: Cambridge University Press.

Schmitt, Norbert, Zoltan Dörnyei, Svenja Adolphs, and Valerie Durow. 2004. "Knowledge and acquisition of formulaic sequences: A longitudinal study." In *Formulaic Sequences: Acquisition, Processing, and Use*, 55–86, edited by Norbert Schmitt. Amsterdam: John Benjamins.

Sheen, Younghee. 2007. "The effects of corrective feedback, language aptitude, and learner attitude on the acquisition of English articles." In *Conversational Interaction in Second Language Acquisition: A Collection of Empirical Studies*, edited by Alison Mackey. Oxford: Oxford University Press.

Shirai, Yasuhiro, and Roger W. Andersen. 1995. "The acquisition of tense-aspect morphology: A prototype account." *Language* 71: 743–62.

Skehan, Peter. 1986. "The role of foreign language aptitude in a model of school learning." *Language Testing* 3: 188–221. doi:10.1177/026553228600300207.

———. 1989. *Individual Differences in Second-Language Learning*. New York: E. Arnold; distributed in the US by Routledge, Chapman, and Hall.

———. 1998. *A Cognitive Approach to Language Learning*. New York: Oxford University Press.

Sparks, Richard, and Leonore Ganschow. 2001. "Aptitude for learning a foreign language." *Annual Review of Applied Linguistics* 21: 90–111. doi:10.1017/S026719050100006X.

Sternberg, Robert J. 2002. "The theory of successful intelligence and its implications for language aptitude testing." In *Individual Differences and Instructed Language Learning*, 13–43, edited by Peter Robinson. Amsterdam: John Benjamins.

11

U-Shaped Development

Definition, Exploration, and Falsifiable Hypotheses

HIROYUKI OSHITA
Ohio University

LINGUISTICS IS AN EMPIRICAL science; second language acquisition, as a branch of linguistics, is an empirical field. To some, this may simply mean that any theoretical claim must be based on actual data, such as learners' linguistic performance. Others may believe that data must be quantified so that claims can be tested and statistically verified in virtual or conceptual replication studies (Hendrick 1990; Mackey and Gass 2005; van der Veer, van IJzendoorn, and Valsiner 1994). To still others, such as the philosopher Karl Popper, a critical requirement for empirical claims is not their verifiability but their falsifiability (Kogawara 1997). According to this view, researchers must formulate testable and falsifiable hypotheses that others can challenge. Thus, if multiple explanations are possible for a particular phenomenon, a theory that can make specific predictions about other phenomena yet to be observed is more valuable than those that do not make such predictions precisely because it is easier to falsify.

This paper is an attempt to meet the falsifiability requirement in a second language acquisition study. The target of investigation is a developmental process in the acquisition of two kinds of intransitive verbs, unergatives and unaccusatives, during which learners occasionally reveal nontarget grammaticality judgments and produce a peculiar ungrammatical sentence pattern. In the literature, a number of accounts have been proposed for these phenomena, but no serious attempt has been made yet to critically evaluate them by considering the overall developmental path. I first discuss split intransitivity based on the proposal made by Perlmutter (1978) and present Oshita's (1997, 2001) unaccusative trap hypothesis (UTH): a three-stage developmental account of phenomena associated with L2 acquisition of intransitive verbs. Next, I review previous L2 studies that tested the UTH—focusing on its prediction of U-shaped developmental patterns—and point out both conceptual and methodological problems inherent in them. I also propose some measures to address those problems, the most important of which is the conceptualization of a relative U-shape. After the review, I describe a grammaticality judgment study conducted on Japanese learners of English, which has produced robust evidence for U-shaped development. In light of the results of this study, the merits of UTH are discussed by comparing it with alternative accounts of L2 acquisition of unaccusatives. The paper concludes with a brief remark on the potential relevance of relative U-shape for language acquisition research. In particular, I foresee such relevance where two competing factors are suspected to be at work in shaping learners' linguistic knowledge (Marcus et al. 1992; Pinker 1999), as well as when superficially similar but linguistically contrasting items appear to initially mislead learners to a wrong representation of one due to the overwhelming influence of the other (Chomsky 1969).

Split Intransitivity and UTH

According to Perlmutter (1978), the intransitive verb class consists of two subtypes called unergatives and unaccusatives. Semantically, unergatives are verbs of controlled processes (e.g., *cry* and *smile*) and unaccusatives are nonvolitional change of state or location verbs (e.g., *melt* and *shift*), existence verbs (e.g., *exist* and *remain*), appearance verbs (e.g., *appear* and *occur*), and so on. Syntactically, unergatives require an external argument (inherent subject), whereas unaccusatives take an internal argument (inherent object); their difference is often masked on the surface because the argument of unaccusative verbs undergoes object-to-subject movement in a way that appears similar to regular passive movement (Burzio 1986). Their difference and similarity are shown below.

a. The guest [$_{VP}$ walked] (unergative derivation)
b. The guest$_i$ [$_{VP}$ arrived *trace$_i$*] (unaccusative derivation)
c. The guest$_i$ was [$_{VP}$ killed *trace$_i$*] (passive derivation)

The division of the two types of intransitive verbs is known as split intransitivity (Sorace 2000).

Oshita's (1997, 2001) unaccusative trap hypothesis (UTH) was proposed to account for various phenomena in L2 acquisition of intransitive verbs such as uneasiness and overpassivization observed in L2 English. Uneasiness refers to learners' reluctance to accept unaccusative verbs in the canonical S-V order (Hirakawa 1995; Kellerman 1978; Oshita 2002). Overpassivization is their tendency to accept and produce them in ungrammatical passive sentences such as, "This problem is existed for many years," and in contextually inappropriate ones such as "The ice in the freezer was melted during the power outage" when "The ice in the freezer melted during the power outage" is more suitable (Ju 2000; Oshita 2000; Zobl 1989). These errors are not very frequent, but they have been observed among relatively advanced learners. They affect mostly unaccusatives.

UTH is a three-stage developmental account of uneasiness, overpassivization, and other phenomena related to split intransitivity. At the first stage, because of the overwhelming instances of unaccusatives appearing in the S-V order in input, learners are believed to misanalyze them as unergatives (subject-taking verbs) and associate them exclusively with the canonical order, making few obvious errors. At the second stage, learners correctly reanalyze unaccusatives as object-taking verbs and face a syntactic challenge to deal with predicates without an external argument. If they associate internal arguments with object position too rigidly, they may hesitate to accept S-V order (uneasiness). If they move the arguments from object to subject position, they may mark the movement superfluously with the auxiliary *be* and the verbs' past participle forms (overpassivization). At the third stage, learners can attain the native-like grammar by expunging the nontarget syntactic intuition from their L2 competence.

Unaccusative Trap Hypothesis
<First Stage>
    Lexicon: unaccusatives misanalyzed as subject-taking verbs
    Syntax: all intransitive verbs used in SV order
        e.g., Unergative: The baby [$_{VP}$ walked]
        e.g., Unaccusative: The baby [$_{VP}$ fell] (nontarget derivation)

<Second Stage>
    Lexicon: unaccusatives correctly analyzed as object-taking verbs
    Syntax: uneasiness and overpassivization observed with unaccusatives
        e.g., Uneasiness: ??? ___ [$_{VP}$ fell the baby] ???
        e.g., Overpassivization: The baby$_i$ was [$_{VP}$ fallen *trace$_i$*]

<Third Stage>
    Lexicon: unaccusatives correctly analyzed as object-taking verbs
    Syntax: uneasiness and overpassivization expunged from L2 syntax
        e.g., Unergative: The baby [$_{VP}$ walked]
        e.g., Unaccusative: The baby$_i$ [$_{VP}$ fell *trace$_i$*] (target derivation)

Additionally, UTH explains why unergatives are immune to the nontarget phenomena: unlike unaccusatives, they are correctly represented from the start and never undergo the lexical or syntactic reanalysis. Finally, because of this contrastive behavior of unaccusatives and unergatives, UTH predicts U-shaped development in the acquisition of unaccusatives in comparison with the unergatives. This highly specific prediction makes the UTH a falsifiable hypothesis.

Previous Research That Tested UTH

A number of studies have examined the claims made by UTH, particularly its prediction of U-shaped development, but most of them have either failed to find evidence for it (Imai 2004; Oshita 1997; Park and Lakshmanan 2007; Wong 2007; Yamakawa et al. 2003) or found only partially supportive evidence for the beginning of a U-shaped development (Hertel 2003; Montrul 2005) or for the end of it (Deguchi and Oshita 2004). A careful review of these studies, however, reveals a number of conceptual and methodological problems.

The first problem is the lack of a clear and unmistakable definition of U-shaped development itself. Most researchers seemed to have in mind something like "[a pattern] whereby early forms appear to be correct, followed by a period of incorrect forms, with a final stage of correct forms" (Gass and Selinker 2008, 522). This conceptualization of U-shape may be called absolute U-shape and can be defined as "a temporary but significant regression from an anticipated steady developmental path followed by a subsequent recovery." Good examples of absolute U-shaped development are the change of a bear's body weight during and after hibernation and the change of a human baby's weight over a few weeks immediately after birth (Vaughan, McKay, and Behrman 1979, 16).

It is important to note, however, that absolute U-shape is not what is predicted by the UTH, which is about potential contrasts between the acquisition of unaccusatives and that of unergatives. To study such contrasts, a different conceptualization of U-shape is necessary: something like "a temporary but significant lag relative to the developmental path of a benchmark item followed by a subsequent recovery." This can be called relative U-shape. An excellent example of relative U-shaped development is an apparent lag in physical growth experienced by boys as compared to girls, which is caused by the delayed inception of the boys' adolescent growth spurt (Steinberg 2008, 28–29). At no point of development do boys shrink or shrivel, so the pattern of their development can be conceived as a U-shape only when it is compared with its benchmark (i.e., the pace of girls' growth). Many cognitive scientists seem to subconsciously look for relative U-shapes when they study human development, as Marcus et al. (1992) tacitly compared children's acquisition of irregularly inflected words (e.g., *ran* and *feet*) with their acquisition of regularly inflected ones (e.g., *walked* and *legs*).[1]

Another problem related to U-shaped development is that most researchers think of it as a holistic image that fortuitously emerges when obtained data are presented visually. This impressionistic notion must be replaced by a more rigorous objective definition. One way is to define it quantitatively as a statistically significant decrease followed by a statistically significant increase. In addition, in the case of a relative U-shape, the target and the benchmark items should show significant differences at the bottom of the U.

A second major problem inherent in most previous studies is that the subjects were recruited from a relatively homogeneous sample, typically college students, and separated into experimental groups by proficiency measures such as their institutional status (Deguchi and Oshita 2004; Hertel 2003), their performance on all or part of a standardized language test (Imai 2004; Ju 2000; Yamakawa et al. 2003), research-internal measurements like cloze tests (Oshita 1997; Park and Lakshmanan 2007), or some combination of the above (Montrul 2005; Yuan 1999). In these studies, different proficiency levels were assumed to correspond to different stages of grammatical development even though the levels were differentiated in a relatively homogenous sample; however, there is no more reason to equate such proficiency scores with different states of the learners' grammar than to assume differences in height or weight among fifteen-year-olds in a school to be somehow indicative of different stages of their physical development. Therefore, the diversity of subjects in terms of the stages of their grammatical development must be based on something other than proficiency alone. Considering that two studies that revealed a clear U-shape used the length of instructed study of the target language as a primary criterion for subject grouping (Kellerman 1978; Yuan 1999; Oshita 2001), this may be a better, though imperfect, measure of estimation of grammatical development. Even then, it is essential that each subject group consist of learners who have experienced the same or similar language instruction as those in the groups preceding them so that the sample as a whole represents the target population.

As important as the criterion for grouping subjects is the number of subject groups. In order to find any developmental trend, including a U-shape, data must be obtained from at least three experimental groups, with a control group aside. Some studies do not meet this minimum requirement (e.g., Park and Lakshmanan 2007) but even those that do (e.g., Montrul 2005; Yamakawa et al. 2003) may have only a slim chance to capture an existing U-shape because the range of the subject groups may not be wide enough to contain the whole sequence of development. For example, the U-shape may have already partially or fully run its course prior to the level of the lowest proficiency group in the study. Therefore, in order to increase the chance of finding a U-shape, the number of subject groups must be as large as possible, covering a wide range of developmental stages (e.g., a wide range of time in instructed study). The more diverse the subjects are and the more levels they are divided into, the better chance there is of finding a U-shape.

Increasing the range and the number of subject groups, however, has important implications on the selection of diagnostics of their grammatical competence. Previous studies used various structures as diagnostics; for example, pseudopassive construction (Hirakawa 2003), resultative construction (Hirakawa 2003; Park and Lakshmanan 2007), absolutive construction (Montrul 2005), and nontarget causativization (Imai 2004; Yamakawa et al. 2003). These, however, may be too complex to use with lower-level subjects. Clearly, diagnostics must be simple enough so that even the lowest subject group can deal with them. One way to address this concern is to use learners' typical errors, like uneasiness and overpassivization, as diagnostics. Of course, as Shan and Yuan (2008) have shown in L2 Chinese, a well-known error such as overpassivization in L2 English may not exist in other nonnative languages. Therefore, the commonness of a certain type of error must be confirmed before it is adopted as a diagnostic (cf Montrul 2005).

Empirical Search for U-Shaped Development

The conceptual and methodological issues discussed in the previous section were taken into consideration in planning the experimental study reported below.[2]

Hypotheses

Five sets of research hypotheses were developed based on the UTH. Every set except for the fifth consists of two parts.

First, according to UTH, unaccusatives and unergatives are assumed to be undifferentiated near the beginning of the developmental path. If this is correct, the unaccusative-related nontarget phenomena should not be observed at this stage: hence, Hypotheses 1-A and 1-B.

> H1-A: Uneasiness will not be observed any more with unaccusatives than with unergatives among subjects close to the beginning of the developmental path.

H1-B: Overpassivization will not be accepted any more on unaccusatives than on unergatives by subjects close to the beginning of the developmental path.

Second, at some intermediate point on the developmental path, unaccusatives are differentiated from unergatives, but their correct syntactic derivation may not be acquired yet. If this is correct, we should find the nontarget phenomena more with unaccusatives than with unergatives at this stage: thus, hypotheses 2-A and 2-B.

H2-A: Uneasiness will be observed more with unaccusatives than with unergatives among subjects at the midpoint of the developmental path.

H2-B: Overpassivization will be accepted more on unaccusatives than on unergatives by subjects at the midpoint of the developmental path.

Third, close to the end of the developmental path (i.e., acquisition of a target-like grammar), the correct syntactic derivation of unaccusatives is acquired. If this is correct, the nontarget phenomena should not appear at this stage: thus, hypotheses 3-A and 3-B.

H3-A: Uneasiness will not be observed any more with unaccusatives than with unergatives among subjects close to the end of the developmental path.

H3-B: Overpassivization will not be accepted any more on unaccusatives than on unergatives by subjects close to the end of the developmental path.

Fourth, if hypotheses 1 through 3 are all correct, a relative U-shaped development (as operationalized above) should be observed with respect to the nontarget phenomena: thus, hypotheses 4-A and 4-B.

H4-A: Uneasiness about S-V order with unaccusatives will produce a U-shape relative to uneasiness about S-V order with unergatives.

H4-B: Overpassivization of unaccusatives will produce a U-shape relative to overpassivization of unergatives.

Finally, the UTH predicts that uneasiness precedes (or, at least, does not follow) overpassivization because the former is hypothesized to appear when learners' grammar has not internalized object-to-subject movement. Since overpassivization marks such movement, when it is internalized in the learners' L2 grammar, uneasiness is expected to disappear. This reasoning leads to the last hypothesis.

H5: Uneasiness will appear before overpassivization.

All the hypotheses are specific and tightly related to one another, which makes them highly falsifiable. For example, even when a significant increase is observed, if it is not preceded by a significant decrease, it will falsify the U-shape prediction. Also, even when both uneasiness and overpassivization emerge, if the latter appears before the former, it will put the proposed theoretical accounts for these phenomena into serious question. Thus, the UTH as a whole meets the falsifiability requirement, especially if it is properly tested with the proposed statistical definition of U-shape.

Method

Five groups of Japanese learners of English (n = 172) and twelve native English speakers participated in the study. The experimental subjects represented a wide range of Japanese learners of English, for whom formal instruction of the language typically started in seventh grade.

Subject Group	Description
Eighth grade (n = 41):	13–14 years old
Ninth grade (n = 34):	14–15 years old
Eleventh grade (n = 36):	16–17 years old
College (n = 34):	college sophomores majoring in English
Functional L2E (n = 27):	adults (college graduates) who use English regularly for professional purposes, and graduate students in the United States
Native (n = 12):	graduate and undergraduate students at an American university

The first three groups of subjects were students in schools run by a private educational foundation where English was taught in a common six-year curriculum. College and functional L2E subjects were all graduates of Japanese high schools; these groups can be considered successful products of the English education in the country's school system. These two groups, along with the native subjects group, were the same as those studied in Deguchi and Oshita (2004), which used the identical experimental materials for data collection.

The diagnostics were uneasiness and overpassivization. Eight verbs were selected based on the split intransitivity hierarchy (Sorace 2000). Three types of unaccusatives, namely, *fall* and *arrive* (change of location), *die* and *appear* (change of state[3]), and *exist* and *remain* (existence), were chosen in order to compare each of them with the most prototypical type of unergatives on the hierarchy; namely, *cry* and *smile* (controlled nonmotional process). Each verb was presented in active and passive sentence patterns and with animate and inanimate subjects.

The test presented thirty-one experimental and six filler sentences with a picture.[4] The subjects were asked to judge the grammaticality of each sentence on a five-point Likert scale (1 = not correct, 2 = unsure but probably incorrect, 3 = cannot decide, 4 = unsure but probably correct, 5 = correct). Prior to the judgment test, the eighth and ninth graders studied a list of difficult words. After the test, the eighth graders translated four passive Japanese sentences into English. Since it is meaningless to discuss overpassivization if the regular grammatical passivization is not acquired yet, only the subjects who correctly translated at least three sentences were included in the analysis. The subjects' responses were scored on their accuracy. For instance, a response of 5 (correct) on a grammatical active sentence and a response of 1 (not correct) on an ungrammatical passive sentence each received five points. A response of 4 (unsure but probably correct) on a grammatical active sentence and a response of 2 (unsure but probably incorrect) on an ungrammatical passive sentence each received four points. And a response of 3 (cannot decide) received three points.

To compare learners' grammatical judgment between groups, a one-way ANOVA was conducted on the five experimental subject groups.[5] To look for absolute U-shapes, groups' mean accuracy scores were compared first on active sentences and then on passive sentences. To find relative U-shapes, groups were compared on how differently they treated unaccusatives and unergatives. Differential treatment was calculated by subtracting the unergative mean from the unaccusative mean. The number is expected to be close to zero (and remain so) when unaccusatives and unergatives are not differentiated or present the same degree of difficulty to learners. On the contrary, if a subject group shows a delay in acquisition of unaccusatives vis-à-vis unergatives, it should result in a negative value considerably lower than that of preceding and following groups. If a relative U-shape was identified, matched-pairs t-tests were used to see if the group(s) at the bottom of the U-shape made significantly more non-target judgment on unaccusatives than on unergatives. These statistical analyses were repeated to compare each semantic subtype of unaccusatives with the two unergatives. Interactions of sentence type and subject group were examined by repeated-measures ANOVA.

Results

Statistical analysis found no absolute U-shape in the obtained data. As expected, there were significant improvements of scores as the subject levels increased, but no significant drops in scores existed between any groups. The result is no surprise. Learners do not experience a drastic regression while they keep learning the target language.

In contrast, robust evidence for relative U-shapes was repeatedly found in the data. Every hypothesis was supported, often with a large effect size. Figure 11.1 shows how the five groups judged active and passive sentences and how their judgments differed from one another.[6]

Let us first look at the subjects' judgment on the grammaticality of active sentences. The result of a one-way ANOVA was statistically significant: $F(4, 167) = 4.35, p = 0.002$; Levene $= 1.93, p = 0.108$. A post hoc LSD identified a clear U-shaped pattern stretching from eighth grade to college. Statistically significant differences were found between eighth and ninth grades (mean difference = 0.46, 95% CI = 0.11, .82, $p = 0.011, d = 0.65$), eighth and eleventh grades (mean difference = 0.59, 95% CI = 0.24, 0.94, $p = 0.001, d = 0.83$), eleventh grade and college (mean difference = –0.59, 95% CI = –0.95, –.22, $p = 0.002, d = 0.83$), and eleventh grade and functional L2E (mean difference = –0.42, 95% CI = –0.81, –0.03, $p = 0.036, d = 0.59$). Matched pairs t-tests confirmed that ninth and eleventh grades (and only these two groups) made significantly more non-target judgments on active unaccusatives than on active unergatives: ninth grade ($M = -0.34, SD = 0.88$, 95%

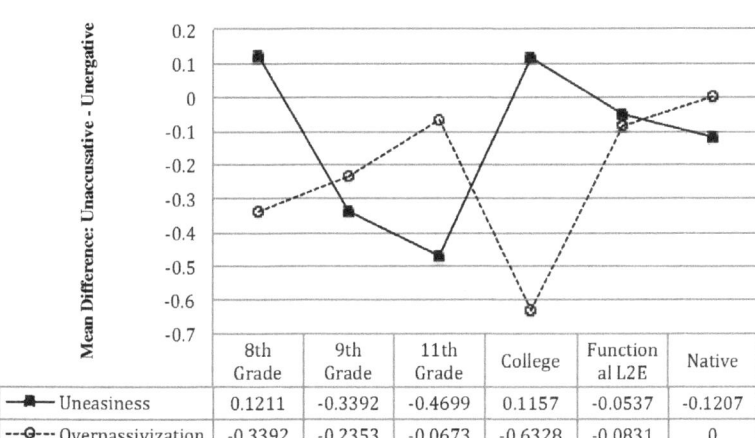

Figure 11.1 Group Differences in Judgment of Active and Passive Sentences

CI = –0.65, –0.03, t = –2.24, p = 0.032, η^2 = 0.13) and eleventh grade (M = –0.47, SD = 0.67, 95% CI = –0.70, –0.24, t = –4.19, p = 0.000, η^2 = 0.33). The results support H1-A, H2-A, and H3-A. The results collectively serve as evidence for a relative U-shape predicted in H4-A: no uneasiness in eighth grade, uneasiness in ninth and eleventh grades, and no uneasiness again in either college or functional L2E.

Next, let us examine how the groups' judgments of passive sentences differed from one another. Statistically significant differences were found among groups: F(4, 167) = 2.49, p = 0.045; Levene = 10.21, p = 0.000. Post hoc Games-Howell identified significant differences between eleventh grade and college (mean difference = 0.57, 95% CI = 0.05, 1.08, p = 0.024, d = 1.88) as well as between college and functional L2E (mean difference = –0.55, 95% CI = –0.92, –0.17, p = 0.001, d = 1.82). Cohen's d statistics indicated very large effect sizes. Matched pairs t-tests on these three groups revealed significantly differential treatment of unaccusatives and unergatives only in college (M = –0.63, SD = 0.69, 95% CI = –0.87, –0.39, t = –5.32, p = 0.000, η^2 = 0.46). The results clearly support H1-B, H2-B and H3-B on overpassivization. In addition, they collectively support H4-B on U-shaped development: no overpassivization in eleventh grade, overpassivization in college, and no overpassivization again in functional L2E.

Furthermore, the analysis of the three semantic subtypes of unaccusatives vis-à-vis the two unergatives (*cry* and *smile*) also produced results highly consistent with the overall patterns observed above. Groups' treatments of the unergatives and the change of location verbs (*fall* and *arrive*) in active sentences were significantly different: F(4, 167) = 3.75, p = 0.006; Levene = 1.21, p = 0.308. Post hoc LSD showed significant differences in the following pairs: eighth and ninth grades (mean difference = 0.54, 95% CI = 0.11, 0.97, p = 0.014, d = 0.59), eighth and eleventh grades (mean difference = 0.70, 95% CI = 0.28, 1.12, p = 0.001, d = 0.78), eleventh grade and college (mean difference = –0.51, 95% CI = –0.95, –0.07, p = 0.023, d = 0.56), and eleventh grade and functional L2E (mean difference = –0.62, 95% CI = –1.10, –0.15, p = 0.010, d = 0.69). Matched t-tests found a statistically significant difference in eleventh grade (M = –0.47, SD = 0.89, 95% CI = –0.77, –0.17, t = –3.15, p = 0.003, η^2 = 0.22) but not in the other groups. Thus, uneasiness was observed in eleventh grade.

Groups' judgments of active sentences with unergatives and the change of state verbs (*die* and *appear*) were significantly different as well: $F(4, 167) = 4.00$, $p = 0.004$; Levene = 1.61, p = 0.173. Post hoc LSD showed significant differences between eighth and ninth grades (mean difference = 0.54, 95% CI = 0.12, 0.95, p = 0.011, d = 0.67), eighth and eleventh grades (mean difference = 0.47, 95% CI = 0.07, 0.88, p = 0.022, d = 0.59), ninth grade and college (mean difference = –0.71, 95% CI = –1.14, –0.28, p = 0.001, d = 0.88), and eleventh grade and college (mean difference = –0.65, 95% CI = –1.07, –0.22, p = 0.003, d = 0.81). Matched t-tests found significant differences in ninth grade (M = –0.49, SD = 0.98, 95% CI = –0.83, –0.15, t = –2.91, p = 0.006, η^2 = 0.20) and eleventh grade (M = –0.43, SD = 0.76, 95% CI = –0.69, –0.17, t = –3.40, p = 0.022, η^2 = 0.25) but not in the other groups. Thus, uneasiness was observed in ninth and eleventh grades.

Groups also differed on judgment of the unergatives and the existence verbs (*exist* and *remain*) in the active sentence pattern: $F(4, 167) = 2.52$, $p = 0.043$; Levene = 2.24, p = 0.067. LSD[7] revealed statistically significant differences between eighth and eleventh grades (mean difference = 0.60, 95% CI = 0.17, 1.03, p = 0.006, d = 0.63) as well as between eleventh grade and college (mean difference = –0.60, 95% CI = –1.05, –0.15, p = 0.010, d = 0.63). Matched pairs t-tests found a significant difference in eleventh grade (M = –0.51, SD = 0.89, 95% CI = –0.81, –0.21, t = –3.47, p = 0.001, η^2 = 0.26). Thus, uneasiness was observed in eleventh grade.

Next, we examined overpassivization with respect to the three types of unaccusatives. Groups differed from one another significantly in their treatment of the change of location verbs and the unergatives: $F(4, 167) = 2.93$, $p = 0.022$; Levene = 11.14, $p = 0.000$). Post hoc Games-Howell revealed significant differences between eleventh grade and college (mean difference = 0.71, 95% CI = 0.16, 1.26, p = 0.005, d = 1.67) and between college and functional L2E (mean difference = –0.60, 95% CI = –1.09, –0.12, p = 0.008, d = 1.43). Matched t-tests identified a statistically significant difference in college (M = –0.77, SD = 0.88, 95% CI = –1.08, –0.47, t = –5.13, p = 0.000, η^2 = 0.44). Thus, a U-shaped development was observed between eleventh grade and functional L2E. In addition, although no statistically significant difference was found, comparisons of groups on their treatment of the change of state verbs and the existence verbs vis-à-vis unergatives in the passive structure produced similar U-like patterns with college at the bottom: $F(4, 167) = 0.85$, $p = 0.494$ and $F(4, 167) = 2.20$, $p = 0.071$, respectively.

In sum, a U-shape was identified in four of the six sets of statistical analysis with respect to the three subtypes of unaccusatives. These results strongly support the U-shaped patterns for uneasiness and overpassivization revealed in the overall comparison between unergatives and unaccusatives.

Finally, to directly confirm the repeatedly observed sequence of the two phenomena—uneasiness in ninth and eleventh grades followed by overpassivization in college—a 2 x 5 repeated-measures ANOVA was conducted and statistically significant interactions of sentence pattern and group were found: $F(4, 167) = 5.56$, $p = 0.000$, $\eta^2 = 0.12$, power = 0.98. Significant differences were identified in the ways uneasiness and overpassivization affected eleventh grade (mean difference = –0.40, 95% CI = –0.78, –0.02, $p = 0.038$) and college (mean difference = 0.75, 95% CI = 0.36, 1.14, $p = 0.000$). In short, uneasiness was evident in eleventh grade whereas overpassivization was characteristic of the college group. Thus, hypothesis 5 was supported.

Discussion

The experiment just reported has given overwhelming evidence for the existence of relative U-shaped development in nonnative acquisition of English intransitive verbs. Considering the complexity of this pattern, its multiple occurrences in the obtained data, and the appearance of uneasiness and overpassivization in the predicted order, it is difficult to regard the finding as a mere fortuitous accident. Still, the merit of this hypothesis becomes even more apparent when alternative hypotheses are considered for comparison.

For example, assume, as in Rosen (1991), that both split intransitivity and object-to-subject movement of the arguments of unaccusatives are present in learners' grammar from the start of L2 acquisition. Or, take the opposite view to Rosen's: that L2 grammar at no point contains split intransitivity and all intransitive verbs remain as syntactically unergative throughout the stages of grammatical development. Neither uneasiness nor overpassivization would emerge in either scenario. These phenomena, however, are real—widely reported in the literature and clearly identified in our data—so the alternative hypotheses must be rejected because they do not match the empirical observations.

The results of the above study also shed light on the inadequacy of some explanations proposed about the cause of nontarget phenomena. For example, Kellerman (1978, 1979) observed a U-shaped development in L1 Dutch speakers' acceptance of "The cup broke" as a translation equivalent of *"Het kopje brak."* Following McCawley's (1978) theory of conversational implicature, he regarded the cause of this phenomenon as learners' failure to acquire an appropriate pragmatic rule on the usage of transitivity-alternating verbs such as *break*. The explanation appears to be accepted by some researchers (e.g., Ortega 2009, 38–39) but is inadequate because his explanation cannot account for a very similar phenomenon: the U-shaped development on uneasiness caused by nonalternating intransitive verbs demonstrated in this study. I suggest that Kellerman's finding should be seen as a case of uneasiness on the intransitive usage of alternating unaccusatives. It should be accounted for in exactly the same way as the uneasiness caused by nonalternating unaccusatives by the UTH. In this way, we do not need to stipulate two unrelated explanations for two identical phenomena.[8]

Similarly, the current data highlight shortcomings of most theoretical accounts proposed as the cause of overpassivization. Some of them, for example, are:

- L1 transfer of a compound tense/aspect structure (Richards 1973)
- overgeneralization of adjectival passive formation (Hubbard and Hix 1988; Hubbard 1994)
- nontarget lexical causativization (Balcom 1995, 1997; Ju 2000[9])
- identification of the passive morpho-syntax with the lack of a logical subject (Zobl 1989)
- nontarget overt marking of syntactic NP movement (Yip 1995; Oshita 1997)

Previous studies (e.g., Oshita 2000, 2001) critically reviewed these alternative proposals and pointed out a number of inadequacies of the first four with respect to their structural and cross-linguistic implications. The last proposal, the syntactic NP movement analysis, was strongly supported and has been incorporated into the UTH. The current data not only show that the incorporation is successful, but also reveal further inadequacy of the alternatives in explaining the acquisition patterns, since none can explain why overpassivization follows uneasiness or how it results in a U-shaped pattern with fairly advanced learners at its bottom. In sum, the UTH appears to be a highly useful collection of hypotheses that can present specific, coherent, and falsifiable predictions on the structural, cross-linguistic, and developmental aspects of the nonnative acquisition of intransitive verbs.

Conclusion

In the past, researchers looked for the conventional notion of the absolute U, which is a pattern that begins with near-perfect performance followed by a mysterious decline and successful recovery. In actual acquisition, however, such a dramatic change is extremely rare. Even regarding children's acquisition of irregular inflectional words, which is often considered to be a textbook case of U-shaped development, Marcus et al. (1992) reported that no clear instance of absolute U-shape was found in the natural utterances of twenty-five children; they over-regularized irregular forms in only 4.6 percent of potential contexts and never did so consistently over an extended period of time. Clearly, norms of language acquisition are progress, not regression. A drastic decline necessary for statistically definable absolute U-shape may not exist in language acquisition after all, at least as part of the normal developmental process.[10]

In contrast, the notion of a relative U is highly compatible with the progressive nature of language acquisition because it does not call for near-perfect performance, either at the beginning or at the end of its pattern. Thus, it has the potential to shed light on previously hidden patterns of the U, which may lead to a discovery of inner mechanisms of language acquisition. The concept appears particularly useful in two types of language acquisition research.

The first is a kind of research that focuses on competing factors suspected to exert major influence in shaping learners' linguistic knowledge (or behavior), but to different degrees at different points of acquisition. Good examples include Marcus et al. (1992) and Pinker (1999), who have demonstrated that children's mastery of inflected words at different acquisition stages can be seen as results of a tug-of-war between two competing psychological processes: access to memorized forms and rule-based computation of target forms. When rules of regular inflection are not acquired yet, children reproduce both regular and irregular forms that are stored in their mental lexicon. However, when the rules are acquired, children start applying them to irregularly inflected words, producing overregularized forms such as *foots* and *goed*. The errors disappear eventually because the access to the memorized irregular forms becomes faster than the rule-based computation as they encounter more and more tokens of them in their daily life. I believe that the long-suspected U-shaped development in the acquisition of irregular inflections can be identified more clearly if it is conceived relative to the acquisition of regular inflectional morphology.

The two conceptualizations of a U-shape may also prove highly relevant in the research that investigates the acquisition of superficially similar but linguistically contrasting items. Chomsky (1969) studied the acquisition of the syntactic properties of *tell* and *promise* by children between the ages of five and ten; her study is a good example of this type of research. The verb *promise* is unusual in comparison with *tell* and many other syntactically similar verbs such as *order, allow, urge,* and so on that take an NP object followed by a *to*-infinitival clause because the covert subject of the subordinate clause is understood as the subject of the main clause, not the object. Chomsky's data suggest that children first mistake *promise* as a *tell*-type verb and gradually recover from this error. What is interesting is that in the recovery process they occasionally mistake *tell* for a *promise*-type verb, although they initially have no problems with the syntax of *tell*. This delayed misanalysis of *tell* appears to lead to a U-shaped development.

In linguistics as well as in cognitive sciences in general, U-shaped development is rarely observed[11] and much less predicted. Generally, it has been regarded as an interesting (and valuable) but fortuitous peculiarity, something that only sheer luck can identify. Therefore, it is almost never a target of rigorous empirical exploration. The conceptualizations of a relative U and an absolute U, coupled with their statistical definitions, may have the potential to change the way developmental data are examined in language acquisition research.

Acknowledgments

I am grateful to the participants of this research, Tatsuya Kurimoto of Taki Gakuen High School and Hiroshi Fujimoto of Nanzan University. Thanks also go to Ayako Deguchi, Scott Jarvis, Yoko Sase, Christina Correnti, and Andrea Johannes for their support and invaluable feedback. All remaining shortcomings are my own.

Notes

1. Due to the practical importance of their differences, I treat absolute and relative U-shapes as different concepts. However, they may be ultimately the same; after all, absolute U can be seen as a self-referenced relative U whose benchmark is its own idealized growth pattern.
2. The experimental study reported here is a part of a larger work that is currently in progress. More detailed information about the experimental materials, data collection procedure, and data is available upon request.

3. Both *die* and *appear* are grouped as change of state verbs here because they denote changes from alive to dead and from invisible to visible.
4. Due to a mistake, the number of experimental sentences was thirty-one, not thirty-two. (There was no inanimate passive sentence for *die* and *cry*, but an additional animate active sentence for *cry*.) However, the influence of this mistake is considered statistically negligible due to the large number of subjects and verbs.
5. Statistical power calculated post hoc was very high (0.89, $n = 33.8$, $k = 5$, $f = 0.3$, $p = 0.05$).
6. The native control group is included in the figure but the statistical analyses were conducted on only the five experimental groups to avoid Bley-Vroman's (1983) comparative fallacy since the focus of the research is on nonnative grammatical development.
7. Here, the obtained p for Levene's test was slightly above .05, but because this test is known to suffer from too much sensitivity with large data sets (Larson-Hall 2010), LSD instead of Games-Howell was used to identify significant group differences.
8. For other problems in Kellerman's pragmatic account of uneasiness caused by alternating unaccusatives, see Oshita (2002).
9. Ju's (2000) account based on the conceptualizable agent can be viewed as a variation of the causativization analysis (see also Kondo 2005).
10. Here I exclude a U-shaped learning path caused by a curriculum of language instruction, such as the one reported by Lightbown (1983) about French learners' acquisition of the present progressive in English.
11. For notable exceptions, see Bever (1982) and Kellerman (1978).

REFERENCES

Balcom, Patricia. 1995. "Argument structure and multicompetence." *Linguistica Atlantica* 17: 1–17.
———. 1997. "Why is this happened?: A passive morphology and unaccusativity." *Second Language Research* 13: 1–9.
Bever, Thomas G. 1982. *Regressions in Mental Development: Basic Phenomena and Theories*. Hillsdale, NJ: Lawrence Erlbaum Associates.
Bley-Vroman, Robert. 1983. "The comparative fallacy in interlanguage studies: The case of systematicity." *Language Learning* 33: 1–17.
Burzio, Luigi. 1986. *Italian Syntax*. Dordrecht: D. Reidel.
Chomsky, Carol. 1969. *The Acquisition of Syntax in Children from 5 to 10*. Cambridge, MA: MIT Press.
Deguchi, Ayako, and Hiroyuki Oshita. 2004. "Meaning, proficiency and error types: Variations in nonnative acquisition of unaccusative verbs." *EUROSLA Yearbook* 4: 41–46.
Gass, Susan M., and Larry Selinker. 2008. *Second Language Acquisition: An Introductory Course,* third edition. New York: Routledge.
Hendrick, Clyde. 1990. "Replications, strict replications, and conceptual replications: Are they important?" In *Handbook of Replication Research in the Behavioral and Social Sciences*, edited by J. W. Neuliep. [Special Issue.] *Journal of Social Behavior and Personality* 5 (4): 41–49.
Hertel, Tammy Jandrey. 2003. "Lexical and discourse factors in the second language acquisition of Spanish word order." *Second Language Research* 19 (4): 273–304.
Hirakawa, Makiko. 1995. "L2 acquisition of English unaccusative constructions." *Proceedings of the 19th Annual Boston University Conference on Language Development*, 291–302.
———. 2003. *Unaccusativity in Second Language Japanese and English*. Tokyo: Hitsuji Shobo.
Hubbard, Philip. L. 1994. "Non-transformational theories of grammar: Implications for language teaching." In *Perspectives on Pedagogical Grammar*, 49–71, edited by Terence Odlin. Cambridge: Cambridge University Press.
Hubbard, Philip L., and Donna Hix. 1988. "Where vocabulary meets grammar: Verb subcategorization errors in ESL writers." *CATESOL Journal* (November): 89–100.
Imai, Atsufumi. 2004. *Against the Unaccusative Trap Hypothesis: Evidence from Adult Japanese Learners of English*. Unpublished MA thesis, Joetsu University of Education, Japan.
Ju, Min Kyong. 2000. "Overpassivization errors by second language learners: The effect of conceptualizable agents in discourse." *Studies in Second Language Acquisition* 22: 85–111.

Kellerman, Eric. 1978. "Giving learners a break: Native language intuitions as a source of predictions about transferability." *Working Papers on Bilingualism* 15: 59–92.
———. 1979. "The problem with difficulty." *Interlanguage Studies Bulletin* 4: 27–48.
Kogawara, Makoto. 1997. *Popaa: Hihanteki Goori Shugi [Popper: Critical Rationalism]*. Tokyo: Kodansha.
Kondo, Takako. 2005. "Overpassivization in second language acquisition." *IRAL* 43: 129–61.
Larson-Hall, Jenifer. 2010. *A Guide to Doing Statistics in Second Language Research Using SPSS*. New York: Routledge.
Lightbown, Patsy M. 1983. "Exploring relationships between developmental and instructional sequences in L2 acquisition." In *Classroom Oriented Research in Second Language Acquisition*, 217–43, edited by Herbert W. Seliger and Michael H. Long. Rowley, MA: Newbury House.
Mackey, Alison and Susan M. Gass. 2005. *Second Language Research: Methodology and Design*. Mahwah, NJ: Lawrence Erlbaum Associates.
Marcus, Gary F, Steven Pinker, Michael Ullman, Michelle Hollander, T. John Rosen, and Fei Xu. 1992. "Overregularization in language acquisition." *Monographs of the Society for Research in Child Development*, vol. 57, no. 4.
McCawley, James D. 1978. "Conversational implicature and the lexicon." In *Syntax and Semantics, volume 9, Pragmatics*, 245–59, edited by Peter Cole. New York: Academic Press.
Montrul, Silvina. 2005. "On knowledge and development of unaccusativity in Spanish L2 acquisition." *Linguistics* 43: 1153–90.
Ortega, Lourdes. 2009. *Understanding Second Language Acquisition*. London: Hodder Education.
Oshita, Hiroyuki. 1997. "'The Unaccusative Trap': L2 Acquisition of English Intransitive Verbs." Unpublished PhD dissertation, University of Southern California, Los Angeles, CA.
———. 2000. "What is happened may not be what appears to be happening: A corpus study of 'passive' unaccusatives in L2 English." *Second Language Learning* 16: 293–324.
———. 2001. "The unaccusative trap in second language acquisition." *Studies in Second Language Acquisition* 23: 279–304.
———. 2002. "Uneasiness with the easiest: On the subject-verb order in L2 English." *Second Language* 1: 45–61. The Japan Second Language Association (J-SLA).
Park, Kyae-Sung, and Usha Lakshmanan. 2007. "The L2 acquisition of the unaccusative-unergative distinction in English resultatives." *Proceedings of the 31st Annual Boston University Conference on Language Development*, vol. 2. Somerville, MA.: Cascadilla Press, 508–19.
Perlmutter, David M. 1978. "Impersonal passives and the unaccusative hypothesis." *Proceedings of the Berkeley Linguistics Society* 4: 157–89.
Pinker, Steven. 1999. *Words and Rules: The Ingredients of Language*. New York: Basic Books.
Richards, Jack C. 1973. "A noncontrastive approach to error analysis." In *Focus on the Learner: Pragmatic Perspectives for the Language Teacher*, 96–113, edited by John W. Oller Jr. and Jack C. Richards. Rowley, MA: Newbury House.
Rosen, Carol G. 1991. "Relational grammar: L2 learning and the components of L1 knowledge." In *Crosscurrents in Second Language Acquisition and Linguistic Theories*, 123–42, edited by Thom Huebner and Charles A. Ferguson. Amsterdam: John Benjamins.
Shan, Chuan-Kuo, and Boping Yuan. 2008. "'What is happened' in L2 English does not happen in L2 Chinese." *EUROSLA Yearbook* 8: 164–90.
Sorace, Antonella. 2000. "Gradients in auxiliary selection with intransitive verbs." *Language* 76: 859–90.
Steinberg, Laurence. 2008. *Adolescence*. Boston: McGraw-Hill.
van der Veer, René, Marinus van IJzendoorn, and Jaan Valsiner. 1994. "General introduction." In *Reconstructing the Mind: Replicability in Research on Human Development*, 1–9, edited by René van der Veer, Marinus van IJzendoorn, and Jaan Valsiner. Norwood, NJ: Ablex Publishing Corporation.
Vaughan, Victor C. III, R. James McKay Jr., and Richard E. Behrman. 1979. *Nelson Textbook of Pediatrics*. Philadelphia, PA: W. B. Saunders.
Wong, Kin Tat. 2007. "Overpassivisation of unaccusative verbs by Malaysian Chinese ESL learners." Unpublished MA thesis, Universiti Putra Malaysia.
Yamakawa, Kenichi, Naoki Sugino, Shinji Kimura, Michiko Nakano, Hiromasa Ohba, and Yuko Shimizu. 2003. "The development of grammatical competence of Japanese EFL learners: Focusing on

unaccusatitve/unergative verbs." *Annual Review of English Language Education in Japan*, The Japan Society of English Language Education 14: 1–10.

Yip, Virginia. 1995. *Interlanguage and Learnability: From Chinese to English*. Amsterdam: John Benjamins.

Yuan, Boping. 1999. "Acquiring the unaccusative/unergative distinction in a second language: Evidence from English-speaking learners of L2 Chinese." *Linguistics* 37: 275–96.

Zobl, Helmut. 1989. "Canonical typological structures and ergativity in English L2 acquisition." In *Linguistic Perspectives on Second Language Acquisition*, 203–21, edited by Susan M. Gass and Jacqelyn Schachter. New York: Cambridge University Press.

12

Using Simulated Speech to Assess Japanese Learner Oral Proficiency

HITOKAZU MATSUSHITA AND DERYLE LONSDALE
Brigham Young University

WE DISCUSS AND EVALUATE simulated speech (SS) as a testing methodology for assessing the oral proficiency of Japanese learners. SS responses are mostly conversational, spontaneous, and open-ended. SS testing is also topic-driven, with the examiner testing the subject's prior knowledge and/or experience with the topic. SS exhibits several features of learner speech that are commonly used in measuring fluency; these include hesitation, fillers, speech burst length, silence, and speech rate. Current automatic speech recognition (ASR) technology is capable of extracting such information from speech. In this paper we discuss a Japanese SS test that was administered to 231 students from a range of Japanese language class levels (100, 200, 300, and native). The recordings were scored using an ASR engine which extracted several features useful for SS evaluation. We describe analyses that led to metrics that identify the most salient speech properties across each of the different SS task types that characterize learners at different levels.

Literature Review

Development of a reliable and time-efficient second language (L2) oral proficiency test is currently of great interest in the field of language testing. One common approach in current L2 speaking assessment is to have a human examiner interview a learner. Measuring speaking ability in this manner involves complex processes: (1) a test taker must be able to produce speech samples recorded for evaluation; (2) two or three human evaluators typically listen to the collected speech samples to evaluate oral proficiency based on a stipulated rubric; and (3) raters' judgments are averaged to produce a single score. These tests are commercially available but are not optimally suited for ongoing L2 speaking ability assessments at large institutions where regular testing of burgeoning populations is necessary for formative and summative purposes.

Much research has gone into developing computerized tests that can be scored using ASR technology. This scoring method requires a system trained on speech samples at a satisfactory level of representativeness. However, ASR systems are not generally able to handle samples of erroneous or unpredictable language usage correctly because their performance depends largely on language data, or corpora, provided for the system training (Nagatomo et al. 2001). In other words, the level of precision in computerized speech processing is likely to be very limited if the input speech samples are outside the domain of the language data on which the machine is trained. The problem is aggravated when processing speech samples from L2 learners, which are even more unpredictable and variable than first language (L1) speakers' speech.

Two dimensions seem important for quantifying oral proficiency: accuracy and fluency (Housen and Kuiken 2009). Over the last fifty years or so, research has focused on the use of elicited repetition (ER) for testing the speaking accuracy of L2 learners (Bley-Vroman and Chaudron 1994). ER is a type of structured response where test takers repeat sentences they hear one by one as completely and thoroughly as possible. The responses are recorded and later analyzed; they are typically graded at the syllable level by indicating which syllables were successfully repeated and which were not. By using carefully engineered sentences (i.e., taking into consideration such features as vocabulary level, syllable count, and morphological and syntactic complexity), language testers are able to administer ER tests to students that gauge the accuracy of their spoken language responses (Christensen, Hendrickson, and Lonsdale 2010).

ER has been used to assess the speaking ability of L1 learners, autistic children, and literate and illiterate L2 learners. When the sentences are long enough and contain multiple targeted linguistic features, they can be repeated only if the test-taker understands the content and is capable of comprehending and producing sentences that exhibit these features. Recent work has shown that ER tests can be effectively scored by current ASR techniques because the range of acceptable responses is comprehensively specified (Graham et al. 2008). We have also shown elsewhere (Matsushita 2011; Matsushita and Tsuchiya 2011) that ER testing is highly effective for evaluating the accuracy of Japanese L2 learners' language knowledge.

However, ER is only capable of giving a partial evaluation—that of accuracy. Another integral aspect of speaking proficiency that must be addressed is fluency. In this article, we discuss using SS to probe the fluency of Japanese language learners.

In prior work, we investigated several fluency factors from ER speech samples, but this attempt was largely unsuccessful because ER speech samples are too short to extract desirable fluency features: ER repetitions produced by typical learners ranged from one to thirteen seconds in a recent Japanese ER test. Although some relevant features were observable in those ER speech samples (e.g., hesitation, fillers, length of repetitions), it is still difficult to retrieve a majority of the relevant fluency features from such short speech samples. On the other hand, SS testing allows us to obtain the full range of fluency features due to the longer responses and less controlled speech environment.

Two main considerations arise when considering using ASR for scoring SS test responses:

1. It is unlikely that precise speech-to-text transcription with such open-ended speech samples will be possible, especially for samples produced by nonnative speakers.
2. Learners' performance in SS depends on a wide variety of latent factors other than their pure L2 capability (e.g., prior knowledge of and/or experience with the topics presented by the test items) thus requiring complex procedures to design appropriate test items for fair grading (Luoma 2004).

We claim that by separating the accuracy and fluency measures and by evaluating the former via ER and the latter via SS, we can overcome these limitations of ASR processing. By employing ER to measure L2 production accuracy via exact syllable-matching of the transcribed response, we can limit SS scoring to fluency features, which can be extracted by ASR processing without having to have an exact transcription, thus overcoming problem (1) above. Although the SS system must process speech samples with a certain level of precision, fluency features do not as crucially depend on the accuracy of the transcription, so this approach enables us to develop an ASR system with more latitude than its ER counterpart. Since the lexical content of the responses is not of primary importance (i.e., a dictation is not required for analysis, but rather recognition of speech runs), the name simulated speech (SS) is used for this type of spoken language processing. The item difficulty issue mentioned in (2) above is beyond the scope of this study and still remains to be addressed in future studies. Therefore, for the sake of simplicity, we chose existing SS test items available for public use rather than creating original items. The following section describes the test items selected for this study.

Research Question

The overall question—and the focus for this paper—thus arises: how well do SS fluency measures correlate with student progress in a program of Japanese language study? To answer this question, we began by recording and selecting responses from a Japanese SS test that was administered to a range of Japanese L2 learners. We then processed the test recordings with an ASR engine to extract fluency features. With these features we were able to examine the performance of the students on their SS tests.

We show that ASR-scored SS gives a good estimate of learner level, at least when evaluating fluency. We conclude by sketching future work, including the prospect of combining SS metrics with other testing modality scores to derive a more comprehensive model that takes into consideration both accuracy and fluency when scoring oral proficiency.

Data Collection

Test items used in this study were selected from the Japanese Simulated Oral Proficiency Interview (SOPI) test (CAL1995), with permission from the Center for Applied Linguistics. The effectiveness of these test items has been thoroughly tested in actual SOPI administrations and they are deemed viable items based on the analyses developed in a series of previous studies on SOPI items for other languages

(Clark and Li 1986; Stansfield et al. 1990). These items are categorized into three groups according to task type: picture tasks, topic tasks, and situation tasks (four picture tasks, five topic tasks, and five situation tasks are enclosed in the test package). In the picture tasks, test takers are asked to provide detailed descriptions of the pictures presented in a test booklet. In the topic tasks, subjects are asked to answer questions on particular topics (e.g., school life) and give justifications for their answers. In the situation tasks, subjects are asked to role-play in hypothetical situations (e.g., offering advice, apologies). These items are classified as Intermediate, Advanced, or Superior based on the anticipated task difficulty. There are three Intermediate, eight Advanced, and three Superior items in the test.

Of these fourteen items, we chose five for the computerized SS test. Table 12.1 provides descriptions of the selected items. The principal criterion for choosing these items was familiarity of the topics to the subjects. All three Intermediate items were chosen for the Japanese SS test to ensure that even low-level learners were able to produce a certain amount of speech. We also selected two high-level items based on consultation with an experienced teaching assistant in the Japanese program, in order to include items with topics that were covered in the class materials. The related assumption is that learners would be able to perform well on the test by applying their experience with these high-level but familiar topics.

The testing procedure used in this study was essentially identical to the Japanese SOPI except for the fact that ours was truncated and administered via computer. The SS items were presented to the subjects as the second portion of a speaking test, following the completion of an ER test as described above. At the beginning of the SS test, general instructions were provided with the test administration tool to briefly explain the nature of SS. Written instructions for each test item taken from the SOPI booklet were displayed on the screen as the audio description of the item started. A picture was also presented in a separate window for the picture tasks. After audio instruction was delivered for each item, the preparation and response time were

Table 12.1
Simulated speech test items selected for administration and analysis

Test item	Level	Prep. time	Response time	Task type
Picture 1	Intermediate	15 sec.	1 min. 20 sec.	Describe a typical shopping mall to a Japanese tourist
Topic 1	Intermediate	15 sec.	45 sec.	Give a description of the kind of weather he or she likes
Situation 1	Intermediate	10 sec.	45 sec.	State what kind of hotel room he or she wants, state the length of stay, and ask about restaurant hours
Topic 3	Advanced	20 sec.	1 min. 15 sec.	Give a step-by-step description of how a Japanese student can find a summer job
Situation 3	Superior	20 sec.	1 min.	Apologize to a host mother for returning home very late after missing the last train home

displayed in a countdown clock on the screen in order for the test takers to be able to pace their thinking and speaking processes. When the test takers reached the final five seconds of the allotted response time, a small warning beep sounded. Once they finished an item, students pressed a button to proceed to the next item.

Data were collected using a custom-programmed Java front-end application. As responses were given, the corresponding SS speech samples were saved as .wav files on the local desktop computer and uploaded to a designated server space with a batch script.

In December 2010, we administered the SS test to 229 L2 learners of Japanese and 14 native Japanese speakers. The students had been placed in four levels corresponding largely to university class levels: 100 (beginner), 200 (high beginner), 300 (intermediate), and native. The first three levels represent about 50, 150, and 250 hours of classroom instruction, respectively.

Analysis and Results

The SS recordings were scored using a state-of-the-art automatic speech recognizer for Japanese, extracting several features useful for SS evaluation. We describe the scoring process, the subsequent machine learning experiments we ran to determine which features were most predictive of students' levels of instruction, and we report on the five features which were most salient below. We also describe analyses across each of the different SS task types and how student levels differed in their fluency characteristics.

For our scoring of the SS responses we used a custom-developed ASR engine for Japanese, which we had also employed previously for scoring ER responses. The system incorporates the Julius ASR engine (Lee and Kawahara 2009), which we extended by creating language and acoustic models trained on the Corpus of Spoken Japanese (CSJ). CSJ is a large-scale spoken language corpus of transcribed utterances (7.5 million words, 658.8 hours) spoken by 1,417 native speakers (947 males, 470 females) of Japanese (Furui et al. 2005). Crucially for us, the corpus also annotates a wide variety of speech-specific language phenomena including disfluencies such as fillers, repairs, fragments, word coalescence, and vowel devoicing. Besides performing speech-to-text (i.e., dictation) processing for Japanese, the engine is also capable of extracting several low-level speech-related features that characterize the properties of the speech samples. Based on previous studies (Higgins et al. 2011; Xi et al. 2008), we identified a set of eleven fluency features that provide critical information on L2 proficiency for English in the evaluation process using semi-direct oral tests such as SS. Table 12.2 shows these eleven features as extracted by Julius that were used in further SS processing.

Since the collected data consisted of open-ended speech, generic ASR components of Julius were used for fluency feature extraction. Pause thresholds were set at four hundred milliseconds, based on prior research (Freed, Segalowitz, and Dewey 2004). The number of pauses, tokens (the total number of morpheme instances), and types (the number of unique morphemes) were counted by parsing the ASR processing results with a Perl script during post-processing. Information on the number of tokens, types, and filled pauses was provided by ASR dictation output, and hence

Table 12.2
Features used for ASR-based fluency analysis

Feature		Description
(1)	# Tokens	Number of morpheme tokens in a test item
(2)	# Types	Number of morpheme types in a test item
(3)	# Pauses	Number of short pauses in speech
(4)	Speech length	Total speech duration in a test item
(5)	Silence length	Total length of silence in a test item
(6)	Speech rate	Number of phonemes per second
(7)	# Fillers	Number of filled pauses in a test item
(8)	# Bursts	Number of fluent speech bursts in a test item
(9)	Tokens per burst	Number of tokens normalized by fluent speech bursts
(10)	Speech time per burst	Speech length normalized by fluent speech bursts
(11)	Types per speech length	Number of types normalized by speech length

regarded to be satisfactorily accurate, if not perfectly precise, for the analyses of L2 fluency in this study. Therefore, it is reasonable to assume that the approximate estimates of these L2 fluency phenomena are readily attainable with this type of generic ASR system.

With the samples scored and features derived for each of the SS tests, several analyses were possible. First, we used a machine learning system to explore how well the raw features derived from a recording could predict which group the corresponding student belonged to. We thus assumed that the learners' class levels indicated their rough proficiency levels, and that fluency was similarly indicative of proficiency level.

To predict the student levels from these features, we treated the task as a classification problem using supervised machine learning. For this step we used the TiMBL system (Daelemans and van den Bosch 2005), widely utilized to address natural language processing problems including speech. TiMBL is a memory-based machine learning system: it makes guesses involving categorization or classification of phenomena based on instances (i.e., examples) that the system has been trained on and has stored in memory. Though the system implements several matching methods, we used the k-nearest neighbor (k-NN) algorithm. This algorithm takes each test instance to be processed and compares it with all of the training examples in memory. It locates the examples that are closest in memory to the instance under consideration, records what their answers (or outcomes) are, and uses the majority answer as the solution to the problem. The user can specify the number of nearest neighbors to consider by setting the value k (hence k-nearest neighbor). For example, with the value $k = 3$, the system will only consider the three nearest neighbors to determine its answer.

TiMBL is desirable for this SS analysis because it has the capability to order the features according to the amount of information gain in the training process, and thus rank the features for their relative contribution to the overall outcome. This capability enables us to identify the most influential features for student level prediction. To analyze the ASR-extracted feature data with TiMBL, the input vectors were created from the eleven features for each recording and stored as input files; the student's class level was the outcome that the system had to predict for each vector. The learning process was conducted on the set of all tests' vectors using the leave-one-out validation process to obtain the results. This means that we trained the system on all of the tests so that it could correlate each test's feature vector with the appropriate outcome. When actually processing any given test, though, we induced the system to forget that test's vector/outcome combination so that it would be forced to compute the answer in detail rather than simply retrieve it from rote memory. This assured that the training process was generalizable, and not just fine-tuned to the particular training instances we had collected. As table 12.3 shows, overall classification accuracy was quite high (70 to 92 percent) using all of the available features. The most important aspect of these results is the five influential factors indicated in the last two columns. Note that for all tasks, the top five most influential features were some permutation of the same features: 1 (# Tokens), 2 (# Types), 3 (# Pauses), 7 (# Fillers), and 8 (# Bursts).

It is worthwhile to observe that the accuracy obtained when processing all of the test items together was significantly higher (at about 92 percent) than when treating each type of test item individually (ranging from roughly 71 to 80 percent). This is due to the fact that, for machine learning, more training data usually results in better prediction.

We sought further confirmation for the role of these five features in predicting student level by processing the same data set in another machine learning system called WEKA (Hall et al. 2009), a data mining system using various decision tree models constructed via support vector machines (Burges 1998). We used the J48 classification method (C4.5 decision tree model) for this second analysis. The data in table 12.4 show the prediction accuracy rates based on the resultant decision trees. Table 12.4 shows that the prediction rates between the trees with all eleven features and with only the five most salient features are almost identical. Therefore, it is safe to say that these five fluency features are the most influential factors in making predictions about learners' proficiency levels and other features are largely inconsequential for score generation. Note that we obtained even higher classification accuracy (82 to 89 percent) with the WEKA system than with the TiMBL system, whether using all eleven features or just the top five features.

Table 12.3
Classification accuracy for k-NN learning of SS test items

Test item	Item level	Classification accuracy	Top 5 influential features
Picture 1	Intermediate	0.754630	2, 7, 8, 3, 1
Topic 1	Intermediate	0.768519	8, 3, 2, 7, 1
Situation 1	Intermediate	0.717593	7, 2, 8, 3, 1
Topic 3	Advanced	0.800926	8, 3, 2, 7, 1
Situation 3	Superior	0.708333	8, 2, 3, 7, 1
All	---	0.922517	2, 8, 3, 1, 7

Table 12.4
Prediction accuracy rate (%) for machine learning of SS test items using decision trees

Test item	All features	5 features
Picture 1	86.1111	82.8704
Topic 1	82.4074	79.6296
Situation 1	80.5556	79.1667
Topic 3	84.2593	81.4815
Situation 3	83.3333	81.9444
All	89.3916	82.0593

Though these results are very promising, recall that we are only using fluency features to predict four outcome classes (100, 200, 300, and native), which is not as informative as one might want to have in a general-purpose evaluation system. A more ideal situation would be to somehow transform the feature values to evaluation scores. Even more desirable would be if these scores could be validated against external measures, such as widely accepted commercial tests. This prompted us to investigate whether we could use the SS scores to generate scores for individual subjects. Since we did not have human-graded fluency scores (something that would be almost impossible given the low-level granularity of the measures), a conventional regression model was not appropriate for this analysis.

Fortunately, with a further processing step, these desiderata are satisfiable given recent language testing research. For example, ETS has developed SpeechRater, a commercial TOEFL iBT product for measuring English oral proficiency. Recent work has shown how ASR-extracted features can map to ETS scores using a multiple regression model (Higgins et al. 2011). Crucially, the features used in the computation for English coincide with the top five features in our work on Japanese using k-NN and decision tree classifiers.

We thus adopted the feature-weighting calculations for the English iBT, though with slight modification. For example, we chose to add the # Fillers feature, which was not used previously. We also chose not to use the # Pauses feature, reasoning that it generally interacts strongly with the # Runs feature. The final features used in predictive generation of SS scores are shown in table 12.5. Factor 1 is a metric roughly equivalent to the number of words per second, Factor 2 is a similar measure but penalized for filled pauses (the equivalent of "um," "uh," and so forth in English), and Factor 3 characterizes the number of words per speech run.

Table 12.5
Factors and their calculation for SS score generation

SS score factor	Calculation
Factor 1 (f1)	2 × # Tokens/ItemTimeLength
Factor 2 (f2)	2 × (# Tokens-# Fillers)/Speech Length
Factor 3 (f3)	log (# Types)/(# Runs)
SS score = $\Sigma_i f_i$	

Based on the formula in table 12.5, we generated SS scores for all subjects. The boxplots in figure 12.1 plot performance of the various levels of students across the various SOPI tasks. Boxes delineate the range of the majority of scores, with outliers indicated by the dotted lines. The horizontal black band in each box indicates the median. Note that for each task the scores rise with the class level, as would be expected. Figure 12.2 visualizes how the means of the SS scores separate nicely by level across the various item types. The interaction between the item type and the class level was computed via a factorial ANOVA. The effects of test item and class level are both statistically significant ($F_{\text{Item Type}}$ (4, 222) = 4.5478, $p < 0.001$ and $F_{\text{Class Level}}$(3, 222) = 311.2628, $p < 0.0001$, respectively). However, the differences in test items are not uniformly significant according to the Tukey post hoc test (only Topic 1–Situation 1 and Topic 3–Topic 1 pairs were significantly different: $p < 0.01$). Therefore, the stipulated item difficulties of the five SOPI items used in this study do not affect subjects' SS scores generated via the calculation method under consideration. The SS test results do not support—and are independent of—the item level difficulty specifications.

Figures 12.3 and 12.4 show the group score differences and the distribution of all scores for the SS items. An ANOVA analysis showed that the differences between

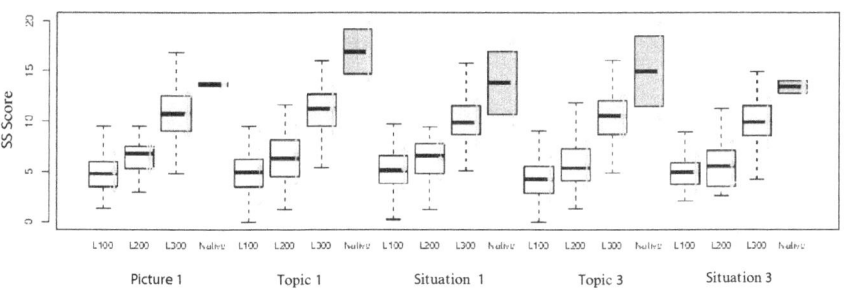

Figure 12.1 Generated SS Scores for Students by Level across SOPI Tasks

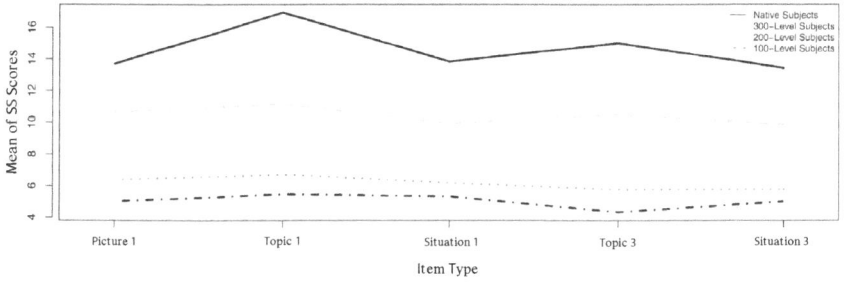

Figure 12.2 Means of Generated SS Scores by Student Level across SOPI Tasks

the class level groups are significant ($F_{\text{Class Level}}(3, 222) = 108.1, p < 0.0001$). Also, the associated Tukey HSD analysis indicated that differences among all the subject groups are significant (the p values range from 0.03 to less than 0.0001). Figure 12.4 plots a histogram of the full spectrum of SS scores along with their distribution of each subrange. Although the score distribution seems bimodal, the Anderson-Darling (AD) test indicates its strong normality with $p < 0.0001$ (A = 2.297). The boxplot across the x-axis shows that most of the scores cluster around 25–55, with the median at about 40. Therefore, it is safe to say that this SS score generation method is useful for measuring learners' performance based on the features selected via machine learning.

Conclusions and Discussion

In this paper we quantified the contribution of several ASR-extracted features to scoring Japanese simulated speech (SS). These features, while not perfectly accurate, were nevertheless very efficient, objective, and consistent in their predictive power. We have demonstrated that it is possible and useful to classify learners according to their proficiency levels using these features.

We also showed that machine-learning-based feature selection can result in highly accurate categorization of test takers' recordings. More importantly, we have demonstrated a method for SS score generation. By adapting calculations from prior work for English, we were able to successfully compute a score for quantifying learners' performance with a few selected fluency features.

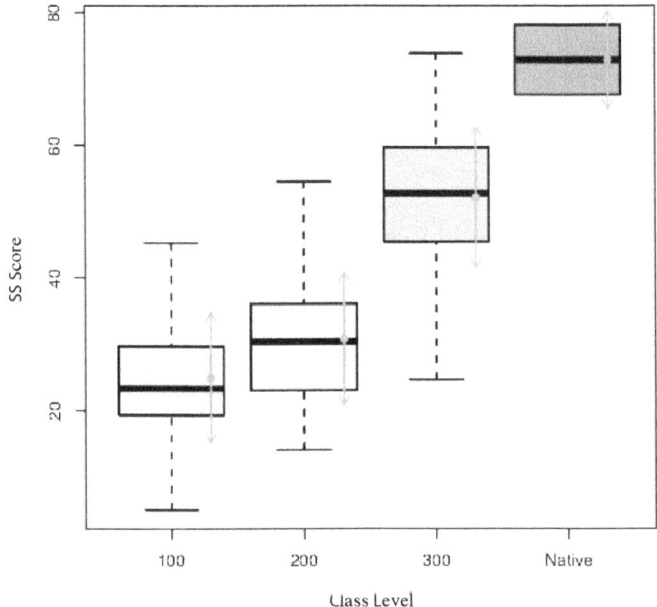

Figure 12.3 Differences in Generated SS Scores across Class Level

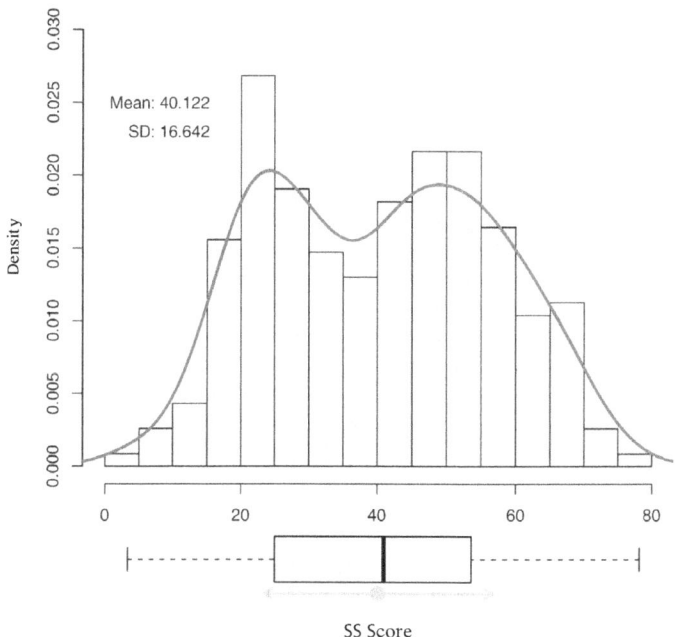

Figure 12.4 Distribution of Generated SS Scores across All Items

This paper has addressed one dimension of oral proficiency, namely fluency. The other dimension is accuracy, which we have addressed extensively elsewhere via ER testing. Given the successful results from both avenues of research, we are optimistic that we can combine these two types of measurements to obtain a more comprehensive metric for Japanese oral proficiency.

REFERENCES

Bley-Vroman, Robert, and Craig Chaudron. 1994. "Elicited imitation as a measure of second-language competence." In *Research Methodology in Second-Language Acquisition*, 245–61, edited by Elaine Tarone, Susan M. Gass, and Andrew. D. Cohen. Hillsdale, NJ: Lawrence Erlbaum Associates.

Burges, Christopher J. C. 1998. "A tutorial on support vector machines for pattern recognition." *Data Mining and Knowledge Discovery* 2: 121–67.

CAL. 1995. "Japanese simulated oral proficiency interview." Center for Applied Linguistics.

Christensen, Carl, Ross Hendrickson, and Deryle Lonsdale. 2010. "Principled construction of elicited imitation tests." In *Proceedings of the Seventh International Conference on Language Resources and Evaluation (LREC '10)*, 233–38, edited by N. Calzolari et al. Valetta, Malta: ELRA.

Clark, John L.D., and Ying-che Li. 1986. *Development, Validation, and Dissemination of a Proficiency-Based Test of Speaking Ability in Chinese and an Associated Assessment Model for Other Less Commonly Taught Languages*. Washington, DC: Center for Applied Linguistics.

Daelemans, Walter, and Antal van den Bosch. 2005. *Memory-Based Language Processing*. Cambridge, UK: Cambridge University Press.

Erlam, Rosemary. 2006. "Elicited imitation as a measure of L2 implicit knowledge: An empirical validation study." *Applied Linguistics* 27: 465–91.

Freed, Barbara F., Norman Segalowitz, and Dan P. Dewey. 2004. "Context of learning and second language fluency in French: Comparing regular classroom, study abroad and intensive domestic immersion programs." *Studies in Second Language Acquisition* 26: 275–301.

Furui, Sadaoki, Masanobu Nakamura, Tomohisa Ichiba, and Koji Iwano. 2005. "Analysis and recognition of spontaneous speech using Corpus of Spontaneous Japanese." *Speech Communication* 47: 208–19.

Graham, C. Ray, Deryle Lonsdale, Casey Kennington, Aaron Johnson, and Jeremiah McGhee. 2008. "Elicited imitation as an oral proficiency measure with ASR scoring." In *Proceedings of the Sixth International Conference on Language Resources and Evaluation (LREC'08)*. 57–67. Marrakech: ELRA.

Hall, Mark, Eibe Frank, Geoffrey Holmes, Bernhard Pfahringer, Peter Reutemann, and Ian H. Witten. 2009. "The WEKA data mining software: An update." *SIGKDD Explorations* 11.

Higgins, Derrick, Xiaoming Xi, Klaus Zechner, and David M. Williamson. 2011. "A three-stage approach to the automated scoring of spontaneous spoken responses." *Computer Speech and Language* 25: 282–306.

Housen, Alex, and Folkert Kuiken. 2009. "Complexity, accuracy, and fluency in second language acquisition." *Applied Linguistics* 30: 461–73.

Lee, Akinobu, and Tatsuya Kawahara. 2009. "Recent development of open-source speech recognition engine Julius." In *Proceedings of the Asia-Pacific Signal and Information Processing Association Annual Summit and Conference*.

Luoma, Sari. 2004. *Assessing Speaking*. Cambridge Language Assessment Series. Cambridge, UK: Cambridge University Press.

Matsushita, Hitokazu. 2011. "Computerized oral proficiency test for Japanese: Measuring comprehensive second language speaking ability with ASR technology." Unpublished MA thesis, Brigham Young University.

Matsushita, Hitokazu, and Shinsuke Tsuchiya. 2011. "The development of effective language models for an EI-based L2 speaking test: capturing Japanese interlanguage phenomena with ASR technology." In *Papers Presented at American Association for Applied Linguistics (AAAL)*, Chicago, IL.

Nagatomo, Kentaro, Ryuichi Nishimura, Kumiko Komatsu, Yuka Kuroda, Akinobu Lee, and Hiroshi Saruwatari. 2001. "Complemental backoff algorithm for merging language models." *IPSJ SIG Notes* 11: 49–54.

Stansfield, Charles W., Dorry M. Kenyon, Ricardo Paiva, Fatima Doyle, Ines Ulsh, and Maria A. Cowles. 1990. "Development and validation of the Portuguese speaking test." *Hispania* 73: 641–51.

Xi, Xiaoming, Derrick Higgins, Klaus Zechner, and David M. Williamson. 2008. "Automated scoring of spontaneous speech using SpeechRater, v1.0." *ETS Research Report No. RR-08-62*. Princeton, NJ: Educational Testing Service.

13

Keys to College

Tracking English Language Proficiency and IELTS Test Scores in an International Undergraduate Conditional Admission Program in the United States

REESE M. HEITNER, BARBARA J. HOEKJE, AND PATRICK L. BRACISZEWSKI
Drexel University

THE DREXEL UNIVERSITY INTERNATIONAL Gateway Program is a year-long conditional admission program designed to prepare international students with low English proficiency for successful matriculation into Drexel University. Administered by the Drexel University English Language Center, the program consists of a foundational sequence of study including intensive English classes and standardized test preparation as well as selected credit-bearing university courses. In addition to progressing through this coursework, participants are required to achieve a standardized testing score mandated by the university for matriculation. In the first year of the program, which ran during the academic year from 2010 to 2011, thirty-two of forty-four total participants enrolled in the program progressed satisfactorily, achieved the required IELTS exit score of 6.0, and entered the university—a fall 2011 matriculation rate of 73 percent. On average, participants achieved IELTS score gains on a term-by-term basis toward the required program exit score of 6.0—data useful for measuring score gains across several intervals. Statistical correlations among term-by-term IEP level progression and term-by-term IELTS scores were consistent, strong, and significant, suggesting that intensive English program course work supported IELTS score gains. Correlations between post-program university matriculated GPAs and pre-program entry scores, however, were slight and not statistically significant, suggesting that matriculated participants had achieved a sufficient level of English language proficiency so that pre-program language abilities did not impact their post-program collegiate performance. Fall 2011 first-year, first-term university GPAs for post-Gateway matriculated students averaged 3.10—higher, but not statistically different than either directly admitted first-term international or first-term domestic students. These initial first-year program results are part of a more comprehensive process of program validation and can provide university administrators with more information by which to plan, execute, and evaluate international conditional admission programs.

International Gateway Program

The Drexel University International Gateway Program (Gateway) is administered by the English Language Center (ELC), a CEA-accredited intensive English language program located in Philadelphia, Pennsylvania. The Gateway program consists of three to four eleven-week terms of intensive English program (IEP) courses, standardized test preparation, periodic IELTS (International English Language Testing System) testing, and credit bearing courses within the Drexel University College of Arts and Sciences (CoAS).[1] Participants are admitted into the program on the basis of an online application, high school transcripts, and standardized English language assessment scores. Whereas direct undergraduate admission to Drexel University requires minimal scores of TOEFL 550, TOEFL iBT 79, and IELTS 6.0 to 6.5, otherwise academically admissible applicants were admitted to the Gateway program in AY 2010–2011 with scores no lower than TOEFL iBT 47 and IELTS 4.5. To graduate from the Gateway program and successfully matriculate as Drexel University students in fall 2011, participants were required to maintain satisfactory performance in their IEP and CoAS courses, achieve minimum standardized exit test scores, and earn a letter of recommendation from their academic advisor.

Research Questions

The current research study was designed to examine the performance of Gateway participants across three measures: IEP coursework, IELTS scores, and university GPAs.[2] These data were collected to track participants' ability to progress through the Gateway program, meet matriculation requirements, and achieve academic standing during their first term of fully matriculated university coursework equivalent or superior to their directly admitted peers. The current research study addressed three questions:

1. What is the relationship between English language proficiency as measured by successive IELTS scores and IEP course level progression?
2. What is the relationship among initial program entry scores and university GPAs?
3. How do first-year post-Gateway matriculated students compare against directly admitted students in terms of matriculated GPAs?

In short, does the Gateway program prepare international students with low English proficiency to meet matriculation requirements and then succeed in their university academic coursework?

Though the focus of the current study was principally internal program evaluation, the data collected also speak to the more general issue of standardized English language proficiency scores, and, in particular, the measurement of IELTS score gains. Given that Gateway participants were required to sit for the IELTS exam each term, the data collected also provide a picture of the magnitude and rate of score gains across several months of intensive English language coursework at a US university. Indeed, it seems this paper is the first published account of IELTS score gains in the United States. For recent IELTS research conducted in the United Kingdom, see, for example, Archibald (2002) and Lloyd-Jones and Binch (2012); in Australia and New Zealand, see Craven (2012), Elder and O'Loughlin (2003), Ingram and Bayliss (2007), O'Loughlin and Arkoudis (2009), and Read and Hayes (2003); and in Canada, see Golder, Reeder, and Fleming (2011). Davies (2008) provides a broad historical overview of the IELTS exam, while Green (2004, 2005, 2007) shares IELTS data across several studies.[3]

Context of Research
AY 2010–2011 Program Design
The year-long Gateway program consists of a sequence of three or four eleven-week terms, with the fall and winter terms emphasizing English language skills and IELTS test preparation, and the spring and summer terms emphasizing content from university credit-bearing courses. Gateway participants were required to take at least ten credit hours—and were eligible to take a total of seventeen credit hours—of first-year level mathematics, chemistry, and humanities CoAS courses while still within the Gateway program. Table 13.1 depicts this Gateway course of study.

AY 2010–2011 Program Participants
Similar to the student population served by Drexel University's English Language Center, AY 2010–2011 Gateway participants were predominantly Middle Eastern or Asian, speaking either Arabic or Chinese as native languages. Figure 13.1 displays native language and gender demographic data of the Gateway participants.

Simple means t-tests—comparing average incoming IELTS scores grouped by native language and gender—were conducted. No statistically significant effects for native language or gender were found vis-à-vis entry test scores or subsequent IELTS scores, IELTS sub-skills, IEP course progression, matriculation rates, or university GPAs.

AY 2010–2011 Program Outcomes
Of the forty-four enrollees in the program during AY 2010–2011, thirty-two completed the program and were admitted as first-year students to Drexel University in fall 2011, a matriculation rate of 73 percent for the program's first year. Seven Gateway students were dismissed from the program for low performance or other issues, and five voluntarily transferred out of the program to begin university study in other programs.

Method
AY 2010–2011 English Language Proficiency
IEP level placement and progression. Participants in the Gateway program were placed and evaluated for promotion within a sequence of listening/speaking and reading/writing IEP classes at Drexel University's ELC. Gateway participants generally advanced through their IEP courses at a rate of one level per term, the expected progression at ELC. Overall, thirty-six of thirty-eight participants taking listening/speaking classes and thirty-six of thirty-eight participants taking reading/writing

Table 13.1
AY 2010-2011 Gateway Curriculum

Program Features	Term 1 Fall 2010	Term 2 Winter 2011	Term 3 Spring 2011	Term 4 Summer 2011
English Language/ Communication Skills (per week)	15 hours ELC ▪ Oral Communication ▪ Written Communication	15 hours ELC ▪ Oral Communication ▪ Written Communication	7.5 hours ELC ▪ Foundations of Academic Writing (CHEM support)	10.5 hours ELC ▪ Skills for College Success ▪ Oral Communication
Test Preparation (per week)	▪ 6 hours IELTS preparation	▪ 6 hours IELTS preparation	▪ 3 hours IELTS preparation or ▪ Skill for College Success	
CoAS Credit Courses (per term)	Math placement test	▪ MATH (3-4 credits)	▪ MATH (3-4 credits) ▪ CHEM (3 credits)	▪ MATH (3-4 credits) ▪ PHIL (3 credits)
End of Term Testing	IELTS December 2010	IELTS March 2011	IELTS June 2011	IELTS August 2011
ELC Support	Advising	Advising	Advising	Advising
University Support		Math Resource Center	Math Resource Center	Math Resource Center

classes in fall 2010 were promoted to the next level in winter 2011, the expected result for the IEP curriculum.

IELTS examination. The standardized IELTS exams were integral to the Gateway program; these exams were administered at the end of each term (approximately every eleven weeks) by the Drexel University IELTS Test Center (#US112). IELTS is the International English Language Testing System, a standardized English language proficiency exam jointly administered by the British Council, IDP Australia, and University of Cambridge (ESOL Examinations). Currently, IELTS scores are accepted by over seven thousand receiving institutions, including an increasing number of institutions in the United States, now numbering some 2,500 (IELTS 2012).

The IELTS exam is a "four skills" exam that independently tests listening, reading, writing, and speaking. Candidates sit for a collectively proctored paper-and-pencil exam consisting of a listening module (thirty minutes), a reading module (one hour), a writing module (one hour), and a live, one-on-one speaking interview (eleven to fourteen minutes). The IELTS exam is offered in two formats: a general training format intended for professional certification and general immigration to English-speaking countries, and an academic format intended specifically for admission to

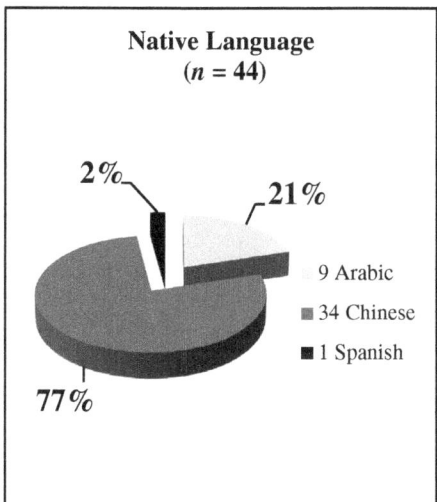 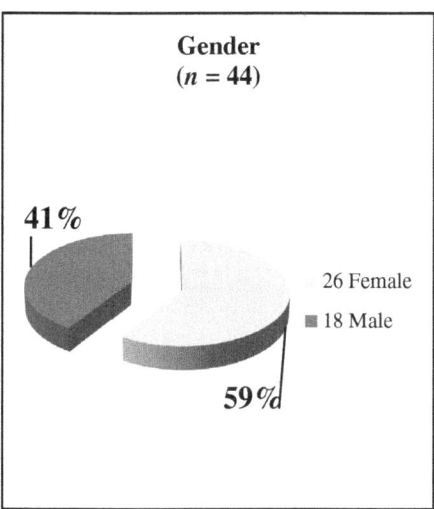

Figure 13.1 Demographic Data of Gateway Participants

institutions of higher education in English-speaking countries. All candidates sit for the same listening and speaking modules, while the reading and writing modules differ between general training and academic formats. Gateway participants sat for the academic IELTS exam. IELTS candidates are awarded a total of five scores, each ranging from one (lowest) to nine (highest) in half-band (0.5) increments (e.g., 4.5, 5.0, 5.5) for each of four skills—as well as an overall IELTS score representing a rounded average of all four subskills. There are no restrictions on the frequency of repeated test taking and scores are valid for two years.

IELTS score progression. Participants entered the Gateway program with IELTS entry scores (or TOEFL scores[4]) generally ranging between 4.5 and 6.0, though two participants entered the program at 6.5.[5] The average entry score for both the full cohort of forty-four participants and for the thirty-two successfully matriculating participants was 5.4. The average entry score of participants eventually dismissed from the program ($n = 7$) was slightly lower at 5.2, and that of participants voluntarily transferring out of the program ($n = 5$) somewhat higher at 5.7.

In addition to supplying pre-program test scores, program participants were required to sit for the IELTS exam each term until cleared for matriculation. As shown in figure 13.2, average IELTS scores for program participants increased each term.

In addition to tracking overall test scores, scores for each of four subskills were also collected and analyzed, save for sub-skill scores from pre-program entry tests, which were not available. Figure 13.3 provides average IELTS scores across all test dates for each of the four subskills of listening, reading, writing, and speaking among the thirty-two matriculated students.

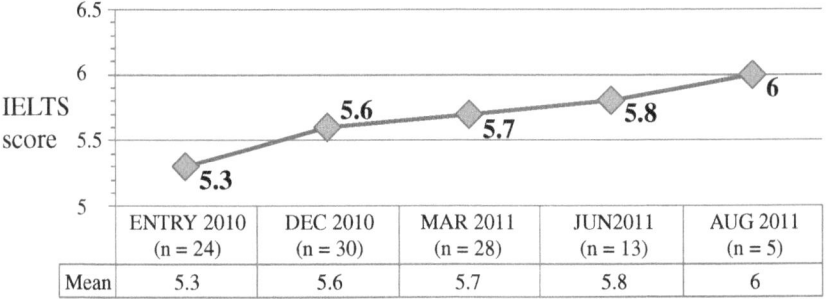

Figure 13.2 Average IELTS Scores of Matriculated Students Grouped by Test Date

Figure 13.3 reveals that participants consistently achieved higher scores on the productive writing and speaking tasks and lower scores on the receptive listening and reading tasks. Indeed, the relative contributions to increases in overall scores were not equal across the four subskills. Increases in overall scores were primarily the result of increases in writing and speaking scores, with listening and reading scores contributing less to improvement in overall test scores.[6]

Relationship between IEP level and IELTS score progression. Since participants sat for the IELTS exam at regular intervals throughout the year-long Gateway program, a total of ninety-two IELTS scores were recorded along with participants' IEP levels at the time of the tests. The average IELTS score rose from a low of 4.5 in level 2 reading and writing to a high of 6.1 in level 6 reading and writing. Figure 13.4 depicts a strong, positive, and significant correlation between IEP course progression and IELTS scores.[7] At a minimum, this correlation indicates that increasing IELTS scores are consistent with ELC course level progression, suggesting the IELTS exam is assessing language skills similar to those measured by ELC placement tests and promotion guidelines.

AY 2010–2011 University Courses

Gateway CoAS performance. In addition to progressing through a sequence of IEP courses, Gateway participants were required to take credit-bearing university CoAS courses. While Gateway participants chose either a calculus-based or non–calculus-based sequence of math courses, all participants were required to take CHEM 201 in the spring 2011 term. Moreover, it is important to note that all winter 2011 and spring 2011 courses were offered in sheltered formats. These math and chemistry courses, though taught by Drexel University CoAS faculty, enrolled only Gateway participants and included additional pedagogical support in the form of content and language assistance. Only summer 2011 courses, the fourth and final term in the Gateway program, were regularly scheduled Drexel University courses.

Figure 13.5 presents the average and range of Gateway student performance in CoAS courses within the Gateway curriculum, as measured by GPA. The eight

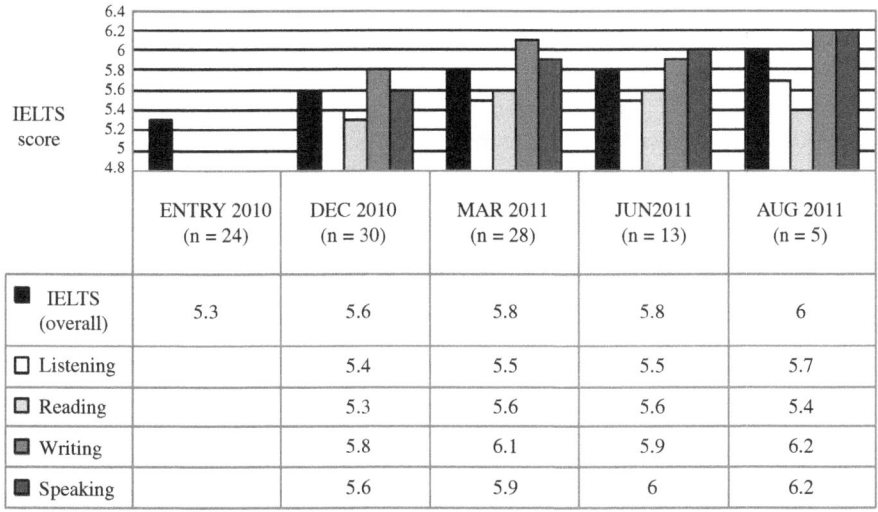

Figure 13.3 Average L/R/W/S IELTS Scores of Matriculated Students by Test Date

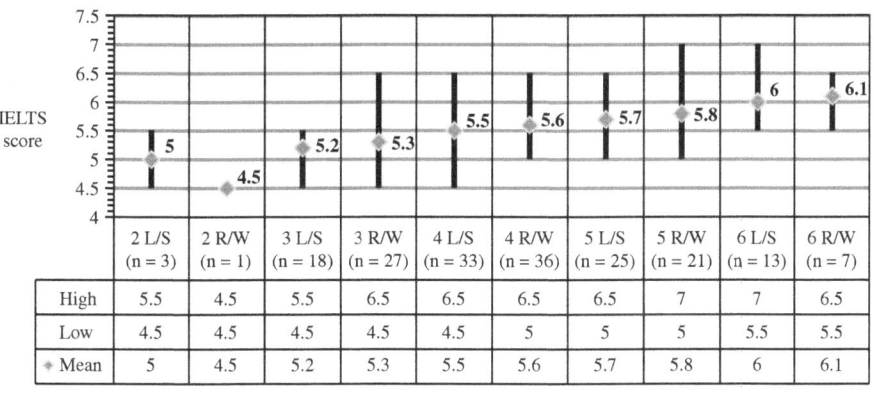

Figure 13.4 Average and Range of IELTS Scores of Full Cohort Grouped by ELC Levels 2-6

Gateway CoAS courses were MATH 100 or MATH 110 (scheduled in winter 2011), CHEM 201 and MATH 101 or MATH 121 (scheduled in spring 2011) and PHIL 105 and MATH 102 or MATH 122 (scheduled in summer 2011). Course GPAs indicate that, as a group, participants performed successfully in their Gateway CoAS courses. The overall cumulative average Gateway CoAS GPA across all courses and participants was 3.25.

Given that participants were also sitting for the IELTS exam on a term-by-term basis, term-by-term GPAs were related to these IELTS scores. However, term-by-term GPAs were largely uncorrelated with (generally increasing) term-by-term IELTS scores.[8] The fact that IELTS scores did not correlate with CoAS course GPAs suggests that participants were achieving at least a threshold level of academic language proficiency to manage their CoAS courses in the sheltered formats of the winter 2011 and spring 2011. In fact, the lowest GPAs were earned in spring 2011, indicative of the specific demands of the math courses offered at that time. By the same token, no significant correlation was obtained between cumulative Gateway CoAS GPAs across terms and entry scores on pre-program tests, suggesting that lower language proficiency upon entry into the program did not adversely affect CoAS course performance.

Matriculated university performance. In addition to tracking the GPAs of participants while still within the Gateway program, the first-year, first-term GPAs of Gateway participants who subsequently matriculated were also collected. The average fall 2011 GPA among the thirty-two post-Gateway matriculated participants was 3.10. Of these thirty-two students, twenty-nine were in good standing at the end of the fall 2011 term, two were placed on the Dean's list, and one was on probation. This fall 2011 post-Gateway GPA of 3.10 is lower than the 3.25 cumulative average GPA for CoAS courses taken during the Gateway program, but like Gateway CoAS GPAs, matriculated fall 2011 GPAs were not significantly correlated with initial entry scores. This average GPA of 3.10 indicates that the Gateway curriculum, including credit-bearing courses, was successful in addressing the needs of lower English proficiency participants.

Moreover, individual student GPAs appear stable over time: pre-matriculation Gateway CoAS GPAs are strongly correlated with post-matriculation fall 2011 GPAs ($r = 0.425$, $p < 0.05$); this further confirms the fact that university performance was largely independent of initial entry scores. Once a threshold level of language proficiency was reached, GPAs appear to be independent of the initial scores with which participants entered the program.

Comparison among Gateway matriculated GPAs and direct admission GPAs. If nine to twelve months of intensive English study and supported university coursework was sufficient

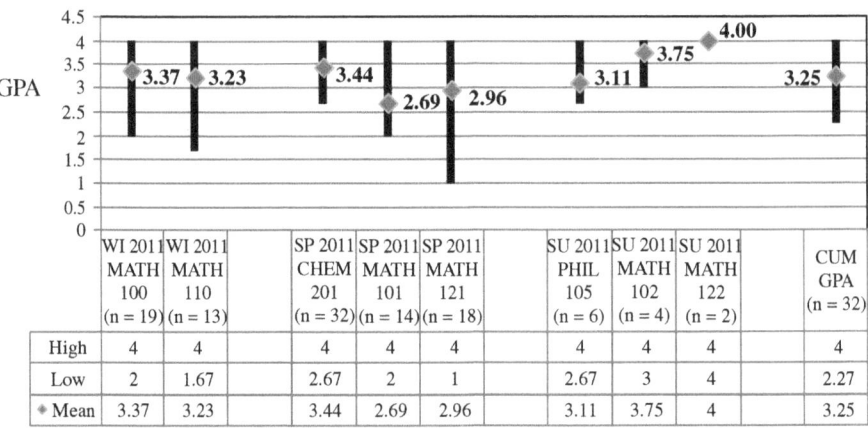

Figure 13.5 Average and Range of Gateway CoAS GPAs for Matriculated Students

to raise English proficiency to a collegiate level, then Gateway alumni students should have performed comparably to their direct admission peers. Comparability is a critical test for any preparatory conditional admission program. Table 13.2 shows that the Gateway alumni were indeed competitive with their direct admission peers during their first three terms of matriculated college study; t-tests confirm that Gateway alumni GPAs and direct admission GPAs were statistically equivalent.

Discussion
Program Validation
Drexel University's International Gateway program was designed to prepare low English proficiency international students for college success. From this perspective, the first year of the AY 2010–2011 Gateway program succeeded, having provided thirty-two out of forty-four participants with the proverbial keys to college. Unlike some college preparatory, foundational, or university-sponsored bridge programs in the United States, the Gateway program required participants to achieve a target exit score on a standardized English language test, in addition to satisfying other program requirements, in order to matriculate. Course progression alone was not sufficient. Approximately 75 percent of the participants achieved the required IELTS exit score of 6.0 within this three- to four-term program, as well as satisfying all other prerequisites for matriculation. This success rate is no doubt attributable to a variety of factors—some related to the Gateway program and its features, and others related to the participants themselves.

One factor that appears to have supported participant success was the intensive English language coursework. IEP course progression was strongly correlated with IELTS scores throughout the program ($r = 0.482$ to 0.486, $p < 0.01$), suggesting coursework was a factor sustaining score gains. The credit-bearing CoAS courses could have also played an important role in supporting language proficiency during the Gateway program. Though offered in sheltered formats in winter 2011 and spring 2011, these university courses demand levels of academic language expected of university students. The sheltered format and additional assistance provided a support structure by which to meet these demands and practice the academic discourse necessary for collegiate studies.

While IELTS score gains advanced alongside IEP coursework, credit-bearing university course GPAs were not correlated with IELTS score gains. Correlations among term-by-term IELTS scores and term-by-term Gateway program CoAS GPAs

Table 13.2
Matriculated Gateway GPA compared to direct admission GPA

Term	Fall 2011	Winter 2012	Spring 2012
Gateway	3.10 ($n = 32$)	3.04 ($n = 31$)	3.18 ($n = 30$)
Direct international	2.96 ($n = 376$)	3.05 ($n = 368$)	3.18 ($n = 361$)
Direct domestic	3.03 ($n = 2,730$)	2.95 ($n = 2,593$)	3.07 ($n = 2,523$)

were inconsistent and often not statistically significant, suggesting that performance in these chemistry, math, and philosophy courses was not directly related to increasing English-language proficiency. Indeed, by the second term of the Gateway program, it was not uncommon for participants to earn significantly different Gateway CoAS course grades within the same term, intuitive confirmation that nonlinguistic factors such as course-specific content, background knowledge, study habits, and other individual factors play an important role in determining course GPA.

The fact that there was no significant correlation between cumulative Gateway CoAS grades and standardized test scores at entry is perhaps another source of program validation; after reaching a basic threshold of English proficiency, cumulative GPAs reflect not only a sufficient level of English language, but content-relevant performance. In this way, the CoAS grades earned during the Gateway program (before matriculation) indicate that with sufficient support in the form of sheltered instruction, tutorial assistance, and reduced academic load (maximum two university courses per term), Gateway participants were generally able to manage their university coursework prior to full matriculation.

Post-Gateway matriculated first-term GPAs did not correlate with entry scores either, but did correlate with Gateway GPAs from courses taken during the Gateway program. The absence of a correlation between test scores at entry and matriculated university GPAs again suggests the matriculated Gateway students had achieved at least a minimum threshold level of English language proficiency so that their initial pre-Gateway language abilities did not appear to have a lasting impact on their collegiate performance. In this way, the Gateway program, having addressed the needs of lower English proficiency participants, mainstreamed a cohort for matriculation.

Several previous studies have investigated the predictive validity of IELTS scores—the relationship between IELTS scores and subsequent academic performance and GPAs—with mixed results. Some studies have reported some significant correlations (Bellingham 1993; Cotton and Conrow 1998; Feast 2002; and Kerstjens and Nery 2000), but, while positive, these correlations between IELTS scores and academic achievement were variable and small. Given that the relationship between English language proficiency and academic performance is mediated by a diversity of factors (motivation, intellect, acculturation, content knowledge, background experience, etc.), these results are not surprising.

Finally, if the Gateway participants were indeed ready for college, then they should have performed comparably to their direct admission peers. The average post-program, first-year matriculated GPAs among Gateway alumni were statistically equivalent to those earned by direct admission international and direct admission domestic students. More information—including longitudinal data tracking this first cohort of Gateway participants throughout their collegiate years as well as successive cohorts of future Gateway participants—is needed, however, to better answer Green (2007, 314), who asks, "Are learners who pursue pre-sessional programs in EAP better able to cope with [the demands of university study] than those accepted on the basis of proficiency scores alone?" Nevertheless, the program overview and data presented here are an indication that pre-university course experience and academic support, especially in sheltered formats, can play a role in supporting college success.

Quantifying IELTS Score Gains

The Gateway data collected here, in addition to providing a basis for evaluating Drexel University's conditional admission program, also speak to the more general issue of standardized test score gains. Since program participants sat for the IELTS at regular intervals, average score gains across multiple sittings were calculated. Four testing intervals were created, corresponding to the periodic IELTS testing which occurred toward the end of each eleven-week term. The average IELTS score gain per eleven-week term—regardless of score and independent of test date—was 0.35 points. Average score gains for longer intervals are predictably greater: 0.58 points across any two terms and 0.83 across any three terms. Table 13.3 presents these score gains as well as more detailed score gain data.

This average score gain of 0.35 per eleven-week term obscures the fact that lower scoring test takers tended to achieve greater score gains than higher scoring test takers. For example, the five participants with a 4.5 score (at any time during the program) experienced an average score gain of 1.30 points over an eleven-week interval. Reading further down the column, the fourteen participants who sat for the exam with a score of 5.0 increased their scores by an average of 0.61 points; those with 5.5 only by 0.26, and those with 6.0 by a mere 0.15 points over eleven weeks. Higher scores resulted in smaller score gains on the subsequent exam. This decreasing score gain dynamic appears to hold for the columns detailing two- and three-term intervals as well. Interval score gains generally decreased as scores increased, consistent with a score gain plateauing dynamic observed by Green (2004, 2005, 2007), which disproportionately advantages lower scoring test takers in comparison to higher scoring test takers.

This average IELTS score gain increase of 0.35 points per eleven-week interval is comparable to score gain data from two previous studies referenced by Green (2004). Though drawing upon much larger pools of IELTS score gain data from among thousands of repeat test takers (with scores ranging from band three to band

Table 13.3
Average 1-term, 2-term, 3-term, and 4-term interval IELTS score gains of matriculated students (one term = 11 weeks)

	1-term interval ($n = 68$)	2-term interval ($n = 38$)	3-term interval ($n = 12$)	4-term interval ($n = 1$)
Average score	5.40→5.75	5.28→5.86	5.13→5.96	4.5→6.0
Average score gain	0.35	0.58	0.83	1.50
4.5	1.30 ($n = 5$)	1.00 ($n = 4$)	0.33 ($n = 3$)	1.5 ($n = 5$)
5.0	0.61 ($n = 14$)	0.75 ($n = 10$)	1.00 ($n = 4$)	
5.5	0.26 ($n = 39$)	0.48 ($n = 23$)	0.50 ($n = 4$)	
6.0	0.15 ($n = 10$)	−0.50 ($n = 1$)	0.00 ($n = 1$)	

seven) over intervals of at least three months, the data were analyzed only for writing score gains. Green (2004) reported average writing score gains from 5.12 to 5.42 (an increase of 0.29) in a sample of 3,052 candidates and from 5.26 to 5.63 (an increase of 0.37) in a sample of 15,380 candidates.

Of course, the Gateway program is not the only IEP to analyze IELTS test scores with an eye toward IELTS score gains, though it seems to be the first in the United States. Comparisons across studies must be approached carefully, as complicating and confounding variables abound: the amount of time between test dates, the nature and amount of instructional contact hours, and the range of initial entry test scores (see, e.g., Ross 1998).

Figures for contact-hours-to-one-band-increase range from a low of ten hours per band to a high of five hundred hours per band (Green 2007, 88). Given these disparities, a once-published IELTS rule of thumb suggesting a timeline of two hundred contact hours per band was removed from the *IELTS Handbook* in 2002. According to the present analysis, an average IELTS score gain increase of 0.35 points per term represents an average score gain increase of slightly more than one full band over the course of three terms, translating to approximately six hundred contact hours per band (given the course structure of the Gateway program). Of course, this score gain figure must be interpreted in light of the specific features of the Gateway program—including the 4.5 to 6.5 IELTS entry score range of the Gateway participants themselves. Test takers drawn from a weaker or stronger pool are likely to present a different score gain profile.

For instance, Read and Hayes (2003) reported that improvement among seventeen participants in a one-month program in New Zealand averaged an increase of 0.36 points on listening, reading, and writing (speaking was not included), advancing from an average of 5.35 to 5.71. Though comparable in terms of average IELTS band range, 0.36 points in one month represents an accelerated learning curve relative to the Gateway participants. In a larger study ($n = 112$), Elder and O'Loughlin (2003) report an average band score increase of 0.59 (from 5.0 to 5.59) during a ten- to twelve-week program consisting of two hundred to two hundred and forty hours of instruction.

Conclusion

As the number of international students seeking undergraduate admission to colleges and universities in the United States continues to increase (now numbering over seven hundred thousand annually[9]), placing these students into appropriate programs becomes more critical for advisors, IEP directors, and university admission officers. The data presented here contribute to this effort by sharing new program data among stakeholders to make better informed academic and policy decisions.

By the same token, as the global reach of IELTS increases and the number of IELTS test centers in the United States multiplies, the research footprint of IELTS testing in the United States correspondingly requires further definition and depth. In contrast to the well-developed research industry surrounding and informing English proficiency testing in the United States generally (see, e.g., Spolsky 1995), and TOEFL testing in particular (see Chapelle, Enright, and Jamieson 2008 for a recent edited volume), IELTS research specifically conducted in the United States is, to date, much more limited. The United States is mentioned only a handful of times in the 2008 volume *Assessing Academic English: Testing English Proficiency 1950–1989: The IELTS Solution* (Davies 2008) and US-based IELTS funded research is only just beginning to appear in IELTS *Research Reports*. Given the history of the IELTS exam, this focus is predictable, but not sustainable.

The present study, then, is a preliminary step toward redressing this IELTS research imbalance. Though an average score gain increase of 0.35 points per eleven-week term is reported here, we agree with Green's (2004, 2005) conclusions that caution should be exercised when relating time of study to increase in scores. Given the interest in and potential utility of such score gain guidelines among test takers, receiving institutions, and IELTS partners, further research among universities and colleges, especially in the United States, is warranted.

Acknowledgments

The authors wish to acknowledge the research compliance granted by the Drexel University Office of Regulatory Research Compliance (IRB Protocol 1206001329) and the financial support offered by the Drexel University College of Arts and Sciences for the funding of a CoAS Humanities Fellowship awarded to Patrick Braciszewski during summer 2011.

NOTES

1. Gateway participants meeting all matriculation requirements by the end of the spring 2011 term were not required to stay for the summer 2011 term. (They could, however, optionally take summer 2011 courses.) In AY 2010–2011, twenty-six participants were cleared for early matriculation by the end of the spring 2011 term. Six participants remained for the summer 2011 term.
2. Since the Gateway program itself consists of a sequence of credit-bearing university courses, there are two sets of university courses and resulting GPAs: university courses and GPAs from CoAS courses taken while still within the Gateway program, and university courses and GPAs from courses taken as first-year fully matriculated students (which include the College of Business and the College of Engineering as well as CoAS courses). All GPA data were provided by the Office of the Provost, Academic Information and Systems, Drexel University.
3. IELTS and its partners sponsor a series of three publications: *Studies in English Language Testing*, *Research Notes*, and *IELTS Research Reports* (where many of these articles can be found; see www.ielts.org/researchers/research.aspx).
4. Sixteen of the original forty-four participants entered the program with TOEFL iBT scores. These TOEFL scores were converted to IELTS scores for the uniform tracking of score gains according to a congruence table provided by Educational Testing Services. See www.ets.org/toefl/institutions/scores/compare. While conversions like this introduce many factors, score conversions from TOEFL iBT (scaled from zero to one hundred and twenty) to IELTS (scaled from zero to nine) are not subject to the same loss of information as are conversions from IELTS to TOEFL given the substantial difference in scale granularity. All subsequent standardized test scores were the result of IELTS examinations conducted at the Drexel University IELTS Test Center (#US112) through regularly scheduled IELTS examinations.
5. These two participants applied for direct university admission too late to be accepted as first-year students and were accepted into the Gateway program as an alternative. These two entry scores were included in the analysis of pre-program entry scores, but given their high entry scores, these two participants were not required to sit for the IELTS exam again (and their scores were not used in analyses related to score gains). Nevertheless, like other participants, both participants were

required to satisfy all other program requirements. While the addition of these two participants raises potential problems related to program evaluation and data analysis, their inclusion reflects some of the realities facing conditional admission programs like Gateway. Of these two participants, one transferred out of the program while the other successfully matriculated.
6. These results contrast with the score gains reported by Craven (2012) where greatest score gains were achieved on the reading and listening modules.
7. The correlation between term-by-term ELC listening/speaking levels and term-by-term IELTS scores is significant, positive, and strong ($r = 0.486$, $p < 0.01$). Similarly, the correlation between term-by-term ELC reading/writing levels and term-by-term IELTS scores is also significant, positive, and strong ($r = 0.482$, $p < 0.01$).
8. The correlation between winter 2011 CoAS grades and December 2011 IELTS scores is just moderately positive and significant ($r = 0.308$, $p < .05$). However, the correlation between spring 2011 CoAS grades and March 2011 IELTS scores is not statistically significant ($p > 0.05$). When each term-by-term IELTS score is correlated with each term-by-term CoAS grade, the correlation between IELTS scores and corresponding CoAS grades is not statistically significant ($p > 0.05$).
9. According to the annually published *Open Doors* report (IIE 2011), the number of international students at colleges and universities in the United States was 723,277 during the 2010–2011 academic year—a five percent increase from the previous year—and a record high. *Open Doors* is published by the Institute of International Education (IIE 2011) in partnership with the US Department of State's Bureau of Educational and Cultural Affairs.

REFERENCES

Archibald, Alasdair. 2002. "Managing L2 writing proficiencies: Areas of change in students' writing over time." *International Journal of English Studies* 1: 153–74.

Bellingham, Lois. 1993. "The relationship of language proficiency to academic success for international students." *New Zealand Journal of Educational Studies* 30: 229–32.

Chapelle, Carol, Mary Enright, and Joan Jamieson. 2008. *Building a Validity Argument for the Test of English as a Foreign Language*. New York: Routledge.

Cotton, Fiona, and Frank Conrow. 1998. "An investigation of the predictive validity of IELTS amongst a group of international students studying at the University of Tasmania." *IELTS Research Reports* 1: 72–115.

Craven, Elizabeth. 2012. "The quest for IELTS Band 7.0: Investigating English language proficiency development of international students at an Australian university." *IELTS Research Reports* 13: 1–61.

Davies, Alan, editor. 2008. *Assessing Academic English: Testing English Proficiency 1950–1989: The IELTS Solution. Studies in Language Testing 23*. Cambridge: UCLES.

Elder, Catherine, and Kieran O'Loughlin. 2003. "Investigating the relationship between intensive English language study and band score gain on IELTS." *IELTS Research Reports* 4: 207–41.

Feast, Victoria. 2002. "The impact of IELTS scores on performance at university." *International Educational Journal* 3: 70–85.

Golder, Katherine, Kenneth Reeder, and Sarah Fleming. 2011. "Determination of appropriate IELTS writing and speaking band scores for admission into two programs at a Canadian post-secondary polytechnic institution." *The Canadian Journal of Applied Linguistics* 14: 222–50.

Green, Anthony. 2004. "Making the grade: Score gains on the IELTS writing test." *Research Notes* 16: 9–13.

———. 2005. "EAP study recommendations and score gains on the IELTS academic writing test." *Assessing Writing* 10: 44–60.

———. 2007. *IELTS Washback in Context: Preparation for Academic Writing in Higher Education, Studies in Language Testing 25*. Cambridge: UCLES.

Ingram, David, and Amanda Bayliss. 2007. "IELTS as a predictor of academic language performance, Part One." *IELTS Research Reports* 7: 137–91.

Institute of International Education (IIE). 2011. "International student enrollment increased by 5 percent in 2010/11, led by strong increase in students from China." *Open Doors Report*, November 11, 2011.

International English Language Testing System (IELTS). 2002. *The IELTS Handbook*. Cambridge: UCLES.
International English Language Testing System. 2012. www.ielts.org.
Kerstjens, Mary, and Caryn Nery. 2000. "Predictive validity in the IELTS test." *IELTS Research Reports* 3: 85–108.
Lloyd-Jones, Gaynor, and Chris Binch. 2012. "A case study evaluation of the English language progress of Chinese students on two UK postgraduate engineering courses." *IELTS Research Reports* 13: 1–56.
O'Loughlin, Kieran, and Sophie Arkoudis. 2009. "Investigating IELTS exit score gains in higher education." *IELTS Research Reports* 10: 95–180.
Read, John, and Belinda Hayes. 2003. "The impact of the IELTS test on preparation for academic study in New Zealand." *IELTS Research Reports* 4: 153–206.
Ross, Steven. 1998. *Measuring Gain in Language Programs: Theory and Research*. Sydney: National Centre for English Language Teaching and Research.
Spolsky, Bernard. 1995. *Measured Words: The Development of Objective Language Testing*. Oxford: Oxford University Press.

14

How Does Foreign Language Proficiency Change over Time?

Results of Data Mining Official Test Records

AMBER BLOOMFIELD, STEVEN ROSS, MEGAN MASTERS, KASSANDRA GYNTHER, AND STEPHEN O'CONNELL
University of Maryland

STUDIES INVESTIGATING CHANGE IN foreign language skills over time have explored a number of factors affecting skill loss, including achieved proficiency in the foreign language, the amount of time since foreign language input markedly decreased (e.g., since the conclusion of formal language training), and use of the foreign language during this period of reduced input. In addition to the general interest in identifying factors that impact the likelihood of losing foreign language proficiency skills over time, there is interest in exploring rate of loss to address language policy questions, such as the frequency with which foreign language skills should be formally tested.

This paper discusses the results of preliminary data mining of test records for more than eight hundred foreign language professionals. Longitudinal analyses explored how listening, reading, and speaking proficiency test ratings change over time. In addition, analyses investigated the extent to which lag time between test occasions (i.e., days between test events), participation in formal language courses, and initial test rating impact the rate of loss in test ratings. Overall trends show patterns of improvement in test ratings for reading and listening; no significant pattern of change was found for speaking skills. Latent growth analyses indicated that individuals who participated in foreign language courses had faster rates of improvement for reading and listening. Event history analyses of cases that showed a loss in ratings found that speaking was the most vulnerable skill, with a sizable proportion of individuals showing loss in their test ratings when the time between tests exceeded two years. Reading and listening proficiency ratings were more stable, with a large proportion of individuals maintaining their rating even when the time between tests exceeded three years. Rate of loss did not significantly differ based on initial reading or listening test score or participation in formal language courses. The paper discusses the implications of these findings for policies on foreign language testing frequency and future research on factors that may mitigate attrition; it also explores the applications of the statistical approach used here to other research questions related to language learning.

Literature Review

The study of how foreign language proficiency changes over time is a relatively new area of research, described as deriving its principal impetus from a conference at the University of Pennsylvania in May 1980 (e.g., Clark and Jorden 1984; De Bot and Weltens 1995; Lambert and Freed 1982; Weltens 1987). Most studies in this area have focused on which aspects of the foreign language are lost, and in what order (e.g., syntax versus lexical knowledge first; Jordens, De Bot, and Trapman 1989). Although this approach is valuable for describing those aspects of language most vulnerable to loss and for comparing the pattern of attrition to the pattern of acquisition, it does not address the question of what factors (e.g., regularly reading newspapers in the L2) affect change in general language abilities, such as reading comprehension over time or how quickly skills begin to show loss.

Studies that have investigated factors influencing change in more general foreign language skills have examined duration of the period of reduced input (e.g., time since the end of formal language training), achieved proficiency level prior to this period, amount of target language use during this period, and other factors. However, as many of these studies involve children or examine language skills at only one or two time points, this research is often difficult to generalize to the language skills of adult speakers over an extended period of time. The current study expands on previous research by examining a database of adult foreign language professionals' proficiency test records, systematically archived over a period of six years, to determine how reading, listening, and speaking skills change over time; the rate at which loss occurs; and how change is affected both by participation in formal language courses and initial proficiency level.

Period of Reduced Input and Change in Language Skills

Duration of the period of reduced input has been defined as the time since the end of formal training (e.g., Bahrick 1984) or since the end of intensive language exposure, such as an immersion experience (e.g., Snow, Padilla, and Campbell 1988). As its name implies, the period of reduced input also assumes that a learner's access to the foreign language is diminished upon completion of a training event or at the conclusion of exposure. More generally, this period has been conceptualized as the amount of time since learners achieved their peak proficiency (Bardovi-Harlig and Stringer 2010), though this characterization can be problematic when learners' abilities improve after the baseline measure of proficiency is obtained (Gardner et al. 1987; Murtagh and van der Slik 2004). The amount of time the learner has had to lose language skills is a particularly intuitive factor in explaining degree of skill loss, with the common sense prediction being that loss increases with elapsed time. Several studies have found evidence for such a relationship (e.g., Murtagh and van der Slik 2004; Nagasawa 1999; Reetz-Kurashige 1999), although some findings suggest that the rate of loss over time may not be linear (Bahrick 1984). It is also important to take into consideration other factors, such as the target language activities the learner has engaged in during the period of reduced input, rather than simply the time elapsed since a benchmark of language learning was attained.

One issue with research on the duration of the period of reduced input is that these studies explore duration as a discrete factor, investigating language skills at a few specific points in time (often at only one or two time points after the period of reduced input has begun). In general, there is a tradeoff between sample size and the number of time points at which the language skills of the participants are measured; those studies with sizable n (e.g., Clark and Jorden 1984; Gardner et al. 1987; Murtagh and van der Slik 2004) tend to measure language skills only twice, once at the beginning of the period of reduced input (i.e., the baseline) and again a set amount of time later. Cross-sectional studies, like Bahrick (1984) and Snow, Padilla, and Campbell (1988), take only one measure of language skills for each participant and compare across groups that have experienced different durations of reduced input. This latter method can be problematic because it does not take into account potential differences in achieved proficiency level between the groups. By contrast, some studies compare language skills for the same individual at a number of time points, but these tend to involve very small groups of participants, generally children (see Russell 1999 for an exception), and to focus on the specific aspects of the language that are lost rather than loss of general language skill (e.g., Hansen-Strain 1990; Reetz-Kurashige 1999; Yoshitomi 1999). The reason for the paucity of studies exploring foreign language attrition at multiple time points with adult learners is likely practical in nature; it is difficult to track and maintain contact with the same group of language learners over a long period of time. Yet, to explore how foreign language skills change over time, it is necessary to examine the skills of the same set of individuals repeatedly during the period of reduced input. The current analyses compare multiple assessments of the same group of adult foreign language learners over time.

Language Use during the Period of Reduced Input
The extent to which the foreign language is used during the period of reduced input is likely to be an important determinant of skill loss because it indicates just how reduced the input during this period is for the learner. Clark and Jorden (1984) found that the learners of Japanese who did not show loss months after formal language training ended reported using the language more regularly than those who did show loss. In a similar study, Murtagh and van der Slik (2004) demonstrated that use of the target language after leaving formal language training predicted strength of language skills for learners of Irish eighteen months after leaving school. In a study with Canadian government employees, French-dominant bilinguals reported more opportunities to use their less dominant language (English) and also showed less skill loss in their weaker language than did English-dominant bilinguals (Edwards 1977, discussed in Oxford 1982). Snow (1982) found that, at the group level, the lowest amount of loss occurred for Spanish immersion student groups with the highest proportion of learners who continued to study the target language after the immersion ended (reported in Snow, Padilla, and Campbell 1988). In the current analyses, participation in formal language courses is included as a variable that captures differing degrees of language use during the period of reduced input.

Proficiency Level and Change in Language Skills

Initial proficiency level in the L2, sometimes referred to as achieved proficiency, is important for assessing change in foreign language skills because it provides the baseline against which to compare current ability. This factor has also been considered as a potential predictor for foreign language loss (Hansen 1999). Having higher proficiency may lead to decreased loss over time (for reviews, see Bardovi-Harlig and Stringer 2010; Weltens 1987). One potential reason for this relationship is that having greater proficiency may provide a learner with more strategies to compensate for loss of specific foreign language knowledge. For example, a learner could use morphological knowledge to uncover the meaning of a forgotten target language lexical item in the same way children use this type of information to comprehend unfamiliar words (Carr and Johnston 2001). In addition, some theories of foreign language acquisition suggest that once language knowledge reaches a critical threshold, it becomes resistant to loss (Bardovi-Harlig and Stringer 2010). However, there are mixed results for the relationship between initial proficiency and change in language skills over time, with several studies suggesting that higher proficiency learners do indeed experience less loss over time (Clark and Jorden 1984; Gardner et al. 1987; Kaufman 1995; Nagasawa 1999), and others suggesting there is no difference in rate of language loss between higher and lower proficiency learners (Bahrick 1984; Weltens and Grendel 1993). To address this ambiguity, the current analyses also investigate how initial proficiency impacts change in foreign language skills.

The Current Study

The current study reports the results of data mining in which a large database of official test records was analyzed to explore change in general foreign language proficiency (reading, listening comprehension, and speaking ability) for more than eight hundred language learners. Individuals were tested multiple times (two to seven tests, with the majority having three or more) as an employment requirement over a period as long as six years. It should be noted that these individuals may or may not use their foreign language skills in their current position and information regarding foreign language use on the job was not available.

Nearly fifty different languages were represented in the dataset; however, because of the small number of people testing in any one language, all analyses were collapsed across languages. In addition to test records, information about participation in formal language courses and the version of the test taken (varied only for listening and reading) was available.

Method

The dataset included 1,084 test histories for listening, 1,085 for reading, and 1,140 for speaking. Each test event was associated with a proficiency rating based on the raw score; raw scores were not included in the dataset. Ratings are on the Interagency Language Roundtable (ILR) scale for that particular skill, with 0 equating to *No Proficiency* and 5 equating to *Functionally Native Proficiency*; between each pair of adjacent levels is a *plus level* (e.g., 2+), which is "assigned when proficiency substantially exceeds one skill level and does not fully meet the criteria for the next level" (Interagency Language Roundtable 2012). For the purpose of analyses, all ratings were recoded as numeric values. Ratings were associated with a test date, enabling calculation of the number of days from the first test administration to each subsequent test.

Initial target language proficiency was defined as the first ILR rating available in the dataset in the relevant skill (i.e., reading, listening, or speaking). It should be noted that the first score in the dataset was not necessarily the individual's first test score for that language; rather, this database was constrained by data availability to include only test scores from 2005 and after. The people in the database may have first learned the target language several years previous to the start date of the available test history. Due to the sparseness of learners at some levels of initial proficiency, a dichotomously coded factor was created: *high* = rating ≥ 2+; *low* = rating ≤ 2. In addition, whether or not the test version changed during the testing history was coded dichotomously (applicable for reading and listening only). This factor was included because the introduction of a new test version may decrease ratings even in the absence of skill loss and could obscure a pattern of improvement in language skills.

A minority of the individuals in the dataset (approximately 14 percent) had at least one formal language course on record. Although the proportion of individuals participating in courses was small, this was the only available information about language use during the test history and so was included to examine the role of this factor in explaining skill loss over time.

Results
Overall Patterns of Change
Latent growth analysis (Bollen and Curran 2006) was used to examine the trajectory of change in skills over time. In these analyses, first rating or intercept (*ICEPT*) and change over time (*SLOPE*) were dependent variables, while participation in formal language courses (*Formalcourse*) and the occurrence of a test version change (*Versionchange*; reading and listening only) were included as independent variables. Since few test histories contained more than four tests, only the first four tests were included in the latent growth analyses.

For listening test histories, 398 cases in the dataset contained at least 4 test records and 729 contained at least 3. The model fit was acceptable ($RMSEA = 0.053$, $CFI = 0.984$; see figure 14.1). The average slope was $M = 1.35$ ($SE = 0.15$; $t = 8.94$, $p < 0.001$), indicating a significant pattern of improvement in listening ratings over test administrations. The correlation between the intercept and the slope was significant and negative for listening ($r = -0.37$, $p < 0.001$), suggesting that people who started with lower ILR ratings had a steeper trajectory of improvement over time than those who started with higher ratings.

Notably, the *Formalcourse* variable had a significant negative relationship (–0.15) to the intercept for listening ratings ($t = -4.27$, $p < 0.001$), suggesting the people who participated in formal language courses had lower initial ILR ratings. This relationship may be due to individuals self-selecting for formal language courses to improve their language skills. In addition, *Formalcourse* had a significant

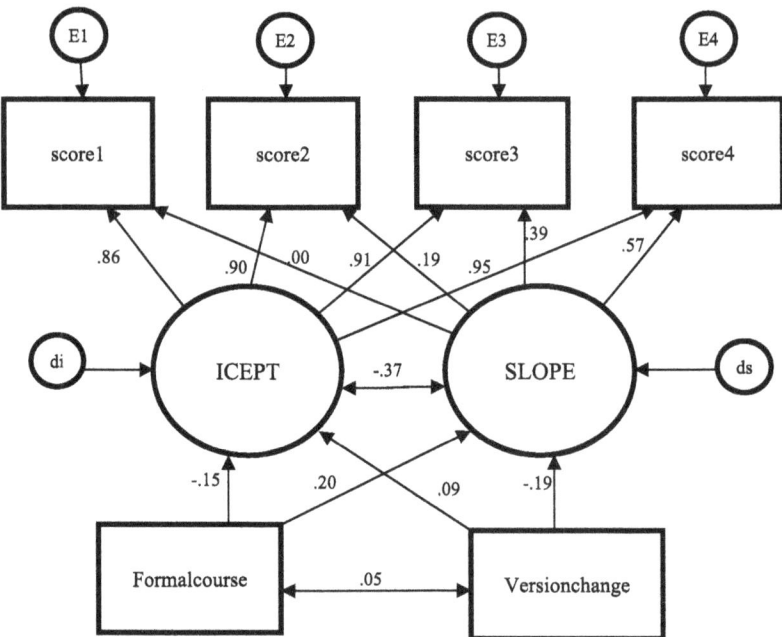

Figure 14.1 Latent Growth Model Fit to the 1–4 Listening Test Administrations in the Dataset

positive relationship (0.20) with slope ($t = 3.09$, $p < 0.01$), indicating that improvement for employees who took formal language courses was steeper over time than for those who had not taken a course. *Versionchange* also had a significant relationship with slope, but this relationship was negative (–0.19; $t = -2.88$, $p < 0.01$). As anticipated, the introduction of a new test version is associated with a decreased degree of improvement shown over time. What is less intuitive, however, is the significant positive relationship (0.09) between the *Versionchange* and the intercept ($t = 2.76$, $p < 0.01$): people who experienced a version change also tended to have higher initial ILR ratings. Since a new test version was introduced for only a subset of languages in the current dataset, it is possible that initial proficiency just happened to be higher in those languages that experienced a version change. Chi-square tests confirm this relationship: more people with starting proficiency of 2+ or above experienced a version change for both listening and reading ($\chi^2(1) = 8.08$ and $\chi^2(1) = 8.32$, respectively; both $ps < 0.01$).

For reading, 400 cases in the dataset contained at least 4 test records and 729 contained at least 3. The model fit of these data was successful (*RMSEA* = 0.027, *CFI* = 0.997; see figure 14.2). The average slope was $M = 1.03$ ($SE = 0.15$; $t = 7.08$, $p < 0.001$), indicating a more modest but significant pattern of positive change over time. Unlike for listening ratings, the significant correlation between the intercept and the slope was positive ($r = 0.24$, $p < 0.05$); this suggests that people with higher initial ILR ratings tended to have a steeper trajectory of improvement over time than people with lower initial ILR ratings. The reason for this difference between listening

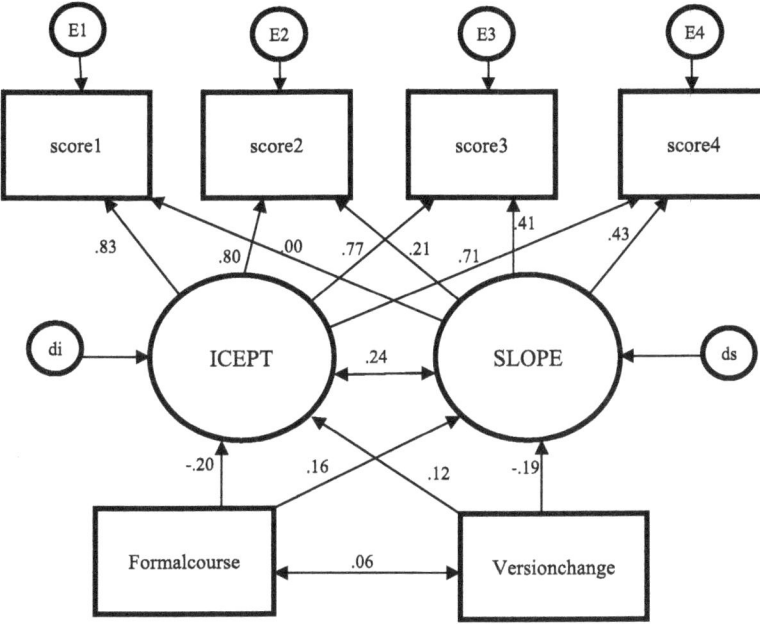

Figure 14.2 Latent Growth Model Fit to the 1–4 DLPT Reading Test Administrations

and reading ratings is not clear, but one possibility is that it is easier for individuals to show improvement in their reading skills than in their listening skills after reaching higher levels of proficiency. This presents an interesting question for future study.

As in the listening analyses, the *Formalcourse* variable had a significant negative relationship (–0.20) with the intercept for reading ($t = -5.71$, $p < 0.001$), indicating that people who participated in formal language courses tended to have lower initial reading ratings; the *Formalcourse* variable also had a significant positive relationship (0.16) with the slope ($t = 2.67$, $p < 0.01$), suggesting that improvement was steeper for those individuals who had participated in at least one course. The *Versionchange* variable had a significant negative relationship (–0.19) to slope ($t = -2.88$, $p < 0.01$); as for listening, the introduction of a new test version is associated with flatter trajectory of growth in reading ILR ratings over time. The same positive relationship between *Versionchange* and the intercept was also present for reading ratings (0.12; $t = 3.42$, $p < 0.001$); as supported by the chi-square test described above, those languages for which a new test version had been introduced also tended to be languages where the individuals had a higher initial rating.

The latent growth model analysis for speaking differed in several ways from those for reading and listening. First, there was evidence that a test vendor change occurring early in the test histories resulted in a drop in test ratings, indicating that the ratings provided by the first vendor may have been inflated compared to subsequent test ratings. To avoid establishing a baseline rating that would exaggerate the initial proficiency of the learners and result in a greater degree of apparent change in ratings over test occasions, analyses excluded the first rating on record. As noted above, the first rating on record was not necessarily the first test rating obtained by these learners, but rather was the first test rating available for them in the current dataset. Therefore, benchmarking proficiency with the second rating on record is not a qualitatively different way of describing the participants' initial proficiency, though this decision avoids the potential noise introduced by the vendor change at the cost of shortening the test histories for speaking.

Another difference between the speaking analyses and those for reading and listening was that the dominant pattern of change observed in the dataset for speaking was loss rather than growth. Consequently, the slope was hypothesized to be negative rather than positive. In addition, unlike for reading and listening tests, there was not a version change to the speaking test, so this variable was not considered.

The model fit to the three speaking ratings was successful ($RMSEA = 0.010$, $CFI = 1.00$; see figure 14.3). The mean slope was $M = -0.23$ ($SE = 0.29$), indicating a slightly negative trajectory across the three test administrations. However, the fact that the slope was not significant ($t = 0.777$, $p = 0.44$) indicates no consistent overall pattern of change in speaking over time. This lack of a significant slope may be due to the smaller number of tests considered in this analysis as a result of the test vendor change. The correlation between slope and intercept was significant ($r = 0.51$, $p < 0.001$), suggesting that the higher the first ILR rating, the steeper the downward trajectory over time. This finding is corroborated in the event history analysis to follow and presents a somewhat contrary picture to previous findings (Clark and Jorden

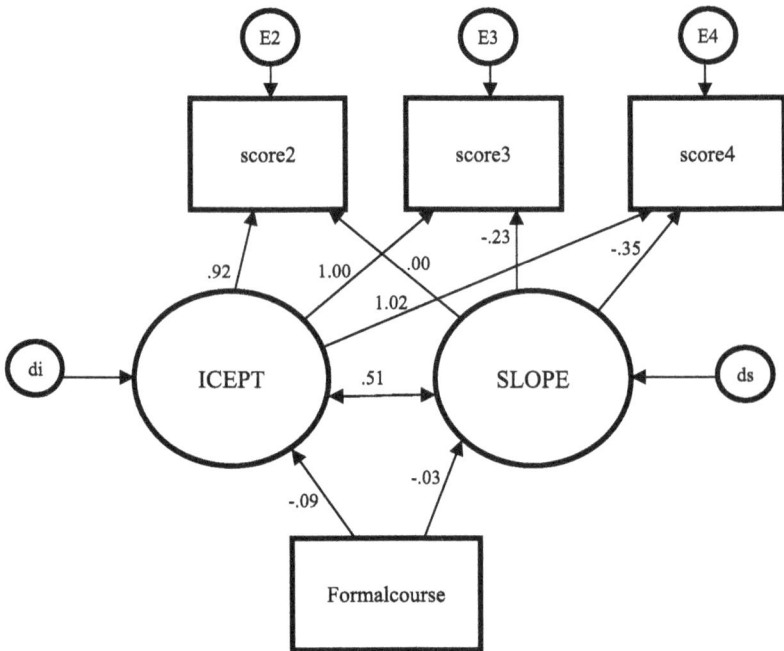

Figure 14.3 The Latent Growth Model Fit to the 2–4 Speaking Test Administrations

1984; Gardner et al. 1987; Kaufman 1995; Nagasawa 1999). This is discussed further below.

The variable *Formalcourse* has a significant negative effect (–0.09) on the intercept ($t = -2.74$, $p < 0.01$), indicating that people with lower second test ratings are more likely to participate in formal language training courses, consistent with the results of the reading and listening analyses. *Formalcourse* did not, however, have a significant effect (–0.03) on the trajectory of change ($t = -0.41$, $p = 0.68$). One possible explanation for this finding is that the speaking skill may not have been targeted by these courses; unfortunately, no information about the skills emphasized by the formal language courses was available in the dataset. Another explanation is that the shorter test histories for speaking (due to excluding the first test) made the trajectories of change less robust, decreasing both the chance of finding a significant overall slope and of finding significant relationships to the slope.

Loss of ILR Ratings

To examine how the amount of time between tests affected the incidence of rating loss, event history analyses were conducted separately for each skill. The event of interest for these analyses is loss of ILR rating. A case was coded as showing a loss if the most recent test occasion produced a lower ILR rating than the first test occasion, ignoring intervening tests; cases where the most recent rating was equal to or higher than the first rating were coded as nonlosses. The goal of the event history analysis is an estimation of the average time lag (i.e., time between the first and most recent test) associated with increasing incidences of loss and the effect of covariates on the observed rate of loss. In the current analyses, initial rating, experiencing a version change, and participating in a formal language course were included as covariates.

Note that the event history analysis focuses on those test histories where the event of interest (i.e., loss) occurs; the results speak to the rate of loss for those individuals who have experienced or will experience a loss. Not every individual in the dataset is expected to experience a loss; in fact, the prevailing pattern for reading and listening, as noted above, is one of improvement over time.

For listening test records, only 10.9 percent of cases show a lower rating on the most recent test than on the first test, consistent with the results of the latent growth analysis. Figure 14.4 displays the baseline rate of survival for listening test ratings. On this figure, the x-axis displays the number of days between the first and most recent test, while the y-axis displays the proportion of the group who will eventually experience a loss but has survived (i.e., retained their initial rating) up to that point in time. Figure 14.4 indicates that the majority of those who would eventually experience a loss are projected to maintain their initial listening rating three years after their first test.

Experiencing a version change was a significant covariate in the event history analysis for listening. Consistent with the results of the latent growth analyses, individuals who experienced a version change did not survive as long as those who did not (i.e., people showed loss faster when there was a version change). In addition, neither initial rating nor participating in formal language courses was significantly related to the rate of loss in listening ratings. This result suggests that while participation in

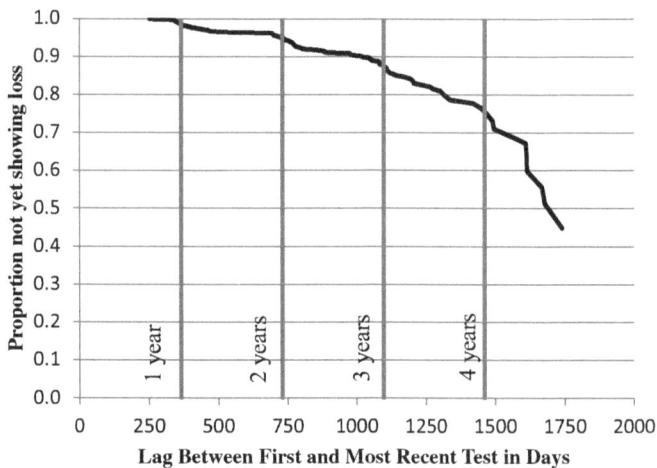

Figure 14.4 Retention of Listening Skills between First and Most Recent Test

these courses encourages improvement in ratings over time, as indicated by the latent growth analysis results, it does not stave off loss of listening ratings. However, given the small number of people in the dataset who had participated in a course and the small proportion who showed a loss in their listening rating, the current analyses may not have had the power to detect a relationship between course participation and the rate of loss over time.

For reading test ratings, a slightly higher percentage of the test histories showed a loss on the most recent test compared with the first test (12.5 percent). However, the rate of loss over time for reading test ratings was very similar to that seen for listening test ratings, with the majority of individuals in the dataset who would eventually experience a loss projected to retain their initial ILR rating three years after their first test (see figure 14.5).

The same variables investigated for listening were investigated for reading ILR ratings: the relationship between experiencing a test version change, initial rating, and participating in a formal language course and the rate of loss over time. Version change was a significant covariate, indicating that individuals who experienced a test version change showed loss faster than those who did not. Again, this result is consistent with the findings of the latent growth analyses. Once version change was accounted for, participation in formal language courses and initial rating did not have significant relationships to the rate of loss for reading ratings. Again, the lack of a significant relationship between course participation and the rate of loss, in conjunction with the results of the latent growth analyses, indicates that course participation encourages improvement of reading skills but does not delay loss of reading skills. However, in regard to listening, it is possible the current analysis did not have the power to detect the relationship between course participation and rate of loss, if it does exist.

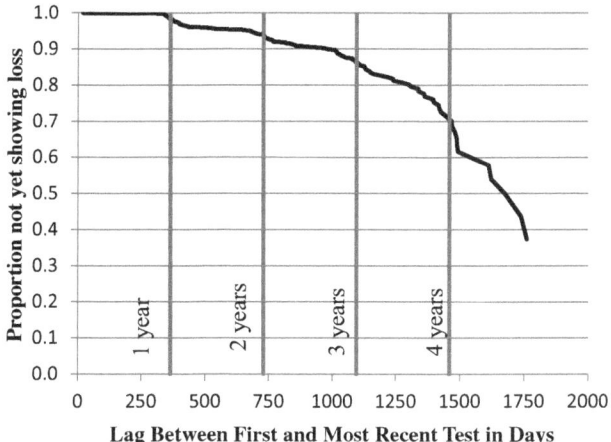

Figure 14.5 Retention of Reading Skills between the First and Most Recent Test

The event history analysis for speaking yielded notably different results than that for reading and listening. There were more cases of loss in the speaking test histories (20.4 percent) than in reading or listening; the rate of loss for speaking ILR ratings was also somewhat faster than for the two other skills (see figure 14.6), with the majority of individuals projected to maintain their initial rating for two years before the rate of loss increases. In addition, the initial rating was a significant covariate in this analysis, with the unexpected pattern that those with higher initial ratings (2+ or higher) are projected to show a faster rate of loss than those with lower initial ratings (2 or lower; see figure 14.7). This pattern is contrary to the relationship between initial proficiency and foreign language skill loss reported in the literature (Clark and

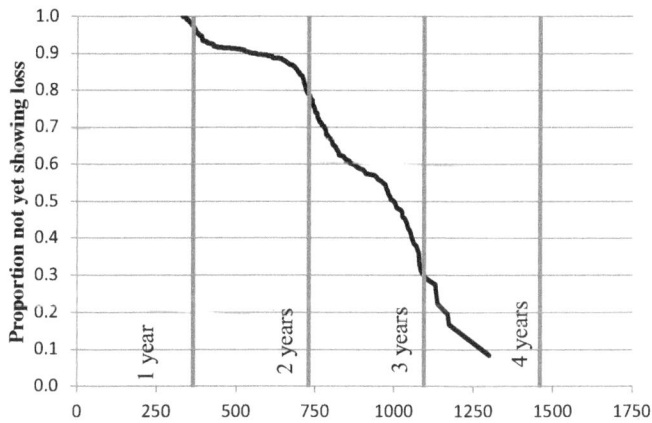

Figure 14.6 Retention of Speaking Skills between Second and Most Recent Test

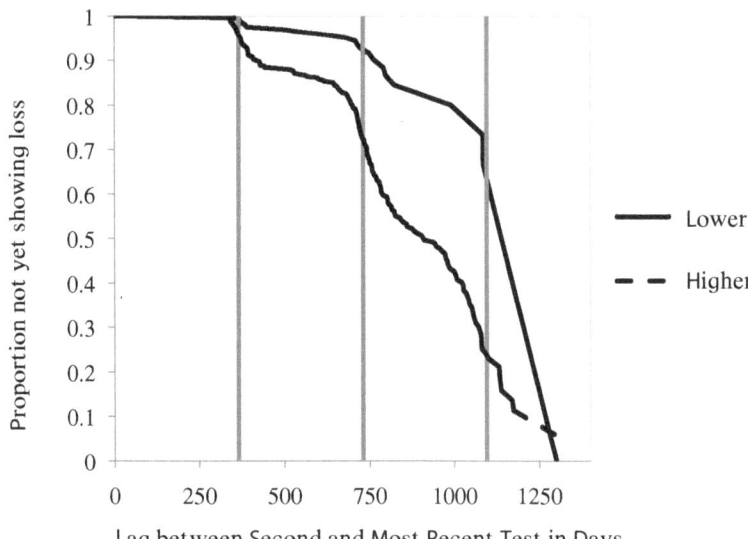

Figure 14.7 Retention of Speaking Skills between Second and Most Recent Speaking Test by Initial Proficiency Level

Jorden 1984; Gardner et al. 1987; Kaufman 1995; Nagasawa 1999) but is consistent with the results of the latent growth analyses.

Discussion

Data mining of test records for a group of foreign language professionals provided an opportunity to investigate change in language skills over time for the same adult learners tested repeatedly. Analyses yielded several results consistent with previous findings. First, retention of initial test rating decreased as time since the first test increased, consistent with previous studies (Murtagh and van der Slik 2004; Nagasawa 1999; Reetz-Kurashige 1999). In addition, language use during the period where change in skills might occur (i.e., in the time since capturing baseline proficiency) is associated with improvement in foreign language skills, as found in previous studies (e.g., Edwards 1977; Murtagh and van der Slik 2004; Snow 1982). Individuals who participated in formal language courses showed a steeper trajectory of improvement in listening and reading test ratings than individuals who did not participate in these courses. As noted above, however, the formal language courses are only one type of language use in which employees in this dataset might have taken part. Further analyses are planned with the current dataset using responses to a survey of language training and use completed by the same individuals; these analyses will provide a more detailed picture of how language use impacts change in skills over time.

Contrary to previous research, individuals in the dataset with higher initial proficiency for speaking showed a faster rate of loss over time than individuals with lower initial proficiency. In addition, overall change over time in speaking ratings was more negative for individuals with higher initial ratings. However, initial proficiency in the current study was defined as the first rating in the dataset for listening and reading and the second for speaking (to avoid the effects of vendor change); previous studies have captured initial proficiency level at the completion of a language training program (Clark and Jorden 1984), course (Gardner et al. 1987), or immersion (Nagasawa 1999). It is possible that attrition immediately following an intensive training or in-country experience may differ from attrition seen later. It is also possible that the "high" proficiency in the current study differed from the "high" proficiency described in previous studies; a level 3 language learner from the current dataset would be capable of using their target language in professional settings. In future studies, defining achieved or initial proficiency relative to some common scale would clarify the relationship between initial proficiency and change in skills over time. Even in the current dataset, however, it is possible that higher proficiency learners were better able to maintain their lower-level skills than lower proficiency learners. For example, to obtain a level 3 rating, a person must apply the skills of a level 3 as well as skills associated with lower ratings; a person who drops from a 3 to a 2+ may have failed to retain their level 3 skills but better retained their lower level skills than someone who drops from a 2 to a 1+. Unfortunately, the dataset did not include information about performance on particular tasks. A finer-grained description of test performance would better address the question of how well higher-proficiency learners maintain their skills over time.

The results reported here suggest that speaking likely needs to be tested more frequently than reading and listening to monitor changes in proficiency rating. Separate testing policies for the three skills may be appropriate given the differences found in rate of loss. However, because other factors affecting retention of these skills may differ, such as the extent to which the skill is used on the job, it is important to investigate language use and maintenance activities before drawing more general conclusions about how quickly these skills show loss.

The statistical approaches taken in the current study have wider applications both for exploring loss of foreign language skills over time and for exploring the acquisition of skills. Latent growth analyses allow the individual trajectories of growth to be considered for learners rather than the pattern of growth at the group level; they have the added benefit of not excluding cases with missing data. Event history analyses allow for the investigation of how covariates impact both the occurrence of an event and the rate at which this event occurs; while loss in test ratings was the focus in the current study, the event could also be defined as gain or even the mastery of a particular sub-skill. This approach could be useful when not only the efficacy of a particular type of material or training technique is of interest, but also its efficiency.

REFERENCES

Bahrick, H. P. 1984. "Semantic memory content in permastore: Fifty years of memory for Spanish learned in school." *Journal of Experimental Psychology: General* 113 (1): 1–29.

Bardovi-Harlig, K., and D. Stringer. 2010. "Variables in second language attrition." *Studies in Second Language Acquisition* 32 (1): 1–45.

Bollen, K.A., and P. J. Curran. 2006. *Latent Curve Models*. Wiley: InterScience.

Carr, L., and J. Johnston. 2001. "Morphological cues to verb meaning." *Applied Psycholinguistics* 22 (4): 601–18.

Clark, J. L. D., and E. H. Jorden. 1984. *A Study of Language Attrition in Former US Students of Japanese and Implications for Design of Curriculum and Teaching Materials*. Retrieved August 4, 2011 from ERIC Document Reproduction Service. www.eric.ed.gov, No. ED243317.

De Bot, K., and B. Weltens. 1995. "Foreign language attrition." *Annual Review of Applied Linguistics* 15 (1): 151–64.

Edwards, G. 1977. "Second language retention in the public service of Canada." Ottawa: Research Section, Official Languages Directorate.

Gardner, R. C., R. N. Lalonde, R. Moorcroft, and F. T. Evers. 1987. "Second language attrition: The role of motivation and use." *Journal of Language and Social Psychology* 6 (1): 29.

Hansen, L. 1999. *Second Language Attrition in Japanese Contexts*: Oxford: Oxford University Press.

Hansen-Strain, L. 1990. "The attrition of Japanese by English-speaking children: An interim report." *Language Sciences* 12 (4): 367–77.

Interagency Language Roundtable. 2012. *Descriptions of Proficiency Levels*. 2011 [cited January 1 2012]. Available from www.govtilr.org/Skills/ILRscale1.htm.

Jordens, P., K. D. De Bot, and H. Trapman. 1989. "Linguistic aspects of regression in German case marking." *Studies in Second Language Acquisition* 11 (2): 179–204.

Kaufman, D. 1995. "Where have all the verbs gone? Autonomy and interaction in attrition." *Southwest Journal of Linguistics* 14: 43–66.

Lambert, R. D., and B. F. Freed. 1982. *The Loss of Language Skills*. Rowley, MA: Newbury House.

Murtagh, L., and F. van der Slik. 2004. "Retention of Irish skills: A longitudinal study of a school-acquired second language." *International Journal of Bilingualism* 8 (3): 279–302.

Nagasawa, S. 1999. "Learning and losing Japanese as a second language: A multiple case study of American university students." In *Second Language Attrition in Japanese Contexts*, edited by L. Hansen. Oxford: Oxford University Press, 169–212.

Oxford, R. 1982. "Technical issues in designing and conducting research on language skill attrition." In *The Loss of Language Skills*, edited by R. D. Lambert and B. F. Freed. Rowley, MA: Newbury House, 119–37.

Reetz-Kurashige, A. 1999. "Japanese returnees' retention of English-speaking skills: Changes in verb usage over time." In *Second Language Attrition in Japanese Contexts*, edited by L. Hansen. Oxford: Oxford University Press, 21–58.

Russell, R. A. 1999. "Lexical maintenance and attrition in Japanese as a second language." In *Second Language Attrition in Japanese Contexts*, edited by L. Hansen. Oxford: Oxford University Press, 114–41.

Snow, M. A. 1982. "Graduates of the Culver City Spanish Immersion Program: A follow-up report." Paper read at Sixteenth Annual TESOL Convention in Honolulu, HI.

Snow, M. A., A. Padilla, and R. Campbell. 1988. "Factors influencing language retention of graduates of a Spanish immersion program." *Applied Linguistics* 9: 182–97.

Weltens, B. 1987. "The attrition of foreign-language skills: A literature review." *Applied Linguistics* (1): 22–38.

Weltens, B., and M. Grendel. 1993. "Attrition of vocabulary knowledge." In *The Bilingual Lexicon*, edited by R. Schreuder and B. Weltens. Amsterdam: John Benjamins, 135–56.

Yoshitomi, A. 1999. "On the loss of English as a second language by Japanese returnee children." In *Second Language Attrition in Japanese Contexts*, edited by L. Hansen. Oxford: Oxford University Press. 80–111.

15

The Development of Complexity in a Learner Corpus of German

COLLEEN NEARY-SUNDQUIST
Purdue University

NORRIS AND ORTEGA (2009) have argued that complexity is a multidimensional construct and that the measurement of complexity must therefore also be multidimensional. This study examines multiple measures of complexity in a learner corpus of German. The data were collected from learners of German ($n = 70$) in their first two years of language study at the university level. The learners completed two writing and two speaking tasks that were identical or similar over the course of a semester of study. The data were examined for complexity by subordination, complexity by coordination, and phrasal complexity. The research questions investigated whether the different measures of complexity rise from one instructional level to another and whether any changes in complexity are consistent across the modalities of speech and writing. The results show that complexity of subordination was the dimension that most clearly distinguished between different instructional levels. Several measures showed more dramatic differences in one modality than in the other. The results are discussed in terms of which measure of complexity best distinguishes among learners at lower proficiency levels.

The understanding of the development of syntactic complexity in second language acquisition is limited by the ability to measure complexity reliably and accurately. As Norris and Ortega (2009) point out, researchers in the field often use redundant measures in their studies of complexity and sometimes seem to lack clarity about how their measures relate organically to the construct of complexity.

This paper attempts to contribute to a more principled approach to complexity research by examining data for three complexity measures which have been carefully chosen to represent three different sub-constructs of complexity. In particular, the study examines both spoken and written data from learners of German at multiple proficiency levels for evidence of complexity by subordination, complexity by coordination, and phrasal complexity.

Background
The Importance of Complexity Measures in Second Language Acquisition Research

In recent years, there has been increased interest in the measurement of fluency, accuracy, and complexity, and in how these three aspects of interlanguage development might be affected by task types and conditions. In a series of studies, Skehan and Foster investigated the trade-offs that occur as learners prioritize one aspect of performance over another (for example, Foster and Skehan 1999).

The potentially important insights into how learners allocate their attentional resources when performing language tasks that can be gleaned from this type of research are limited by our ability to accurately measure complexity, accuracy, and fluency.

Norris and Ortega (2009) argue that complexity is a multidimensional construct that also must be measured multidimensionally. They maintain that studies of the complexity of learner language have made use of a perplexing variety of different measurements, and these measurements are not selected carefully enough to match the questions and goals of the particular research study. Norris and Ortega argue further that many of the distinct measures used in complexity studies often index the same behavior without realizing this or at least without making it clear to the reader.

The problems with complexity studies that Norris and Ortega outline are troubling because they can lead to problems comparing results of different studies, as well as generalizing results to other contexts. For research on the development of complexity to progress, there needs to be greater agreement on what constitutes syntactic complexity and how it is measured.

The Relationship among Measures of Complexity

The first step in choosing measures of complexity is to consider what subconstructs might constitute the construct of complexity. Norris and Ortega (2009) argue that complexity is a multidimensional construct that is composed of overall complexity, subordination, phrasal complexity, and variety of forms. Consequently, they propose measures that they argue correspond to the different subcomponents of the complexity construct. The first measure is complexity through the use of coordinate clauses. The second measure is complexity through the use of subordinate clauses. The third measure is average clause length, to capture complexity at the phrasal, rather than the clausal level. They note that each of these measures might be particularly helpful for distinguishing learners at different proficiency levels: coordination for lower-level learners, subordination for intermediate learners, and phrasal complexity for advanced learners. Norris and Ortega conclude that " . . . it will be wise to measure all three dimensions of complexity in the same data, and this will require minimally the combined use of one measure from each of the three families in the same study" (Norris and Ortega 2009, 564).

Norris and Ortega's recommendations dovetail with observations from Wolfe-Quintero, Inagaki, and Kim's (1998) large-scale review of measures of fluency, accuracy, and complexity. Wolfe-Quintero, Inagaki, and Kim (1998) propose that complexity will first appear as coordination in interlanguage, then as subordination, and finally in increased clause length. The measurement of all three of these components of complexity in a study of learners at multiple proficiency levels should be able to shed some light on how the development of complexity proceeds among second language learners.

We now review some previous research on each of the subcomponents of complexity that are measured in this study.

Complexity by Subordination
A number of previous studies of L2 writing have shown that the rate of subordination appears to level off or decrease at more advanced levels of proficiency (Bardovi-Harlig and Bofman 1989; Cooper 1976; Perkins 1980). This evidence accords with the suggestion by Wolfe-Quintero, Inagaki, and Kim (1998) that the expression of complexity moves from coordination to subordination to longer phrases. They also speculate that complexity measures might exhibit "omega-shaped" behavior, with an increase in the behavior followed by a decline as students deemphasize the behavior for another type of complexity. This would be the inverse of the famous U-shaped behavior for accuracy.

Hirano (1991) found that the ratio of dependent clauses to total clauses did increase with proficiency level, but the correlation between the dependent clause ratio and the subjects' proficiency test scores was weak. Kameen (1979) also did not find significant results for this measure between writing samples that had been rated either good or poor. A related but different measure—dependent clauses divided by T units—was used in other studies. Homburg (1984) found a significant relationship between this measure and holistic ratings, but Vann (1979) found none.

For spoken data, Iwashita et al. (2008) found that the dependent clause ratio did not increase with proficiency level. But in a study of high and low proficiency Japanese learners, Iwashita (2006) found that the high proficiency group produced significantly more dependent clauses than the low proficiency group.

Since this study operationalizes the difference between levels not just in terms of statistical significance, but also in terms of effect size, it is important to consider the effect sizes for the studies above. Unfortunately, effect sizes were not published as part of the results of these studies, so I have calculated them myself based on the data available. For rates of dependent clause use, Iwashita et al. (2008) showed effect sizes ranging from 0 and 0.13 between groups. Iwashita (2006) showed an effect size of 0.66 between the high and low proficiency groups. In contrast, Hirano (1991) displayed effect sizes from 0.64 to 1.15 in written data.

To summarize the previous research on subordination measures, we can expect subordination to drop at higher levels of proficiency. Whether subordination correlates well with holistic levels or distinguishes between adjacent levels is unclear. Lower effect sizes are evident in the spoken data than in the written.

Complexity by Coordination
Previous research on the use of coordinate clauses by learners has been conducted using a variety of different measures of coordination. Bardovi-Harlig (1992) proposed the coordination index (CI), which is calculated by dividing the total number

of independent clause coordinations by the total number of combined clauses. The coordination index should reveal what percentage of clauses are coordinate clauses and not subordinate clauses.

Previous studies using the coordination index have found mixed results. Bardovi-Harlig (1992) found a regular decrease in CI with an increase in program level. Casanave (1994), however, did not find a linear progression in the coordination index. Sharma (1980) and Homburg (1984) both found that CI increased at the intermediate level and dropped at the advanced level.

I have chosen not to use the coordination index in this study. Although this measure is clearly very useful for expressing the ratio of combined clauses that are coordinate rather than subordinate, it does not capture how much subordination or coordination learners at different levels are using relative to how much language they are producing. For this reason, I use subordinate clauses per clause and coordinate clauses per clause to measure coordination and subordination, respectively.

Iwashita (2006) found that high proficiency learners of Japanese produced significantly more independent clauses per clause than low proficiency learners. The effect size (calculated by me for this study) was –0.66 between the high and low proficiency groups.

The discussion above has generally shown an increase in coordination followed by a decrease during later interlanguage development. It is important to note, however, that the majority of these studies have been conducted using written data from learners of English. The generalizability of these results to L2 German written and spoken data is investigated below.

Complexity by Increased Clause Length
The use of some measure of clausal length is suggested by Norris and Ortega (2009) as a way to measure phrasal complexity, or an increase in the length of phrases rather than the addition of clauses to an utterance.

Many previous studies have made use of some kind of measure of clause length, although these studies did not do so to explicitly measure phrasal complexity compared with other types of complexity. The results of these studies have been mixed. A number of studies have found that mean clause length gradually increases and that it distinguishes between learners at different levels but not between two adjacent levels (Cooper 1976; Hirano 1991; Monroe 1975; Yau 1991).

I calculated the effect sizes from data when they were available in previous studies. Iwashita (2006) showed an effect size of 0.01 between high and low proficiency groups for mean length of clause. Hirano (1991) showed effect sizes ranging from 0 to 1 among low, middle, and high-proficiency groups.

The previous research into mean clause length can give some indication of what to expect in the current study. In the previous studies, mean clause length varied from 5.2 words per clause at the lowest levels of proficiency to 10.8 words per clause at the most advanced levels. Since the subjects of this study are lower-level learners of German, we can expect their mean clause length to be at the lower end of this range. Based on previous results that have shown that mean clause length did not distinguish between learners at adjacent levels, we expect that it will not distinguish between learners at adjacent levels, but that it will distinguish between learners at non-adjacent levels. Kameen (1979) found that mean clause length did distinguish between levels, but these levels were holistically scored and not related to program level. A few additional studies found no relationship between clause length and test scores (Hirano 1991; Sharma 1980). Even when the differences between levels were not significant, previous research has generally shown that words per clause increases linearly with proficiency level (Wolfe-Quintero, Inagaki, and Kim 1998). In terms of effect sizes, previous research has shown more substantial differences in writing than in speaking.

Spoken and Written Modalities
Learning to write in a second language has often been considered secondary to learning to speak, and there has been relatively little research done on the role that L2 proficiency plays either in L2 writing (Williams 2008) or in the study of speech and writing simultaneously (Weissberg 2000). Harklau (2002) argues that we need to pay more attention to modality both in research on second language acquisition and in how this research affects theory-building: "Research needs to address the relative contributions of each modality to classroom second language development and how modality affects what is acquired" (338).

The few studies that have been done on both L2 speaking and writing have produced intriguing results. Weissberg (2000) looked at the appearance of novel morphosyntactic forms in speech and writing samples from ESL learners. He found that 57 percent of these forms appeared in writing before speech. This led him to suggest that writing may function as a kind of staging area for speech that allows learners to try out new forms. However, since a substantial percentage of the forms did not appear first in writing, this assertion should be considered provisional and evaluated through further research.

In a study of twenty-eight Arabic-speaking adult learners of English, Vann (1979) found a number of substantial differences between spoken and written production gathered from the same learners. Written discourse was shorter in terms of the overall number of words, had a longer average T-unit length, and had fewer errors. T-unit length and the percentage of dependent clauses did not correlate highly on speaking and writing samples.

Research Questions
In light of the research on complexity in second language production so far, this study proposes the following research questions in order to explore the development of different types of complexity and to examine the relationship between speech and writing.

1. How do three measures of complexity (subordination, coordination, and clause length) differ among four levels of German learners?
2. Do these measures follow the same or similar patterns in speech and writing?

Methodology

The data in this study come from a larger-scale study of lower-proficiency learners in their first two years of university-level language instruction. The purpose of the larger study was to investigate multiple measures of language development in speech and writing over a year of instruction.

Participants

The participants were all students at an American university in their first four semesters of German language study. Many of the students take these classes to fulfill a language requirement. Although some of the students receive all of their instruction at the university, beginning with the first semester and continuing through to the fourth, many of them also place into one of the later semesters through a placement test. Students in their first two semesters of study at this university generally range from Novice-Mid to Intermediate-Mid on the ACTFL speaking scale. Data were gathered from a total of seventy students: eighteen in their first semester of German (level 1), seventeen in the second semester (level 2), sixteen in the third semester (level 3), and nineteen in the fourth semester (level 4).

Instrument

The students completed two writing tasks and two speaking tasks over the course of the semester. The focus of the present study is on only the first writing and first speaking task in order to minimize possible task-type effects. The students at different levels did not perform exactly the same task later in the semester since they were given tasks that corresponded to some degree to the topics being covered in their courses at the time the tasks were completed.

The tasks the students were asked to complete were part of their regular curriculum. The task given to the students at all levels and in both modalities was to describe someone they know. The written task and the speaking task were completed during the second or third week of the semester, with no more than a week separating the two tasks. The only exception to this was the first semester course, where the tasks were delayed until approximately the sixth week of instruction; otherwise, the students would not have been able to produce enough language for analysis. Both the written and spoken tasks were completed in a computer lab, where participants were shown the prompt on a computer screen. They typed their response for the writing task and recorded their responses through a microphone for the speaking task. No dictionaries or other supporting materials were allowed during the completion of either task. The recorded responses from the speaking task were then transcribed according to the principles of transcription outlined in Allwright and Bailey (1991).

Measurement

The data were examined for three different types of complexity. Complexity by subordination was measured as the ratio of subordinate clauses to total clauses. Complexity by coordination was measured as the ratio of coordinate clauses to total clauses. Phrasal complexity was measured as mean length of clause, obtained by dividing the number of words by the number of clauses.

The first research question asks how rates of subordination, coordination, and average mean length of clause differ among students at four levels of German. In this study I operationalize difference not only as a significant difference according to an analysis of variance, but also in terms of the effect size.

As Durlak (2009) points out, effect sizes should be reported for all results, whether they are statistically significant or not. Snyder and Lawson (1993) showed that in the case of a study with a small sample size, adding one subject might push the *p*-value into the range where it would be considered significant (below 0.05). However, such a change did not similarly change the effect size. Similarly, Thompson (2007) offers the example of eleven hypothetical studies with varying numbers of subjects in which ten of the studies show positive results for a treatment. According to his calculations, only one of the studies—the single study with negative results— would achieve statistical significance and therefore have a good chance of publication. In this case, the reliance on statistical significance to the exclusion of other metrics, such as effect size, would lead the research in the wrong direction.

In interpreting effect sizes, many researchers rely on Cohen's (1988) guidelines characterizing effect sizes of 0.2 or lower as small, 0.5 as medium, and 0.8 as large. However, these points of reference should not be relied upon for the interpretation of the importance of any particular effect sizes; rather, effect sizes should be interpreted in context by comparing them with results in similar previous research (Thompson 2007; Cohen 1988).

Comparing the effect sizes in this study with those in previous research is difficult, since most of the previous studies discussed above do not report effect sizes. To have some indication of how to interpret the effect size results in this study, I have calculated the effect sizes where possible, using the data available in previous studies. These calculations are found in the review of previous research above.

Results
Complexity in Writing
The results for the three complexity measures in writing are summarized in table 15.1. Each of the individual complexity measures are discussed separately below.

Analysis of variance showed a significant effect of course level on the rate of subordination in writing: $F(3, 66) = 7.8$, $p = 0.00002$. Post-hoc analyses using Tukey's HSD indicated that level 1 students used subordination at a significantly lower rate than both level 3 ($p < 0.01$) and level 4 ($p < 0.05$) students. Post-hoc analyses also showed that level 2 students used subordination at a significantly lower rate than both level 3 ($p < 0.01$) and level 4 ($p < 0.05$) students.

The ANOVA showed that course level did not have a significant effect on the rate of coordination in writing: $F(3, 66) = 1.51$, $p = 0.22$.

The ANOVA showed a significant effect of course level on the mean length of clause (MLC) in writing: $F(3, 66) = 5.48$, $p = 0.002$. Post-hoc analyses using Tukey's HSD indicated that level 1 students had a lower MLC than level 2 ($p < 0.05$) and level 4 ($p < 0.01$) students.

Table 15.2 shows the results of effect size calculations and ANOVAs and compares the different levels in the study with each other. The effect sizes that are reported

Table 15.1
Grammatical complexity in writing

Level	N	Subordination Rate M	Subordination Rate SD	Coordination Rate M	Coordination Rate SD	MLC M	MLC SD
1	18	0.01	0.02	0.06	0.07	5.7	0.89
2	17	0.02	0.03	0.07	0.07	6.6	1.12
3	16	0.09	0.07	0.20	0.10	6.4	0.69
4	19	0.07	0.11	0.13	0.12	6.9	0.76

are Hedge's g. The statistical significance was first calculated through a one-way repeated measures ANOVA. The independent variable was the level of the subjects, and the dependent variables were the rate of coordination, the rate of subordination, and the average mean length of clauses. If statistical significance was found for a measure, Tukey HSD post-tests were conducted to locate the source of the significance. Those measures that were statistically significant are marked with asterisks.

Subordination in writing. The rate of subordination in writing is very low for both of the first-year groups (levels 1 and 2). However, a dramatic increase in subordination is seen in the second year groups (levels 3 and 4), from two to nine subordinate clauses per one hundred clauses. The highest rate of subordination is found in the third semester group; the rate of subordination drops slightly for the fourth semester group.

The effect sizes for subordination in writing show large differences between level 1 and both levels 3 and 4, and between level 2 and level 3. There were medium effect sizes for levels 1 and 2 compared to level 4. These effect sizes reflect the fact that the subordination rate rises sharply from level 2 to level 3 and then drops slightly for the level 4 group. The terms small and large are relative when discussing effect sizes. When compared with effect sizes from previous research on subordination in writing, these results are largely similar to those found using data from Hirano (1991) for English.

Table 15.2
Effect sizes and statistical significance for complexity measures in writing

Pairs	Effect Size (Hedge's g) Subordination	Coordination	MLC
Level 1_Level 2	0.39	0.14	0.93*
Level 1_Level 3	1.56**	1.60	0.94
Level 1_ Level 4	0.89*	0.69	1.42**
Level 2_ Level 3	1.28**	1.47	0.20
Level 2_ Level 4	0.59*	0.59	0.25
Level 3_ Level 4	0.21	0.61	0.58

* significant ($p<.05$)
** significant ($p<.01$)

Coordination in writing. The coordination rates for the first-year groups are very similar. A dramatic increase in coordination is evident for the second-year groups, from seven to twenty coordinated clauses per one hundred clauses. This is similar to the pattern for subordination. However, there is a much larger drop in coordination between the third and fourth semesters than there was for subordination rate.

The effect sizes for coordination in writing were very large for level 1 and level 2 as opposed to level 3. The effect sizes for levels 1, 2, and 3 as compared with level 4 were medium. The effect size comparing the two first-year groups was negligible.

Mean length of clause in writing. The pattern for clause length differs considerably from that of subordination and coordination. The largest difference in mean length of clause occurs not between the first and second years of instruction, but between the first and second semester: from 5.6 to 6.6 words per clause. Clause length drops slightly at the third semester of instruction and then rises at the fourth semester. By the end of four semesters, a change of slightly over a word per clause can be observed.

The effect size for the first semester group as compared with the fourth semester was very large (1.42). The effect sizes for the first semester group as compared with the second and third semester were large (0.93 and 0.94). The effect size for the third as compared with the fourth semester was medium (0.58). All other effect size pairings were small. The effect size for levels 1 and 4 was higher than that calculated for the high and low groups in Hirano (1991). The lowest effect sizes in this study for MLC were still higher than that in Hirano (1991), which showed an effect size of zero for the low and middle groups.

Summary of writing results. The results show that complexity by subordination and coordination undergoes significant development from the first year of instruction to the second year. Rates of both subordination and coordination roughly tripled from the second to the third semester.

The results from mean length of clause tell a slightly different story. In this case, the initial jump in clause length occurred during the first year of instruction, between the first and second semesters of study. The gains in clause length then hesitantly dipped at the third semester before a healthy rise at the fourth semester.

Complexity in Speaking

Descriptive statistics for the three complexity measures in the students' speaking task are summarized in table 15.3. Each of the individual complexity measures are discussed separately below.

Analysis of variance showed a significant effect of course level on the rate of subordination in speaking: $F(3, 66) = 3.28$, $p = 0.03$. Post-hoc analyses using Tukey's HSD did not find any significant differences between groups, which can be attributed to the relatively conservative nature of the Tukey test.

Analysis of variance showed a significant effect of course level on the rate of coordination in speaking: $F(3, 66) = 3.68$, $p = 0.02$. Post-hoc analyses using Tukey's

Table 15.3
Grammatical complexity in speaking

Level	N	Subordination Rate		Coordination Rate		MLC	
		M	SD	M	SD	M	SD
1	18	0	0	0.06	0.07	5.2	0.69
2	17	0	0.01	0.14	0.11	5.5	0.65
3	16	0.03	0.05	0.16	0.11	5.8	0.92
4	19	0.03	0.06	0.15	0.10	5.5	0.66

HSD indicated that students at level 1 had a significantly lower rate of coordination than level 3 students ($p < 0.05$).

Analysis of variance showed that course level did not have a significant effect on the mean length of clause in speaking: $F(3, 66) = 1.61$, $p = 0.19$.

Table 15.4 shows the effect sizes for the three complexity measures in the spoken data. All of the effect sizes reported here are Hedge's g.

Subordination in speaking. The first-year students produced no subordinate clauses; the second-year groups barely produced any subordinate clauses. All of the effect sizes for the first-year groups compared to the second-year groups are either large or medium, as seen in table 15.4. In the context of previous research, these effect sizes are much larger than those found in Iwashita et al. (2008), where the largest difference in effect sizes among five proficiency groups was 0.13 (according to my calculations). Iwashita (2006) shows an effect size of 0.66 between high and low proficiency groups, which corresponds to the difference between levels 2 and 4 in this study.

Coordination in speaking. The results for coordination rate show that the use of coordinate clauses increases dramatically after the first semester of instruction. The coordination rate for the second semester is more than double that of the first. After the second semester, the coordination rate stays fairly stable through the second year of instruction.

The effect sizes for coordination rate likewise highlight the differences between the first semester and the other three semesters. The effect sizes comparing level 1 with levels 2, 3, and 4 were either large or very large. All other effect sizes were negligible. From previous research, I have calculated an effect size of 0.66 between the high and low proficiency groups. Three of the effect sizes in this study were higher, and three were lower.

Mean length of clause in speaking. Mean clause length rises from the first semester through the third, and then drops slightly in the fourth semester of instruction. There were no large effect sizes for any of the pairs. The effect size for level 1 compared to level 3 was medium; all others were small or negligible. Compared to previous research, these effect sizes are larger than what was calculated for Iwashita (2006),

Table 15.4
Effect sizes and statistical significance for complexity measures in speaking

Pairs	Effect Size (Hedge's g)		
	Subordination**	Coordination	MLC
Level 1_Level 2	—	0.85	0.36
Level 1_Level 3	0.86	1.07*	0.67
Level 1_ Level 4	0.68	1.01	0.30
Level 2_ Level 3	0.82	0.17	0.37
Level 2_ Level 4	0.66	0.09	0.06
Level 3_ Level 4	—	0.09	0.42

* significant (p<.05)
** The ANOVA showed statistical significance ($p=.026$). However, due to the conservative nature of the Tukey HSD post-test, none of the pairs were found to be significantly different from each other.

0.01, but generally smaller than the differences in Hirano's (1991) data, which ranged from 0 to 1.

Summary of speaking results. The use of subordinate clauses distinguishes clearly between the first and second years of instruction. The use of coordinate clauses, however, instead distinguishes between the first semester and the later semesters. Mean length of clause did not distinguish well between the different program levels.

Speaking and Writing Compared

The subordination rate for the spoken and written data is summarized in figure 15.1. Subordination distinguishes well between the first and second year groups in both the spoken and written modalities. However, there was substantially more subordination in writing than in speaking. Learners in the first two semesters used no subordination in speaking at all, and the second-year groups' rate of subordination in speaking was only slightly higher than the first-year groups' rate of subordination in writing.

The percentage of coordinate clauses used in the speaking and writing samples is summarized in figure 15.2. Coordination rose dramatically between the first and second years in writing, with a peak occurring at level 3. In the spoken data, however, the rise in coordination rate is evident instead at level 2, between the first and second semesters. The coordination rate then levels off, with little difference between levels 2 through 4.

The results for mean clause length for the spoken and written production are summarized in figure 15.3. At first glance, the graphic shows that mean length clause was more similar in speaking and writing than coordination or subordination. However, when the effect sizes are taken into account, it is clear that MLC distinguished more clearly between the different levels in writing than in speaking.

Discussion and Conclusion

The results show that the complexity measure that differentiated most clearly among the different instructional levels was the rate of subordination, with medium to large

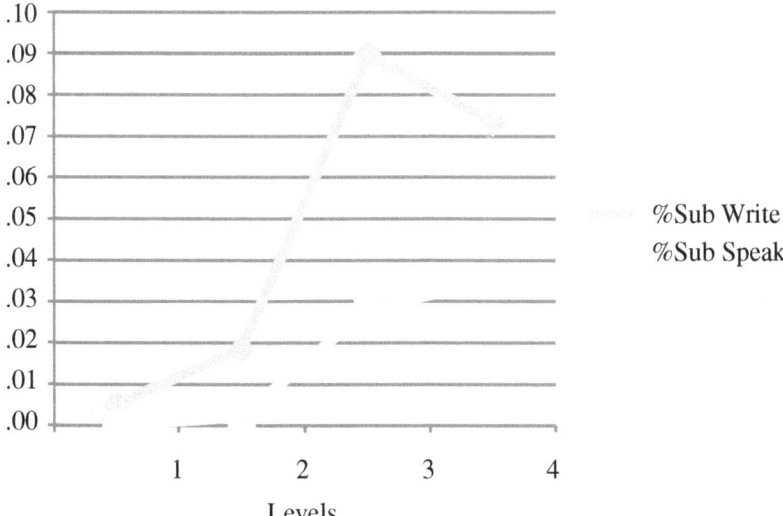

Figure 15.1 Subordination Rate for Speaking vs. Writing

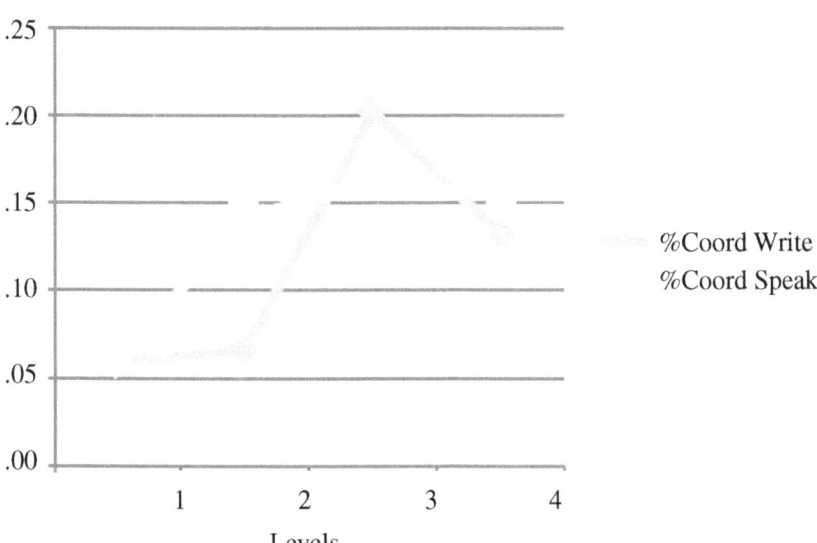

Figure 15.2 Coordination Rate for Speaking vs. Writing

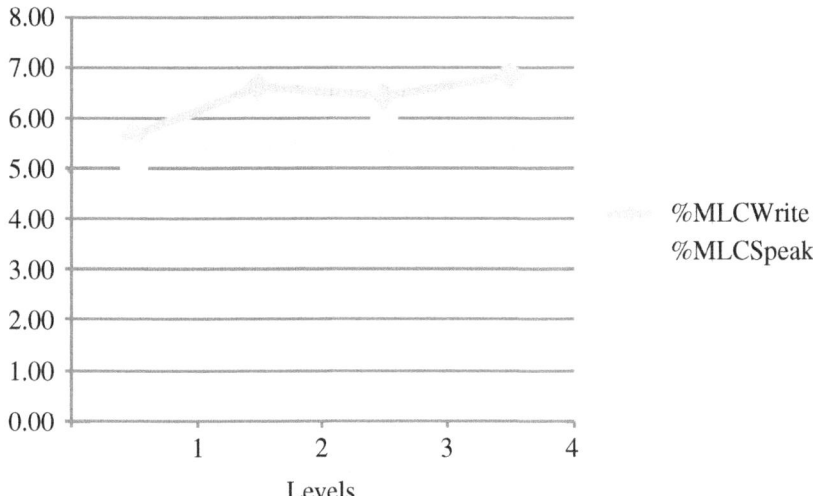

Figure 15.3 Mean Length Clause for Speaking vs. Writing

effect sizes and statistical significance. This measure was not perfect, as it did not differentiate the first-year groups from each other or the second-year groups from each other. It did, however, distinguish between the two years of instruction, and therefore between the adjacent second and third semesters of instruction. The results for subordination were generally similar in speech and writing, although the written data showed larger effect sizes and statistically significant differences between groups. These results provide additional support to Weissberg's (2000, 2006) findings that syntactic innovations appear first in writing.

The strong results for subordination are somewhat surprising; based on previous research, we might have expected complexity by coordination to distinguish better among low-proficiency learners. Coordination did not distinguish between groups as well as subordination, although it produces some of the largest effect sizes in the data. The large differences between some of the groups suggest that some kind of change in complexity by coordination takes place after the second semester in the written data, but after the first semester in the spoken data. This result seems to constitute counter-evidence to Weissberg's (2000, 2006) suggestion that syntactic innovations first appear in writing. But Weissberg (2000) also noted that some types of morphosyntactic structures may have an affinity in particular with the spoken or written modality. If this is the case, it could be one possible explanation of the earlier development of coordination in speech.

Mean length of clause, like coordination, seems to undergo a substantial change between the first and second semesters of instruction in the written data. In the spoken data, MLC instead rises gradually and the differences between the different levels are not as considerable.

Almost all of the measures showed signs of a flattening or drop at level 4 compared to level 3. This could be evidence the omega-shaped behavior (Wolfe-Quintero et al. 1998) that is indicative of learners leaving one complexity behavior for another. This might suggest an interesting area for future research, although the current data are too similar in proficiency level to get a clear idea of whether the rates will stay flat, drop, or perhaps rise. The only exception to the flattening of complexity behavior at level 4 was mean length of clause in the written modality, which continued to rise from level 3 to level 4. This may indicate that this type of complexity, which Norris and Ortega (2009) suggested for the study of more advanced learners, may continue to rise among higher proficiency levels.

The results of the different measures of complexity in this study are mixed, but this is to be expected if complexity truly is a multidimensional construct. Moreover, we should not expect complexity to develop among learners in a simple linear fashion. Norris and Ortega (2009) remarked that one of the reasons that the measurement of complexity poses such problems is that complexity, accuracy, and fluency constitute a dynamic system. Furthermore, Wolfe-Quintero et al. (1998) point out that the proposed different stages of complexity would overlap in any one individual's writing sample. These suggestions also offer interesting possibilities for the investigation of the development of complexity in individual learners.

Using the effect sizes to compare the results in this study with the data from previous research showed both similarities and differences among the different complexity measures. In this way, the results of this study highlight the importance of cross-linguistic research when measuring a phenomenon such as complexity. Although effect sizes offer a useful metric for assessing the impact of a difference (and not just the reliability of the result), the generalizability is limited by the fact that the previous studies that I have used for comparison were not conducted on the same language as this one (German). It is, therefore, impossible to determine at this point whether the differences between this study and others are due to differences inherent in the language being learned, the conditions under which the study was done, or some other factor. This highlights the importance of using and reporting a standard set of measures, so that future research in the area can dialogue with current studies.

REFERENCES

Allwright, Richard, and Kathleen M. Bailey. 1991. *Focus on the Language Classroom: An Introduction to Classroom Research for Language Teachers*. Cambridge University Press.

Bardovi-Harlig, Kathleen. 1992. "A second look at T-unit analysis: Reconsidering the sentence." *TESOL Quarterly* 26 (2): 390–95.

Bardovi-Harlig, Kathleen, and Theodora Bofman. 1989. "Attainment of syntactic and morphological accuracy by advanced language learners." *Studies in Second Language Acquisition* 11 (1): 17–34.

Casanave, Christine Pearson. 1994. "Language development in students' journals." *Journal of Second Language Writing* 3 (3): 179–201.

Cohen, Jacob. 1988. *Statistical Power Analysis for the Behavioral Sciences*. Mahwah, NJ: Lawrence Erlbaum Associates.

Cooper, T. C. 1976. "Measuring written syntactic patterns of second language learners of German." *The Journal of Educational Research*: 176–83.

Durlak, Joseph A. 2009. "How to select, calculate, and interpret effect sizes." *Journal of Pediatric Psychology* 34 (9): 917–28.

Foster, Pauline, and Peter Skehan. 1999. "The influence of source of planning and focus of planning on task-based performance." *Language Teaching Research* 3 (3): 215–47.

Harklau, Linda. 2002. "The role of writing in classroom second language acquisition." *Journal of Second Language Writing* 11 (4): 329–50.

Hirano, Kinue. 1991. "The effect of audience on the efficacy of objective measures of EFL proficiency in Japanese university students." *Annual Review of English Language Education in Japan* 2 (1): 21–30.

Homburg, Taco Justus. 1984. "Holistic evaluation of ESL compositions: Can it be validated objectively?" *TESOL Quarterly* 18 (1): 87–107.

Ishikawa, Sandra. 1995. "Objective measurement of low-proficiency EFL narrative writing." *Journal of Second Language Writing* 4 (1): 51–69.

Iwashita, Noriko. 2006. "Syntactic complexity measures and their relation to oral proficiency in Japanese as a foreign language." *Language Assessment Quarterly: An International Journal* 3 (2): 151–69.

Iwashita, Noriko, Annie Brown, Tim McNamara, and Sally O'Hagan. 2008. "Assessed levels of second language speaking proficiency: How distinct?" *Applied Linguistics* 29 (1): 24–49.

Kameen, Patrick. 1979. "Syntactic skill and ESL writing quality." *On TESOL* 79: 343–64.

Monroe, James H. 1975. "Measuring and enhancing syntactic fluency in French." *The French Review* 48 (6): 1023–31.

Norris, John M., and Lourdes Ortega. 2009. "Towards an organic approach to investigating CAF in instructed SLA: The case of complexity." *Applied Linguistics* 30 (4): 555–78.

Perkins, Kyle. 1980. "Using objective methods of attained writing proficiency to discriminate among holistic evaluations." *TESOL Quarterly*: 61–69.

Sharma, Alex. 1980. "Syntactic maturity: Assessing writing proficiency in a second language." In *Occasional Papers in Linguistics*, edited by R. Silverstein. Carbondale, IL: Southern Illinois University.

Snyder, Patricia, and Stephen Lawson. 1993. "Evaluating results using corrected and uncorrected effect size estimates." *The Journal of Experimental Educational*: 334–49.

Thompson, Bruce. 2007. "Effect sizes, confidence intervals, and confidence intervals for effect sizes." *Psychology in the Schools* 44 (5): 423–32.

Vann, Roberta J. 1979. "Oral and written syntactic relationships in second language learning." *On TESOL* 79: 322–29.

Weissberg, Bob. 2000. "Developmental relationships in the acquisition of English syntax: Writing vs. speech." *Learning and Instruction* 10 (1): 37–53.

Weissberg, Robert. 2006. *Connecting Speaking & Writing in Second Language Writing Instruction*. Ann Arbor: University of Michigan Press.

Williams, Jessica. 2008. "The speaking-writing connection in second language and academic literacy development." *The Oral/Literate Connection: Perspectives on L2 Speaking, Writing, and Other Media Interactions*: 10–25.

Wolfe-Quintero, Kate, Shunji Inagaki, and Hae-Young Kim. 1998. *Second Language Development in Writing: Measures of Fluency, Accuracy, and Complexity*. Honolulu: University of Hawaii Press, 17

Yau, Margaret. 1991. "The role of language factors in second language writing." *Language, Culture and Cognition: A Collection of Studies in First and Second Language Acquisition*: 266–83.

Index

Numbers in italics indicate a table or figure.

absolute U-shape, 157–58, 162, 166, 167n1
abstract/impersonal style, 5
academic stance, 17
accuracy, evaluating, 172–73, 181, 214, 215, 226
acquisition of language. *See* automatization and speedup in foreign language acquisition; learning conditions and language analytic ability; robust language acquisition and English verb-argument constructions; second language acquisition (SLA) theory; U-shaped development
ACTFL speaking scale, 218
adaptive control of thought theory, 112
Airasian, Peter, 97, 99
Akamatsu, Nobuhiko, 114, 117
Aksu-Koç, Ayhan, 81
Albro, Elizabeth R., 87
Aline, David, 142
Allwright, Richard, 218
Ambon-Timor subgroup, *64,* 65, 66, 75
Amoroso, Luke Wander, xiii
Andean Spanish, cross-linguistic influence from Quechua to. *See* Quechua to Spanish cross-linguistic influence
Anderson, John R., 112
ANOVA, 121, 123, 134–35, 146–48, 162, 165, 179–80, 219–20, 223
Archibald, Alasdair, 185
argumentation, overt expression of, 5
Arkoudis, Sophie, 185
Artificial Grammar Learning (AGL) tasks, 128
assessment of language ability, xvi–xvii. *See also* change in foreign language skills over time; Drexel University International Gateway Program; simulated speech (SS) to assess Japanese learner oral proficiency; subjective assessments
Atlas van Tropisch Nederland (1938), 65
Austronesian Basic Vocabulary Database (ABVD), 69–70, 76n4
Austronesian language family, 63, *64,* 74
automatic speech recognition (ASR) technology. *See* simulated speech (SS) to assess Japanese learner oral proficiency
automatization and speedup in foreign language acquisition, xv, 111–23
    all proficiency levels, evidence of speedup and automatization at, 120, 121, 122
    coding and operationalizations, 120
    DELE *(Diploma de Español como Lengua Extranjera),* 118, 120
    difference between automaticity and speedup, evidence for, 113–15
    extent of speedup/automatization by proficiency level, 121–23
    Familiarization Quiz, 119, 120
    first language, controlling for, 117
    Fisher's z scores, 111, 121, 122–23
    independent assessment of L2 proficiency, 111, 116
    LCP, use of, 119
    lexical items, controlling for participant knowledge of, 117
    limitations of earlier studies of, 116–17
    measuring automaticity and speedup, 112
    methodology of study, 118–19
    participants in study, *118*
    relationship to proficiency levels, evidence for, 111, 115–16
    research questions, 117
    semantic decision tasks used in study, 119, 120
    theoretical foundations of, 111–12

Bahrick, H. P., 201
Bailey, Kathleen M., 218
Bamberg, Michael, 80
Bardovi-Harlig, Kathleen, 215–16
basic categories and language acquisition, 34
Bayesian modeling, xiv, 63, 69, 71, 72, 73, 75–76
Bayliss, Amanda, 185
Besnier, Niko, *15*
Biber, Douglas, xiv, 1, *12–13,* 13–14, *14, 16,* 17
bilingual/multilingual children, narrative development in, 79, 81–82, 90–91
Bima-Sumba-Flores (BSF) subgroup hypothesis, 63, 65, 66, 75–76
Bima-Sumba (Bi-Su) subgroup, 63, *64,* 65–66, 75
Binch, Chris, 185
Bloch, Maurice, 2
Bloomfield, Amber, xvi–xvii, 199
Blust, Robert, 63, 65, 66, 75
Bonk, W. J., 56
Bowern, Claire, 69
Braciszewski, Patrick L., xvi, 183
Brazilian Portuguese, MD studies of, 13
British National Corpus (BNC), 41, *42, 44*
burnouts, gender, and negative concord, 21–23, *22, 23*
Butler, Yuko Goto, xiv, 79

C-units, 84
Calderòn, Anne M., xv, 111
Calque-Weighted Total Cross-Linguistic Feature (CLF) Score, 95, 96, 99–100, 104
Campbell, R., 201

229

Casanave, Christine Pearson, 216
Casenhiser, D., 46
Celaya, M. Luz, 105
Central Malayo-Polynesian (CMP) language subgroups. *See* subgrouping in CMP languages
change in foreign language skills over time, xvi–xvii, 199–211
   data mining of test records to determine, 199, 202–3, 210
   dependent and independent variables, 203
   duration of period of reduced input and, 200–201, 210
   formal coursework, as independent variable, 203–5, 207–8, 210
   ILR ratings, 202–3, 204, 205, 207–10, *208–10*
   initial proficiency level and, 202, 203, 207, 208, 209–11
   latent growth analysis, xvii, 199, 203, *204–6*, 205–6, 207–8, 210
   listening, 203–5, 206, 207–8, *208*
   literature review, 200–202
   methodology of study, 202–3
   overall patterns in, 203–7, *204–6*
   reading, 203–5, 206, 208, *209*
   speaking, 205–6, *209*, 209–10, *210*
   test version change, as independent variable, 203, 204, 205, 207, 208
   use of foreign language use during period of reduced input and, 201, 210
change of state or location verbs, 34, 156, 161, 164, 168n3
Chicano English, 25–28, 30–31
The Chicken Thief (Rodriguez), 83
Chinese
   narrative development in. *See* narrative development in first (Chinese) and foreign (English) languages
   word, what constitutes, 105
Chinese yuppies, 24
Chomsky, Noam, 167
CI (coordination index), 215–16
clarification requests (CR) versus recasts (RE), oral corrective feedback in form of, 141, 144, *147–49*, 147–51
Clark, J. L. D., 201
class. *See* socioeconomic status
CLI (cross-linguistic influence) and CLF (cross-linguistic features). *See* Quechua to Spanish cross-linguistic influence
cloze tests, 158
Clyne, Michael, 104–5
co-occurrence relations, xiv, 6, 14, 17
Coastal California Shift, *25*, 27
COBUILD project, 40, 41
cognates, 69–70
cognitive linguistics, 34–35
Cohen, Jacob, 219

complex adaptive systems (CAS), 34, 40
complexity in German learner corpus, xvii, 213–26
   comparison of speaking and writing data, 223, *224, 225*
   coordination, complexity by, 213, 215–16, 218, 221, 222, 223, *224*, 225
   different measures of complexity, 214–15
   effect size, 219, *220*, 221, 222, 223, *223*, 226
   importance of studying complexity, 214
   methodology of study, 218–19
   as multidimensional construct, 213, 214, 226
   omega-shaped development in, 215, 226
   participants, 218
   phrasal complexity (mean length of clause or MLC), 213, 216–17, 218, 221, 222–23, *225*, 225–26
   research questions, 217
   in spoken language, 217, 221–23, *222, 223–25*
   subordination, complexity by, 213, 215, 218, 220, 222, 223–25, *224*
   in writing, 217, 219–21, *220*, 223, *224, 225*
confidence judgments, 128–29, 132
Connor-Linton, Jeff, xiii
consistency or reliability of measurement, 51–52
construction frequency, 37
construction grammar, 36–37, 39
construction learning determinants, 37–39
content-focused discourse, 17
contingency of form-function mapping, 39
conversational implicature, 165
conversational text types, MD analysis of, 17
coolness, ethnicity, and peer-based social order, 24–31, *25, 29–30*
coordination, complexity by, 213, 215–16, 218, 221, 222, 223, *224*, 225
coordination index (CI), 215–16
corpus linguistics and corpus-driven research, 1–2, 35
Corpus of Spoken Japanese (CSJ), 175
correlation evidence, 52
Cox, Jessica G., xv, 111
Cox regression, 57, 58
CR (clarification requests) versus RE (recasts), oral corrective feedback in form of, 141, 144, *147–49*, 147–51
Craven, Elizabeth, 185
criterion validity, 52
Cronbach's Alpha, 96, 97, 99, 100, 103
cross-linguistic influence (CLI). *See* Quechua to Spanish cross-linguistic influence
culture and narrative development, 81

Index

Currie, Thomas, 69
Czech, MD studies of, 13, *15*

Dagbani, MD studies of, 13, *15*
Davies, Alan, 185
De Bot, K. D., 200
declarative/procedural model of language, 136
Deguchi, Ayako, 161
DeKeyser, Robert, 125, 142, 143
demographic categories and speech patterns, xiv–xv, 21–31
   Chinese yuppies, 24
   ethnicity and ethnolects, 24–31, *25, 29–30*
   gender and class, 21–23, *22, 23*
   Linda, case study of, 28–30, *30*
   Martha's Vineyard, use of dialect features on, 23–24
   negative concord, high schoolers' use of, 21–23, *22, 23*
Dienes, Zoltan, 128–29
Dollo model, stochastic, 71, 72, 73, *74,* 75
Domino, George, 81
double-object ditransitive (VOO) construction, 36, 38, 39
Drexel University International Gateway Program, xvi, 183–95
   comparison of Gateway matriculated and direct admission students, 190–91, *191*
   credit-bearing CoAS (College of Arts and Sciences) courses, 184, 185, *186,* 188–90, *190,* 191–92, 195n2, 196n8
   GPA scores, effect on, 183, 184, 188–92, *190, 191*
   IELTS (International English Language Testing System) exam, 183, 184, 186–88, *188, 189*
   IEP (intensive English program) courses, 184, 185–86, *186,* 188, 191, 196n7
   literature review of IELTS research, 184–85, 194–95
   matriculated university performance of former Gateway students, 190
   methodology of study, 185–91
   participants, 185, *187,* 195–96nn4–5
   program design and content, 183, 184, 185, 195n1
   program validation, 191–92
   relationship between coursework and IELTS score progression, *188,* 191–92, 196nn7–8
   research questions, 184
   score progression on IELTS, 184–85, 187–88, *189,* 191–92, *193,* 193–94
Drummond, Alexei, 63, 65, 66, 72
dual-mechanism views of language learning, 136
Dunn, Michael, 72

Durlak, Joseph A., 219

Eckert, Penelope, xiv–xv, 21
Eckes, T., 56
Edgeworth, Francis, 52
effect size in complexity measurement, 219, *220,* 221, 222, 223, *223,* 226
elaborated versus situation-dependent reference, 5
Elder, Catherine, 185
elementary school
   ethnicity, coolness, and peer-based social order at, 24–31, *25, 29–30*
   MD analysis of register variation in oral and written English, 16
   narrative development in. *See* narrative development in first and foreign languages
elicited repetition (ER) testing, 172–73, 175, 181
Ellis, Nick C., xv, 33, 45
Ellis, Rod, 142
emergentist approach to language, 126
Engelhard, G., Jr., 56
English. *See also* demographic categories and speech patterns; Drexel University International Gateway Program; multidimensional (MD) analysis of register variation in oral and written English; narrative development in first (Chinese) and foreign (English) languages; robust language acquisition and English verb-argument constructions; U-shaped development
   automatization and speedup in foreign language acquisition of, 113, 114–16
   change in foreign language skills over time, 201
   complexity measures, 216, 217
   learning conditions and language analytic ability, 143
ER (elicited repetition) testing, 172–73, 175, 181
Erlam, Rosemary, 143
Escobar, Alberto, 104
Esser, S. J., 63, 65, 66, 75
ethnicity and ethnolects, 24–31, *25, 29–30*
Ethnologue, 63, 65, 66, 67, *69,* 75
explicit and implicit knowledge, relationship of frequency effects to, 125, 126, 128–29, *135,* 136, 137

factor analysis, xiv, 3–4, 17
"fair average" metric, 56
falsifiability requirement, 155, 166
fast processing, 112
Feke, Marilyn S., 99
Finnish-Swedish bilingual children, narrative development in, 81–82, 90–91
Fisher's z scores, 111, 121, 122–23
FL (Flores-Lembata) languages, 63, 66, 74–75

Fleming, Sarah, 185
Flores-Lembata (FL) languages, 63, 66, 74–75
fluency, evaluating, 172–73, 175–76, *176*, 178, 180–81, 214, 226
foreign language acquisition. *See* automatization and speedup in foreign language acquisition; learning conditions and language analytic ability; robust language acquisition and English verb-argument constructions; second language acquisition (SLA) theory; U-shaped development
foreign language assessment, xvi–xvii. *See also* change in foreign language skills over time; Drexel University International Gateway Program; simulated speech (SS) to assess Japanese learner oral proficiency; subjective assessments
Foster, Pauline, 214
Fought, Carmen, 27
four-alternative forced-choice (4AFC) picture matching task, 132, 133, 134
Francis, G., 40, 45
Freed, Barbara F., 114, 117, 119
French
  automatization and speedup in foreign language acquisition of, 114, 115
  language analytic ability in L2 acquisition. *See* learning conditions and language analytic ability
frequency effects, xv, 125–37
  confidence judgments, 128–29, 132, 133
  conscious state of acquired knowledge and, 129, 133–34
  exposure phase, *131*, 132
  4AFC picture matching task, 132, 133, 134
  future research avenues, 137
  implicit and explicit knowledge, relationship to, 125, 126, 128–29, *135*, 136, 137
  incidental versus intentional learning conditions, 125, 126–27, 135–36, 137
  interaction with other factors, 125–26
  measuring implicit and explicit knowledge, 128–29
  methodology of study, 129–32, *131*
  participants in study, 130
  source attributions, 132, 134, *135*
  subjective measures of awareness and, 128, 137
  test phase, 132
  verbal reports, 128, 134, 137
Friginal, Eric, *12*
Frog, Where Are You? (Mayer), 83

Galton, Francis, 52
Games-Howell, 163, 168n7
gang orientation and gang culture, 25, 26, 27
Gasser, Emily, xiv, 63

Gay, L. R., 97, 99
gender and speech patterns, 21–23, *22, 23*
Generalizability Theory, 55–56, 61
German. *See* complexity in German learner corpus
Goldberg, A. E., 36, 46
Golder, Katherine, 185
Goldschneider, Jennifer, 125
grammaticality judgment test (GJT), 142
grammaticality judgments, xvi, 129, 142, 155, 162
Gray, Bethany, *12*
Gray, Russell, 63, 65, 66, 69, 72, 74
Green, Anthony, 185
Greenhill, Simon, 63, 65, 66, 69, 72, 74
Guttman procedure, 96, 100, 103
Gynther, Kassandra, xvi–xvii, 199

Halverson, John, 2
Hamrick, Philip, xv, 125
Hannah, Mo Therese, 81
Hared, M., *16*
Harklau, Linda, 217
Harley, Birgit, 142
Harrington, Michael, 115, 116, 117
Hart, Doug, 142
Hatch, Eveyln, 103
Hayes, Belinda, 185, 194
Hedges' *g, 220, 222, 223*
Heitner, Reese M., xvi, 183
heterosexual desirability, ethnicity, and peer-based social order, 26–30, *30*
high schoolers' use of negative concord, 21–23, *22, 23*
Hirano, Kinue, 215, 216, 223
Hoekje, Barbara J., xvi, 183
Homburg, Taco Justus, 215, 216
Hornberger, Nancy H., 2, 96
Hulstijn, Jan H., 111, 113, 114–15, 116, 117, 122, 123
Hunstan, S., 40, 45

idea units, xiv, 84, 89–92, *90, 91*
IELTS (International English Language Testing System) exam. *See* Drexel University International Gateway Program
IEP (intensive English program) courses. *See* Drexel University International Gateway Program
impersonal/abstract style, 5
Implicational-Weighted Total Cross-Linguistic Feature (CLF) Score, 95–96, 100–104, *101, 102*
implicit and explicit knowledge, relationship of frequency effects to, 125, 126, 128–29, *135*, 136, 137
Inagaki, Shunji, 214–15, 226
incidental versus intentional learning conditions, frequency effects under, 125, 126–27, 135–36, 137

Index

inductive learning ability, 142
informational versus involved production, 4, 6–9, *8,* 10–11, *12–13,* 17
Ingram, David, 185
intensive English program (IEP) courses. *See* Drexel University International Gateway Program
intentional versus incidental learning conditions, frequency effects under, 125, 126–27, 135–36, 137
Interagency Language Roundtable (ILR)
  base level sets, 52–54
  change in language proficiency over time, rating, 202–3, 204, 205
International English Language Testing System (IELTS) exam. *See* Drexel University International Gateway Program
involved versus informational production, 4, 6–9, *8,* 10–11, *12–13,* 17
Irish, change in ability to use over time, 201
irregular and regular forms, acquisition of, 167
Iwashita, Noriko, 215, 216, 222

Jang, Shyue-Chian, *15*
Japanese
  complexity measures, 215
  simulated speech assessment of learners of. *See* simulated speech to assess Japanese learner oral proficiency
  U-shaped development in Japanese speakers' acquisition of English. *See* U-shaped development
jocks, gender, and negative concord, 21–23, *22, 23*
Jorden, E. H., 201
Jordens, P., 200
judgment knowledge, 129
Julius ASR engine, 175

Kachergis, George, 127, 136
Kameen, Patrick, 215, 217
Kanoksilapatham, Budsaba, *13*
Kellerman, Eric, 165
Kendall's tau, 41
Kiesling, Scott, 24
Kim, Hae-Young, 214–15, 226
Kim, Y. H., 56
Klee, Carol, 104
Kodytek, Vilem, *15*
Korean
  MD studies of, 13, *14*
  narrative development in, 81
KR (Kuder-Richardson), 97
Krashen, Steven D., 142
Kuder-Richardson (KR), 97
Kurjian, J., 16

L2 acquisition. *See* automatization and speedup in foreign language acquisition; learning conditions and language analytic ability; robust language acquisition and English verb-argument constructions; second language acquisition (SLA) theory; U-shaped development
L2 assessment, xvi–xvii. *See also* change in foreign language skills over time; Drexel University International Gateway Program; simulated speech (SS) to assess Japanese learner oral proficiency; subjective assessments
Labov, William, 23–24
language acquisition. *See* automatization and speedup in foreign language acquisition; learning conditions and language analytic ability; robust language acquisition and English verb-argument constructions; second language acquisition (SLA) theory; U-shaped development
language analysis test (LAT), *146*
language analytic ability. *See* learning conditions and language analytic ability
language aptitude, 142, 152
language assessment, xvi–xvii. *See also* change in foreign language skills over time; Drexel University International Gateway Program; simulated speech (SS) to assess Japanese learner oral proficiency; subjective assessments
language contact profile (LCP), 119
language, measuring. *See* quantitative methods of measuring language
latent growth analysis, xvii, 199, 203, *204–6,* 205–6, 207–8, 210
Lawson, Stephen, 219
Lazaraton, Anne, 103
learning conditions and frequency effects, 125, 126–27, 135–36, 137
learning conditions and language analytic ability, xv–xvi, 141–52
  CR (clarification requests) versus RE (recasts), oral corrective feedback in form of, 141, 144, *147–49,* 147–51
  data collection and analysis, 145–46
  definition of language analytic ability, 141–42
  inductive learning ability, 142
  language aptitude, 142, 152
  LAT, *146,* 146–47
  limitations of study, 151
  methodology of study, 144–47
  MLAT, 141–42, 143, 144
  passé composé and imparfait, as target structures, 141, 145
  relationship between, 142–44, 152
  research questions, 144
Lee, Tae Yoon, 104
Lee, Y. W., 55
Lee, Young-ja, 81, 85
Leichtman, Michelle D., 81

Levene's test, 162–64, 168n7
Lipski, John M., 104
literacy. *See* written language
Lloyd-Jones, Gaynor, 185
loanwords, 67, 69, 70
LOB Corpus, 4
loess method, 85
Logan, Gordon D., 112
London-Lund Corpus, 4
Lonsdale, Deryle, xvi, 171
LSD, 162, 163, 164, 168n7
Lynch, B., 56

Manley, Marilyn S., xv, 95
Manning, E., 40, 45
Many-Facet Rasch model, 56, 57, 59, 60
Marcus, Gary F., 158, 166
Markov Chain, 73
Martha's Vineyard, use of dialect features on, 23–24
Martingale Residuals, *59*
Masters, Megan, xvi–xvii, 199
Matsushita, Hitokazu, xvi, 171
Matthews, Stephen, 105
McCawley, James D., 165
McNamara, T., 56
MD. *See* multidimensional (MD) analysis of register variation in oral and written English
mean length of clause (MLC; phrasal complexity), 213, 216–17, 218, 221, 222–23, *225, 225–26*
measuring language. *See* measuring language; quantitative methods of measuring language
Meister, G., 127
middle school, narrative development in. *See* narrative development in first and foreign languages
Miralpeix, Immaculada, 105
Modern Languages Aptitude Test (MLAT), 141–42, 143, 144
Monte Carlo method, 73
multidimensional (MD) analysis of register variation in oral and written English, xiv, 1–18
 abstract/impersonal style, 5
 academic stance, 17
 conversational text types, 17
 dimensions of variation, 3, 4–9, *8, 10*
 earlier findings on orality/literacy distinctions, 2
 elementary student registers, 16
 involved versus informational production, 4, 6–9, *8,* 10–11, *12–13,* 17
 languages other than English, comparison of MD studies of, 13–14, *14–16,* 17
 methodology, 3–9, *8*
 narrative versus nonnarrative discourse, 4, *10,* 16, 17
 other-directed idea justification, 16
 other MD studies of English discourse domains compared, 9–11, *12–13*
 overt expression of argumentation, 5
 patterns and conclusions emerging from, 3, 16–18
 procedural versus content-focused discourse, 17
 real time information elaboration, 5
 situation-dependent versus elaborated reference, 5
 stance-focused or procedural versus context-focused discourse, 17
 text samples used in study, 5–6
 unique dimensions in certain discourse domains or languages, 16–17
 university registers, 17
multidimensional construct, complexity as, 213, 214, 226
multilingual/bilingual children, narrative development in, 79, 81–82, 90–91
Murtagh, L., 201

Nagata, Hirota, 142
narrative development in first (Chinese) and foreign (English) languages, xiv, 79–93
 analytical methods, 84–85
 book used in study, 83
 challenges in analyzing narrative, 80–82
 conclusions regarding, 92–93
 content analysis, 89–92, *90, 91,* 93
 figurative and poetic expressions, use of, 92
 idea units, xiv, 84, 89–92, *90, 91*
 literature review, 79, 80–81
 methodology of study, 83–84, 93
 models for analyzing narrative, 80
 mother's education level and, 82–83, 87
 participants in study, 82–83
 PPVT scores, 83, 87–88
 relationships between narrative coherence and other variables, 87–89, *88, 89*
 research questions, 82
 story grammar, 80–81, 84, 85, 87, 92
 structural coherence results, *85,* 85–87, *86, 87,* 93
narrative versus nonnarrative discourse, in MD analysis, 4, *10,* 16, 17
Nation, I. S. Paul, 127
Navés, Teresa, 105
Neary-Sundquist, Colleen, xvii, 213
negative concord, 21–23, *22, 23*
NeighborNet, *71,* 73, 74
neurocognitive approach to language, 126
Nicopoulou, Ageliki, 81
Norris, John M., 213, 214, 216, 226
Nukulaelae Tuvaluan, MD studies of, 13, *15*

object-to-subject movement, 156, 160, 165
Ocampo, Alicia, 104

Index

Ockey, G., 56
O'Connell, Stephen, xvi–xvii, 199
Odlin, Terrence, 104
O'Donnell, Matthew Brook, xv, 33, 45
O'Loughlin, Kieran, 185
omega-shaped development in complexity, 215, 226
OPI, *53*, 53–54, 56–60
orality. *See* spoken language
Ortega, Lourdes, 213, 214, 216, 226
Oshita, Hiroyuki, xvi, 155, 156, 161
other-directed idea justification, 16
Ottó, Istvan, 146
overpassivization, as diagnostic of U-shaped development, xvi, 156, 157, 159, 160–61, *163*, 164–66
overt expression of argumentation, 5

Padilla, A., 201
Peabody Picture Vocabulary Test (PPVT), 83, 87–88
Pearson, Karl, 52
Pearson product moment coefficient, 147
Pellicer-Sánchez, Anna, 127
Perlmutter, David M., 155
Phillips, Natalie A., 111, 115, 116
phrasal complexity (mean length of clause or MLC), 213, 216–17, 218, 221, 222–23, *225*, 225–26
Pica, Teresa, 145
Pinker, Steven, 166
Popper, Karl, xiv, 155
procedural/declarative model of language, 136
procedural versus content-focused discourse, 17
Profozic, Nadia Mifka, xv–xvi, 141
Proto Austronesian, 74
Proto Malayo-Polynesian, 74
prototype exemplars, 34, 39
pseudowords, 125, 127, *130*, 130–32, 133, 134, 135, 136
psychology of learning and robust language acquisition, 33–34, 37
Purvis, Tristan M., 15

quantitative methods of measuring language, xiii–xvii
    automatization versus speedup, xv, 111–23. *See also* automatization and speedup in foreign language acquisition
    change over time, xvi–xvii, 199–211. *See also* change in foreign language skills over time
    classification and comparison of phenomena via, xiv
    complexity, xvii, 213–26. *See also* complexity in German learner corpus
    constructs, operationalizing and measuring, xiv–xv
    cross-linguistic influence, xv, 95–107. *See also* Quechua to Spanish cross-linguistic influence
    demographics and, xiv–xv, 21–31. *See also* demographic categories and speech patterns
    at different developmental stages, xvi
    different scales, using, xv
    Drexel University International Gateway Program, xvi, 183–95. *See also* Drexel University International Gateway Program
    frequency effects, xv, 125–37. *See also* frequency effects
    historical background and development of, 51–52
    language assessment, xvi–xvii
    learning conditions and language analytic ability, xv–xvi, 141–52. *See also* learning conditions and language analytic ability
    MD analysis, xiv, 1–18. *See also* multidimensional (MD) analysis of register variation in oral and written English
    narrative development, xiv, 79–93. *See also* narrative development in first and foreign languages
    qualitative differences, quantitative differences indexing, xv
    reliability, assessing, xvi
    robustness of language acquisition and VACs, xv, 33–46. *See also* robust language acquisition and English verb-argument constructions
    scientific value of, xiii–xiv
    simulated speech, xvi, 171–81. *See also* simulated speech (SS) to assess Japanese learner oral proficiency
    subgrouping, xiv, 63–76. *See also* subgrouping in CMP languages
    subjective assessments, xv, xvi, 51–61. *See also* subjective assessments
    U-shaped development, xvi, 155–67. *See also* U-shaped development
Quechua to Spanish cross-linguistic influence, xv, 95–107
    amount of speech produced by participants, 105
    Calque-Weighted Total CLF Score, 95, 96, 99–100, 104
    future research avenues, 105–6
    Implicational-Weighted Total CLF Score, 95–96, 100–104, *101, 102*
    language attitudes interview used in, 96, 106–7
    limitations of measures of, 104–5
    number of participants using thirty-one features, 100, *101*
    participants and data collection, 96, *97*

Quechua to Spanish cross-linguistic influence (cont'd)
  reliability analyses of measures, 96, 97, 99, 100, 103–4
  single instances of thirty-one cross-linguistic features, use of, 104–5
  thirty-one cross-linguistic features analyzed, 95, 97, *98*
  Total CLF Score, 95, 96, 97–99, 100, 104
  transfer, defined, 104–5
Quinceañera, 26, 28

Ranta, Leila, 143
Rasch analysis, 53, 54, 59–61
RASP parser, 41
Read, John, 185, 194
real time information elaboration, 5
Rebuschat, Patrick, xv, 125
recasts (RE) versus clarification requests (CR), oral corrective feedback in form of, 141, 144, *147–49*, 147–51
Reeder, Kenneth, 185
registers. *See* multidimensional (MD) analysis of register variation in oral and written English
regular and irregular forms, acquisition of, 167
relative U-shape, 158, 162–65, *163*, 166, 167n1
reliability or consistency of measurement, 51–52
Reppen, Randi, *12*, 16
Robinson, Peter, 143, 144, 150
robust language acquisition and English verb-argument constructions (VACs), xv, 33–46
  CAS, 34, 40
  construction frequency, 37
  construction grammar, concept of, 36–37, 39
  construction learning determinants, 37–39
  contingency of form-function mapping, 39
  corpus used to study, 41
  definition and description of VACs, 35–36
  future research avenues, 45–46
  grammar of verbs and VACs used to study, 40–44
  latent structure of VACs, 44–46
  lexical constituency of verbs in VACs, 41–42, *42*
  literature review of language acquisition studies, 33–36
  prototype exemplars, 34, 39
  psychology of learning and, 33 34, 37
  semantic network, 43–44, *44*
  type and token frequency, 33, 37–38
  usage-based acquisition, 33, 37, 39–40
  verb-VAC contingency, 42–43
  Zipfian distribution of word frequencies, xv, 33, 38, 40, 41, 43, 44–45, 46
Roget's thesaurus, 44
Römer, Ute, xv, 33, 45
Rosch, E., 34
Rosen, Carol G., 165
Rosenthal's Higher-Order Thought Theory, 129
Ross, Steven J., xvi–xvii, 51, 199

Saffran, Jenny, 127
Sakai, Hideki, 84
Saragi, Thomas, 127
Saussure, F. D., 36
Sawaki, Y., 55
Schmitt, Norbert, 127, 146
Schoonen, Rob, 111, 113, 114–15, 116, 117, 122, 123
Scott, Ryan, 128–29
second language acquisition. *See* automatization and speedup in foreign language acquisition; learning conditions and language analytic ability; robust language acquisition and English verb-argument constructions; U-shaped development
second language acquisition (SLA) theory, 33–34, 111, 123, 125, 126, 136, 137
second language assessment, xvi–xvii. *See also* change in foreign language skills over time; Drexel University International Gateway Program; simulated speech (SS) to assess Japanese learner oral proficiency; subjective assessments
Segalowitz, Norman S., 112, 113, 114, 115, 116, 117, 119, 122
Segalowitz, Sidney J., 112, 113, 114, 115, 116, 117, 122
semantic network for VACs, 43–44, *44*
SES. *See* socioeconomic status
Sethuraman, N., 46
Shan, Chuan-Kuo, 159
Sharma, Alex, 216
Sheen, Younghee, 144
Shiffrin, Richard, 127, 136
Simulated Oral Proficiency Interview (SOPI) test, 173, 174, *179*
simulated speech (SS) to assess Japanese learner oral proficiency, xvi, 171–81
  accuracy, evaluating, 172–73, 181
  analysis of data, 175–80, *176–81*
  current tests and research for oral proficiency assessment, 171–73
  data collection and methodology, 173–75, *174*
  ER (elicited repetition) testing, 172–73, 175, 181
  fluency, evaluating, 172–73, 175–76, *176*, 178, 180
  research question, 173

single-mechanism views of language learning, 125, 136
situation-dependent versus elaborated reference, 5
Skehan, Peter, 142–43, 151, 214
SLA (second language acquisition) theory, 33–34, 111, 123, 125, 126, 136, 137
small-world networks, 44
Smith, Linda, 127
Snow, M. A., 201
Snyder, Patricia, 219
socioeconomic status (SES)
  narrative development and, 81, 83
  negative concord and, 21–23, 22, 23
Somali, MD studies of, 13, 16
SOPI (Simulated Oral Proficiency Interview) test, 173, 174, 179
Spanish. *See also* Quechua to Spanish cross-linguistic influence
  automatization and speedup in foreign language acquisition of, 111, 114, 118–23
  change in foreign language skills over time, 201
  MD studies of, 13, 14
Spearman coefficient, 147
SpeechRater, 178
speedup. *See* automatization and speedup in foreign language acquisition
split intransitivity, 155, 156, 161, 165
SplitsTree, 71
spoken language. *See also* multidimensional (MD) analysis of register variation in oral and written English; narrative development in first (Chinese) and foreign (English) languages; simulated speech (SS) to assess Japanese learner oral proficiency
  change in foreign language speaking skills over time, 205–6, 209, 209–10, 210
  clarification requests (CR) versus recasts (RE), oral corrective feedback in form of, 141, 144, 147–49, 147–51
  complexity in German learner corpus, 217, 221–23, 222, 223–25
Spolsky, Bernard, xvi
SS. *See* simulated speech (SS) to assess Japanese learner oral proficiency
stance
  academic stance, 17
  context-focused versus stance-focused discourse, 17
  Martha's Vineyard, use of dialect features on, 24
  negative concord, high schoolers' use of, 21–23, 22, 23
Standard Indonesian, 67
statistical learning, frequency-driven. *See* frequency effects

Stein, Nancy, 80, 81, 84, 85, 87, 92
Steyvers, M., 44
stochastic Dollo model, 71, 72, 73, 74, 75
story grammar, 80–81, 84, 85, 87, 92
storytelling. *See entries at* narrative
structural knowledge, 129
subgrouping in CMP languages, xiv, 63–76
  Ambon-Timor subgroup, xiv, 63–76
  analysis of study, 71–74
  Bayesian modeling, use of, xiv, 63, 69, 71, 72, 73, 75–76
  Bi-Su subgroup, 63, 64, 65–66, 75
  BSF hypothesis, 63, 65, 66, 75–76
  Cebuano and Dayak Bgaju (Western Malayo-Polynesian outgroup), 66, 67, 75
  choice of languages analyzed, 66, 67, 68–69
  coding decisions, 69–71, 70
  data and methodology of study, 66–71
  FL languages, 63, 66, 74–75
  geographic orientation of study, 66–67, 67, 75
  hypotheses for, 63–65, 64
  maximum clade credibility tree, 74
  MCMC phylogenetic models, 72–74
  NeighborNet, 71, 73, 74
  results of study, 72, 74, 74–75
  stochastic Dollo model, 71, 72, 73, 74, 75
  Sula-Bacan subgroup, 64, 65
  unrooted distance-based network, 72, 74–75
  word lists, 67–69
subjective assessments, xv, xvi, 51–61
  Generalizability Theory, 55–56, 61
  literature review, 56
  Many-Facet Rasch model, 56, 57, 59, 60
  proficiency gains over time and rater severity differences, 60–61, 58–61
  Rasch analysis, 53, 54, 59–61
  rater co-calibration systems, 59–60, 60, 61
  score variation, sources of, 52–54, 53, 55
  strategies for dealing with, 54–56
subjective measures of awareness, 128, 137
subordination, complexity by, 213, 215, 218, 220, 222, 223–25, 224
Sula-Bacan subgroup, 64, 65
SuperLab 4.0, 119
surfers, 25, 27
Swedish-Finnish bilingual children, narrative development in, 81–82, 90–91
syntactic complexity. *See* complexity in German learner corpus
syntactic NP movement analysis, 166

T-units, 84, 217
Taiwanese, MD studies of, 13, 15
Tennebaum, J., 44
Thompson, Bruce, 219

TiMBL, 176–77
time, change in proficiency over. *See* change in foreign language skills over time
TOEFL, 55, 56, 178, 184, 187, 194, 195n4
TOEIC, 54, 55
Tognini-Bonelli, Elena, 1
Total Cross-Linguistic Feature (CLF) Score, 95, 96, 97–99, 100, 104
Tracer program, 75
Trapman, H., 200
Tukey's HSD, 178, 180, 219, 220, 221–22, *223*
type and token frequency, 33, 37

U-shaped development, xvi, 155–67
　absolute U-shape, 157–58, 162, 166, 167n1
　future applications of, 166–67
　grammaticality judgment study, xvi, 155, 162
　hypotheses based on UTH formed and examined, 159–61
　methodology of study, 161–62
　object-to-subject movement, 156, 160, 165
　omega-shaped development for complexity versus, 215
　overpassivization, as diagnostic, xvi, 156, 157, 159, 160–61, *163,* 164–66
　previous research, conceptual and methodological problems with, 157–59
　relative U-shape, 158, 162–65, *163,* 166, 167n1
　split intransitivity, 155, 156, 161, 165
　uneasiness, as diagnostic, xvi, 156, 157, 159, 160–61, *163,* 164–65, 166, 168n8
　unergatives and unaccusatives, acquisition of, 155, 156
　UTH (unaccusative trap hypothesis), 155, 156–57, 165–66
unaccusative trap hypothesis (UTH), 155, 156–57, 165–66
unaccusatives, acquisition of, 155, 156
uneasiness, as diagnostic of U-shaped development, xvi, 156, 157, 159, 160–61, *163,* 164–65, 166, 168n8
unergatives, acquisition of, 155, 156
universities
　complexity measures. *See* complexity in German learner corpus
　international gateway programs. *See* Drexel University International Gateway Program

MD analysis of register variation in oral and written English, 17
UPGMA distance-based tree, 74
usage-based acquisition, 33, 37, 39–40
UTH (unaccusative trap hypothesis), 155, 156–57, 165–66

VACs. *See* robust language acquisition and English verb-argument constructions
van der Slik, F., 201
van Gelderen, Amos, 111, 113, 114–15, 116, 117, 122, 123
Vann, Roberta J., 215, 217
Vassberg, Liliane M., 96
verb-argument constructions. *See* robust language acquisition and English verb-argument constructions
verb locative (VL) construction, 36, 38, 39
verb object locative (VOL) construction, 38, 39
verbal reports, use of, 128, 134, 137
Viberg, Åke, 81–82, 90–91

Wang, Qi, 81
Watson, Vivien, 113, 115
web text types, 16
Weissberg, Robert, 217
WEKA, 177
White, M., 12
Wolfe-Quintero, Kate, 214–15, 226
Wood, Anthony G., 114, 115, 116
word frequencies, Zipfian distribution of, xv, 33, 38, 40, 41, 43, 44–45, 46
word, what constitutes, 105
WordNet, 43, 44
written language. *See also* multidimensional (MD) analysis of register variation in oral and written English
　change in foreign language reading skills over time, 203–5, 206, 208, *209*
　complexity in German learner corpus, 217, 219–21, *220,* 223, *224, 225*

Yamaguchi, Y., 144
Yip, Virginia, 105
Yu, Chen, 127, 136
Yuan, Boping, 159
Yule prior, 74

Zavala, Virginia, 104
Zeng, Wei, xiv, 79
Zhang, Qing, 24
Zipfian distribution of word frequencies, xv, 33, 38, 40, 41, 43, 44–45, 46